Racism and God-Talk

Racism and God-Talk

A Latino/a Perspective

Rubén Rosario Rodríguez

NEW YORK UNIVERSITY PRESS

New York and London

NEW YORK UNIVERSITY PRESS
New York and London
www.nyupress.org

Library of Congress Cataloging-in-Publication Data
Rodríguez, Rubén Rosario.
Racism and God-talk : a Latino/a perspective / Ruben Rosario
Rodríguez.
p. cm.
Includes bibliographical references (p.   ) and index.
ISBN-13: 978-0-8147-7610-0 (cl : alk. paper)
ISBN-10: 0-8147-7610-8 (cl : alk. paper)
ISBN-13: 978-0-8147-7611-7 (pb : alk. paper)
ISBN-10: 0-8147-7611-6 (pb : alk. paper)
1. Racism—Religious aspects—Christianity. 2. Race relations—
Religious aspects—Christianity. 3. Racism—North America.
4. Race relations—North America. 5. Theology—Latin America.
6. Theology—North America.   I. Title.
BT734.2.R625 2008
277.0089—dc22   2008004085

New York University Press books are printed on acid-free paper,
and their binding materials are chosen for strength and durability.

Manufactured in the United States of America

c 10 9 8 7 6 5 4 3 2 1
p 10 9 8 7 6 5 4 3 2 1

For EAB

Contents

Acknowledgments

My thanks to the Department of Theological Studies at Saint Louis University for encouraging and supporting faculty research. The Louisville Institute's First Book Grant for Minority Scholars facilitated completion of this book; its generosity of resources and time—especially the consultation with Institute staff and other grant winners in Louisville, Kentucky—proved invaluable to the writing process. I would also like to thank the Hispanic Theological Initiative for nurturing a community of Latino/a scholars and church people whose wisdom and encouragement midwifed this project and many others like it, as well as the many friends and colleagues at Princeton Theological Seminary—especially Mark Taylor, Daniel Migliore, and Luis Rivera Pagán—for their enduring support. Special thanks to my department chair, Wayne Hellman, for accommodating a last-minute request for a one-year research sabbatical; to colleagues Brian Robinette, Belden Lane, and Dan Finucane for being such willing, open, and supportive sounding boards when I needed to think aloud or just plain vent; and to my graduate research assistants, Christine Baudin and Erick Moser, without whose help this project might never have gotten off the ground. Sections of chapter 3 appeared as "Calvin or Calvinism: Reclaiming Reformed Theology for the Latin American Context," in *Apuntes: Reflexiones teológicas desde el margen hispano* 23 (Winter 2004); chapter 4 was published in somewhat different form as "Beyond Word and Sacrament: A Reformed Protestant Engagement of Guadalupan Devotion," in *Journal of Ecumenical Studies* 42, no. 2 (Spring 2007). It goes without saying, but I will say it anyway: completion of this book would not have been possible without advice and expert direction from Jennifer Hammer, my editor at New York University Press. Finally, special thanks to my wife, Dr. Elizabeth Blake, secret weapon and in-house editor: words cannot express my gratitude for everything you are and everything you do.

Introduction

Nearly all the wisdom we possess, that is to say, true and sound wisdom, consists of two parts: the knowledge of God and of ourselves. But, while joined by many bonds, which one precedes and brings forth the other is not easy to discern.

—John Calvin, *Institutes of the Christian Religion*

The future begins in the dream of what could and ought to be.

—Virgilio Elizondo, *The Future Is Mestizo*

The Fundamental Contradiction

The apostle Paul writes, "As many of you were baptized into Christ have clothed yourselves with Christ. There is no longer Jew or Greek, there is no longer slave or free, there is no longer male or female; for all of you are one in Christ Jesus" (Gal. 3:27–28, NRSV). Today's church, while recognizing that questions of ethnic identity in the ancient world differ greatly from modern conceptions of race, embraces Paul's eschatological vision of a community in which distinctions of race, class, and gender are transcended in Christ as a normative statement for understanding Christian identity. However, in the North American context, race consciousness plays a central role in the theological constructions of racially marginalized and oppressed communities. Given Paul's vision of God's kingdom defined by the breakdown of all distinctions and relationships of domination—no longer Jew or Greek, slave or free, male or female—how do we make sense of ethnic particularity within the church's theological formulations?

The tendency toward group inclusion/exclusion at the intersection of two or more cultures has persisted throughout human history. Cultural identity, an intangible and fluid reality, often solidifies in response to threats to the unifying identity of a group, stimulating the formation of values and practices that maintain the "purity" of the social grouping. Since classical antiquity color difference has been an established category for defining group identity, distinguishing "us" from "them." Yet only in the modern period have these physiological differences been linked to certain moral and intellectual traits as part of a biologically distinct and inherited group identity. Shrouded in the taxonomical language of science, the categories "Caucasoid," "Negroid," and "Mongoloid," legitimated "real" (i.e., biological) differences between ethnic groups and established a hierarchy that valued the "white" European while devaluing and objectifying the dark-skinned "other" as demonstrated by the reluctance to sanction intermarriage.[1] Over time slavery became almost synonymous with blackness as the practice of using physical traits to differentiate the conquerors from the conquered became an accepted and essential part of the cultural matrix. While the Christian church was often a willing accomplice in this history of domination and submission, many voices of resistance and transformation have arisen from within this tradition, such as those of Bartolomé de Las Casas during the Spanish conquest of the Americas and the church-led abolitionist movement in the antebellum United States. Despite the advances of the civil rights movement, we continue to live in an age of racial disparity. As a religious body that embraces the breakdown of all relationships of domination in God's kingdom, the church must draw upon its own traditions of resistance to effectively counter racism.

In an effort to support the church's critical self-examination, this book explores the biblical and religious dimensions of North American racism while highlighting examples of resistance within the Christian religious tradition. The Bible—a complex collection of documents from various sources reflecting a multiplicity of social, historical, and cultural locations —lends itself to many, often contradictory, interpretations. At no point in church history has this been more evident than in the antebellum United States when abolitionists in the North read and interpreted Galatians 3:1– 29 as a manifesto for human freedom while Southern theologians cited Paul's letter to Philemon in defense of the Fugitive Slave Law of 1850. If political historians have interpreted the Civil War as the nation's first major constitutional crisis (arising from the fundamental contradiction of the three-fifths compromise), then these conflicting interpretations of the Bible constitute the young nation's enduring moral crisis. In 1852

Frederick Douglass exposed the nation's religious hypocrisy in his Fourth of July address:

> Americans! your republican politics, not less than your republican religion, are flagrantly inconsistent. You boast of your love of liberty, your superior civilization, and your pure Christianity, while the whole political power of the nation (as embodied in the two great political parties), is solemnly pledged to support and perpetuate the enslavement of three million of your countrymen. . . .
>
> Fellow-citizens! I will not enlarge further on your national inconsistencies. The existence of slavery in this country brands your republicanism as a sham, your humanity as a base pretence, and your Christianity as a lie.[2]

This uniquely American moral crisis remains conspicuous in world history because it arose in a nation and culture committed to the idea of human equality, a belief emanating both from the egalitarian ethos of the Christian doctrine of justification (with Christ on the cross establishing a new community in which all who are in Christ are equal before God) and from the Enlightenment belief in universal human rights grounded in natural law (in tacit rejection of biblical and ecclesial authority). Ultimately, this contradiction became manifest in both the public and private spheres as bitter armed conflict was preceded and even precipitated by religious schism over the issue of slavery. Long before the first shot was fired at Manassas, all the major American Protestant denominations had split into Northern and Southern communions—the Methodists in 1844, the Baptists in 1845, and the Presbyterians in 1857[3]—foreshadowing the political divide that eventually threatened to destroy the nation.

Nevertheless, social historians have seldom analyzed the problematic of race from a primarily theological perspective. Within academic discourse there exists a consensus opinion that the Industrial Revolution and the growth of capitalism are directly responsible for the rise of American racist thought;[4] however, recent scholarship challenges this prevailing thesis. Historian James H. Sweet argues that the identification of blackness with servitude characteristic of American racism was part of the western European cultural matrix long before the discovery of the New World and the rise of the Atlantic slave trade.[5] Medieval and premodern prejudices traceable to Jewish, Christian, and Muslim attitudes about ethnic and religious otherness gave rise to the notion of European cultural superiority that eventually manifested itself as racial prejudice based on skin color. At some point in each of their histories, all three Abrahamic faiths have espoused the view that sub-Saharan Africans were culturally inferior and therefore naturally suited for slavery, yet few studies have explicitly examined how the confessional commitments of these faith traditions might contribute to—or counter—a racist worldview. This project undertakes a critical examination of explicitly theological perspectives for understanding and transforming North American racism. Employing a method that is both confessional and public—grounded in the distinctively Christian discourse of the faith community while actively conversing with a plurality of critical perspectives in civil society—I examine racialized readings of the Bible not only to highlight the church's role in perpetuating racist social structures but also to articulate a Christian response to the problem of racism that draws upon the U.S. Latino/a[6] experience of *mestizaje*. In this book I articulate a transcultural theology of human liberation by interjecting the insights of Latino/a theology into the ongoing conversation on race in the public arena by offering the metaphor of *mestizaje,* or mutual cultural exchange, as a challenge to the church that it recognize the effects of racial and ethnic particularity in all theological construction.

Toward a Theological Response

Theological anthropology—the Christian understanding of what it means to be human in light of our relationship to the Creator—is central to any discussion of the church's response to the problematic of race. A Christian doctrine of humanity draws upon various aspects of traditional church teaching—especially the doctrines of Creation, Christ, and the Trinity —in order to present an understanding of humankind grounded in the knowledge of God. Still, the depth and breadth of human sin call into question the very possibility of reliable knowledge of God as evidenced by Christianity's troubled relationship with such dehumanizing institutions as slavery and apartheid. The second half of this book presents a creative reconstruction of traditional doctrines through the lens of U.S. Latino/a experience in order to advocate a theological anthropology that transforms and transcends a cultural heritage tainted by the sin of racism. First, however, it is important to provide a theological analysis of racism that honestly confronts the church's responsibility in perpetuating racist structures yet also identifies a methodological direction for liberating Christian doctrine from theological racism.

Christian identity is formed at the nexus of many, often competing, relationships incorporating (but not limited to) ethnic, gender, economic, biological, linguistic, moral, and religious factors. Consequently, it is vital for theology to adequately understand the complex interaction between Christianity and culture and account for the role of cultural factors in theological construction. At stake is an understanding of God's revelation in the world—does revelation transcend culture, or is revelation a cultural phenomenon? The problem with the former view is that when revelation is understood as independent of culture, it can quickly become irrelevant to culture, while the problem with the latter view is that when revelation is equated with culture, it becomes impossible to offer divine judgment upon the sins of a culture. H. Richard Niebuhr's classic text, *Christ and Culture* (1951), establishes five paradigms for understanding Christ's relationship to culture: Christ against culture, Christ of culture, Christ above culture, Christ and culture in paradox, and Christ as the transformer of culture.[7] Niebuhr accepts the historical and cultural particularity of all theological narratives yet makes room for God's transcendent and transformative Word in the world. His fifth paradigm, Christ transforming culture, provides an attractive option for political theologies advocating for a more just society.

If racism is a product of cultural factors, and particular theological traditions are necessarily part of the cultural matrix that generates racism, to what extent do deep theological commitments foster or resist racist worldviews? While at certain times in its history the Christian church has perpetuated racist attitudes and practices, Christian theology is not intrinsically racist; the thesis here developed is that Christian doctrines remain open to interpretation and can be manipulated for good or evil. Recognizing both the temporal and the spiritual realities embodied in the church, Christian theology acknowledges the sinfulness of the faith community without abandoning its core salvific message. Accordingly, the role of the contemporary theologian parallels that of the prophets of ancient Israel, men and women who arose within the faith community, exhorting it to remain faithful to its true identity while proclaiming God's judgment upon the community's disobedience. Ultimately, Christian identity is inseparable from Christian community, for it is only as *ecclesia* that the Christian life is properly understood. Thus, tradition and canon become crucial concepts for a Christian understanding of what it means to be human—especially when unraveling the place of racial/ethnic particularity in the divine providence—for it is in the context of the historical church that God has chosen to reveal God's self.

Canon has both formative and normative functions because it involves a continual exchange between the individual and the communal spheres circumscribed by an explicit catalog of authoritative texts, narratives, and practices. While a tradition's canon is in great part constitutive of that tradition, it is to some degree contestable given the diversity of interpretations within any single tradition. This investigation defines canon as a "core" set of beliefs and practices that preserve the historical continuity of a given tradition yet remain fluid enough to allow for change. Since mere repetition proves inadequate as a tradition encounters new situations, theology is an inherently hermeneutical undertaking that continually "makes sense" of the world in a narrative relation to its "original" story. Accordingly, theological interpretation always takes place within a specific tradition and in a particular social location involving a process of participation and distanciation.[8] Given that no neutral standpoint exists from which to extricate oneself from one's own tradition, it becomes necessary to view tradition in general as a highly contextualized social praxis. Believers affirm their identity as members of a particular tradition by active participation in the life of that community of faith and reform this tradition by distancing themselves—through intersubjective discourse with other members of one's faith community (both past and present)—from those aspects of the tradition they find objectionable. For this reason, the theological anthropology proposed here respects the role of collective identity and cultural inheritance on the formation of personal identity yet affirms the role of dissension in reforming religious traditions by defending individual freedom over against authoritarian collective forces.

The present work originates within the theological self-reflection of the U.S. Latino/a community of faith but also incorporates external critical perspectives, embodying a model of theological reasoning that presupposes cooperation and coordination between conversation partners who do not necessarily share the same interpretive framework as a safeguard against every culture's tendency to create a false idol out of its particularity. While U.S. Latino/a theology recognizes that its particular cultural perspective provides valuable insights and interpretations of the Christian tradition, Latino/a theologians also honor the traditional sources of Christian theology (Scripture, Tradition, Reason, and Experience). Accordingly, there is a methodological concern about the role of culture in defining Christian theological identity. Great care must be taken so that no single cultural perspective defines the tradition and so that our theological constructions do not favor one particular group or culture over others. In the words of the apostle Paul, "We have this treasure in clay jars, so that it may be made clear that this extraordinary power belongs to God and does not come from us" (2 Cor. 4:7, NRSV).

Every theology must unravel the relationship of Christ to culture. The word *culture* has many connotations, but I choose to employ the terms *culture* and *cultural* to refer to those attitudes, ideas, languages, practices, and institutions that differentiate specific populations from one another while recognizing that the very factors that constitute cultural identity are socially constructed and continually negotiated. Theology cannot reduce Christianity to culture without accepting Feuerbach's reductionist critique that Christian theology is really anthropology, but neither can it embrace what Bonhoeffer has termed "revelational positivism." From a classical Reformed theological perspective, theological statements are possible because God reveals God's self.[9] More to the point, God is both the content of that revelation and the only means by which humans can know this content. Christian theology, because of this unyielding commitment to Scripture as its *norma normans,* is often judged by its critics to be blatantly foundational. However, theologies whose experiences and explanatory narratives are never subjected to external criticism weave elaborate discourses that are little more than *idioglossia*—private languages. Without undermining the normative function of Scripture this investigation accepts as axiomatic that revelation is always mediated through culture. Christocentric and Trinitarian in orientation, the constructive theology articulated herein affirms the particularity of God's self-revelation in Jesus of Nazareth through the power of the Holy Spirit in order to argue that the act of revelation always takes place in concrete historical situations by means of particular cultural symbols. Even though knowledge of God begins with God's self-revelation, all attempts to understand this divine act are themselves human acts of interpretation and by definition culturally specific.

Because theological discourse is human language about God, it cannot limit God's freedom, so God's self-revelation always remains mystery. Accordingly, theological language is not the language of absolute certainty but that of faithful and humble acknowledgment. Recalling Anselm's classical formulation, "faith seeking understanding," theology is the search for a deeper understanding of the subjective (individual and collective) religious experience. Therefore, as the human search for knowledge of God, theology cannot have the "last word" on God but must propose answers to the questions of faith that are always *provisional*. Such open-endedness does not eliminate the possibility of certainty in the church's teaching, but rather than equating theological assurance with Cartesian epistemological certainty, this conception of theology locates dogmatic certainty in the obedient act of continual self-criticism in light of the Word of God.

The task of theology remains abundantly clear: theology serves the church by informing and correcting its proclamation of the Word of God in an ever-changing world. Given that God's self-revelation is known only indirectly—that is, always mediated by Scripture and the church's procla-mation—great care must be taken not to equate the church's teaching with the Word of God. Still, it is possible to affirm the unequivocal authority of Scripture over tradition while recognizing that Scripture, like church doc-trine, is the Word of God only by an act of God. Scripture bears witness to God's self-revelation, but this does not warrant a direct identification of the Bible with revelation, since Scripture's authority over the church rests not in itself but in the One to whom it bears witness by the power of the Holy Spirit. The only unquestionable foundation for Christian theologi-cal reflection is the living Lord Jesus Christ, who as the incarnate Word of God is himself the truth of the Gospel. However, naming Jesus Christ as its absolute norm does not relieve Christian theology of the difficult task of articulating what this norm is or how it is to be applied. While the norm of faith is outside us (*extra nos*), God chooses to speak through hu-man words (Scripture, tradition, confessional statements, etc.); therefore, systematic theology is burdened with the awesome task of instructing the church. Church teaching is a human word that serves the divine Word, so from a human perspective there is no guarantee that church doctrine will not slip into error and disobedience. Theological proclamation is always uncertain action. Only insofar as the church continues to listen faithfully to the living Word by always remaining open to the possibility that it has misheard the Word is it able to proclaim and teach faithfully.[10]

The church's dogmatic theology functions as both gateway and barrier, though authentic church theology never instructs by force. Rather, by lis-tening to the Word of God and constantly reminding the church of the revelation attested in Scripture, it calls the church to faithfulness. While its content is grounded in the biblical witness, accepting the Scriptures as God's command, theology remains free to take up questions and concerns not directly addressed by the biblical witness (though always with an eye toward Scripture). Recalling the four-part description of *ecclesia* in the Nicene Creed ("We believe in one holy catholic and apostolic church"), the church is "one" although visibly and lamentably divided because it acknowledges Christ as its only Lord; "holy" when the church adopts the proper humility by doing penance before God for its sins and praying for a new and better hearing of the Word by the power of the Holy Spirit; "catholic" in the sense that particular theologies serve the whole Christian church and ought to listen to different perspectives, even those labeled heretical; and "apostolic" insofar as its teaching is in part determined by the faith of the ecumenical councils and creeds. Finally, dogmatics is called to be contemporary and contextual in that it must address the struggles and sufferings of the church in the world today.

The critical question that systematic theology in every generation needs to answer is whether as a human word it truly serves the divine Word or is governed by lesser cultural, historical, and political idols. God's promise to the church is that God will speak in the preaching and proclamation of the church. Unless the church wants to disown this promise, it must accept its role as the teaching church in such a way that it does not elevate the human word alongside, or in place of, the Word of God. To this end, dogmatics must continually listen to the Word of God, which requires a particular attitude where the church teaches with authority yet respects the limits of its authority. The reality of a divided church confirms that —in spite of shared sources and norms—inherited cultural frameworks indelibly shape theological traditions. Therefore, recognizing the existing plurality of perspectives within the church remains a *necessary* theological task.

The present-day eruption of theological pluralism is linked to the dramatic emergence across the globe of local theologies resisting the hegemony of Western academic and ecclesial norms. By "Western" theology I mean the dominant theological traditions of Europe and North America that have, until recently, defined doctrine and practice for world Christianity, as contrasted to the emergent theologies of Asia, Africa, and Latin America as well as marginalized voices within Europe and North America. This movement toward contextual and local theologies is characterized by the realization that particular experiences, contexts, and traditions play a vital role in theological construction.[11] Accordingly, contextual theologies like U.S. Latino/a theology undertake the tasks of theology aware that the Christian tradition is not singular. Rather, constructive and systematic theology is expected to provide an ordered account of Christian belief and practice from a particular location while engaging in critical dialogue with the diachronic and synchronic plurality called "church." By viewing the history of Christianity as a series of local theologies grounded in the historical "Christ event" that all communities self-identified as "Christian" purport to proclaim and embody (while also acknowledging that no single tradition is the privileged interpreter of this Christ event), contextual approaches also affirm a set of *loci communes* (common places) identifiable as the Christian tradition—even when these are expressed symbolically and culturally in diverse ways.

Accordingly, a method more faithful to the diversity found within the Christian tradition is one that lives with dissensus while working toward theological convergence. When theology adopts this mind-set, particular confessional and cultural traditions are no longer viewed as mutually exclusive but can become mutually corrective. Recognizing that these inherited cultural frameworks encompass all aspects of human life—not just the religious sphere—demands an approach that enables us to critique our traditions while standing inside them. As human beings, we are neither determined selves nor autonomous isolated egos, but always exist as a self in community; given the understanding of canon previously articulated, this understanding of religious community includes our predecessors, our contemporaries, and our successors. Since God is a living subject, who approaches us in the midst of our particularity, it is methodologically important that we listen to how the "other" has encountered the living Word. Not because God is many—for God is one even in God's triunity—but because of the simple fact that all our conversations about God run the risk of becoming internal monologues. By conversing with the plurality that is the Christian tradition, past *and* present, while also engaging external (non-Christian) critical discourses, we are rescued from solipsism and provincialism, and can perhaps avoid dogmatically rejecting or denying potential avenues of God's revelation. Adopting an intentionally inclusive methodology allows theologians to recognize cultural distortions of God's self-revelation while at the same time affirming that *every* cultural manifestation of the Gospel is a potential vessel of God's self-revelation. The goal is an ecumenical theology respectful of the differences within catholic Christianity in which genuine conversation and mutual exchange are demanded.

This commitment to mutually beneficial exchange transcends particularity and helps illuminate the cross-cultural permeability linking confessional traditions with their surrounding cultural milieu. The implications for a theological analysis of racism stemming from this view of the relationship of theology to culture are profound. First, by understanding theology as culturally mediated yet distinguishable from culture, it becomes possible to analyze racist theological interpretations without dismissing an entire tradition. Second, by recognizing that multiple and overlapping spheres of human experience are constitutive of culture—the religious, moral, racial/ethnic, and so forth—it encourages genuine pluralism by welcoming previously silenced or marginalized perspectives to the interdisciplinary conversation without privileging any one narrative for the very reason that no *one* perspective is capable of representing reality in its fullness. Because cultural/ethnic identity is intertwined with religious/theological identity, a comprehensive academic study of race and racism in the United States ought to include insights from Christian theological anthropology.

Theology in the Public Arena

There is no universally accepted Christian confessional statement that confronts the problem of racism by affirming the full humanity of all persons as *imago Dei* regardless of national origin or differences in physical appearance. While all the major Christian denominations in the United States have adopted language and policies denouncing racism since the advent of the civil rights movement, Christian doctrines of humanity—in their analysis of the human condition—have largely ignored the role of racial prejudice in perpetuating sinful social conditions. In 1985 the *Kairos* document—a theological statement issued by an anonymous group of primarily black theologians in South Africa—challenged that nation's churches to oppose the vicious policies of the apartheid state.[12] While this document is generally considered too controversial to serve as an ecumenical confessional statement on human differentiation, ethnic conflict, and racial reconciliation, it does serve as a historical guidepost for future Christian political engagement of—and theological reflection on—the challenges of global racial disparity. Arguably an instance of a *status confessionis* for the whole Christian church,[13] the *Kairos* document serves as a prime example of a local and contextual theology that informs and illuminates our understanding of the Word of God across contexts and cultures. As a Christian, biblical, and theological analysis of the political crisis in

South Africa in the mid-1980s, the document condemns political domination and oppression on the basis of race, gender, and/or socioeconomic status and calls for all Christians to choose sides against oppression in the historical struggle for liberation because God "works vindication and justice for all who are oppressed" (Ps. 103:6, NRSV).

Fully aware that explicitly theological reasoning can sometimes stifle —even end—political debate, this theological exploration of the problem of racism engages both the Christian community and the broader civil society in the hope that theological analysis can foster and nurture genuine conversation.[14] While a comprehensive history of racism in North America lies beyond the scope of this investigation, an exploration of the historical development of racial discourse demonstrates how contemporary contextual theologies have come to affirm both ethnic/cultural particularity and the universality of the Gospel while empowering marginalized faith communities to resist political and cultural domination. However, before North American Christianity can confront its own racial *kairos* situation, the church must overcome the widespread fallacy—especially in the United States, with its constitutional separation of church and state —that "political theology" is the bringing together of two incompatible realities.

Embodying an alternative model of theology—one that openly expresses its deepest theological commitments, remains respectful of pluralist concerns, and rejects coercion as a means of affecting political change in a democratic society—this work addresses the religious-secular divide that characterizes much contemporary public discourse. One response to the marginalization of theology in the public arena is to produce theologies that intentionally incorporate critical perspectives external to the Christian tradition but do so by surrendering that which is uniquely "Christian" about their discourse.[15] Critical theories, while having a place in theological reflection, are not the *primary* discourse of faith communities. Therefore, a more effective means of transforming a faith community's praxis—or of understanding that community's distinct contribution to the social well-being—begins with an appreciation of that community's deep doctrinal commitments.[16] This particular task of theology—differentiating specifically Christian doctrine from other sociopolitical discourses —may inevitably increase the Christian community's isolation from the public discourse. Still, in a free and democratic society, theologians have a responsibility to make the faith community's deepest commitments intelligible to outsiders as honestly and authentically as possible, as well as the freedom to engage in political debate from an openly confessional stance.[17] Thus, while the theologian utilizes diverse theories of explanation in conversing with those who do not share the same confessional commitments, his or her *unique* contribution to the public discourse is to offer critical analysis of social issues informed by the rich resources of his or her own distinct tradition.

In *Remembering Esperanza,* Mark Taylor develops critical guidelines for doing theology in the contemporary North American context by recognizing a threefold tension among tradition, pluralism, and liberation as constitutive of theological content.[18] By refusing to limit theology to a single starting point and instead suggesting that contemporary theologians are entangled in a threefold tension of equally compelling demands, Taylor develops a "thick" description of the North American context.[19] This description recognizes "three demands that we often wish to respect simultaneously: to acknowledge some sense of tradition, to celebrate plurality, and to resist domination. As compelling as each of these demands seems to be, pursuing any one of them makes highly problematic the realization of the other two."[20] A singular focus on tradition results in a culturally irrelevant and myopic theology; a singular attention to plurality can result in political impotence (when all perspectives are equally valid, how does one resist injustice?). Furthermore, the postmodern emphasis on pluralism without tradition only recognizes those aspects of tradition that perpetuate political domination without acknowledging how tradition can also create an appreciation of difference that provides vital resources for political resistance. Finally, focusing on liberation alone (to the exclusion of tradition and pluralism) can result in a failed struggle against oppression, since a sense of tradition nurtures and sustains liberation struggles over time, and a healthy sense of pluralism prevents the divisiveness that so often destroys resistance movements. Taylor's program, with its concerted effort to retain some sense of tradition, to develop a healthy pluralism, and to empower the community of faith to resist domination, has much in common with the inclusive vision of U.S. Latino/a theologies. It also provides analytical tools for evaluating the public character of theology. Unfortunately, the suspicion within the academy that a theologian committed to the doctrinal claims of his or her faith is incapable of the same degree of objectivity as "secular" scholars impedes the effectiveness of "public" theologies. This characterization of the confessional theologian as "partisan" over against the academic as "nonpartisan" hampers genuine interdisciplinarity by granting epistemic privilege to one type of rationality over another. It also illustrates how theology's perspective is not always welcome in the academy, even when theology enters public discourse committed to making its confessional claims intelligible to all conversation partners on the basis of shared rational criteria.

During the period of modernity, an era most often identified with Descartes's search for self-evident and universal epistemological foundations, the natural sciences were elevated to a position of epistemic privilege and theology marginalized to the realm of the private and personal. The postmodern moment, by rejecting totalizing metanarratives and emphasizing the contextualization of all human knowledge, allows theology to reenter the interdisciplinary conversation. I claim a public voice for confessional theology by emphasizing interdisciplinary conversation as the means of achieving authentic pluralism. Such discourse does not demand that interlocutors share the same assumptions but only that they intentionally develop ways to talk with one another by emphasizing shared experiences. Given that Christian and cultural commitments overlap and often merge, theology cultivates the proper relation between participation and distanciation in order to maintain the cultural relevance of its message while at the same time affirming its particularity. As a theology of liberation this work employs a "hermeneutics of suspicion" that questions and challenges received theological traditions and cultural frameworks of interpretation in order to show how unconscious motivations, socioeconomic interests, political ideologies, and cultural biases shape all interpretations of history, science, philosophy, and theology. While recognizing that a theologian's role is often prophetic—exposing a particular tradition's sins or calling the community toward a "new" understanding of itself—the confessional theologian nevertheless acts from a deep sense of commitment to and respect for the tradition. In other words, prophetic theology faces a two-tiered challenge: (1) to critique and transform the tradition while speaking *within* the community of faith, and (2) to defend the tradition's ideas as effectively as possible—by means of shared rationality—when speaking *outside* the community. Therefore, what the contemporary situation demands is a "hermeneutics of trust" to accompany our hermeneutics of suspicion. Such an approach does not alienate the faith community by imposing external ideas upon it, but undertakes the difficult task of reconstruction *by reclaiming the tradition's own resources in order to address new situations and contexts.* In other words—in spite of all our cultural and confessional differences—it is important to identify shared *loci communes* that distinguish particular local traditions as belonging to the broad Christian tradition. For example, while *mestizaje* is an integral part of my personal Christian experience, I contend that the reality of *mestizaje* (understood as mutual exchange between two or more cultures) has always been a vital part of the Christian tradition (though not always identified by that name). All of us inhabit multiple communities and begin life with a cultural inheritance informed by many sources. Not surprisingly, as a theologian shaped by both the Reformed/Calvinist tradition and Latin American liberation theology, I intentionally bring both perspectives together in theological reflection. Thus, what follows is an analysis and creative reconstruction of Christian doctrines shaped as much by John Calvin and Karl Barth as by Gustavo Gutiérrez and Virgilio Elizondo.

Interjecting a Mestizo Perspective

In recent years the place of religion in the public arena has been greatly debated, whether in reaction to U.S. president George W. Bush's "faith-based initiatives" approach to social problems or in the aftermath of the religiously motivated terrorist attack on September 11, 2001. However, a quick survey of post-9/11 academic literature on the subject gives the mistaken impression that religious fundamentalism—whether militant Islamists or the U.S. "Christian Right"—has a chokehold on religion in the public arena,[21] as popular news media coverage singles out best-selling author Jim Wallis as the lone voice for progressive Christianity in the United States.[22] This book introduces the insights of U.S. Latino/a theology into the ongoing conversation on religion in the public arena, optimistic that the metaphor of *mestizaje*—despite its ethnocentric and nationalist undertones—can contribute to a transcultural theology of human liberation. This refreshing optimism challenges Samuel Huntington, who identifies Mexican immigration and what he terms "Hispanization"[23] as the greatest threat to American national identity and national security in the post-9/11 United States. I engage the discourse on race as a Protestant Hispanic American by advocating a notion of cultural *mestizaje* that transcends ethnocentric categories and challenges the church to recognize the effects of racial and ethnic particularity upon all theological construction. In conversation with U.S. Latino/a theology, this investigation proposes a more inclusive conceptualization of *mestizaje* that moves beyond its Latino-specific usage. Focusing on the mutual exchange between cultures allows us to employ the term as an interpretive tool for resisting racism and transforming communities while critically evaluating past uses of *mestizaje* as a theological metaphor in light of the inclusive vision of community found in Galatians 3:27–28.

Interjecting the work of U.S. Latino/a theologians in the public discourse serves to break down the black-white dichotomy that has dominated the conversation on race in North America. Given that the experience of living as a marginalized minority within a dominant majority population frames the interpretive horizon of most Latino/as in the United States—specifically the experience of bilingualism and biculturalism arising from navigating two cultures while never fully belonging in either—U.S. Latino/a theologians seek to develop discourses that build bridges between different cultures, languages, and perspectives. Accordingly, *mestizaje* has become a central category for U.S. Latino/a theological reflection. The terms *mestizo* and *mestizaje* refer to the process of cultural and biological mixing of Iberian and Amerindian peoples. Originally a denigrating label, *mestizaje* has been transformed and appropriated by Latino/as as a term of self-identity and cultural pride. Theologians employ the term broadly—as descriptive of "the U.S. Hispanic ethos that seeks inclusion of the other"[24]—emphasizing the possibility of dialogical and mutually enriching relationships at the intersection of two or more cultures. The challenge for Latino/a theology is to encourage and value cultural distinctness without denigrating other cultures or perpetuating exclusionary practices. Recognizing the limits of *mestizaje* as a transcultural symbol of liberation, many U.S. Latino/a theologians continue to reinterpret *mestizaje* so that it remains both a symbol of Christian hope and a paradigm of universal human liberation. The eschatological dimension of Christian thought (its "already-not yet" aspect) reminds the church that while it is renewed in the Spirit and called by God to live in inclusive community, where there is no longer Jew or Greek, slave or free, male or female but all are one in Christ Jesus, our present reality is tainted by sin and relationships of domination persist. Therefore, a genuinely Christian use of *mestizaje* must not only trust in the unseen hope of faith but also foster strategies for resisting and transforming relationships of domination here and now.

Today "race" is no longer considered a valid descriptive category in the natural sciences, yet race has been embraced by marginalized and oppressed groups as a necessary descriptive category for political discourse in order to resist white cultural and political dominance. Fully aware of the temptation every community faces to make a false idol of its ethnic particularity, I nonetheless argue that the Christian church's response to racism must embrace liberating aspects of the "race consciousness" movement in its theological constructions. In my opinion, the work of Hispanic theologians in the United States—especially their creative use of the concept of *mestizaje*—provides a transcultural paradigm for resisting racism in our increasingly globalized society. The U.S. Latino/a experience of racism is that of being objectified, categorized, and left without a cultural identity. Constantly treated like an alien—even if born and raised in the United States—leaves one feeling emotionally isolated, politically impotent, and vulnerable to economic exploitation. Latino/as seek to broaden the discourse on race to include the "browning" of America without minimizing the long, tragic history of enslavement and exploitation of blacks in this country in order to bring to light the similarities and shared struggles of the subjugated other—whether that other is African American, Native American, Asian American, or Latino/a—within the dominant Euro-American culture.[25] This discourse demands brutal honesty, challenging Latino/as to come to terms with their participation in and perpetuation of racist structures. For example, we cannot deny the fact that it is possible for many light-skinned Hispanics to shed their cultural/ethnic identity in order to assimilate and succeed in U.S. society, an opportunity denied many African Americans solely because of the color of their skin, the texture of their hair, or the shape of their noses. Nor can Latino/as pretend they are immune from becoming racist by virtue of having experienced discrimination themselves. In my own Puerto Rico one finds a spectrum of racial types that include *blanco* (white), *indio* (dark skinned and straight haired), *moreno* (dark skinned with a mix of black and white features), *negro* (black or African American in appearance), and *trigueño* (wheat-colored), reflecting both the biological diversity of our ancestry (*mestizaje*) and that part of our Spanish cultural heritage that elevates white/European traits, culture, and lineage to the detriment of all things African and Amerindian.

Throughout this investigation *mestizaje* is understood in one of three ways: (1) the historical and biological reality of mixing between two or more human groups, (2) the complex interaction and mutual exchange between two or more cultures, and (3) a distinctly Christian theological anthropology grounded in Christ's own historical identity as "mestizo" that advocates a liberating vision of human equality distinguished by active resistance to various forms of cultural, political, and religious domination. U.S. Latino/a theology posits a communal notion of personal identity grounded in a complex web of social relationships and historical commitments that attempt to make sense of the cruel history of *mestizaje*. At the same time, Latino/a theologians seek to protect individual self-determination over against the potential encroachment of tradition and culture. So while *mestizaje* is at its core the mixing of different cultures, to identify oneself as *mestizo* in the way most Latino/a theologies employ the term entails something more than just being the offspring of parents from two different cultures—it entails a spiritual conversion from the old way of viewing human relationships as relationships of domination to a new, Christ-centered vision of human relationships where "There is no longer Jew or Greek, there is no longer slave or free, there is no longer male or female; for all of you are one in Christ Jesus" (Gal. 3:28, NRSV).

Structure of the Book

The book is divided into two parts: the first part focuses on theoretical and methodological questions raised by the problematic of race while the second part articulates a theological response to the problem of racism. Chapter 1, "Beyond Black and White: Understanding Race in North America," traces the history of theological and scientific racism, then presents three race-conscious responses to the "persistent problem of race."[26] In analyzing Western notions of race and identity I accept as axiomatic that race is a cultural construct inextricably linked to European colonial expansion, that race is not a valid descriptive category in the natural sciences, and that race has been embraced by marginalized and oppressed groups as a necessary descriptive category for political resistance. After a brief history of racist interpretations of biblical texts within Judaism, Christianity, and Islam, the chapter examines the so-called curse of Ham (Gen. 9:18–27) and its role in the development of theological racism in the United States. To highlight scientific racism's deep and long-lasting influence on popular beliefs about race, I trace the history and eventual rejection of scientific racism within academic discourse in addition to detailing the recent resurgence of biological theories of race in the North American academic context. Because this persistence of racism in contemporary society has not yet allowed for the abandonment of race as a descriptive category, the chapter concludes with an analysis of three contemporary race-conscious responses to racism—Cornel West's genealogy of racism, critical race theory (arising out of critical legal studies), and the contributions of U.S. Latino/a theologians.

Chapter 2, "Exploring *Mestizaje* as Theological Metaphor," defends *mestizaje* as a vital concept for fostering racial reconciliation by analyzing the work of three Latino/a theologians in the United States, Virgilio Elizondo, Ada María Isasi-Díaz, and Luis G. Pedraja. First, the chapter focuses on the central role of *mestizaje* in the development of U.S. Latino/a theology. Then it responds to the criticism that Latino/a theologies embrace essentialist notions of race (*mestizaje* is a concept most often associated with pan-Hispanic nationalist and ethnocentric movements) by arguing that Latino/as risk further "ghettoizing" politically marginalized minority populations when they appropriate *mestizaje* as both a religious *and* a nationalist symbol. My analysis of Elizondo's theology exposes the primary risk in employing *mestizaje* as theological metaphor—namely, that by emphasizing the biological/historical understanding of *mestizaje* Latino/a theologies encourage identity-based politics that further contribute to the marginalization of U.S. Latino/a perspectives by giving the false impression such theologies are unable to "break out" of a specifically Hispanic location. Finally, the work of theologians Ada María Isasi-Díaz and Luis G. Pedraja provides strong examples of how *mestizaje* has been transformed from a source of personal and group identity into a politically empowering model of religious social activism and dialogic encounter with the other.

Chapter 3, "The Public Relevance of Theology," confronts the primary crisis of spirituality within North American Christianity: the privatization of faith. The dominant view of religion in the United States marginalizes confessional perspectives in public discourse by limiting faith to the domain of private religious experience with little or no relevance in matters of policy. I articulate a Christian political theology informed by both the Calvinist Reformed tradition and Latin American liberation theology that is grounded in the community's lived faith yet remains receptive to external critical voices by analyzing New Testament narratives in order to gain a deeper understanding of Jesus' relationship with civil authorities, to discern Jesus' teachings concerning slavery, and to describe his resistance to the dominant political and religious authorities of his day. These narratives then serve as prototypes for contemporary political action, informing the development of a transcultural theology of human liberation that is public and confessional, spiritual and temporal, revolutionary and nonviolent.

The second part of the book draws upon the insights of U.S. Latino/a theology in order to demonstrate the emancipatory potential of doctrine by reconstructing major Christian doctrines through the hermeneutical lens of *mestizaje*. Chapter 4, "Guadalupe: *Imago Dei* Reconsidered," utilizes Guadalupe—an instance of *mestizaje* often associated with Mexican nationalism—as a case study for the encounter between Christ and culture by defending the Guadalupe theophany as a valuable resource for a theology of human liberation. As a Latino Protestant writing about the most recognized Latin American and U.S. Latino/a Catholic devotion, I trace Protestant discomfort with (and objections to) Guadalupan devotion to iconoclastic tendencies among sixteenth-century Protestant Reformers, as well as to the strict Christocentric understanding of divine revelation in the theology of John Calvin. Recovering resources within the Reformed theological heritage that allow Protestants like myself to approach Guadalupe as a vehicle of divine self-communication (i.e., a new cultural manifestation of the Gospel), I argue that some readings of the Guadalupan tradition are compatible with a Reformed Christocentric theology. The chapter ends with constructive proposals for reconstructing the doctrine of Creation by creatively incorporating Guadalupan insights that remind the ecumenical church that our identity as creatures made in the image of God necessarily includes the historically marginalized "other."

Chapter 5, "The *Mestizo* Christ," explores *mestizaje* as a Christological metaphor by allowing us to see how in Jesus of Nazareth God became incarnate as *mestizo*. Since Jesus—as a marginalized Galilean—identifies with the racialized other, the church must affirm and actively struggle to preserve the full humanity of those marginalized and oppressed because of their race or ethnicity. The metaphor of *mestizaje* applied to the person and work of Christ yields a Christology that focuses on the nature of Jesus' relationships with his neighbors, his relationship to God, and his relationship to the dominant religious and civil authorities. After an examination of classical Christology in which five thematic loci are identified as important for an emancipatory reconstruction of the doctrine of Christ, I defend an understanding of the person and work of Christ indivisible from his liberating praxis. The chapter concludes by arguing that *mestizaje* is not just a source of cultural and ethnic identity but also provides a strong theological argument for understanding the Christian life as the communally embodied continuation of Christ's saving work in the world today.

In an effort to see how humans are reconciled with one another, chapter 6, "The Spirit of Community," discusses the work of the Holy Spirit in founding and empowering the community of faith. The Holy Spirit is shown to empower humanity for the ministry of reconciliation, and our theological metaphor is enriched through the recognition that moral agency is a crucial dimension of *mestizaje*. Since traditional understandings of justification and sanctification emphasize that the Christian life begins with a conversion experience made possible by the indwelling of the Holy Spirit, a liberationist understanding of Christian conversion as political solidarity is needed before the whole church can embrace *mestizaje* as a model of liberative praxis. I then raise a question implied (but never adequately stated) in both chapter 4 (on the doctrine of Creation) and chapter 5 (on the person and work of Christ): *Does the church community exclusively mediate reliable knowledge of God, or is reliable knowledge of God available independent of the teachings of the one, holy, catholic and apostolic church?* By focusing theological reflection upon the work of the Holy Spirit, I seek to help the church embrace God's presence in human cultures beyond the Christian community and thereby address the problems raised by the encounter with other world religions.

The conclusion, "Toward a *Mestizo* Church," shows how the paradigm of *mestizaje* as descriptive of the work of the Holy Spirit yields concrete liberating practices that must be embodied by the Christian community. Broadly, these "marks" of a *mestizo* church include resistance to racism, sexism, and classism. Such a prophetic Christian community would emphasize a liberative reading of Scripture that empowers the church to engage in positive social transformation while preserving a distinct cultural identity that does not denigrate or exclude other cultures. Part 2's exploration of doctrine as a source of liberating praxis presents Christian practices that might constitute "marks" of the *mestizo* church, including (1) engaging in political activism to resist racism grounded in a belief that the racially and ethnically "other" shares in the *imago Dei,* (2) continuing Christ's ministry of reconciliation by fully embodying the "way of the cross" as adversarial politics, (3) broadening our definition of spiritual community to recognize God's liberating work wherever it occurs, and (4) working together with new manifestations of spiritual community located outside traditional understandings of *ecclesia*.

Arguing that dominant theological traditions can benefit from an open and receptive encounter with different, even apparently incompatible, perspectives, I ultimately intend this investigation to contribute a deeper appreciation within North American theology for the integral role of liberation in the formation of Christian doctrine. This investigation undertakes a major task of theology, to preserve the diachronic and synchronic unity of the church in the face of pluralism by identifying those doctrines and practices without which a tradition cannot name itself Christian. In this continuing theological conversation, the task of marginalized perspectives is often to correct historical errors by emphasizing neglected or silenced aspects of doctrine—not to supplant one perspective with the other but to articulate a richer, more authentic comprehension of divine mystery. By reconstructing major Christian doctrines through the lens of mestizo experience, my goal is to enrich the Christian tradition by reminding the dominant theological perspective of long-neglected, important, and integral liberative themes essential to the biblical and doctrinal heritage of ecumenical Christianity through the ages.

PART I

The Fundamental Contradiction

1

Beyond Black and White
Understanding Race in North America

Two apparently inconsistent axioms shape this investigation's conception of race: (1) there is only one human race, and (2) racial particularity remains a necessary aspect of political discourse. In North American public discourse *race* and *racism* are widely used terms open to a variety of interpretations and vulnerable to imprecision between technical and popular usage. Nevertheless, within academic discourse there is, despite the vagaries of language, some consensus as to their technical use: (1) the most common yet outdated usage of "race" refers to the existence of biologically distinct human subspecies (i.e., Negroid, Mongoloid, Caucasoid), a view now rejected by the disciplines of biology and anthropology; (2) in contrast to this first use, "race" is often used as a synonym for the entire human species, emphasizing the genetic unity of humankind in spite of somatic differences; (3) a third meaning of "race" is closer to the term *ethnicity* insofar as it is used as a synonym for a nation or ethnic group (Jewish, Irish, etc.); and (4) social scientists use *race* to identify a group of people who share a collective identity on the basis of physical markers (skin color, hair texture, facial features, etc.) and/or analogous social locations in their respective societies, even when belonging to distinct national or ethnic groups (black, Asian, white, Hispanic, etc.).[1] By this schema, the concept of race does not refer to any singular identifying trait but encompasses such diverse factors as national origin, skin color, cultural traditions, and familial bloodlines. Accordingly, the term *racism* describes a broad range of negative or hostile attitudes by one social group toward another on the basis of these same factors.

By defining *ethnocentrism* as the almost universal human tendency to prefer members of one's own social group, and *racial prejudice* as the irrational hatred toward members of another group (often on the basis of physical differences such as skin color), this investigation reserves the term *racism* for a very particular set of attitudes and behaviors. *Racism* is distinguished by the systemic imposition of ethnocentrism or racial prejudice by one social group upon social structures and cultural practices that not only foster racial discrimination but also produce long-term racial disadvantage for another social group. By this definition, whenever one social group exercises political power over against another group with the intention of advancing its own political advantage and cultural domination while limiting the political, economic, and cultural opportunities of the other, we have an instance of racism. Historically, the oppressed group is often an ethnic minority within a larger population, but as evidenced by South Africa under apartheid, a minority population can dominate and oppress a majority population. A spectrum of social realities can be considered "racist" beyond the more obvious authoritarian racist regimes of the nineteenth and twentieth centuries (e.g., slavery and Jim Crow laws in the United States, the genocidal ideology of Nazi Germany, and South African apartheid), given that a society not overtly structured to benefit one group over another can nonetheless perpetuate cultural attitudes and behaviors that lead to the racial disadvantage of others. At stake in this definition of racism is the oppressed social group's access to political power and ability to positively transform its own socioeconomic reality, a crucial distinction when addressing theorists who claim that racism is a modern phenomenon linking European colonial expansion, the rise of capitalism, and the dominance of scientific rationalism to the creation of totalitarian racist states without accounting for the premodern, culturally embedded roots of modern racism.

By emphasizing the social power dynamics that constitute racism, I do not minimize the role of moral agency in perpetuating racism, but seek to highlight individual acts of irrational racial prejudice within a particular cultural and historical matrix. This definition allows for the possibility that the victims of racism can themselves institute racist structures and practices, countering those theorists who argue that, for example, in a white-dominated society only whites can be racist. The justification for the latter is based upon the assumption that since racism is structural and institutional, since we live in a society defined by white cultural privilege, and since blacks do not have an equal share of institutional power, only whites can be racist (most of this literature speaks only in black-white polarities).[2] This approach rightly emphasizes the institutional dimension of racism but posits a rather narrow view of power. For example, the tendency within minority populations of color to create hierarchies in which lighter skin is valued and darker skin stigmatized ("colorism") might have arisen as a consequence of white European racism, but the fact that these tendencies have been internalized and perpetuated by the very victims of racism demonstrates that the oppressed are also capable of instituting practices of domination. Furthermore, this definition does not adequately account for racism in nonwhite societies. Take the tragic history of conquest and oppression of Koreans by the Japanese, grounded on the long-held belief that Koreans are inherently different from and inferior to the Japanese. To label this an "ethnic" conflict over cultural differences as opposed to a "racist" conflict on the assumption that both populations belong to the same "race" (i.e., they are both "Asian") is to impose Western theoretical concepts on the situation. Finally, there is something imperialistic and paternalistic about any view of humanity that treats the victims of oppression as less than human by denying them the capacity to act as sinfully as their oppressors. We must resist the temptation to romanticize the victims of oppression as saintly on the basis of their social location, since to define racism as solely institutional at the cost of individual moral agency or group self-determination is in itself an act of domination.

While the racial attitudes of the biblical world reveal an awareness of color difference that does not necessarily lead to the enslavement or oppression of other people, there is a long history of postbiblical interpretation within Judaism, Christianity, and Islam that rationalizes and justifies the subjugation of sub-Saharan Africans. In modern Euro-American racial discourse the so-called curse of Ham (Gen. 9:18–27) stands out as the chief example of racist misuses of the Bible, one with clear precursors in Talmudic, Patristic, and early Muslim exegesis. A brief survey of the history of interpretation of such racialized texts is warranted in order to better understand the racist contradiction embodied in antebellum Christianity in the United States. While Christian belief and practice have contributed to the legitimization of racial stratification, scientific racism has also exerted a deep and long-lasting influence on popular North American beliefs about race. Therefore, this chapter traces the history and eventual rejection of scientific racism within academic discourse, highlighting the recent resurgence of biological theories of race in the North American academic context. While race is no longer considered a valid descriptive category in the natural sciences, it has been embraced by marginalized and oppressed groups as a necessary descriptive category for political discourse in order to resist white cultural and political dominance. Historically, racial descriptive categories were forced upon minority groups by the dominant culture ("racialization"), yet these groups have appropriated and transformed such labels in their search for cultural identity and political liberation. To unilaterally abandon the language of race now that science has recognized the error of its ways is to ignore and minimize a long and painful history of oppression. Consequently, I contend that the Christian church's response to racism ought to embrace liberating aspects of the "race consciousness" movement in its theological reflection.

The Biblical Background

When did color prejudice enter the biblical exegetical tradition? Two landmark studies, Frank Snowden's *Blacks in Antiquity* (1970) and Lloyd Thompson's *Romans and Blacks* (1989), evaluate the culture of Western classical antiquity and conclude the ancients were not racist in the modern sense of the term. Nevertheless, both studies acknowledge the presence of negative color prejudice and identify a cross-cultural tendency toward ethnocentrism. Still, the consensus among classical and biblical scholars is that most references to skin color and ethnicity in classical texts are examples of literary color symbolism not motivated by racial prejudice. This investigation contends there is evidence of an accumulative consequence upon Western culture resulting from the continual use of negative color symbolism, which, while not originating in color prejudice, gave rise to racial prejudice and racism. Given that Christianity originated as a persecuted sect within the Roman Empire and became the official state religion, serious questions also need to be asked concerning the "rhetoric of empire" in the formation and spread of Christianity.[3] If, indeed, the spread of Christianity in the West follows the general history of empire, theology faces the arduous task of unraveling how the rhetoric of empire transformed the New Testament message and, more important (for the current investigation), how Christianity accepted and spread Greco-Roman "ethno-political rhetorics" that contributed to the rise of modern racism.[4]

The Theological Roots of Modern Racism

Both Snowden and Thompson presume a definition of racism—as the creation and perpetuation of totalitarian structures by a dominant group to subjugate another group perceived as inferior—that leads them to conclude classical antiquity was not racist. However, this definition of racism does not adequately account for the more subtle forces that shape cultural attitudes in order to create racial/ethnic stratification without the overt use of political domination. In general, references to skin color in non-Christian and early Christian Greco-Roman literature disclose a rhetorical use of color symbolism in which black is negative/evil and white is positive/good, but such metaphors are not considered instances of color prejudice insofar as this anthropological phenomenon appears cross-culturally (even in some black African cultures).[5] Nevertheless, Thompson acknowledges antiblack sentiment—attributing it to an almost universal response to the unfamiliar other ("ethnocentrism")—while Snowden documents the Greco-Roman aesthetic bias against both very dark and very light skin color that certainly contributed to classical attitudes about sub-Saharan Africans.[6]

In the wake of Snowden's research, the accepted consensus among classicists and biblical scholars states that color prejudice (as we know it today) did not exist in antiquity. I am troubled by the sweeping generalization that racism is a modern phenomenon because it fails to recognize those important aspects of classical aesthetic and moral norms equating beauty and goodness with whiteness that contributed to the formation of modern racist worldviews.[7] It is worth noting that several of Snowden's peers (Thompson included) have critiqued his emphasis on positive portrayals of blacks in classical literature to the exclusion of more negative and grotesque representations.[8] Regardless, Hellenistic culture left its indelible mark on Judeo-Christian theological traditions. Biblical and post-biblical perceptions of blacks by Jews, Christians, and Muslims illuminate the cross-cultural permeability of confessional traditions with their surrounding culture and provide a baseline comparison for deciphering the various "rhetorics" of empire that have interacted with the biblical tradition. Images of black Africans in the Hebrew Bible correspond to Snowden's evaluation of ancient Greco-Roman attitudes. In other words, there is no historical evidence of negative color prejudice in the Bible. Based on the limited textual evidence, the ancient Israelite perception of black-skinned Africans (specifically references to "Kushites" in the Hebrew Bible, "Ethiopians" in the LXX) can be cataloged under three distinct categories: (1) a proverb about skin color that does not reveal any negative sentiment toward black skin but merely refers to skin color as a metaphor for that which is unchangeable (Jer. 13:23), (2) statements about specific Kushites (Num. 12:1; Jer. 38:7–13; Jer. 36:14; Zeph. 1:1; Ps.

7:1), none of which reveal an attitude of color prejudice or other negative sentiment based on ethnicity, and (3) a passage in Isaiah (18:1–2, 7)
that describes the land of Kush and its people in positive terms.[9] Ironi-
cally, the Hebrew text most often associated with biblical justifications of
racism, Genesis 9:18–27, contains no reference to ethnicity or skin color,
pointing to a postbiblical origin for the interpretive tradition that viewed
the curse of Ham etiologically as the rationalization for the enslavement
of sub-Saharan Africans.

Analysis of postbiblical Jewish and Jewish-Hellenistic sources also reveals a lack of negative evaluations of black Africans. Rabbinic and tar-
gumic literature preserves the biblical image of Kush as the "land at the
farthest southern reach of the earth" becoming the basis "for various expressions denoting geographic extremes, just as in classical writings."[10]
Thus, within the Judaism of late antiquity, the idea that Ethiopia was literally the end of the earth "gave rise to two contradictory images of the
people who lived there: they are pious, unsullied by civilization; and they
are barbaric, unenlightened by civilization."[11] In other words, while postbiblical Jewish literature does reveal some negative attitudes toward Kushites, they are not based on skin color but reflect a general Mediterranean
attitude toward all barbarian cultures, or merely echo the negative color
symbolism present within all ancient literature (Greco-Roman and Near
Eastern).

Not surprisingly, early Christian literature—both New Testament and
Patristic writings—reflects the same cultural norms of aesthetic beauty
and perpetuate the same ethnocentric tendency toward one's own social
grouping as the rest of ancient Mediterranean culture. The most influential early Christian interpreter of "blackness" in the Bible was Origen. He
interpreted Song of Songs 1:5 ("I am black but beautiful") allegorically,
employing the common metaphor of darkness as sin. Origen's identification of the maiden speaking in verse 5 as an Ethiopian, and his use of this
and other biblical Ethiopians as symbols for those still in sin and outside
God's covenant (i.e., unbaptized Gentiles), became widely accepted, thus
establishing the pattern for all future Christian exegesis.[12] The church
fathers from Origen to the sixth century "saw the biblical Ethiopian as
a metaphor to signify any person who, not having received a Christian
baptism, is black in spirit and without light."[13] While not a completely
negative valuation—insofar as "unbaptized" implies there is still hope of
salvation in Christ—the fact remains that Origen and other church fathers equated "Ethiopia" and black skin with a spiritually unregenerate

state, even extending the metaphor to the point that salvation becomes linked with whiteness.[14] The church fathers allegorized biblical references to Ethiopians (in the LXX and New Testament) as symbols for sin, going so far as to depict devils as black Ethiopians; nevertheless, historians still view them as inheritors of the classical literary tradition that employed black-white color symbolism to represent good and evil instead of as proto-racists.

So when did color prejudice enter the biblical exegetical tradition? Postbiblical Jewish exegesis had a strong influence on Christian and Islamic exegetical traditions, yet it is disingenuous to conclude that Western color prejudice and racism originated in Jewish literature. The evidence is inconclusive as to whether or not Rabbinic interpretation influenced Origen's reading of Song of Songs or was itself a reaction to Origen. The link is stronger between Philo of Alexandria, the first-century Jewish philosopher and contemporary of Jesus, and Patristic exegesis. Although Philo was not a major source in the development of Rabbinic Judaism, he is frequently cited in early Christian literature, especially in reference to his allegorical method of exegesis (and the allegorization of Ethiopian/blackness as evil). Classical historian Raoul Lonis has argued that Philo is the only exception to the prevailing view that racism and color prejudice did not exist in the ancient world.[15] Given Philo's influence upon Patristic exegesis, and the Christian appropriation of the metaphor of the Ethiopian as sinner and as devil, it is understandable how—with the rapid spread of Christianity—the use of color symbolism had a negative effect over time and contributed to racist cultural attitudes in the West.

What apparently rescues early Christian theology from being labeled racist is its commitment to the equality of blacks within the church, a belief grounded in the New Testament account of the Ethiopian eunuch's conversion (Acts 8:26–40), which has become symbolic of the Christian belief in the universality of the Gospel "as a means to emphasize their conviction that Christianity was to include all mankind."[16] However, recent scholarship challenges this naïve reading of the New Testament text and questions the prevailing view of racism in antiquity by arguing that the rhetorical use of ethnicity and skin color implies a deprecating view of the black-skinned other. Thus, while the customary exegesis of Acts 8:26–40 correctly affirms the inclusiveness of the Christian church insofar as salvation is offered to all humankind, the text's rhetorical effectiveness relies upon the dominant sociopolitical and cultural prejudices existing in antiquity to make the point that "Christianity can extend to every nation

—*even* Ethiopia."[17] Gay Byron argues that early Christians naturally adopted the ethnopolitical rhetorics of the dominant Greco-Roman culture and concludes that when New Testament and Patristic writers manipulate popular perceptions of Ethiopians for theological and evangelistic purposes they disclose much about the sociopolitical realities underlying these discursive patterns.

Patristic narratives about the desert father Ethiopian Moses (who became an exemplar of ascetic virtue) demonstrate how references to the otherness of his skin color or ethnic identity signify more than literary color symbolism or allegorical allusions to sin but reveal real antipathy toward the black-skinned other in Greco-Roman society. One story, in which Moses is ordained and then tested spiritually by being rebuked for his blackness, employs both an ethnic identifier ("Ethiopian") and a color description ("Black one") for Moses, who responds humbly by internalizing the color-symbolic language of his religious superiors: "Rightly have they treated you, *ash skin, Black One* (*spododerme melane*). As you are not a human, why should you come among humans?"[18] Lloyd Thompson attributes Moses' self-deprecation to the caste system present in classical antiquity in which "there is often a tendency among the upper ranks to see the lower orders as 'non-men' or 'less than human.'"[19] Byron questions Thompson's interpretation: "I agree with Thompson's class-based assessment of the references to humans in this text. But I do not agree with his claim that this class-based prejudice has nothing to do with race prejudice," since "the editor of this text is appealing to attitudes about ethnic and color difference in order to shape an understanding of ascetic virtue."[20] In other words, the very rhetorical structure of the narrative as a test of Moses' humility and patience depends upon an appropriate response to verbal insults; the use of the terms *Ethiopian* to refer to Moses and *white* to refer to his new status following ordination, and the monastic community's consequent treatment of Moses (driving him out because of his skin color and ethnicity), are deliberate acts of humiliation. This rhetorical use of skin color and ethnicity as insults rests upon a sociopolitical reality in which the dominant classes frequently disparage and discriminate on the basis of skin color and nationality. Only then does the narrative—in which the spiritually appropriate response is for Moses to demonstrate the ascetic virtues of self-control, indifference, and dispassion when his blackness is disparaged—make sense. The implication in this text (and others that make a moral exemplar of Ethiopian Moses) is that spiritual perfection is attainable only by ignoring oppressive social realities. Moses' silence in the face of these insults—long praised as an example of spiritual humility—also reveals much about ancient Mediterranean culture: "The rhetorics work only if the authors assume that the audiences would respond to the conversion stories based on accepted perceptions about ethnic and color difference. That is, Ethiopians had to be perceived not only as other or foreign, but also as inferior from the perspective of the audiences addressed in the texts."[21]

The Western viewpoint equating slavery with blackness confirms the ancient Greco-Roman cultural hegemony and points to the long-lasting influence of the rhetoric of empire in spreading color prejudice. In the ancient world slavery was a universally accepted fact of life, and it is well documented that there were black slaves in ancient Greece and Rome. In the Hellenistic and Roman periods of Western antiquity, prisoners of war were the primary source of slaves; however, there is also historical evidence of a black slave trade originating in East Africa and Arabia and extending as far west as Greece and Rome in the earliest centuries of the Common Era. Consequently, among the lighter-skinned peoples of the Mediterranean and the Near East, the visibly different skin color of African slaves contributed to the gradual cultural association of blackness with slavery that spread with the growth of the Roman Empire.[22] Furthermore, the Arab slave trade during the early Islamic period (eighth century CE) was extensive and well established, suggesting it had existed in the pre-Islamic era. Historian James Sweet argues that the racist ideologies of the fifteenth-century Atlantic slave trade can be traced to the development of African slavery in the Islamic world as far back as the eighth century CE: "From North Africa to Persia, blackness equaled slavery (*'abid*) and the degradation that slavery implied."[23]

At the height of Islamic cultural influence the Muslim world extended from Iberia across southern Europe and North Africa east into China. From 711 to 1492 CE Muslims controlled the Iberian Peninsula, producing long-lasting effects upon the racial attitudes of Iberians and by implication the entire Atlantic slave trade. By the ninth century Muslim culture differentiated between black (*'abd*) and white (*mamluk*) slaves in great part because the white European "*mamluk* commanded a higher price than the black *'abd* because he could bring a substantial Christian ransom or be exchanged for a Muslim captive."[24] Ultimately, this disturbing economic reality shaped cultural attitudes in the Arab world, justifying the belief that black Africans were little more than a cheap and expendable source of labor in much the same way Greco-Roman aesthetic norms and general attitude of cultural superiority had, in earlier centuries, spread color prejudice across the Mediterranean world. Thus, in spite of religious commandments protecting Islamic black Africans, the myth of black inferiority perpetuated Arabic cultural superiority:

> Negative racial stereotypes crystallized in the minds of whites over the duration of the trans-Saharan slave trade. As reflected in Arabic linguistic constructions, religious assumptions, and literary records like Ibn Battuta's diary, blacks, regardless of their legal status, were always viewed as morally and culturally inferior. The Muslim world expected blacks to be slaves.[25]

And, like their Jewish and Christian antecedents, Muslim exegetes also appealed to the Old Testament—specifically the so-called curse of Ham (Gen. 9:18–27)—to justify the enslavement and dehumanization of sub-Saharan Africans.

This brief picture of Western classical antiquity allows us to draw certain conclusions about the incidence of color prejudice during the formative years of the Christian religion. First, without imposing a modern definition of racism onto the ancient world, we can accept Gay Byron's thesis that prejudice based on skin color and/or ethnicity was commonplace, otherwise numerous texts that depend on negative stereotypes about the ethnically "other" for their rhetorical effectiveness are rendered meaningless. Second, we can also accept Snowden and Thompson's conclusions about the inclusiveness of early Christian theology while nonetheless recognizing that Christians shared the prejudices of the dominant culture. Finally, we must acknowledge the hegemonic influence of the dominant Greco-Roman culture on all the cultures of the Mediterranean and Ancient Near East.[26] Therefore, without labeling all ancients as proto-racists, we can nonetheless identify a developing pattern that strongly suggests Greco-Roman cultural norms and ethnocentric attitudes—either embraced by or forced upon local cultures wherever Roman legions established political domination (be it Europe, North Africa, or the Near East)—created a fertile environment for antiblack sentiment that, given the foundational influence of classical antiquity upon Western culture and history, ultimately manifest itself as modern racism.

Rather than identify a single historical source for the exegetical tradition that links the curse of Ham to the enslavement of black Africans, this investigation has described the multiple cultural factors present in classical antiquity that contributed to the creation of Western racism. Given that any ethnic group is partial to its own skin color (an anthropological phenomenon found in all cultures throughout human history), and given the political and cultural dominance of Rome, it is no surprise that as Christianity developed from a sect within Judaism into a legally recognized religion and eventually the official state religion of the Roman Empire, it came to embrace the dominant ethnopolitical rhetoric that viewed the ethnic other as "barbarian," asserted the Mediterranean/European physical type as the aesthetic norm, and equated blackness with slavery. Ethnocentrism is not color prejudice or racism, but neither is it harmless. Consequently, without precisely identifying a date when Western postbiblical exegesis first linked slavery to race, it is evident that the building blocks of New World racialized readings of Genesis 9 were present in the earliest exegesis of the Jewish, Christian, and Muslim traditions.

The Biblical Justification of Slavery in the United States

The previous section examined how the cultural seeds of modern racism were planted in late classical antiquity as evidenced by similar racialized readings of biblical texts in the Rabbinic, Patristic, and Muslim exegetical traditions. Although Genesis 9:18–27 makes no reference to ethnicity or blackness, the curse of Ham has been employed as the biblical justification for the enslavement of black Africans since the earliest centuries of the Common Era, forever linking dark skin and slavery in the collective consciousness of Western culture. This section explores the way in which nineteenth-century proponents of slavery manipulated the biblical story of Noah's drunkenness and the resulting curse on Ham's son Canaan to defend the institution of slavery.

The biblical text makes no mention of a curse relating to blackness; it only names slavery as the curse Noah uttered against Canaan. Still, the King James Version of the Bible (the most common and widely used English translation in the antebellum United States) contributed to theological justifications for enslaving black Africans by condemning Ham's descendants to lives of subjection:

And Noah awoke from his wine, and knew what his younger son had done unto him. And he said, "Cursed be Canaan; a servant of servants shall he be unto his brethren." And he said, "Blessed be the Lord God of Shem; and Canaan shall be his servant. God shall enlarge Japheth, and he shall dwell in the tents of Shem; and Canaan shall be his servant." (Gen. 9:24–27, KJV)

While the belief that this story provides a historical explanation for the origins of slavery as well as evidence that Ham was the progenitor of sub-Saharan Africans has roots in the earliest periods of Western theological interpretation, it is only with the growth of the transatlantic slave trade and the increased demand for slave labor that Western interpretations of the curse of Ham as justification for black enslavement became part of the popular consciousness.

The racialized readings of Genesis 9 in the United States not only embrace the text as an explanation for slavery but also explicitly link blackness with slavery as rationalization for the institution of slavery upon which the agricultural economy of the Southern states depended. One such popular reading from Southern Presbyterian minister James A. Sloan concludes that enslavement and blackness are the result of Ham's sin:

> Ham deserved death for his unfilial and impious conduct. But the Great Lawgiver saw fit, in his good pleasure, not to destroy Ham with immediate death, but to set a *mark of degradation* on him. . . . All Ham's posterity are either *black* or dark colored, and thus bear upon their countenance the mark of *inferiority* which God put upon the progenitor. . . . *Black, restrained, despised, bowed down* are the words used to express the condition and place of Ham's children. Bearing the mark of degradation on their skin.[27]

After the Civil War and well into the twentieth century, the curse of Ham continued to inform Southern cultural attitudes about blacks, despite the fact that the biblical curse of Ham did not mention blackness. In the text Ham's descendants were cursed to enslavement; African blacks are slaves; therefore, Ham's curse must have involved the darkening of his skin. The circular logic of such racialized readings exposes the strong ideological drive to provide divine and moral legitimization for the Southern social order.

During the Patristic era the interpretation of Genesis 9:18–27 cast Ham as the villain deserving the punishment of forced servitude. Augustine of Hippo (354–430 CE), perhaps the most influential theologian in Western Christendom, traced the origins of slavery to Ham's transgression without linking blackness or ethnicity to the curse: "For it is understood, of course, that the condition of slavery is justly imposed on the sinner. That is why we do not hear of a slave anywhere in the Scriptures until Noah, the just man, punished his son's sin with this word; and so that son deserved this name because of his misdeed, not because of his nature."[28] Not surprisingly, this tendency to interpret the Genesis 9 text etiologically persisted through the Middle Ages and into the Reformation, perpetuating the interpretive paradigm that viewed Noah as righteous and Ham as villainous and therefore deserving punishment for dishonoring his father. Contrary to Southern racialized readings, however, Augustine rejected slavery as a natural condition for any human being regardless of skin color: "And yet by nature, in the condition in which God created man, no man is the slave either of man or of sin."[29]

While racialized readings of this text predate the founding of Islam and were already part of the Western cultural matrix, it is possible to trace the proliferation of these cultural attitudes in Europe (and eventually the New World) to the Muslim conquest of the Iberian Peninsula because of the central role the African slave trade played in the imperialist expansions of Islam. Stephen Haynes makes the controversial claim that enslavement and blackness were first overtly linked in the Muslim Near East: "The so-called Hamitic myth was first invoked as a justification for human thralldom. In fact, it appears race and slavery were first consciously combined in readings of Genesis 9 by Muslim exegetes during the ninth and tenth centuries, though these authors claim to draw on rabbinic literature."[30] Sweet makes similar claims about the Muslim origins of this racialized reading of Genesis 9:18–27, citing a tenth-century Arab history that identifies Ham as the father of "all blacks and people with crinkly hair . . . [for] Noah put a curse on Ham, according to which the hair of his descendants would not extend over their ears and they would be enslaved wherever they were encountered."[31] Predictably, these cultural prejudices spread over time as Iberian Christians adopted the Muslim justification for black slavery, added arguments of their own, and then disseminated these attitudes by means of the Atlantic slave trade.

Still, the tendency to racialize Ham—while present throughout every period of Western exegetical history—was only part of the ideological justification for black slavery in the antebellum defense of slavery. A brief assessment of antebellum proslavery literature reveals that the story of Ham dishonoring his father resonated with the deep-seated culture of honor, order, and patriarchy of the Old South. The widespread use of Genesis 9:18–27 in popular antebellum proslavery tracts confirms the central role of Noah's curse in theological justifications of slavery. However, the fact that so many of these texts link slavery to Ham's sin without describing the nature of that sin demonstrates a willingness to accept the enslavement of blacks without an explicitly theological justification. In fact, there were differences of opinion among proslavery exegetes regarding the very nature of Ham's sin, but universal agreement on the moral rectitude of slavery and the belief that black Africans—as descendants of Ham—deserve enslavement. According to Haynes, an important insight for understanding antebellum proslavery interpretations of Genesis 9:18–27 is found by reading those texts that not only recount the narrative of Noah's curse on Ham and Canaan but also clearly identify the nature of Ham's sin. Haynes argues that for "proslavery intellectuals who were also devout Christians, Genesis 9 seems to have become an intellectual nexus where religion and honor commingled in support of a common cause."[32]

Although not an exclusively Southern trait, honor (personal and familial) played a central role in the development of Southern culture in the United States—especially among Southern males. Accordingly, the emphasis upon honor and shame in describing the nature of Ham's moral failing taps into the Southern patriarchal psyche and can help explain why proslavery readings of Genesis 9 place so little importance on the exact nature of Ham's offense yet focus on the necessity of satisfaction for dishonoring his father.[33] As agricultural patriarchies, many analogies exist between the biblical world of Noah and the antebellum South, which contribute to the popularity of this biblical text for explaining the origins of slavery. Not surprisingly, abolitionist attacks on the Southern institution of slavery—in which the plantation owner is revered as the patriarch of family and slaves alike—demanded an honor-bound defense of the status quo in order to restore what was perceived as the divinely instituted order. Thus, while not accounting for all the inconsistencies between antebellum proslavery interpretations of Genesis 9:18–27 and the biblical text itself, the role of honor in defending slavery helps to understand the fervor with which such strained and immoral interpretations were defended.

The manipulation of Genesis 9 as a theological justification for slavery demonstrates the need to understand the role of religion in the development of Western racism. Still, the text itself never links blackness to Ham's sin, or to Noah's curse of perpetual enslavement for all of Ham's descendants, so we must look to the gradual association of blackness with slavery in the history of the West to locate the cultural genesis of such racialized readings. Thus, while the curse of Ham became a powerful tool for maintaining the status quo of slavery, proslavery writers were not the only ones to rely on the divine authority of the Bible to bolster their position. The abolitionist movement in the antebellum United States offers liberative counterreadings of the Bible that can inform contemporary theological resistance to racism.

Traditions of Theological Resistance to Racism

In spite of strong voices for separatism and Black Nationalism, the dominant African American abolitionist perspective emphasized the ideal of human unity under God's grace and used the Bible to expose the fundamental contradiction and hypocrisy of American Christianity. The goal was a fully integrated society in which African Americans were recognized as human beings, citizens, and Christian brothers and sisters. In the nineteenth century no voice was more respected—while still remaining highly critical of white Christian America—than Frederick Douglass, who, with a few swift words, effectively undermined the proslavery racist reading of the Curse of Noah:

> Every year . . . a very different-looking class of people are springing up at the south, and are now held in slavery, from those originally brought to this country from Africa; and if their increase will do no other good, it will do away the force of the argument, that God cursed Ham, and therefore American slavery is right. If the lineal descendants of Ham are alone to be scripturally enslaved, it is certain that slavery at the south must soon become unscriptural; for thousands are ushered into the world, annually, who, like myself, owe their existence to white fathers, and those fathers most frequently their own masters.[34]

Among antebellum abolitionists the most important biblical text for providing a counterreading of the Bible was the apostle Paul's liberating vision in Galatians 3:27–28 in which distinctions of race, class, and gender are transcended in Christ, and which continues to serve as a normative statement for understanding contemporary Christian responses to the problem of racism.

Galatians 3:28 became the key passage for Christian moral and social thinking about slavery in the antebellum United States, and many African American orators used this passage to "level prophetic judgment against a society that thought of itself as biblical in its foundation and ethic."[35]

While the African American prophetic tradition sought to remain true to the biblical vision of a community transcending distinctions of race, class, and gender, the realities of North American society in the nineteenth and twentieth centuries gave rise to the ethnically segregated church:

> Irony must be seen in the fact that it was from the situation of institutional separatism that the prophetic call went out for the realization of the biblical principles of universalism, equality, and the kinship of all humanity. Perhaps African Americans had begun to see the inevitability of America's irony: the call for oneness could be made only apart from others, lest particularity be lost; but since particularity in America often meant being left out or discriminated against, exhortation for inclusion was made.[36]

Nevertheless, the theme of radical Christian inclusion and the use of this text to justify Christian unity "was embraced and referred to over and over again even as the African-independent or separate church movements got under way."[37]

Contemporary biblical scholarship affirms the inclusive and emancipatory dimension of Paul's letter to the Galatians. Judith M. Lieu's study of the origins of Christian communal identity uses Galatians 3:27–28 to frame her discussion of "race" (*genos*) and ethnicity/nationality (*ethnos*).[38] Lieu explores ancient notions of personal and group identity within Judaism, the New Testament, early Christianity, and the wider Greco-Roman world before concluding that in the nomenclature of the first century the three major religious groupings—Greco-Roman polytheism, Judaism, and the upstart Christian movement—were understood to constitute three distinct "races" (*genos*). While the earliest Christians belonged to the Jewish nation (*ethnos*), Christian identity became a distinct grouping that transcended both nationality and biological heritage. Although this use of "race" is far removed from the modern understanding of race grounded in physical differences, her study affirms a common reading of Paul's words in Galatians 3:28 that understands Christian identity as somehow transcending established hierarchical relationships in favor of relationships of equality.

Elisabeth Schüssler Fiorenza names this text the "Magna Carta of Christian feminism," and grounds her feminist liberation theology in the "eschatological vision of freedom and salvation" described by the apostle Paul.[39] Yet Fiorenza is careful to differentiate the promised eschatological kingdom from the realities of church life, lamenting the "failure of the church to realize the vision of Galatians 3:28–29 in its own institutions and praxis" and the rise of a "sexist theology of the church, which attempted to justify the ecclesial practice of inequality and to suppress the Christian vision and call of freedom and equality within the church."[40] I would add that the church has also manifested a racist theology, and argue that Fiorenza's "theological reconstruction of the early Christian movement as a discipleship of equals" remains incomplete until the church also comes to terms with its long history of racism.[41]

In Galatians Paul is merely expressing the radical understanding of discipleship held in common by the earliest Christian communities:

> As one leaves the old world, a world in which separation and domination are essential, and enters the new, the old hierarchical values based on the differences in people are left behind. Within the eschatological community, people, no matter of what background, shape, or form, are seen and accepted as equals. While three pairs in the passage point to only three of the greatest separations and sources of inequality in the ancient world, it is legitimate to broaden the perspective and to suggest that the formula implies that *all* superior-inferior relationships are destroyed in the body of Christ.[42]

While it remains unclear whether or not Paul advocated for the emancipation of all slaves in the ancient world, Paul's advice to Philemon concerning Onesimus gives the impression that the slave participated on an equal footing with the master within the life of the Christian community. Without glossing over the troubling fact that Paul's letter to Philemon once served as a central text for slaveholders in the Americas,[43] there is enough textual evidence to support a liberative reading of Paul, especially Galatians 3:27–28, in which all relationships of domination are overcome "in Christ Jesus."

If the church as the body of Christ is our foretaste of the promised kingdom, then when Paul tells us that God, through Christ, "has given us the ministry of reconciliation" and that "we are ambassadors for Christ," he clearly intends for humanity to participate in God's reconciling work (2 Cor. 5:17–21, NRSV). Granted, humankind does not add or contribute to Christ's work of justification, yet we have been entrusted with the message of reconciliation and by our example bear witness to Christ's transforming work in the world. Therefore, before the church can offer a critique of culture it should evaluate its own praxis according to the very standard it proclaims. The apostle Paul recognizes distinctions among people but rejects any social stratification derived from these distinctions. Given the Gospel's call to "Go therefore and make disciples of all nations, baptizing them in the name of the Father and of the Son and of the Holy Spirit" (Matt. 28:19, NRSV), what justification remained for the enslavement of black Africans once they had converted to Christianity? The hollowness of theological justifications for slavery begs the question as to what other cultural factors shaped racist thought in the United States; aside from religious belief, no other force has had a deeper or longer-lasting influence on popular beliefs about race than scientific racism.

The Eclipsing of "Race" and Its Troubling Return

Without a doubt Christian theological construction has been tainted by racism, and sadly Christian practice has often contributed to the legitimization of racially stratified societies. However, to argue that modern American racist thought is primarily a product of religious bigotry ignores the influence of Darwinian evolutionary theory in North America—especially the historical conflict between nineteenth-century Christianity and the scientific worldview. Without denying the formative role of Christianity upon the culture of the United States, I contend that scientific racism currently has a deeper influence on popular beliefs about race.

The Use and Abuse of the Natural Sciences

Biological determinism, the view that shared behavioral patterns within human groups arise from inherited genetic distinctions (that can then be used to legitimize social stratification according to race), came under sharp criticism and was in great part discredited in the latter half of the twentieth century. Stephen Jay Gould in *The Mismeasure of Man* (1981) denies the existence of a general factor for intelligence as an independent and verifiable biological phenomenon and suggests that determinist arguments about human intelligence are a form of scientific racism. By demonstrating how social prejudice shapes and alters so-called objective and disinterested knowledge, he explores whether or not a priori commitments to a racist worldview shaped the "scientific" questions asked and colored the data gathered to support an already foreordained conclusion. Gould argues that the "scientific" data undergirding the psychological tests that today quantify and measure intelligence arose in a cultural context where white Europeans were considered the pinnacle of human evolution, Indians (Native Americans) were below whites on the evolutionary scale, and blacks below everyone else. Hence, IQ tests do not measure a universal genetic human trait ("intelligence") but merely reflect the cultural bias of a white racist society. Gould's landmark study demonstrates how the "scientific" data of the recent past—used to rationalize racist "ranking" and even to designate certain races as subhuman—were the product of unconscious social prejudice or, worse, deliberate manipulation and fabrication of "empirical" evidence.

An example of the former is the work of Samuel George Morton, a respected nineteenth-century scientist and practitioner of craniometry, whose empirical measurements of human skulls reveal an unconscious racist bias since he often omitted data that might discredit his theories about Caucasian superiority (Gould concludes such omissions were unintentional). An example of the latter is *Types of Mankind* (1854) by Nott and Gliddon, a leading North American textbook of its time on the subject of human racial differences that disseminated Morton's data to the popular culture and which Gould cites as a blatant example of deliberate fraud, as evidenced by the manipulation of skull diagrams in order to emphasize similarities between "Negroid" skulls and those of lower primates.[44] However, it was not until the advent of evolutionary theory popularized by Charles Darwin's *Origin of Species* (1859) and *The Descent of Man* (1871) that "arguments for slavery, colonialism, racial differences, class structures, and sex roles would go forth primarily under the banner of science."[45]

While Gould acknowledges the role of religious institutions in disseminating racist ideology, he argues that scientific racism became widely accepted and ultimately more influential because it was presented to the public as "scientific" truth—supposedly arrived at through a disinterested and objective method. Before Darwin, the dominant views on race in North America depended upon a literal reading of the Bible. The main issue dividing the biblical racism dominant in the Southern states from the new scientific racism was the theory of *polygeny* that classified the different human races as different species with distinct biological origins, in contradiction to the biblical teaching that all humans are the children of Adam and Eve. Belief in *monogenism* was so prevalent that racist Southern preachers resorted to rather strained interpretations of Genesis 9:18–27 (the curse of Ham) in order to rationalize the enslavement of black Africans.[46] After Darwin, the Bible (and creationism) quickly lost its authority for settling scientific debates in the public arena (though not in certain fundamentalist circles), and popular opinion on matters of race came to rely more and more upon "scientific" fact. Because scientific racism, in the form of the hereditary theory of IQ, has maintained a veneer of respectability well into the present, it is vital to expose the hidden prejudice underlying contemporary intelligence testing.

The very concept of intelligence is so ethereal it defies definition. IQ tests, as well as other "aptitude" tests like the SAT college entrance exam, are culturally biased; they do not measure innate intelligence but are merely reflections of the intellectual tools necessary to succeed in the dominant culture administering the exams. Consequently, such tests label and stigmatize those not properly assimilated into the culture and further marginalize and hamper the social progress of the already socioeconomically disadvantaged. Given that there is no demonstrable direct correlation between particular mental skills (such as spatial memory) and biological reality (there is no one gene for intelligence), mental tests have been misused to justify belief in the hereditarian theory of IQ. Rejecting this theory is not a blanket dismissal of all intelligence testing insofar as IQ tests are useful tools for identifying children with learning disabilities or for recognizing educational deficiencies in a particular population. Still, such tests have been used to provide evidence for biological determinism in order to argue (1) that intelligence is not only inherited, but inevitable, meaning that intelligence cannot be significantly improved through proper education, and (2) that if genetics can explain variation in intelligence within a racial group, it can also explain variation between racial groups without properly accounting for socioeconomic and other cultural factors. Societies that uncritically adopt biological determinism and let it guide policy on social issues like welfare reform and public school funding are dangerously close to repeating the sins of the past.

The Rejection of Race as a Biological Category

After the Second World War the scientific community confronted the ascendancy of racist ideas that led to the genocidal horrors of the Holocaust. The postwar global situation was altered by the process of decolonialization that led to increased involvement by formerly colonized nations in the United Nations and its international agencies. The United Nations Educational, Scientific and Cultural Organization (UNESCO) focused its energies on the problem of racism, addressing the structures of power that perpetuate racism—especially the international political implications of race relations. These academic responses were in great part motivated by changing social forces, such as the rise of race consciousness among formerly subordinate populations, but also produced a major paradigm shift in theoretical perspective expressed most clearly in the 1950 "Statement on Race" and the 1967 "Statement on Race and Racial Prejudice."

The first statement affirms that scientists "have reached general agreement in recognizing that mankind is one: that all men belong to the same species, *Homo sapiens,*"[47] and accounts for "racial" differentiation among different groups as a result of evolutionary factors. The second UNESCO statement goes further, not only emphasizing the genetic unity of the human race but acknowledging that the very concept of "race" is an arbitrary convention: "Many anthropologists stress the importance of human variation, but believe that 'racial' divisions have limited scientific interest and may even carry the risk of inviting abusive generalization."[48] Asserting that racism is a social construct arising from unchecked prejudices and irrational cultural attitudes, the 1967 statement concludes that the primary means of "coping with racism involve changing those social situations which give rise to prejudice, preventing the prejudiced from acting in accordance with their beliefs, and combating the false beliefs themselves."[49]

Given this major paradigm shift within the scientific community following the Second World War, Stephen Jay Gould's *Mismeasure of Man* reflects the accepted orthodoxy for scientific discussions of what—in the modern era—has been called race. In fact, Gould questions the continuing use of "race" for biologically distinct branches of the human species: "But biologists have recently affirmed—as long suspected—that the overall genetic differences among human races are astonishingly small. Although frequencies for different states of a gene differ among races, we have found no 'race genes'—that is, states fixed in certain races and absent from all others."[50] For example, the official position of the American Association of Physical Anthropologists (AAPA) states:

All humans living today belong to a single species, *homo sapiens,* and share a common descent. . . . Human populations have never genetically diverged enough to produce any biological barriers to mating between members of different populations. . . . *Pure races, in the sense of genetically homogeneous populations, do not exist in the human species today, nor is there any evidence that they ever existed in the past.*[51]

The American Anthropological Association has taken a similar position: "All human beings are members of one species, *Homo sapiens*. . . . Differentiating species into biologically defined 'races' has proven meaningless and unscientific as a way of explaining variation (whether in intelligence or other traits)."[52]

Accordingly, the biological sciences no longer recognize "race" as a legitimate subdivision of the human species, arguing that those physical traits historically defined as racially distinctive (skin color, facial features, hair type, etc.) actually represent—on the level of DNA—a spectrum of possibilities at the same genetic location. Thus, in explaining differences between human groups, science now looks at historical factors like migration and intermarriage, *not* the existence of genetically distinct branches of *Homo sapiens,* to account for such factors as gradations of hair color and texture. Given the widespread acceptance of Gould's position, this raises the question: *Why does academic discourse continue to use the term* race *when referring to different human groups?* While race is no longer a biologically meaningful category, race still matters as "an anthropological and political category."[53] The reasons will become more evident in the following sections, where I discuss Cornel West's genealogy of racism and the rise of "race consciousness" as political resistance against white cultural dominance. Still, there is another reason that the academy has not abandoned the language of biological racism, namely, the resurgence of scientific racism and biological determinism within North American academic discourse. I am referring specifically to the renaissance of psychometric research inaugurated with the publication of *The Bell Curve* (1994) by Richard J. Herrnstein and Charles Murray.

The Resurgence of Race in the Social Sciences

The authors of *The Bell Curve* set out to analyze "differences in intellectual capacity among people and groups and what those differences mean for America's future," well aware of the fears that such research "will promote racism."[54] As expected, response to their claims was extremely passionate: "Most of the published reaction was virulently hostile. The book was said to be the flimsiest kind of pseudoscience. A racist screed.

Designed to promote a radical political agenda. An angry book. Tainted by the work of neo-Nazis."[55] Most published criticism—including Stephen Jay Gould's highly critical review in the *New Yorker*—charged Herrnstein and Murray with uncritically embracing a nineteenth-century essentialist notion of racial difference. That is, instead of exploring fully the sociocultural reasons why a certain human group tends to score lower on a particular IQ test, the authors were quick to embrace a biological explanation.

While the book has become one of the most controversial works of social science in recent history, primarily because of what is says about race, the work is a cautiously presented contribution to social science that identifies a particular problem in contemporary society, analyzes it, and offers a solution. Herrnstein and Murray's argument says that *if* intelligence has a role in determining social status and economic success, *and if* intelligence is inherited through a combination of genetic and environmental factors over which we as individuals have no control, *then* society has a responsibility to organize itself in such a way that steps are taken to compensate the intellectually (and thus economically) disadvantaged. Therefore, however much critics disagree with the claims made by both authors, we need to be fair about their intentions. In fact, once we remove race from the equation, their study is not out of place within the Anglo-American school of political liberalism (Mill, Rawls, Singer, etc.). But we *cannot* remove race from any discussion of social policy in the United States. Intentional or not, the claims made in *The Bell Curve* have racist consequences that the authors have made little or no effort to address.

Briefly, what Herrnstein and Murray have said about ethnic differences in cognitive ability can be summed up as follows: (1) both genetic and environmental factors contribute to cognitive ability in unknown quantities, but psychometric research indicates that much of the observed variation in IQ between ethnic groups can be attributed to genetics; (2) the environmental impact on intelligence is negligible given that educational programs have never raised cognitive ability on a permanent basis (as measured by IQ tests); (3) any discussion of social problems in the United States must take into account the cognitive differences among ethnic and racial groups; and (4) public policy that strives for economic and social equality is misguided—the more realistic goal is a society structured so that everyone can find a "valued place" according to his or her abilities. The guiding mantra of *The Bell Curve* is that public policy cannot significantly change cognitive ability:

Inequality of endowments, including intelligence, is a reality. Trying to pretend that inequality does not really exist has led to disaster. Trying to eradicate inequality with artificially manufactured outcomes has led to disaster. It is time for America once again to try living with inequality, as life is lived: understanding that each human being has strengths and weaknesses, qualities we admire and qualities we do not admire, competencies and incompetencies, assets and debits; that the success of each human life is not measured externally but internally; that all of the rewards we can confer on each other, the most we can confer on each other, the most precious is a place as a valued fellow citizen.[56]

The dangerous presumption of the entire work is the naïve belief that in the United States (or any other modern state) all persons are equally valued as fellow citizens.

Repeatedly the authors state that acceptance of genetic explanations for cognitive differences among ethnic and racial groups does not justify racist behavior. They also claim it is "bad science" to ignore well-documented differences in intelligence or the position that these differences are best explained by genetic factors. Yet, when confronted with the possibility that their research could be used to justify racist behavior or shape racially biased public policy, their response is to minimize the consequences of such an act:

The evidence about ethnic differences can be misused, as many people say to us. Some readers may feel that this danger places a moral prohibition against examining the evidence for genetic factors in public. We disagree, in part because we see even greater dangers in the current gulf between public pronouncements and private beliefs.[57]

The authors recognize that racism, sexism, ageism, and other forms of discrimination are real. However, they are also committed to a libertarian political ideology that limits governmental intrusion into the lives of its citizens and highly values individuality. Accordingly, they argue that programs like affirmative action cannot guarantee equal outcomes by race. Indeed, the most a society can hope for is equal access, since inequality in performance arising from genetic differences in ability will always exist. Recognizing that public policies that attempt to compensate for genetic or environmental disadvantages are "overly optimistic," the authors conclude that much "can and should be done to improve education, *especially for those who have the greatest potential.*"[58] At best, such views maintain the nation's status quo; at worst, they help widen the gap between the haves and have-nots by benefiting the already economically and socially advantaged.

While I disagree with both the scientific conclusions and the policy proposals made in *The Bell Curve,* I cannot deny that the authors' statistical analysis of empirical data is thorough and impressive. Yet, they have done little to address Gould's initial concern about psychometric research —IQ tests do not measure a biological reality but primarily measure individual performance in a culturally biased test. Furthermore, I fail to find any beneficial social consequences for claiming that cognitive differences between human groups are genetic. Discussing whether or not difference in cognitive ability is attributable to environment or genetics, the authors state that the "*existence* of the difference has many intersections with policy issues. The *source* of the difference has none that we can think of."[59] Having said this, they still conclude that the source is primarily genetic. Why? What purpose does it serve? Turning their argument against them, I grant the existence of differences—any analysis of social problems in the United States must come to terms with and account for the fact that there are social and economic inequalities in our country attributable to the complex intersection of many environmental and genetic factors—but contend that accepting the existence of these differences does not commit one to biological determinism. Therefore, given the negative social consequences of espousing a biological determinism that essentializes racial differences (thus providing "scientific" rationalization of racist beliefs and attitudes), I see no benefit in accepting a primarily genetic explanation for these differences.

Race-Conscious Responses to Racism

A fundamental assumption of this investigation is that theology has as much right as evolutionary biology or physical anthropology to participate in and contribute to the public discourse on race. Accordingly, theologians discussing racism in the North American context need to critically engage the resurgence of scientific racism and its consequences for public policy. U.S. Latino/a theologians who find liberation from racism in the concept of biological *mestizaje* should proceed cautiously so that their efforts to establish a distinct Latino/a ethnic identity do not perpetuate a nineteenth-century racial essentialism. Furthermore, biological determinism and racial stratification based on cognitive ability create problems for a theological anthropology grounded in the doctrine of *imago Dei*. If all human beings are created in the image of God, then our basic human dignity remains unaltered whether a person is mentally retarded or intellectually a genius. For that reason, a society ordered according to this doctrine ought to resist social stratification based on genetic inheritance. I argue that the metaphor of *mestizaje* yields a better description of human reality than outdated (and scientifically vacant) racial categories. Still, I take issue with certain usages of *mestizaje* that essentialize Latino/a identity as a biologically distinct human grouping. Race is a social construct and not a biologically distinct reality; there is one human race manifest in a rich diversity of outward physical appearances, and *mestizaje* is a very apt metaphor for describing the biological richness of human genetic mixing. The question I am pursuing is whether or not the racial categories that predominate in social science can be transcended and abandoned in favor of *mestizaje,* or is it the case that—given our long history of racism—our society is not ready to embrace such a universally descriptive category?

Cornel West's Genealogy of Racism

A very important theological text for dismantling the dominant paradigm of modern scientific racism is Cornel West's *Prophesy Deliverance! An Afro-American Revolutionary Christianity* (1982). In this work West reexamines the Western canon and traces the evolution of racism within the dominant academic discourse, he analyzes four traditions of response to modern racism, and then makes concrete recommendations as to which of the four traditions best serves the emancipatory interests of the African American community. African American liberationist thought is influenced by evangelical and pietistic Christianity, the American tradition of political pragmatism, and Marxist social analysis, while also possessing a healthy respect for constitutional democracy. Accordingly, black liberation theology stresses the need for African Americans in North American society to rediscover and affirm a distinctively African American self-identity in light of the painful history of dehumanization and exploitation at the hands of the dominant white culture, and champions the struggle for African American political control of the major institutions that regulate people's lives.

On the twentieth anniversary of the publication of *Prophesy Deliverance!*, Cornel West reaffirmed his intentions for articulating an African American religious philosophy: "To put forward a prophetic interpretation of the Christian tradition rooted in the Afro-American struggle against white supremacy, informed by progressive Marxist theory and fallibilist pragmatic thought and tempered by a profound tragic sense of life."[60] A burning existential question underscores West's often overwhelmingly theoretical language:

> To prophesy deliverance is not to call for some otherworldly paradise but rather to generate enough faith, hope, and love to sustain the human possibility for more freedom. For me, to be a Christian is not to opt for some cheap grace . . . but rather to confront the darker sides, and the human plights, of societies and souls with the weak armor of compassion and justice. The fundamental human mystery is how and why this weak armor—in a cold and cruel world—is not snuffed out just as the Christian mystery is, how and why love so thoroughly crushed by evil force is not fully extinguished.[61]

For most of Western history black people have been treated as less than human, and their cultural contributions to human history have been ignored, marginalized, or silenced. For much of that history Christianity has been woefully silent about the sin of racism if not outright complicit in perpetuating racist social structures. Accordingly, West's history of the black "creative appropriation of Christianity" is a crucial text for any Christian wrestling with the church's racist history.

Resisting and transforming racist theologies demands a rereading of Western intellectual history from the perspective of the oppressed and marginalized—those whose voices have been ignored by or removed from the dominant narrative—which is why West embraces a *genealogical* approach (à la Nietzsche and Foucault) that seeks to describe the rise to dominance of certain ideas and explores the role of power (cultural and political) in the formation of knowledge. While not fully embracing Foucault's philosophical project West recognizes that

> the Foucaultian model and project are attractive to black intellectuals primarily because they speak to the black postmodern predicament, defined by the rampant xenophobia of bourgeois humanism predominant

in the whole academy, the waning attraction to orthodox reductionist and scientific versions of Marxism and the need for reconceptualization regarding the specificity and complexity of Afro-American oppression. Foucault's deep antibourgeois sentiments, explicit post-Marxist convictions and profound preoccupations with those viewed as radically "other" by dominant discourses and traditions are quite seductive for politicized black intellectuals wary of antiquated panaceas for black liberation.[62]

With Foucault, he is committed to a detailed analysis of the complex relations of knowledge and power, is aware of how intellectual discourses shape (and are shaped by) politics, and argues that social control of persons is often the unrecognized goal of both knowledge and power. As pertains to racism, a Foucaultian analysis of power is particularly problematic since these

> powers are subjectless—that is, they are the indirect products of the praxis of human subjects. They have a life and logic of their own, not in a transhistorical realm but within history alongside yet not reducible to demands of an economic system, interests of a class, or needs of a group . . . a history made by the praxis of human subjects which often results in complex structures of discourses which have relative autonomy from (or is not fully accountable in terms of) the intention, aims, needs, interests, and objectives of human subjects.[63]

Thus, while the social construction of ideologies like racism has long been recognized—for example, Stephen Jay Gould's analysis and rejection of scientific racism is predicated on the belief that social prejudice shapes and distorts scientific observation—the social structures of racism are so incredibly complex that even those progressive voices within a particular society that seek to eliminate racism can unintentionally serve the interests of a racist worldview.

A dominant characteristic of modernity is the ability of human reason to find order in the contingent appearance of reality. Postmodernity, on the other hand, "swims, even wallows, in the fragmentary and the chaotic currents of change as if that is all there is."[64] Michel Foucault, reflecting on the constructed nature of knowledge and the role of power relations in the formation and continuation of cultural traditions, views all political praxis with equal suspicion:

Liberty is a *practice*. So there may, in fact, always be a certain number of projects whose aim is to modify some constraints, to loosen, or even to break them, but none of these projects can, simply by its nature, assure that people will have liberty automatically, that it will be established by the project itself. The liberty of men is never assured by the institutions and laws that are intended to guarantee them. This is why almost all of these laws and institutions are quite capable of being turned around.[65]

Foucault emphasizes the inherently ambiguous tendency of all cultural traditions to foster either liberating praxis or horrible oppression:

I think that the central issue of philosophy and critical thought since the eighteenth century has always been, still is, and will, I hope, remain the question: *What* is this Reason that we use? What are its historical effects? What are its limits, and what are its dangers? How can we exist as rational beings, fortunately committed to practicing a rationality that is unfortunately crisscrossed by intrinsic dangers. . . . One should not forget—and I'm not saying this in order to criticize rationality, but to show how ambiguous things are—it was on the basis of the flamboyant rationality of social Darwinism that racism was formulated, becoming one of the most enduring and powerful ingredients of Nazism. This was, of course, an irrationality that was at the same time, after all, a certain form of rationality.[66]

Unfortunately, Foucault stresses irrationality to such a degree that he undermines the capacity of human reason to distinguish between legitimate and illegitimate uses of power and therefore lacks a cohesive model for liberation. Cornel West's prophetic pragmatism, while indebted to Foucault's analysis of power relations, rejects Foucault's tendency to downplay human agency and devalue moral discourse: "For prophetic pragmatists, human agency remains central—all we have in human societies and histories are structured and unstructured human social practices over time and space."[67] Like Foucault, prophetic pragmatists constantly criticize and resist all forms of subjection, exploitation, and domination, but "these critiques and resistances, unlike his, are unashamedly guided by moral ideals of creative democracy and individuality."[68]

West's genealogy of racism focuses on the evolution of modern intellectual discourse and identifies three moments in Western history as particularly important for the formation and rise to dominance of modern scientific racism: (1) the scientific revolution associated with the pioneering work of Copernicus, Galileo, and Newton in the natural sciences, (2) the Cartesian "turn to the subject" in philosophy, and (3) the classical revival arising from the "Enlightenment revolt against the authority of the church and the search for models of unrestrained criticism."[69] While all three events contributed to the formation of white cultural dominance, West contends that the classical revival in particular emphasized white European standards of beauty and cultural achievement, so much so that

> even if race prejudice did not exist in classical antiquity, the minority status of black people in Greece and Rome still rendered black statues, proportions and measurements marginal to cultural life. Hence, the black presence, though tolerated and at times venerated, was never an integral part of the classical ideals of beauty.[70]

Thus, when classical ideals were grafted onto the modern scientific obsession with classifying, categorizing, and imposing order upon the natural order, it gave rise to what West calls the "normative gaze" of Western culture. Consequently, the "role of classical aesthetic and cultural norms in the emergence of the idea of white supremacy as an object of modern discourse cannot be underestimated."[71] European (white) standards of beauty, intelligence, and cultural creation became the unquestioned norms of modern scientific investigation—the ideal by which all of the observations of "natural" history were categorized.

Racism based on physical differences in the modern West originated with the invention of "race" as a classificatory category for describing differences between human groups. In much the same way that physical differences were used to categorize lower-order animals into different species, physical differences between different human groups were used to rationalize belief in the racial inferiority of the nonwhite other. Thus, while the natural sciences recognized infertility as the test for classifying different species (members of the same species produce fertile offspring), many scientists continued to categorize Africans as a different species than Europeans (in spite of much racial mixing), revealing an irrational, even pathological, commitment to the ideal of white superiority.

By employing a Foucaultian genealogical analysis, West is not trying to find the causal origin of modern racism, since such a foundationalist approach is precisely the type of scientific methodology Nietzsche and

Foucault were trying to undermine and supersede. Rather, by demonstrating how the idea of white supremacy has become an integral part of the fabric of modern science, West exposes the insidiousness of modern racism. To reduce this history to a simple cause-and-effect relationship ignores the complex web of power relations that underlie Western science, art, politics, religion, and all other social practices. It is not enough to identify racist attitudes (cause) and actions (effect) and then attempt to eliminate them through legislation (or some other form of social control), since the more dangerous and pervasive aspect of racism is its ability to shape the self-image of the victims of racism:

> The deep human desire for existential belonging and for self-esteem—what I call the need for and consumption of *existential capital*—results in a profound, even gut-level, commitment to some of the illusions of the present epoch. None of us escapes. And many Western peoples get much existential capital from racist illusions, from ideologies of race.[72]

What is needed is a method that exposes—layer by layer, like an archaeologist painstakingly unearthing an ancient ruin—the ideas that our culture has enshrined and upon which our notions of truth and knowledge rest. Therefore, it is not a simple matter of diagnosing a cause and prescribing a cure (although this is possible on the micro-institutional level), but of constantly critiquing the false foundations upon which we have built our cultural discourses. West's genealogical method is not just a history of ideas or a search for origins but is primarily a deconstructive endeavor that seeks to unmask the pretensions to universality of the dominant scientific discourse.

However, unlike Foucault's, West's philosophy is also a *re*constructive undertaking. Cornel West not only exposes the false pretensions of the dominant academic discourse but also brings to light discourses of resistance that have been ignored or purposefully silenced in order to create a fuller history that can provide guideposts for contemporary liberating praxis:

> Modern racist discourse did not go unanswered by Afro-Americans. . . .
> I shall put forward an interpretation and a description of the Afro-American experience in the light of the black reactions and responses to the modern justifications of the idea of white supremacy initiated in enlightened Europe and inseminated in the slavery-ridden United States. The

interpretation and the description are essentially a reconstruction of the black counter discourse to modern European discourse.[73]

Unlike the dominant intellectual history of the West, this new history treats African Americans not as passive objects but as the active subjects of their own history struggling against political, economic, and cultural exclusion and exploitation. Cornel West's analysis of this African American history of resistance recognizes four ideal types or theoretical models under which the various African American resistance movements and intellectual traditions can be categorized: the (1) exceptionalist, (2) assimilationist, (3) marginalist, and (4) humanist traditions of response to modern racism.

The *exceptionalist tradition* can be described in either a weak or a strong form of ethnocentrism that extols the uniqueness of Afro-American culture and identity. Historical examples of this tradition include W. E. B. Du Bois and James Weldon Johnson, although West (surprisingly) categorizes Martin Luther King Jr. as an example of "weak" exceptionalism insofar as Dr. King viewed his God-given mission as an attempt to teach and positively transform (the implicitly inferior) white society through nonviolence. Whether in its strong or weak form, the exceptionalist tradition is a response to white supremacy and is an attempt to build African American self-worth by emphasizing the cultural accomplishments of successful African Americans. This tradition is linked to the rise of an African American middle class and has not always worked to improve the social conditions of all African Americans.

If the exceptionalist tradition is an attempt to create a positive self-image over against the degradation experienced at the hands of a white racist society, then the *assimilationist tradition* can be seen as an internalization of this degradation: "The self-image of Afro-Americans in both types of the assimilationist tradition is one of self-hatred, shame, and fear. Afro-Americans are viewed as morbid subhuman monsters. This tradition posits Afro-American inferiority, not against everyone, but specifically to white Americans."[74] In effect, the assimilationist tradition rejects the notion of an autonomous African American culture and promotes the acceptance of and acculturation into the dominant (and superior) white culture. Cornel West sees many similarities between the exceptionalist and assimilationist responses to racism, not least of which is their dependence upon the rise of a black middle class and with it a black secular intelligentsia, and consequently both traditions ignore the poverty-stricken conditions in which the majority of African Americans live. The intellectual founder of the assimilationist tradition is E. Franklin Frazier, who tended to view much of African American culture as superstition and ignorance and proposed assimilation into white society as the only viable means of cultural and political liberation. West identifies this tradition as "an ideology of Afro-American uplift" whose goal was to "civilize, refine, and modernize Afro-Americans," although later in life Frazier became disappointed with the direction of black assimilation into white bourgeois society and called for "Afro-American intellectuals to provide positive self-images for black people and not to confuse assimilation with self-effacement."[75] Ultimately, West finds the assimiliationist response to modern racism unacceptable as a model for contemporary African American critical thought.

The *marginalist tradition* differs from both the exceptionalist and assimilationist responses to racism insofar at it manages to value and extol a unique African American culture while at the same time feeling confined and limited by this culture. West characterizes members of this tradition as marginalized from Afro-American culture *and* from the dominant white society, thus maintaining a critical distance from both. Accordingly, this tradition is not an organized movement so much as it is descriptive of certain rebellious black intellectuals or alienated community leaders. Of particular relevance to a study of *mestizaje* in U.S. Latino/a culture are the contributions of two archetypal examples of the marginalist tradition, Sutton Griggs and Charles Chestnutt, who reflected extensively on the marginal status of *mulattoes*—"the physically marginal person between Afro-American culture and American society."[76] As persons of mixed backgrounds, Griggs and Chestnutt experienced rejection from both parent cultures and created characters in their fiction who maintain a distance from African American culture while also rejecting and distrusting mainstream American society. Yet it is Richard Wright whom West identifies as the marginal man par excellence whose revolt, while intense, "never crystallized into any serious talk of concerted action, partly because such talk presupposes a community, a set of common values and goals, at which a marginal man like Wright can only sneer."[77] This emphasis on private and personal identity at the expense of communal identity makes the marginalist tradition unsuitable as a model for African American political struggle, although West recognizes that this sense of alienation (usually manifest as rebellion against one's own community) is a prevalent modern attitude.

The best example of the *humanist tradition* of resistance is African American music—spirituals, gospel, the blues, jazz, and hip-hop—because it is a sincere expression of African American experience without romanticizing Afro-American culture (like the exceptionalist tradition) or rejecting its unique contributions (like the assimilationist and marginalist traditions). These different musical styles are grounded in the African oral and musical traditions yet are indelibly marked by the painful history of enslavement and dehumanization in America, becoming "the expression of an oppressed human community imposing its distinctive form of order on an existential chaos, explaining its political predicament, preserving its self-respect, and projecting its own special hopes for the future."[78] While music is one of the most important forms of distinctively African American culture, the Afro-American humanist tradition is also present in literature as expressed in the works of Langston Hughes, Zora Neale Hurston, and Ralph Ellison. At its core, the humanist tradition strives to create a distinctively African American cultural identity (unlike the assimilationist tradition) that does not seek to denigrate other cultures (unlike the marginalist or exceptionalist traditions), while at the same time it avoids essentializing African American identity, which can often limit individual expression.

Central to the humanist understanding of African American history is the open-ended character of the search for personal and cultural identity. While some critics have criticized this obsession with cultural self-identity, Cornel West lifts up Ralph Ellison as the paradigm for the Afro-American literary humanist because he asks the perennial existential questions: "Who am I?" "What is a human being?" "What is an American?" "What is an African American?" The humanist tradition is the best model for contemporary African American critical thought because it links this quest for personal and cultural identity to the equally important struggle for political liberation. These various Afro-American humanist thinkers share a healthy respect for the democratic process and recognize

the necessity for the democratic control over institutions in the productive and political processes. The basic assumption of this Afro-American humanist political viewpoint is that the present economic system and social arrangements cannot adequately alleviate the deplorable socioeconomic conditions of the Afro-American masses. This assumption is linked to a corollary claim, namely, that the circumstances of the black poor and those of the black working class (including both blue- and white-collar workers) are qualitatively similar and only quantitatively different.[79]

What makes the humanist tradition the preferred model of African American resistance to modern racism is its commitment to the liberation and advancement of *all* African Americans. This commitment is grounded in the realization that while it is possible for a small black middle class to flourish, unless the political process in the United States is radically altered, even the wealthiest Afro-Americans still lack "meaningful participation in the decision-making process as to who gets hired or fired, nor any control over the production of goods and services."[80]

Latino/a theology in the United States can benefit greatly from a critical exchange with Cornel West, as evidenced by the work of Benjamin Valentín.[81] Of particular relevance for an analysis of *mestizaje* are West's personal struggle with the Christian faith as a source of both oppression and liberation of African Americans, and West's recognition of the delicate balance between group identity and individual freedom. West's investigation of African American critical thought begins by asking: "Why did large numbers of American black people become Christians? What features of Protestant Christianity persuaded them to become Christians?"[82] While acknowledging Friedrich Nietzsche's critique of Christianity as an ideology of *ressentiment,* West resists attempts to reduce the Christianizing of African slaves to this one cause. Instead he acknowledges that the Scriptures—especially the exodus of Israel out of slavery and Jesus Christ's earthly ministry with the socially outcast and marginalized—provided a unifying identity for African slaves whose historical experiences mirrored the biblical narratives. Of equal importance is the realization that

> Christianity is first and foremost a theodicy, a triumphant account of good over evil. The intellectual life of the African slaves in the United States—like that of all oppressed peoples—consisted primarily of reckoning with the dominant form of evil in their lives. The Christian emphasis on against-the-evidence hope for triumph over evil struck deep among many of them.[83]

For many African Americans the act of embracing Christianity is intellectually and emotionally difficult, given the long history of racism by white Christians and their institutions. Thus, it is not surprising that African

Americans created their own churches in order to ensure "autonomous control over the central institution in the Afro-American community."[84] The theological worldview of prophetic Christianity—grounded in God's many acts of liberation on behalf of the poor and oppressed as recorded in the Scriptures—is a necessary aspect of African American critical thought. Nonetheless, this worldview is mediated by the Afro-American tradition of humanism discussed earlier, and subjected to a thorough progressive Marxist analysis.

One can find many similarities between the work of Cornel West and those U.S. Latino/a theologies that emphasize a liberating reading of Scripture in order to transform our present reality, value a distinctive cultural identity without denigrating other cultures, and struggle against the tendency to essentialize cultural identity at the expense of individual freedom of expression. Chapter 2 will explore the conceptualization of *mestizaje* as a continuous dialogic encounter that parallels Cornel West's Afro-American humanist tradition of response to racism, insofar as both approaches seek to define political liberation as protective of individual identity against the potential tyrannization of an essentialist view of cultural/ethnic identity. However, to value and protect individual autonomy does not diminish the importance of group identity, especially when discussing racism in the North American context. Therefore, it is important to discuss the rise of race consciousness as an empowering concept for both cultural identity *and* political praxis.

Critical Race Theory and the Rise of "Race Consciousness"

Critical race theory (CRT), a movement that began within legal scholarship but now affects the broader society, provides a new paradigm for analyzing race by identifying white supremacy as the defining ideology of North American society. CRT challenges the ways in which race and racial power are constructed and presented in the American legal system and in American society as a whole. This movement's most important contribution to the public discourse on race is its critique of liberal/progressive notions of racial justice as color blindness. Coining the term *racialism* to describe structures and systems that continue the practices of racial domination, CRT argues against the traditional liberal position that favors abandoning race consciousness because liberalism ignores critiques of racial power that expose the normativity of the dominant white perspective. Given our nation's history of racism, dreams of a color-blind society are dangerous, since "certain conceptions of merit function not as a neutral basis for distributing resources and opportunity, but rather as a repository of hidden, race-specific preferences for those who have the power to determine the meaning and consequences of 'merit' . . . under a regime of uncontested white supremacy."[85]

Although the scientific community no longer views race as a legitimate biological distinction, our society has not transcended the language of race to become a color-blind utopia. Now that the contemporary discourse on race recognizes the historical contextuality of racist attitudes and actions, our analysis of race must focus on the manipulation of power in society. Critical race theory analyzes racism as a system, the product of human cultural creativity, reflecting the prejudices, beliefs, and economic interests of the dominant social group. In accord with this view of history, the only possible explanation for the subjugation and marginalization of one group of people by another—apart from an irrational hatred for the other—is the former group's desire to preserve its current socioeconomic status. Racism persists in our society, even now that the false science behind categorical racism has been exposed, because we are, all of us, too deeply enmeshed within the racist structures created by the ideology of European expansion, an ideology that has played a normative role for both the church and the academy since the Enlightenment. Consequently, political action is needed to end racism.

The emphasis on *race consciousness* by critical race theory is an attempt to address problems left unresolved by the earlier civil rights movement. The civil rights movement of the 1950s and 1960s fought primarily for expanded legal representation for minorities and was characterized by faith in the legal system and a belief in social progress. CRT is distinguished by its dissatisfaction with liberalism and civil rights litigation. Specifically, CRT is an effort to expose white cultural domination in all its forms —legal, economic, religious, and so on—since matters of justice and socioeconomic well-being are inextricably linked to the cultural milieu. The dream of the civil rights movement was a society in which no single race or ethnic group asserted its particular heritage as normative for national identity. The reality uncovered by critical race theory is that the United States is *foundationally* structured and organized to benefit the dominant white majority. Therefore, even the most well-meaning attempts at social reform by the dominant population ultimately benefit the dominant population. Girardeau Spann, a professor of law at Georgetown Law Center, argues that communities of color that have historically pursued racial justice through the courts are better served by pursuing what he calls "pure politics"—in which elected representatives (in both the legislative and executive branches of government) are held accountable to the minority community through an organized movement of "grassroots" mobilization to elect local officials and establish genuine representation.

According to Spann, political solutions are more effective because in the present system the judiciary has almost unchecked power:

> Because justices are socialized by the same majority that determines their fitness for judicial office, they will arrive at the bench already inculcated with majoritarian values that will influence the manner in which they exercise their judicial discretion. Accordingly, unless judicial discretion can be reduced to acceptably low levels, justices can be expected to rule in ways that facilitate rather than inhibit majoritarian efforts to advance majority interests, even at minority expense.[86]

Consequently, the civil rights movement's emphasis on expanding legal representation through the courts is misguided. Instead, Spann contends that

> a rational minority response to the veiled majoritarian nature of the Supreme Court would be to abandon efforts to influence the Court and to concentrate minority political activities on the representative branches, because minorities are more likely to secure concessions from an overtly political branch of government than from one whose political dimensions are covert.[87]

Comparing the history of the representative branches with the history of the Supreme Court tends to support his position, since the representative branches have done more to advance minority interests. After all, the Supreme Court does not write the law but merely interprets it according to a vague and changing standard of constitutionality.

Sociologist Joseph Tilden Rhea provides an insightful history of race consciousness in *Race Pride and the American Identity* (1997). His thesis states that the rise of multiculturalism and ethnocentrism has fueled a demand for public recognition of our nation's racial injustices and in the process "changed the national collective memory of the past."[88] The various assertions of race pride and minority cultural identity (Black Power, Chicano Pride, etc.) arose in response to a long history of oppression in which the racial and ethnic diversity of American citizenry was denied and overt steps were taken to deny minorities not only full citizenship but also full human status:

> The collective memory of a nation is that set of beliefs about the past which the nation's citizens hold in common and publicly recognize as legitimate representations of their history. Collective memory is important because shared beliefs about the past provide citizens with common landmarks or examples which can be referred to when addressing the problems of the present. As in other nations, collective memory in America is structured through political interaction of groups seeking to position themselves in relation to one another. Thus one way to demean another group is to deny the value of its history. Written out of the national past, the group is denied the collective landmarks which signify its importance. A public history which promotes negative views of a group, or simply excludes it from consideration, does real harm to the living members of that group.[89]

Rhea contends that while the various ethnocentric movements primarily seek national cultural recognition for their particular communities, the rise of identity politics has also resulted in the positive transformation of the overall American national identity. Rhea's analysis differs from CRT in very important ways: (1) Rhea believes that no "one race or ethnic group in America can now securely assert that its particular heritage is the one that defines the national identity,"[90] whereas CRT maintains that the United States is a white supremacist culture; and (2) Rhea believes the ethnocentric celebration of difference has caused ethnic fragmentation, and calls us to transcend race consciousness in order to affirm what the various groups share for the sake of a unified national identity, whereas CRT rejects integrationism and sees race consciousness movements as the only way to advance minority interests in a white racist society. Nonetheless, both agree that the nation's collective memory shapes present public policy, and that a collective memory that recognizes the racial and ethnic diversity of our shared history and respects the positive contributions of previously ignored groups is important for the health and future well-being of the nation.

Paramount to all contextual theologies (and thus to all theologies) is the task of recognizing that no neutral standpoint exists from which to extricate oneself from the formative influence of culture or from one's particular social location within that culture. Therefore, it is important to develop an interpretive methodology that enables the theologian to properly describe and critique the effects of racial and ethnic particularity in theological construction. Critical race theory can provide theologians with a theoretical vocabulary for addressing the issue of racial inequality. In fact, a similar criticism already exists within U.S. Latino/a theologies, whose deconstruction of the "melting pot myth" exposes racism as the fatal flaw in the liberal dream of assimilation and color blindness. According to the discourse of racialism, successful integration into mainstream U.S. culture has been achieved only by sacrificing ethnic and cultural identity. CRT seeks to establish a framework for social transformation that embraces race consciousness by providing a genuine political alternative for contemporary America.

The theoretical vocabulary of CRT has extended beyond the insular world of critical legal studies into the public arena as more scholars recognize the need to move past the postmodern preoccupation with deconstruction toward the more difficult task of reconstruction. Anthony Cook's positive appraisal of the reconstructive theology of Dr. Martin Luther King Jr. serves as a model for a viable political alternative to racialism. In fact, the lack of political viability for much race-conscious political activism can be attributed to its lack of "grassroots" support. Consequently, Cook calls for an alternative vision of community that respects ethnic particularity and is therefore better able to protect people from the oppressive structures of racism, sexism, and economic inequality:

> This can only be achieved through the detailed examination of American institutions and the systematic development of alternative institutions designed to rectify present oppression and injustice. . . . we must meet and walk together, appreciating our respective histories and experiences of alienation and oppression. We must talk specifically about the kind of community we would fashion and how the rules, laws, and rituals defining the roles we adopt can be mutually empowering and facilitative of a community of equals. We must talk specifically about how we should organize, protest, agitate, and struggle to achieve our objectives, realizing that we are perennially engaged in a dialectic in which the program shapes our practices, which in turn refine and redefine our program.[91]

Without question, CRT and U.S. Latino/a theologies share similar concerns, since both (1) value the role of ethnic particularity in political praxis, (2) emphasize the need to revisit history in order to give voice to previously silenced discourses, and (3) recognize the need for marginalized communities to "name" themselves.[92] U.S. Latino/a theology, specifically the movement called *teología en conjunto,* possesses the kind of communal grounding Cook describes as necessary for successful race-conscious activism.

Mestizaje *in U.S. Latino/a Theology*

I have briefly surveyed the literature of CRT in order to gain a fuller understanding of the relevant issues and challenges posed by race consciousness for theological reconstruction. My hope is to use the insights gathered here to develop a theological critique of North American racial hegemony that is grounded in U.S. Latino/a particularity yet remains relevant for all of Christianity. U.S. Latino/a theology is unabashedly contextual, speaking to a universal audience from a particular context, while presupposing and demanding openness toward other particular traditions. Thus, instead of perpetuating a modern totalizing narrative, or a postmodern radical relativism that leads to chaos and conflict, Hispanic theology models a collaborative method for ethical and theological discourse:

> The task confronting us, therefore, is one of neither assimilation nor repudiation; it is, rather, a task of critical appropriation. Such a task requires that we approach and critique traditional sources and methods, whether European or Latin American, from the perspective of U.S. Hispanics *in order to be able to articulate the significance of that perspective for the life of our communities, the church, and society.*[93]

Modern political philosophy equates freedom with the individual's ability to do as he or she pleases under the guise of self-determination. Such a belief is grounded upon the erroneous notion that human beings are autonomous subjects who enter into social relationships voluntarily—we *choose* to love our neighbor but are not *required* to. U.S. Latino/a theology posits a communal notion of personal identity grounded in a complex web of social relationships and historical commitments. At the same time, Latino/a theologians also seek to protect individual self-determination over against the potential encroachment of tradition and culture. The metaphor of *mestizaje,* as Latino/a theologians have employed it, provides a race-conscious foundation for individual and group identity that also seeks to transcend the particularities of culture, race, and socioeconomic status. *Can U.S. Latino/a theology make St. Paul's vision of the eschatological community "in Christ"—in which all relationships of domination are eclipsed and replaced by relationships of mutuality—a present reality and not just a utopian dream?*

Most Hispanics share a heritage greatly influenced by Spanish culture and language, yet we are not a single "race," having in our lineage European, Amerindian, African—even Arabic and Asian—ancestry. The descriptive terms *Hispanic* and *Latino* are artificial constructs imposed by the U.S. Census Bureau to classify a growing, primarily immigrant population that does not fit the biracial dichotomy of U.S. society. However, over time these objectifying terms have been appropriated by Hispanics/ Latinos/as seeking a collective identity—in spite of great diversity of religious beliefs, cultural experiences, economic realities, and national backgrounds—for the purposes of political survival. Yet, despite many differences, most who identify themselves as Latino/a or Hispanic in the United States share a similar experience of socioeconomic and cultural marginalization. *Mestizaje* can serve as a starting point for developing strategies of resistance and liberation because in our collective history Latino/ as have been both oppressed and oppressor in much the same way that the church has contributed both to the formation of racist ideologies and to the rise of progressive social movements that seek to dismantle racism. U.S. Latino/a theology is united by a biblical vision of liberation and strives to work for political empowerment and positive social transformation within the church and in the broader society. *Mestizaje* can serve as a living reminder that God loves all of humanity in its great diversity and does not condone social stratification and relations of domination.

Hegel's analysis of the master-slave relationship introduced in the *Phenomenology of Spirit* can illumine our discussion of relationships characterized by subordination and dominance.[94] We need not embrace the entirety of Hegel's philosophical system in order to find his analysis of relationships of domination instructive for our discourse on race. Hegel argues that a human being is a subject aware of objects as *its objects* as well as aware of itself as a "subject-object," since the self can be an object for itself (not to mention other subjects). This notion of personal identity strives to overcome the Cartesian object-subject split by emphasizing that for subjects there is no experience of the self apart from its relationship to the external world of objects. Not only are we aware of the self in relation to objects, a higher degree of self-consciousness is available to us in our relationship with other subjects: "Self-consciousness exists in and for itself when, and by the fact that, it so exists for another; that is, it exists only in being acknowledged."[95] A subject can control objects as it wills, and it can also do this in relation to other subjects insofar as the other person is an object of its consciousness. Unlike objects, however, subjects have the freedom and ability to contradict the wishes of other subjects. Thus, since all human beings are subjects, conflict is an inevitable aspect of human relationships. The appropriate relationship between the self and the other is one of mutual respect in which every participant is both subject and object for the other. Yet, human relationships become relationships of domination when one subject evades the reciprocity of allowing itself to become an object for the other, seeking instead to control and "objectify" the other.

This model of human self-consciousness poses a great challenge for theology, since it reduces all human relationships to a struggle for domination. How, then, do we actualize the divine command to love our neighbor as ourselves? How do we make real Paul's eschatological vision of a community free from relationships of domination? As noted earlier, the most insidious aspect of racism is the tendency for the subjugated group to internalize the dominant group's negative objectification of itself. In Hegel's terms, the self-identity of the oppressed group originates in the experience of being treated as an object-for-others at the expense of self-determining subjectivity. A Christian theology interested in overcoming the prevailing racist ideology must embrace two equally important tasks: (1) to expose and transcend all manifestations of cultural idolatry, and (2) to foster the development of historical agency and positive cultural identity among the victims of oppression. Only when we as Christians recognize the full humanity of the "other" by allowing the other to define itself *as* other do we glimpse the prophetic vision of God's kingdom, where there is neither Jew nor Greek, slave nor free, male nor female. So long as racism persists, and one group lives in subjugation to another, the church is called to resist the ideologies and structures that perpetuate racism.

Virgilio Elizondo is rightly credited with developing *mestizaje* as the chief theological metaphor employed by U.S. Latino/a theology for resisting North American cultural hegemony.[96] In the next chapter, I will identify three different—though often confused—uses of *mestizaje* to argue that U.S. Latino/a theologians have inadvertently fostered a cultural and biological essentialism that impedes liberating praxis. My concerns with

Elizondo's emphasis on biological *mestizaje* stem from the fact that his attempts to articulate an alternative to the language of modern racism —which views various human groups as distinct biological entities—can perpetuate an essentialist view of human groups by insisting that *mestizaje* describes a new and distinct biological reality. I support his emancipatory project and strongly believe that *mestizaje* is a vital concept for racial reconciliation, but not as the source of a distinct Latino/a genetic identity. Rather, by emphasizing the universality of *mestizaje* as a more accurate scientific description of human biological diversity, Latino/a theology can resist racism and positively transform racial discourse.

2

Exploring *Mestizaje* as Theological Metaphor

Globalization, understood as accelerated cultural interaction facilitated by technological advances that have de facto reduced geographic boundaries between nations and peoples, has elevated the category of hybridity to the forefront of theoretical discourse on culture.[1] Still, a backlash against hybridity as a social scientific paradigm has developed, in great part because of the shallowness of its analysis, as demonstrated by those who conceive of hybrid persons as "lubricants in the clashes of culture."[2] Not only has much of this analysis focused on the everyday multiculturalism of popular culture,[3] but its optimistic presentation of the fusion of cultures has ignored long-standing cultural conflicts and also avoided questions of power and inequality: "The triumph of the hybrid is in fact a triumph of neo-liberal multiculturalism, a part of the triumph of global capitalism."[4] In other words, such analyses gloss over the historical conflicts between cultures by appealing to the intermarriage and blending of cultures as a means of overcoming conflict without adequately addressing the reality that such conflicts are perpetuated—often to a heightened degree—by the "mixed" offspring of cross-cultural unions. *Mestizaje,* as a subset of hybridization, must engage the anti-hybridity backlash in order to provide some clarity about its distinct contribution to the discourse on globalization and multiculturalism.

Mestizaje: *Critical Issues and Fundamental Concerns*

While *mestizaje* has proved a useful locus for Latino/a theological reflection, the concept has come under scrutiny for uncritically adopting essentialist notions of race and ethnicity, for glossing over the ethnic and cultural diversity within U.S. Hispanic experience, and for contributing to the insularity of U.S. Latino/a theology. For example, Andrew Irvine has argued that the use of *mestizaje* as a nationalist/liberative symbol within U.S. Latino/a theology can lead to a form of cultural essentialism that "hinders dialogue and solidarity between theologies and cultures."[5] In 1988, John P. Rossing suggested that if "North American Christians listen to the voices of Hispanic Christians speaking from the intersections in our society, we can learn to see the entire church as a *mestizo* community, in which people from all nations are reconciled to God and to each other."[6] Many years later *mestizaje* remains marginalized and overlooked by mainstream academic theology, and, as Benjamin Valentin contends, the Latino/a community contributes to this marginalization by employing *mestizaje* primarily as a means of establishing a unique Latino/a cultural identity and by isolating itself within an explicitly ecclesiocentric discourse.[7] Despite such criticism, I remain optimistic that the metaphor of *mestizaje* can serve as a transcultural paradigm for resisting racism in our increasingly globalized society.

This investigation is written from the perspective of a Puerto Rican in the North American diaspora who, in spite of being born in the Caribbean and raised in Central America, received his formal theological education in the hallowed halls of Union Theological Seminary in New York and Princeton Theological Seminary and has served as pastor for white, middle-class congregations in the midwestern United States. Consequently, my point of reference for discussing *mestizaje* and all its complexities is the North American context, specifically, theoretical work of primarily Roman Catholic, Mexican American theologians whose work dominates the landscape of Latino/a theology in the United States. While cherishing the contributions of such pioneers as Virgilio Elizondo and Andrés Guerrero, I am critical of the myopia afflicting much U.S. Latino/a theology in promoting *mestizaje* as theological metaphor without accounting for the fact that in the Hispanic Caribbean there is another vision of *mestizaje* that romanticizes the mixing of Spanish, African, and indigenous peoples in order to conceal the tragedies of genocide and exploitation that accompanied racial mixing in the sixteenth century.[8] Consequently, I employ the term *mestizaje* fully aware that it is potentially harmful to an emancipatory theology, yet optimistic about its promise as a liberating theological metaphor. Within U.S. Latino/a theology there is a tendency to view biological *mestizaje* as the creation of a new "race"—that is, a new people of God[9]—by which "God and humanity come together to create a new reality."[10] This work challenges these ethnocentric and nationalist undertones by defending a complex notion of *mestizaje* that involves a conscious moral decision—an act of political solidarity—as a counterbalance to those theological uses of the term that have unintentionally appropriated the language of racial/ethnic exclusion, thereby compromising the socially transforming and inclusive vision of U.S. Latino/a theology.

Responding to the Anti-hybridity Backlash

Mestizaje draws criticism for essentializing Latino/a identity, and thus failing to transcend established models of cultural interaction characterized by domination of the racialized other. Cuban anthropologist Fernando Ortiz, in describing the complexities of *mestizaje,* coined the term *transculturation* to account for the mutuality of exchange between cultures.[11] He prefers this term to *acculturation* because the latter term suggests that the transition from one culture into another demands the loss of one's original cultural identity, "which could be defined as a deculturation."[12] Transculturation, on the other hand, understands that even dominant cultures are influenced by the conquered and colonized, "always exerting an influence and being influenced in turn."[13] Furthermore, transculturation is preferable, since, like *mestizaje,* it makes room for cultural innovation: "In the end . . . the result of every union of culture is similar to that of the reproductive process between individuals: the offspring always has something of both parents but is always different from each of them."[14] Still, Walter D. Mignolo, while appreciative of Ortiz's critique and correction of acculturation, ultimately rejects transculturation for its strong resemblance to *mestizaje.* Instead, he develops the concept of "border gnosis" or "border knowledge" to counter the direct linkage to the biological/cultural mixture of people in articulating a more inclusive and fluid model of cultural interaction. In other words, Mignolo seeks a "transculturation without mestizaje."[15]

Catholic theologian Orlando Espín has developed an "intercultural" theology of tradition that captures what the term *transcultural* conveys in my reconceptualization of *mestizaje* as theological paradigm:

An intercultural theology of tradition must squarely face the difficulties implied in relating, on the one hand, intercultural dialogue with its risks and its "contrasting" approach, and, on the other hand, the myriad particularizing and universalizing cultural horizons of humankind, as a means of constructing a multilayered, polyphonic, and non-innocent model of

Catholic tradition. An intercultural theology of tradition, furthermore, must do all of this within the globalized and globalizing world context. And an intercultural theology of tradition should also reflect on the possibilities and contours of intercultural interpretations of revelation (not forgetting to also develop an intercultural definition of revelation).[16]

Espín challenges dominant Catholic models of tradition as "inculturation" (the foundationalist belief in a cultural "something" that exists independent of culture and is transmitted in particular cultures) by appealing to the theoretical work of Raúl Fornet-Betancourt on "intercultural" discourse[17] in order to argue that even the truth of the Gospel, grounded as it is in the divine act of revelation, is nonetheless received and interpreted in culturally specific forms. Consequently, since all traditions are themselves culturally specific acts of interpretation, it is more accurate to describe traditions not as static receptacles of truth but as dynamic social practices through which "every generation attempts to construct, in its present, that corporate identity for itself in continuity with preceding generations of believers."[18] Such an open-ended and polyphonic understanding of tradition as the "present interpretation of the past in reference to the future"[19] moves beyond merely recalling the past and necessitates *transcultural* or *intercultural* discourse.

While Mignolo favors transculturation to *mestizaje* as descriptive of the complex and multidirectional character of cultural exchange, he questions Ortiz's use of the term to create a distinct *mestizo* culture, which in his opinion perpetuates the cultural essentialism Ortiz sought to overcome: "This is the main reason why I prefer the term colonial semiosis to transculturation, which, in the first definition provided by Ortiz, maintains the shadows of 'mestizaje.'"[20] This concern also guides Orlando Espín's articulation of an intercultural theology:

> Instead of inculturation we should perhaps speak of "intertransculturation," whereby another "witnesses" to me, in an open inter-discursive dialogue, what he/she understands and lives as truth; and I within and from my own cultural perspective, will contrast and perhaps assume that truth, because I have discovered it as truth (within and from within my cultural horizon). And I in turn, upon my discovery of truth (possible within and from within my cultural perspective), "witness" to the other, again in an open inter-discursive dialogue, what I have come to understand and live as truth, inviting the other to question and/or grow in what he/

she understands and lives as truth—thereby moving the process into an ever deepening and continuing dialogue where truth is discovered and affirmed, over and over, through mutual witnessing, contrasting dialogue, and non-colonizing reflection.[21]

Still, in spite of misgivings about Ortiz's use of transculturation as descriptive of mutual cultural exchange, Mignolo recognizes that

> the advantage of the term transculturation over mestizaje is not only its power to move us away from racial consideration, but also its ability to invite a second move toward the "social life of things." It allows for the detachment of specific cultural entities from specific communities of people, identified either in ethnic or national terms (e.g., Cubans, Indians, white, Negroes, and Mongols).[22]

Mignolo's underlying concern with *mestizaje* is that it perpetuates the modern/colonial world system by creating the idea of a homogeneous Latin American *mestizo* identity as "other" to the colonial power without fully recognizing the cultural heterogeneity of Latin America. The problem with all such essentializing terms used to define ethnic/cultural identity is that "they reveal and they occlude. They are also the grounding of a system of geopolitical values, of racial configurations, and of hierarchical structures of meaning and knowledge."[23] There is risk in using the term *mestizaje*. Nevertheless, this investigation argues this term reveals something very important about racism in the North American context that Mignolo has not properly accounted for, and can therefore be utilized to subvert the dominant discourse on race.

Kathryn Tanner, in *Theories of Culture: A New Agenda for Theology* (1997), questions the notion that "cultures are self-contained and clearly bounded units, internally consistent and unified wholes of beliefs and values simply transmitted to every member of their respective groups as principles of social order."[24] Instead, she advocates a view of cultural identity as something fluid, "what we might call a postmodern stress on interactive process and negotiation, indeterminacy, fragmentation, conflict, and porosity."[25] Before reformulating the notion of culture from a postmodern perspective, Tanner attempts a postmodern reconstruction of culture that shares many of the same qualities ascribed to *mestizaje,* in which differences "are not marked by boundaries separating self-contained cultures" and "cultural elements may cross such boundaries without jeopardizing the distinctiveness of different cultures."[26] Her goal is to "de-center" dominant conceptualizations of culture in order to give greater attention to the role of humans as culture-creating agents and view culture itself as an open-ended and continually changing historical process. Within this complex web of social relationships theorists are still able to identify stable cultural forms that give a particular culture its distinct identity, with the understanding that a culture is not defined solely by the dominant forms but is best understood as a "community of argument" involving many perspectives.

Given this understanding of culture as something that is constantly negotiated within a culture, between cultures, and between the community and the individual, it is not surprising that Tanner embraces the notion of hybridity:

> The distinctiveness of cultural identity is therefore not a product of isolation; it is not a matter of a culture's being simply self-generated, pure and unmixed; it is not a matter of "us" vs. "them." Cultural identity becomes, instead, a hybrid, a relational affair, something that lives between as much as within cultures. What is important for cultural identity is the novel way cultural elements from elsewhere are now put to work, by means of such complex and ad hoc relational processes as resistance, appropriation, subversion, and compromise.[27]

Mestizaje is a particular instance of such hybridity, suggesting that—in much the same way that scientific descriptions of racial/ethnic difference have rejected the notion of racial purity and the existence of distinct racial groups in favor of a view of human biological difference as variations along the same genetic location—culture is best described as a communal and relational process of appropriation and distanciation that is neither social determinism nor autonomous self-determination. Accordingly, Tanner looks to instances of ethnic mixing as examples of what she means by a postmodern view of cultural identity: "Creoles and exiles, colonized peoples who 'write back' to colonizing nations using those nation's own literary forms, ethnic or racial minorities who revel in their own mixed heritage, become models for this interrelational notion of identity."[28]

This investigation chooses to employ the term *mestizaje* because it is the dominant metaphor for cultural identity employed by U.S. Latino/a theologians, and because it reminds the dominant culture that existing social stratifications are built upon an ideology and history of white cultural domination. In other words, while acknowledging that hybridity and transculturation are suitable conceptual alternatives, the use of *mestizaje* is a subversive political act that empowers those labeled racially "other" (and therefore less than human) to resist cultural and political domination by valuing their difference. Admittedly, linking biological and cultural identity to liberative uses of the term *mestizaje* is problematic. However, because of its emancipatory value as a tool for resisting racism, *mestizaje* remains a flexible enough concept to include the valuation of a previously despised biological heritage without devolving into a narrow ethnocentrism, racial essentialism, or nationalism.

Globalization as *Mestizaje*

Sociologist Jan Nederveeen Pieterse conceptualizes globalization as a process of hybridization in order to counter the view that globalization is a form of cultural homogenization. Given a nonessentialist view of human cultures, defining cultural interaction as hybridization (or *mestizaje*) seems almost tautological. Nonetheless, in spite of widespread theoretical acceptance of these two paradigms for racial and cultural mixing, there remains social resistance to the realities of biological and cultural mixing in the North American context, as evidenced by the ongoing furor over Latin American immigration and the challenge it poses to American cultural homogeny (Huntington). Hybridization remains a meaningful paradigm for combating existing cultural and ethnic essentialisms because it unsettles received and static conceptualizations of culture while simultaneously rejecting "easy" forms of multiculturalism: "Structural hybridization, or the increase in the range of organizational options, and cultural hybridization, or the doors of erstwhile imagined communities opening up, are signs of an age of boundary crossing, not, surely, the erasure of boundaries."[29] *Mestizaje,* as a form of cultural hybridization, not only challenges nationalism, racism, ethnocentrism, and other forms of cultural essentialism but also addresses the fundamental inequality of global capitalism by focusing on the historical relationships that perpetuate domination and exploitation.

Nevertheless, the theoretical language of *mestizaje* employed by U.S. Latino/a theology does not always adequately focus on the historical and political dimensions of *mestizaje* but is plagued by a persistent eschatology.[30] This is evident in the work of Mexican philosopher José Vasconcelos (1882–1959), whose views have influenced many Latino/a theologians, and the theology of Virgilio Elizondo, the first U.S. Latino/a theologian to employ *mestizaje* as *locus theologicus*, since both thinkers seek emancipatory social transformation yet entrust it to a gradual process of racial/ethnic mixing rather than to some more immediate political agenda. Given that Christian thought is inherently eschatological, it is not surprising to find Elizondo placing so much emphasis on a future hope, but a messianic dimension of *mestizaje* also permeates the philosophy of Vasconcelos, whose short manifesto, *La raza cósmica* (The Cosmic Race) provides a pseudotheological narrative advocating Latin American—and specifically Mexican—racial superiority. Vasconcelos, a Mexican philosopher who countered the prevailing positivism[31] of his age with an aesthetic and prophetic vision of the future, develops the thesis "that the various races of the earth tend to intermix at a gradually increasing pace, and eventually will give rise to a new human type, composed of selections from each of the races already in existence."[32] The text recounts the mythical prehistoric origins of racial diversity, describes the gradual mixing of races, and argues for the mutual enrichment of racial groups through the process of *mestizaje*. According to Vasconcelos, the present age is dominated by two groups, the Saxons (England) and the Latins (Spain), who embody the evolution of the human race through a process of gradual world unification that originates in war and conflict but finds its fulfillment in a beautiful Utopian vision of racial harmony made possible by historical/biological *mestizaje*: "A mixture of races accomplished according to the laws of social well-being, sympathy, and beauty, will lead to the creation of a type infinitely superior to all that have previously existed."[33] He argues that while the English conquered and destroyed the natives of the New World (whom Vasconcelos links to the "original" Atlantean race of mythical prehistory), the Spanish colonization created *mestizaje*, in accord with "their divine mission in America . . . the mission of fusing all peoples ethnically and spiritually."[34] In effect, the racial and cultural mixing of Latin America is interpreted as a prophetic vision of humanity's global future, a way forward that transcends those conflicts arising from difference by positing biological and cultural mixing as a divinely guided historical process that will yield a new messianic "race."

Vasconcelos's interpretation of the horrific realities of *mestizaje* in Latin America (violent conquest, rape, and genocide of entire peoples) through the hermeneutical lens of eschatological hope has had a great influence upon U.S. Hispanic theology, especially as mediated by the work of Chicano theologian Andrés Guerrero.[35] The attraction of *La raza*

cósmica for many Latino/a theologians is that it provides a model for understanding biological and cultural mixing that values the contributions
of all cultures without dissolving the uniqueness of each race and culture. Its great weakness is that the creation of this new mixed "race" does
not necessarily lead to the end of human conflict. There is a naïve presumption in the work of both Vasconcelos and Elizondo that *mestizos,*
by having experienced marginalization and oppression at the hands of
both parent cultures, will heed their divine election and accept the yoke
of liberation for all peoples. Vasconcelos hoped for the dissolution of conflict and disagreement between peoples through the ongoing mixture of
races and cultures, a process that would result in a new humanity, the
cosmic race that would incorporate all the biological and cultural gifts of
each human grouping for the benefit of all humanity. According to Vasconcelos, Latin American *mestizaje* is a foretaste of this new humanity,
which helps explain both the strong messianic dimension and the emphasis upon Latin American—and specifically Mexican—national identity in much U.S. Latino/a theology. However, great care must be taken to
avoid categorizing Virgilio Elizondo as one of those Hispanic theologians
writing in the North American context who is heavily influenced by the
philosophy of Vasconcelos. In fact, none of his major works on *mestizaje*
cite or discuss *La raza cósmica,* and when pressed by colleagues to discuss
the influence of Vasconcelos on his own understanding of *mestizaje,* Elizondo affirms that his conceptualizations were nurtured and grew in the
fertile ground of the popular religiosity of his childhood with its focus on
Nuestra Señora de Guadalupe.[36] Accordingly, this investigation—without
denying the influence of José Vasconcelos as mediated through the theology of Andrés Guerrero and more recently Roberto Goizueta[37]—begins
its conceptual analysis and criticism of *mestizaje* with an exploration of
the theology of Virgilio Elizondo in recognition of his unparalleled influence upon U.S. Latino/a theology.

The Role of Ethnic Identity in U.S. Latino/a Theologies

While *mestizaje* has played a central role in the development of U.S.
Latino/a theology, many Latino/a theologies minimize the ethnic and
cultural diversity within U.S. Hispanic communities for the sake of a
pan-ethnic Latino/a identity. In fact, outside the very small world of U.S.
Latino/a academic theology, *mestizaje* is most often associated with pan-

Hispanic nationalist and ethnocentric political movements. Two important works, an article in the *Journal of Hispanic/Latino Theology* by Andrew Irvine (August 2000) and a book by Benjamin Valentin, *Mapping Public Theology: Beyond Culture, Identity, and Difference* (2002), attempt to rehabilitate *mestizaje* as a potentially liberating metaphor.

Andrew Irvine, an Australian living and teaching in the United States, has written about his affinity for Latino/a theologies, arguing that due to his experience as a foreigner in the United States he finds more in common with Latino/a and African American colleagues than he does with "Anglo" Americans.[38] While acknowledging that his skin color (not to mention linguistic heritage) has allowed him greater acceptance among white Americans, Irvine's experiences as both insider *and* outsider in mainstream North American culture have fostered an appreciation for— and empathy with—the Latino/a experience of *mestizaje*. With this personal confession as background, Irvine asks some key critical questions about U.S. Latino/a theological reflection on *mestizaje*:

> It is above all the diverse and densely lived situations of *mestizaje* that force the theological problematic of authority to our attention. How, and to what extent, has attention to *mestizaje* authorized theological contributions as distinctively Hispanic or Latino theology? How, and to what extent, has attention to *mestizaje* made such theologies distinctively authoritative for Latinas and Latinos?[39]

He then proceeds to develop a typology that catalogs the ways in which *mestizaje* has been appropriated by U.S. Latino/a theologians over the last thirty years in order to illuminate the key question confronting Latino/a theologies—*what makes a particular theological contribution distinctively Hispanic?* Irvine concludes the article with a discussion of *mestizaje* as a nationalist religious symbol in order to critique a potentially limiting and dangerous tendency in some U.S. Latino/a theologies.

Irvine is careful to acknowledge that, like any typology, his proposal is neither comprehensive nor final; his analysis is intended to challenge U.S. Latino/a theologians to think through their categories of thought systematically in order to "discern whether and where the various types of appropriation of mestizaje are in fact harmonious, in tension, or in outright contest."[40] Yet, as someone outside the Hispanic community, Andrew Irvine admits the risk he takes in writing such a piece and declares that whatever "authority this piece possesses will be in large part a function of the authority Hispanic/Latino theologians grant it."[41] Irvine's discussion is useful, since it highlights many of the same concerns motivating the present investigation. Nonetheless, while his typology is an important conversation partner, ultimately I propose a different framework for evaluating the use of *mestizaje* as theological metaphor—one that not only describes the various ways U.S. Latino/a theologians have appropriated *mestizaje,* but also traces the evolution of the concept *from* its earliest appearance as a unifying force in the creation of a shared Hispanic ethnic identity *to* its more emancipatory and dialogical manifestations.

Irvine describes five distinct ways in which *mestizaje* is employed by U.S. Latino/a theologies: (1) *historical mestizaje* as descriptive of the history of conquest and domination that gave rise to a mixture of cultures and ethnicities and the continuing experience of belonging to two or more cultures while not fully belonging to any; (2) *biblical mestizaje* as the hermeneutical perspective from which to read and interpret the life of Jesus of Nazareth as the source of Latino/a cultural identity, since in Jesus God elected one of the marginalized to reveal the divine will, a mission continued in the life of *mestizos* who represent (some of) today's marginalized; (3) *liberating mestizaje* as a way of broadening the concept of God's preferential option for the poor to encompass not just the economically oppressed but also those marginalized by virtue of race or ethnicity; (4) *eschatological mestizaje* as the future hope by which the human community is transformed into God's kingdom—used analogically to describe God's work of redemption within the *mestizo* church; and (5) *nationalist mestizaje* to describe its pan-Hispanic nationalist uses.[42] Irvine contends this last type creates a crisis for U.S. Latino/a theology by emphasizing identity-based politics to the detriment of those uses of *mestizaje* that embrace an ethos of inclusion.

The danger inherent in appropriating *mestizaje* as both a religious *and* a nationalist symbol is that the latter discourse can perpetuate the notion that ethnic differences are irreconcilable and can also be used to justify exclusionary practices—further "ghettoizing" an already politically marginalized minority population. Consequently, Irvine seeks to transcend those uses of *mestizaje* that facilitate a cultural essentialism in which only those who are ethnically or biologically *mestizos* are capable of bridging cultural divides:

> I propose an alternative interpretation of the relation of intellectual work to the life-labors of the poor. Intellect can reach out to share imaginatively

in another's experience, regardless of social or existential situation. Or, intellect can refuse any such imaginative encounter. This is the force behind the well-established position in liberation theology that the call to make a preferential option for the poor is issued to both the rich and poor. Without that possibility, the option cannot be binding.[43]

While Andrew Irvine's fifth descriptive category correctly diagnoses the crisis within U.S. Latino/a theology, and may help explain why *mestizaje* has not been embraced by the theological mainstream, he does not propose a viable alternative to the nationalist discourse underlying so many Latino/a theologies. Instead, he merely suggests that such an understanding of *mestizaje* may be incompatible with other theological uses of the term. Perhaps Irvine is purposely cautious, since he is writing about U.S. Latino/a theology as an outsider looking in. Still, I agree with Irvine that *mestizaje* must be reconceptualized in such a way that its emancipatory potential is not forever linked to a literal or nationalist understanding of *mestizaje* but is interpreted as a moral and political possibility regardless of a person's biological heritage.

Like Irvine, Benjamin Valentin—a Puerto Rican born and raised in the United States—is concerned with the insularity of U.S. Latino/a theology; however, his analysis of this emerging theological movement moves beyond *mestizaje* to also include popular religious practices. Furthermore, as a U.S. Latino/a theologian, he can offer a comprehensive critique of the most insular aspects of Latino/a theology without evoking the negative reactions an outsider like Irvine would likely face. Valentin's constructive proposal espouses a pragmatic and progressive public theology that seeks to provide a "spiritual basis for the integration of the struggle for equality and justice into broader spheres of everyday life."[44] His primary thesis is that Latino/a theologians, by focusing almost exclusively on *mestizaje* and popular religion, have created an ethos that emphasizes matters of personal and group cultural identity to the detriment of political and economic liberation.

While acknowledging that the search for both a positive self-identity and collective cultural identity is a crucial component of liberation in the United States, Valentin argues that the challenge facing U.S. Hispanic theologies is no longer the creation of a unifying ethnic identity but "that of finding ways to construct discourses that can simultaneously help excluded groups to establish themselves as distinctive communities with distinct social claims, while also situating these claims and concerns in the broader context of the continental 'American' society."[45] He concludes that "Latino theological scholarship as a whole is driven by this fervor to promote cultural affirmation and the achievement of positive self-identity and group identity,"[46] while demonstrating an "inability to break out of a specifically Hispanic/Latino localism."[47] In order to help U.S. Latino/a theology break out of its provincial shell, Valentin identifies two dominant trends contributing to the insularity of U.S. Latino/a theological reflection and suggests a more "public" direction grounded in the constructive theology of Gordon Kaufman, the critical social theory of Nancy Fraser, and the "prophetic pragmatism" of Cornel West. According to Valentin, U.S. Latino/a theology exhibits a general *ecclesiocentrism* that limits its ability to affect the national public discourse, and a tendency to focus discussion on issues of culture and identity to the detriment of broader emancipatory political projects.[48]

This work agrees with Valentin's assessment that U.S. Latino/a theology needs to engage various "publics" or risk cultural and political irrelevance, yet disagrees with his overall characterization of U.S. Latino/a theology as an insular conversation solely concerned with matters of personal and group identity and therefore incapable of contributing to the common moral discourse. Granted, *mestizaje* within U.S. Hispanic theology can (1) contribute to exclusionary practices within Latino/a churches, (2) perpetuate the self-marginalization of an already politically disenfranchised minority population, and (3) undermine efforts at political and economic liberation by focusing almost exclusively on issues of cultural and ethnic identity. Nevertheless, U.S. Latino/a theology—by employing *mestizaje* as a multivalent theological metaphor—contains *within its own distinctive discourse* a model for public theology capable of transforming the public discourse on social justice in very positive ways.[49]

In *Mapping Public Theology,* Benjamin Valentin examines the theology of Virgilio Elizondo only when discussing *mestizaje* as a source of Latino/a cultural identity. His choice to focus on Elizondo is made primarily for the sake of expediency:

> Virgilio Elizondo was in fact the first theologian to employ Latino/a mestizaje, specifically Mexican American mestizaje, as a starting point for Hispanic theological reflection in the United States. As pioneer of the theological translation of lived mestizaje, his texts have come to be influential and are frequently cited by Hispanic theologians writing on the subject.[50]

However, by neglecting contributions from other theologians, Valentin's analysis and criticism ignore those uses that envision *mestizaje* as a liberating and politically empowering metaphor for public discourse. While his analysis of Elizondo's use of *mestizaje* exposes many of the same flaws identified earlier in this chapter—namely, that emphasizing the biological/literal use of *mestizaje* encourages identity-based politics that may contribute to the marginalization of U.S. Latino/a theology—his conclusion, that all Latino/a theologies embracing the discourse of *mestizaje* are unable to "break out" of a specifically Hispanic location, is unwarranted. The works of theologians like Ada María Isasi-Díaz and Luis G. Pedraja provide strong examples of how *mestizaje* has been transformed from a source of personal and group identity to a politically empowering model of social activism and dialogic encounter. When Benjamin Valentin argues that a "theology that aims to promote social justice cannot be limited to discussions of symbolic culture, local identity, subjectivity, and difference,"[51] this investigation argues that U.S. Latino/a theology's *distinctive* contribution to the public discourse on social justice is to link political and economic liberation to matters of ethnic and cultural identity.

Three Perspectives on Mestizaje

Over the last three decades U.S. Hispanic theologians have articulated an intentionally ecumenical (Roman Catholic, mainline Protestant, Pentecostal) and multicultural theology. This movement, *teología en conjunto*, exemplifies a communal approach to doing theology involving the cooperative efforts of theologians, pastors, and laypeople.[52] Arising from the social reality of an oppressed and marginalized group within North American society, *teología en conjunto* has developed a critique of the dominant culture (grounded in the pioneering work of Latin American liberation theology)[53] critical of the North American "melting pot" myth that minimizes racial and ethnic differences for the sake of cultural assimilation. Nevertheless, the relationship of U.S. Latino/a theology to the broader Christian tradition is neither assimilation nor outright rejection. Instead, *mestizo* Christianity values *both* its marginalized ethnic identity *and* its cultural inheritance from the dominant Western Christian tradition, as demonstrated by the collective effort of Latino/a theologians to make the biblical message and the dominant theological traditions relevant to the Hispanic community while simultaneously developing a prophetic critique of these dominant traditions from the margins. This emergent theological movement is recognized for valuing ethnic particularity while denouncing social structures that perpetuate exclusion on the basis of race and ethnicity. By reconceptualizing *mestizaje* as a moral and political act, some Latino/a theologians heighten the transcontextual relevance of *mestizaje* and answer those critics who would argue that the contributions of U.S. Latino/a theology "merely reflect back the horizons of the community of protest in self-affirmation."[54]

Justo L. González asserts that the most important contribution of U.S. Latino/a theology is a "new ecumenism" characterized by a liberating reading of Scripture that seeks to transcend the particularities of culture, race, and socioeconomic status with a vision of the kingdom of God capable of transforming our present reality. Such a reading of the Bible "must throw light on our current situation, help us understand it, and support us in the struggles for justice and liberation."[55] However, if Latino/a theological reflection does not extend beyond the church's confessional walls, "our emancipatory discursive praxis will fail to accomplish any significant changes in the sociopolitical arena."[56] In spite of confessional differences it is possible to examine U.S. Latino/a theology as a single entity because of a common linguistic/cultural heritage and a shared experience of marginalization implicit in the term *mestizaje*. I selected three theologians, representing different traditions, genders, national/ethnic backgrounds, and methodological perspectives, to provide a brief survey of U.S. Latino/a theology and to support the claim that Latino/a theology embodies an ethos of inclusion. Moving beyond an understanding of *mestizaje* as merely the mixing of biological heritages, Latino/a theology also explores the intricacies of cultural mixing; more important, it attempts to understand the role of this biological and cultural mixing within the context of God's salvific plan for humanity. By recognizing the interested perspective of every explanatory narrative, Latino/a theology encourages intersubjective conversation as a corrective against the tendency to universalize particular points of view, making the task of theology a *necessarily* public endeavor. Accordingly, U.S. Latino/a theology works to establish its distinctive voice in mutually enriching conversation across boundaries of belief, culture, gender, race, and ethnicity, or risk cultural irrelevance and political impotence.

Virgilio Elizondo and the Birth of *Mestizo* Theology

Virgilio Elizondo, a Mexican American priest from San Antonio, Texas, is perhaps the most influential figure within Roman Catholic Hispanic theology whose works have contributed much to the development of *teología en conjunto.* The discourse on *mestizaje* within U.S. Latino/a theology cannot be understood without reference to his seminal text, *Galilean Journey: The Mexican-American Promise* (1984), in which Elizondo interprets the life and witness of Jesus Christ through the lens of Mexican American experience and then develops a theological critique of the dominant North American culture. *Galilean Journey* begins with an interpretation of the Mexican American experience that presupposes a particular understanding of the relation of faith to culture in which culture is the medium through which God is revealed. Elizondo interprets the history of Mexican American culture from a faith perspective as the journey from oppression toward liberation. Accordingly, *mestizaje* is viewed as the means through which God transforms the world—the eschatological future breaking into the human present.

In part 1 of *Galilean Journey,* Elizondo develops the thesis that the people of Mexico (including what is now the American Southwest) have experienced a double conquest that produced the historical and cultural *mestizaje* that defines contemporary Mexican American reality. The first wave of *mestizaje* refers to the Spanish-Catholic conquest of Mexico, the second wave to the nineteenth-century conquest and annexation of Mexican territory by the United States.[57] In this historical context, *mestizaje* connotes half-breed and impure status (presupposing the existence of a superior "pure race") and contributes to a harmful psychological internalization of the dehumanizing objectification experienced at the hands of the dominant powers. From the perspective of the conqueror, to be *mestizo* is to be less than human. During the oppression phase of Elizondo's history of *mestizaje,* Mexican Americans internalized the oppressor's degrading image of them and accepted it as their own cultural identity. A fundamental tenet of Elizondo's conceptualization of *mestizaje* is his belief in the uniqueness of this event in recorded human history: never before has such a massive biological mixture, clash, and confluence of human cultures occurred.[58] From this tenet Elizondo is able to draw positive consequences for *mestizaje*: what was basically the violent conquest and subjugation of a people is transformed into a salvific act of God. Thus, in the liberation phase of Elizondo's cultural history, *mestizo* identity becomes a source of personal empowerment and social renewal.

In tracing the historical development of Mexican American cultural identity from oppression to liberation, Virgilio Elizondo develops a cultural anthropology that explains why dominant, homogeneous cultures fear cultural and biological mixing, given the fact that as "a biological phenomenon, *mestizaje*—the generation of a new people from two disparate parent peoples—has been very common in the evolution of humankind."[59] Elizondo observes three tendencies (which he terms "anthropological laws of human behavior") that are always present at the intersection of two distinct cultures. These are (1) the tendency toward group inclusion/exclusion in order to preserve group purity, (2) the tendency to create social distance at the individual/personal level, and (3) the elimination of those who threaten the barriers that preserve group purity. Cultural identity is the result of social self-definition; threats to the unifying cultural identity of a group result in the formation of values and practices that maintain the purity of said social group. Historically, certain concrete characteristics like "race, class, language, family name, education, economic status, social position, [and] religion" have been used to distinguish "us" from "them."[60] Furthermore, this process of self-definition as a negation of the other permeates all levels of cultural interaction, so much so that even "when deep personal friendships or love relationships develop, social barriers interfere with harmonization."[61] Certain essentialist categories become so internalized that even within the most intimate relationships (e.g., between a husband and wife, parent and child), the "superior/inferior" dichotomy of domination is preserved, undermining the possibility of relationships of true equality. Finally, Elizondo argues that this tendency toward "group purity" is so prevalent that the dominant culture develops discourses to justify the elimination of anyone who threatens or obscures the barriers that preserve purity.

Mestizaje as a cultural force is most destabilizing and threatening at the nexus of two conflicting tendencies in human behavior—the social drive toward "group purity" versus the formation of individual relationships that transcend divisive barriers—perhaps best embodied in the loving relationship between a husband and wife of different cultures, and, specifically, in the children of such unions. The *mestizo* is a concrete reminder of the inadequacy of existing categories of self-definition employed by both parent cultures. To be *mestizo* "is to have closeness to and distance from both parent cultures," to be both insider and outsider in both cultures; consequently, by breaking down the barriers that preserve self-identity and social stability, *mestizaje* threatens both the dominant and the conquered cultures.[62] Yet, precisely because it is a force for social instability, *mestizaje* can become a force for *universal* liberation. According to Elizondo, the process of cultural maturity reaches its apex when, instead of simply assimilating itself into one of the two parent cultures, thereby perpetuating the history of oppression, the *mestizo* group transcends its parent cultures and becomes a new humanity—that is, it embodies a new way of relating one to the other that is not based on exclusion and the preservation of relations of domination.

Part 2 of *Galilean Journey* begins with a methodological caveat about the relation of Scripture to culture that states that the religious experience of Mexican American people must be judged by the Word of God: "We must be aware that we, like all Christians, are historico-culturally conditioned and that we read the gospels from within our conditioned perspective. This is both our limitation and our originality."[63] In other words, a careful reading of the Scriptures in which the foundational events of Christianity are read and interpreted by emphasizing the meaning of these events in their original cultural and historical context provides a corrective against the tendency to "confuse the cultural expression of *our* faith with *the* faith, and begin to impose our cultural expressions of the gospel on *the* gospel."[64] At the same time, Elizondo emphasizes the importance of judging the Scriptures through the hermeneutical lens of the contemporary community's lived faith. Otherwise, "If the gospel is not reinterpreted through the expressions, language, and symbols of the faith community, it will appear as foreign, lifeless, or even destructive doctrine, not an incarnated, life-giving power."[65]

Not surprisingly, the Incarnation becomes a central doctrine for a *mestizo* reading of the New Testament: "The overwhelming originality of Christianity is the basic belief of our faith that not only did the Son of God become a *human being,* but he became *Jesus of Nazareth.*"[66] According to Virgilio Elizondo, it is of great theological import that God chooses what the world rejects—Jesus, a Jew of questionable parentage, living in an insignificant region of the country (Galilee), who fraternizes with social outcasts and women—in order to bring about reconciliation and salvation. Elizondo identifies the "Galilee principle" as the first principle for understanding the cultural and historical context of the New Testament: "*what human beings reject, God chooses as his very own.*"[67] If the possibility of reversing the effects of generation upon generation of domination begins with the cultural acceptance of *mestizaje,* the interpretation of Jesus as a marginalized Galilean is crucial to Elizondo's eschatological vision in which Mexican Americans "discover their ultimate identity as God's chosen people."[68] Although Elizondo's language often functions like the language of group self-definition (i.e., by implying some sort of "us" versus "them" dichotomy), he is careful to always link the language of *mestizaje* to Christ's liberating mission, suggesting that *mestizo* identity differs significantly from past conceptualizations of group identity. The good news of liberation as the ultimate unifying characteristic of *mestizaje* transcends both parent cultures—transcends *all* cultures—for it is "in Christ that the heads of the rejected can truly be raised high with the pride that it is in and through them that the expected liberation and peace of the world is now beginning."[69]

In Elizondo's history of *mestizaje*—understood as the journey from oppression to liberation, from rejection to election, and from marginalization to new creation—the ultimate identity of an oppressed people is located in the Galilean identity of Jesus. Thus, the second hermeneutical principle for understanding the New Testament context is the "Jerusalem principle," in which the oppressed people's mission to the world is viewed as the continuation of Christ's self-sacrificing public ministry. In the Scriptures Jesus undertakes a journey from Galilee to Jerusalem, culminating with his death on the cross, yet Elizondo wants to view Jesus' *entire* public ministry as salvific (and not just the cross). In the same way that the oppressed and marginalized find their identity in Jesus' "mixed" Galilean background, their lives find meaning and purpose in his life-affirming and world-transforming ministry: "God chooses an oppressed people, not to bring them comfort in their oppression, but to enable them to confront, transcend, and transform whatever in the oppressor society diminishes and destroys the fundamental dignity of human nature."[70] Jesus confronts the oppressors, but unlike most revolutionaries, Jesus brings genuine liberation by inaugurating a new creation—a new way for human beings to relate one with another. A *mestizo* people, while experiencing marginalization and subjugation, are called by God to build bridges between the oppressor and the oppressed.

In the same way that Jesus lived and ministered at the margins of society, himself one of the marginalized, Elizondo interprets the calling and mission of oppressed peoples, and specifically Mexican Americans, as continuing Jesus' struggle for liberation. Throughout the history of Christianity the church has always existed *within* culture while differentiating itself *from* culture. Sometimes the church has committed the sin of identifying itself too much with the dominant culture; at other times it has risked hampering its evangelical mission by removing itself entirely from culture. Elizondo argues for an understanding of church that does not settle for an easy resolution of this dialectical tension but instead prefers to live "between the times"—God's kingdom breaking into the present but not yet fully realized—as the body of Christ incarnated in our communal existence: "The church is the *mestizo par excellence* because it strives to bring about a new synthesis of the earthly and the heavenly (Eph. 1:10). It is the 'third' or new people, which assumes the good that was there before and gives it new meaning, direction, and life: faith, hope, and charity."[71] Thus, for Virgilio Elizondo *mestizaje* is not an accident of birth but a prophetic vocation.

Part 3 of *Galilean Journey* completes the pattern at the heart of Elizondo's cultural history of *mestizaje*: the journey from Galilee (marginalization) to Jerusalem (struggle for liberation) ends in death (crucifixion), but from death comes new life (resurrection). The third interpretive principle for understanding the Gospel matrix is the "resurrection principle" upon which the hope of the believing community rests. In God's act of salvation and reconciliation through Jesus Christ the world witnessed a revaluation of all values, in which love triumphs over evil, weakness is exalted as truly powerful, and death becomes the gateway to life. The cross, once a symbol of shame, becomes the symbol of divine election:

> The poor and marginated of society can be transformed in their encounter with the risen Lord. In him, they can come to life and overcome their fears. They will no longer be enslaved or silenced, nor will they hide away in their ghettos. As the "new" Galileans of the Acts of the Apostles, they will not hesitate to speak openly and make the truth be heard by all. Concrete manifestations of sin will be exposed. Such denunciations are part of the divine mandate constitutive of discipleship of Jesus on his way to Jerusalem. In the encounter with the risen Lord, the powerless of society are now reborn so as to become a new power *for the salvation of all.*[72]

The Latino/a emphasis upon the cross and resurrection, far from becoming a panacea for suffering, strengthens us in our suffering for others.

Elizondo characterizes the current period of Christian history as the beginning of a new universalism originating in *mestizaje*. What appears a contradictory statement—universal Christian salvation born from the particular experience of the Mexican American people—is in fact a profound statement about God's preferential option for the poor and oppressed as the means for liberating *all* of humanity: "This new love came through many cultures (the way of the incarnation) but at the same time transcended them by opening them up to the wealth and riches of other cultures (the way of transcendence)—to respect local cultures but not to canonize new ghettos."[73] God has acted in the world through *mestizaje* to overcome the barriers human cultures create to exclude the other. *Mestizaje* represents neither the victory nor the defeat of an established people, but the creation of a new people of God: "the proclamation in flesh and blood that the longed-for kingdom has in fact begun."[74]

Methodologically, in spite of the central role given to the public ministry of Jesus Christ as recounted in the Gospels, Elizondo gives preference to the historical/cultural dimension of *mestizaje*. Virgilio Elizondo's theological project falls well within the camp of contextual theology, since, in spite of efforts to maintain the dialectical tension between a theological critique of culture and a cultural critique of theology, inevitably the cultural history of *mestizaje* as the Mexican American journey from oppression to liberation takes precedence. While Elizondo attempts to read the current situation through the lens of Scripture, his reading of Scripture presumes a "canon within a canon"—that is, certain texts become more normative than others in order to preserve Jesus' Galilean (i.e., *mestizo*) identity. Further evidence that the direction of interpretation in Elizondo's theology is from extrascriptural realities to the Scriptures rests in his use of popular religious practices (those practices that do not originate in "official" doctrine and thrive without the presence of clergy) when defining Latino/a cultural identity: "For a suffering and oppressed people, there is nothing more powerful than one's collective religious symbols."[75] Among the symbols central to Mexican American cultural identity Elizondo lists the solemn celebrations of Ash Wednesday and Good Friday, the Christmas posadas that reenact the journey of Joseph and Mary from Nazareth to Bethlehem, and meditation on the Sacred Heart.[76] However, one celebration stands out above all others as uniquely Hispanic, the fiesta of Our Lady of Guadalupe (Nuestra Señora de Guadalupe), which Virgilio Elizondo identifies as proclaiming the "collective resurrection of a new people."[77]

Virgilio Elizondo was the first to articulate *mestizaje* as a primary *locus theologicus,* a typology now used by most U.S. Latino/a theologians. While Elizondo's cultural analysis originated within the *mestizo* reality of Mexican Americans, specifically the relationship between the Roman Catholic Church and the popular religiosity of Mexican Americans converging around Our Lady of Guadalupe, he asserts that this very particular event has now become normative for all Latino/a Christians. He also links the Latino/a struggle for liberation to issues of race and culture, developing *mestizaje* as the chief theological metaphor for resisting North American cultural hegemony. Without ignoring the complex realities that produce marginalization (which include but are not limited to the interaction of race, gender, and class, etc.), Elizondo centers Latino/a cultural identity in *mestizaje* to underscore that we live in a race-conscious society. Accordingly, Virgilio Elizondo's eschatological vision presents *mestizaje* as an empowering and positive cultural and theological identity with concrete political consequences.

Unfortunately, certain inconsistencies within Elizondo's conceptualization of *mestizaje* impede the full realization of his emancipatory goals. Virgilio Elizondo's anthropological and theological project as presented in *Galilean Journey, The Future Is Mestizo,* and *Guadalupe: Mother of the New Creation* contains at least three often blurred uses of *mestizaje*: (1) as biological/genetic identity, (2) as source of cultural/ethnic identity, and (3) as source of universal Christian identity. While all three distinct uses of *mestizaje* are for Elizondo potentially liberating, the last category transcends all others, since at "the core of Christianity is the conviction that a universal human family is truly possible and desirable, one that transcends the blood and ethnic bonds which usually identify us and divide us."[78] Nonetheless, the multivalent character of *mestizaje* is problematic and raises questions about its usefulness as a theological metaphor: *Can U.S. Latino/a theologians continue using the same term for three very different, and perhaps contradictory, realities?*

Elizondo presents a beautiful eschatological vision of a universal *mestizaje*—what Gustavo Gutiérrez has described as a "hermeneutics of hope"[79]—announcing a future humanity in which differences are not suppressed but celebrated. He writes that the "future begins in the dreams of what could and ought to be."[80] Revealing a kinship with Latin American liberation theology, and drawing specifically upon Jon Sobrino's Christological reflections on the "crucified people," Elizondo emphasizes the evangelical role of the world's oppressed and marginalized peoples:

Creative dreams can and will transform reality from battlefields to farm-lands, from opulence at the cost of starvation of others to a new family of concerned neighbors. . . . However, these creative dreams will not emerge from those whose present-day wealth and security are safeguarded by the cultural and socio-economic structures of today's world. They will struggle and fight to maintain the *status quo*. The creative dreams can only come from where they have always come: the prophetic cries and the utopian imagination of the victims.[81]

An underlying question left unanswered by Elizondo—even in his more recent work—concerns how this new humanity brings about the desired social transformation. Clearly there is a moral and political dimension to *mestizaje*. Yet throughout his discussion of the prophetic and liberating mission of the new *mestizo* humanity Elizondo gives the impression that, simply by virtue of being oppressed, the marginalized will want to partici-pate in politically transforming action.

Elizondo shares José Vasconcelos's naïve optimism that a gradual proc-ess of biological mixing is sufficient to overcome cultural conflicts and thus fails to articulate a practical political solution to the problem of racism. Arturo J. Bañuelas, whose book *Mestizo Christianity: Theology from the Latino Perspective* (1995) collects seminal articles by first-generation U.S. Latino/a theologians, raises similar concerns about Elizondo's project:

> Viewed from the perspective of *mestizaje,* the historico-cultural dimen-sion takes precedence for Elizondo. This does not mean that he ignores the political dimension, but further elaboration would help show how ac-ceptance of the other is integrally linked to new structures and public policies that promote the new universalism.[82]

Elizondo himself recognizes that his works provide a vision of what could be rather than concrete steps for getting there: "I have no formulated ide-ology or plan of action, neither do I have any timetable of what will and must take place. I am aware of the vast complexities of nationalistic and cultural identities. Yet I see things beginning to happen, as I equally see profound obstacles to be worked through."[83]

Elizondo's call for the marginalized to continue Christ's saving work in the world would be strengthened by a discussion of the challenge that comes with accepting God's preferential option. Gustavo Gutiérrez in *We Drink from Our Own Wells* discusses at length the difficult process of conversion that rich and poor alike must undertake. He describes the process as a complete break with the past, characterized as an ongoing process of spiritual growth in response to "the call and action of the Spirit who requires a decision that leads us to think, feel, and live with Christ in our day-to-day lives (Phil. 2:5)."[84] Hence, while solidarity is not possible without God's grace, it nonetheless demands a human response; in the U.S. Latino/a context it requires that we choose and embrace the concrete political consequences of *mestizaje*:

> The solidarity required by the preferential option for the poor forces us back to a fundamental Christian attitude: a grasp of the need for continual conversion. We are then able to find in the break with former ways and in our chosen new way deeper dimensions of a personal and social, material and spiritual, kind. The conversion to the Lord to which solidarity with the oppressed brings us calls for stubbornness and constancy on the road we have undertaken.[85]

Elizondo and many others influenced by him have fostered a cultural essentialism linked to a genetic understanding of *mestizaje* that undermines emancipatory political action because it does not adequately call the Latino/a community to conversion. Particularly problematic are those essentialist tendencies within Latino/a churches that tend to conflate ethnic and theological identity.

Mestizaje serves a valuable purpose as a source of both group/cultural identity and personal identity. Elizondo, by grounding his discussions of *mestizaje* within the framework of evolutionary biology,[86] risks impeding his project's liberative goals. While he recognizes both a biological and a cultural dimension to *mestizaje,* he does not always distinguish one from the other, giving the impression that the historical mixing of different peoples is sufficient to bring about his eschatological vision of a universal *mestizaje*. Given the resurgence of biological theories of race in the North American academic context, as exemplified by the work of Herrnstein and Murray (*The Bell Curve*), an uncritical use of biological/genetic language as the basis for ethnic identity can give credence to the new scientific racism.[87] As Irvine, and other allies of U.S. Hispanic theology have noted, U.S. Latino/a theologians may inadvertently foster racial stereotyping when they embrace biological *mestizaje* as a source of Hispanic/Latino/a cultural identity.

Still, any notion of *mestizaje* necessarily retains a biological aspect, since it was coined as a derogatory racist term to distinguish the "superior" Spanish blood from the "inferior" mixed offspring. Hence, any definition or conceptualization of *mestizaje* must account for the fact that it originated as a racist term and is reflective of a social order in which a dominant group marginalizes and oppresses another on the basis of racial/biological differences. However, an undue emphasis on the biological aspects of *mestizaje* can and does contribute to an uncritical ethnocentrism within Latino/a communities. A short selection of passages from Virgilio Elizondo's *The Future Is Mestizo*, in which he articulates the concept of universal *mestizaje*, demonstrate how biological *mestizaje* as a defining characteristic of U.S. Latino/a ethnic particularity undermines his liberating vision of a human community that transcends racial difference.

For example, Elizondo uncritically borrows the language of evolutionary biology for use in the anthropological and sociological arena: "Nature seems to demand differentiation but this does not have to be opposed to universalization."[88] This leads him to make pseudoscientific claims like "the culture of our parents is so deep it is transmitted in an almost biological way. We can adjust to a new culture and even assume into ourselves many of the traits of the new culture we have moved into, but we can never cease being who we are."[89] There is little difference between this kind of biological and cultural essentialism and racist statements about all Latino/as being born with rhythm and able to dance. When Elizondo states that the European conquest of the Americas marks the beginning of "a new and totally unprecedented stage in the evolution of humanity through *mestizaje*," it is clear Elizondo is using the language of evolutionary biology analogically to discuss cultural development—a wholly appropriate move.[90] Still, Elizondo's use of evolutionary terminology ignores the fact that evolutionary change within a species is measured in millions —not hundreds—of years, substantiating the claim that he is not always careful to differentiate between biological and cultural evolution.

Twelve years after the original publication of *The Future Is Mestizo*, Elizondo revisited the work and in a new epilogue reaffirmed the biological use of *mestizaje*: "Biologically, mestizaje is an enriching of the genetic pool and therefore very positive."[91] To be fair, Elizondo's use of *mestizaje* is not a one-dimensional emphasis on the biological aspects of race and ethnicity: "Biologically and culturally, mestizaje is an important process in the evolution of the human race into a truly human family—from divided and fighting tribes, clans, nations, and races to a united human family."[92] Yet too much emphasis on the biological reality of *mestizaje* undercuts the eschatological vision of a new identity grounded in Christ that transcends all other identities without negating them. In other words, the liberating aspect of embracing our mixed biological heritage and therefore valuing it as a fully human reality (as opposed to a less-than-human racial slur) can quickly become an ethnocentric nationalism. Recalling Elizondo's own "anthropological laws of human behavior"—in which one inevitable aspect of cultural interaction is the perpetuation of an "us" versus "them" dichotomy in order to foster group cultural identity—some forms of U.S. Latino/a theology unintentionally subvert the desire for an inclusive community for the sake of a unique and unified cultural existence over against the dominant culture by essentializing Latino/a identity. In summary, there are two major shortcomings to using *mestizaje* as a liberating theological metaphor: (1) *mestizaje* as a source of biological/ racial, and ethnic/cultural, identity can easily deteriorate into a nationalist project by fostering an exclusionary and uncritical ethnocentrism, and (2) the previously mentioned search for a pan-Hispanic identity (rooted in a shared experience of marginalization due to our *mestizo* biological and cultural inheritance) conceals vital differences within the Hispanic community. For an example of the latter, consider Elizondo's emphasis upon certain distinctly Catholic religious practices as *constitutive* of Latino/a identity, which raises concerns among Elizondo's Protestant critics (myself included). When Elizondo writes, "I do not want to say that every Hispanic has to remain a member of the Roman Catholic Church in order to be a Hispanic, but I am saying that when a Hispanic ceases to be catholic (to participate in the religious-cultural expressions of our people), he or she ceases to be a Hispanic,"[93] he seems to impose a particularly Mexican American and Roman Catholic popular religiosity as normative for *all* Latino/a Christians. For Elizondo, the Guadalupe event is foundational for Latino/a cultural *and* religious identity, and it is granted the same authority as Scripture, a move that *creates* rather than *eliminates* barriers between Roman Catholic and Protestant Latino/as.

Recently, a new generation of Latino/a scholars has suggested abandoning *mestizaje* as a liberating theological metaphor.[94] By looking at how two Latino/a theologians influenced by Elizondo, Ada María Isasi-Díaz and Luis G. Pedraja, have reconceptualized *mestizaje,* this investigation evaluates whether or not *mestizaje* is a fluid enough metaphor to contain the tensions outlined earlier without hampering Elizondo's beautiful eschato-logical vision of a "new humanity which will be inclusive of everyone."[95]

Ada María Isasi-Díaz: A *Mujerista* Reconceptualization of *Mestizaje*

Ada María Isasi-Díaz, a Cuban-born Roman Catholic theologian best known as an ardent advocate of *mujerista* theology,[96] has taken Virgilio Elizondo's understanding of *mestizaje* and broadened it to describe Latino/a realities beyond the Mexican American experience. In her most recent scholarly work Isasi-Díaz prefers the more inclusive hyphenated term *mestizaje-mulatez* to describe the U.S. Latino/a reality of racial and ethnic mixing in order to also include the cultural and racial mixing between European and African peoples. However, as Fernando F. Segovia has argued, *mestizaje-mulatez* ignores the mixing of Amerindian and African peoples, as well as those who identify themselves as criollo (the children of Spaniards or Africans born in the Americas).[97] Therefore, Segovia offers a more inclusive term, *mezcolanza* (mixture), to encompass the plurality of racial/cultural mixing characteristic of Latino/a reality. However, given the prevalence of the term *mestizaje* in U.S. Latino/a theology, and the fact that this term has been broadened to include the dialogical and mutually enriching relationship between two or more cultures, I continue to use the term *mestizaje* throughout as descriptive of *all* the complex realities of racial and cultural mixing because of its ability to disconcert the black-white dichotomy that dominates North American racial discourse.

Like Elizondo, Isasi-Díaz recognizes a first wave of *mestizaje* coinciding with the Spanish conquest of the Americas, and a second wave of cultural and ethnic mixing now taking place in the North American context. Yet, while Elizondo's discussion of *mestizaje* focuses on the Mexican American experience, Isasi-Díaz opts to broaden *mestizaje* to include "the present day mixtures of people from Latin America and the Caribbean both among ourselves and with people of other ethnic/racial and cultural backgrounds here in the United States."[98] Furthermore, while Isasi-Díaz affirms Elizondo's overall vision of a new *mestizo* humanity, she adds a vital new dimension to his concept of *mestizaje,* since for her *mestizo* identity is not grounded in genetic mixing (although biological factors cannot be ignored), but depends upon an act of moral choice and political solidarity:

Being thrown together into a pile labeled Hispanic, however, can also be helpful for us in our process of self-definition and self-determination. . . . Experiencing what it means to be considered totally other helps us to understand and reject the dynamics of cultural imperialism. Being considered a homogenous group in a way forces us to face up to our own prejudices: our own racism, classism, and sexism. That we are looked upon as all being the same, as a homogenous group, can become an opportunity for us to make a conscious choice of what it does mean that we are Hispanics living in the U.S.A. as well as the role we want to have in this society. In a word, we have the opportunity of defining ourselves, of opting to be *mestizos*, opting *for* Hispanics, opting to be Hispanics.[99]

Isasi-Díaz, in discussing the experiences of Latina women, is able to cross borders that Elizondo leaves unexplored, such as the diversity of national and ethnic backgrounds that constitute U.S. Latino/a identity or a conception of popular religiosity that transcends Mexican American popular Catholicism.

According to Isasi-Díaz, the central task of theology is liberation—*political liberation* from oppression and marginalization, *personal-psychological liberation* from the lack of self-worth resulting from political powerlessness, and *spiritual liberation* from religious teachings and institutions that impede the aforementioned modes of liberation. Comparing her theological method to that of Virgilio Elizondo, Isasi-Díaz also develops a contextual theology in which the direction of interpretation originates with extrascriptural social realities before moving to the Scriptures. However, if Elizondo's project privileges a "canon within a canon," then the theological approach developed by Ada María Isasi-Díaz completely relativizes the canon. Theological reflection begins with the lived experience of a particular faith community, which in the case of *mujerista* theology means the lived experience of Latina women in the North American context, and the "correctness" of doctrine is established by how well these beliefs contribute to the community's liberation:

> This is to say that *mujerista* theology recognizes as its source the faith of Hispanic women, faith that is intrinsically linked to our struggles for liberation. . . . This is why our theological enterprise struggles to be a community process committed to listening to and articulating the beliefs of the communities of Latinas who struggle for liberation. These communities whose experiences are the source of *mujerista* theology have a

long history of Christian belief and practices. They are communities with a long religious tradition which is central to our culture. In other words, because present-day Hispanic women communities continue the traditions and religious beliefs of our ancestors, we are provided with an important way to evaluate contemporary theological elaborations. However, tradition is not the main criterion of *mujerista* theology. A holistic liberation is our main criterion.[100]

Accordingly, Isasi-Díaz understands divine revelation as ongoing, not "completed and closed when the canon of Christianity was determined," but taking place "through the faith and religiosity of the poor and oppressed of this world."[101] Thus, while Elizondo grounds his theology in the Galilean Jesus as presented primarily in the synoptic Gospels, Isasi-Díaz considers the praxis of liberation as the very basis upon which to select a canon.

While liberation is the chief locus, Isasi-Díaz identifies two "preoccupations" that define *mujerista* theology: *marginalization* as one of the most dangerous forms of oppression confronting Latinas, and *economic exploitation* as the concrete manifestation of this marginalization. *Mujerista* theology systematically addresses these concerns by focusing on four major themes: (1) the need to demystify academic theology by insisting that all theology is "contextual" theology, (2) the importance of grounding theological reflection in the day-to-day struggle of Latina women (*lo cotidiano*)[102] in order to challenge the dominant Western notions about what constitutes legitimate academic work, (3) recognition that sin is essentially social and that justice is achieved by transforming society such that relationships of oppression and domination are replaced by relationships of mutual respect and accountability, and (4) a methodological commitment to the understanding that divine revelation is ongoing, not limited to the biblical canon, and manifest in the daily struggles for liberation of the politically and economically marginalized.[103] Not surprisingly, even though Elizondo spends considerable time analyzing particular popular practices, popular religiosity proves an even more important theological source for Ada María Isasi-Díaz given her focus on the daily struggle for survival of Latina women. Specifically, Isasi-Díaz suggests that the resources for liberating praxis are found in the community's traditions and religious beliefs; however, just as in the *mujerista* understanding of Scripture, popular religious practices gain their authority only insofar as they contribute to the community's liberation.

In her book *En la Lucha/In the Struggle: Elaborating a Mujerista Theology* (1993, rev. 2004), Ada María Isasi-Díaz builds upon an innovative methodology first explored in the book *Hispanic Women: Prophetic Voice in the Church* (1988), cowritten with Yolanda Tarango, in order to articulate her notion of *mujerista* theology. This approach, grounded in the "ethnomethodology" developed by Harvard social psychologist Harold Garfinkel, involved a decade of sociological research during which time the two researchers met with groups of Latina women and carefully listened to and recorded their testimonies in order to understand their beliefs about God.[104] From these data they sought to identify recurring themes; however, since both Isasi-Díaz and Tarango define *mujerista* theology as liberating praxis, their research inevitably focused on the ethical dimensions of these women's beliefs. Finally, the two researchers allowed for participant feedback to ensure that their conclusions accurately reflected these women's beliefs.

The closing chapter of the earlier book, *Hispanic Women*, introduces the framework that Isasi-Díaz develops further in *En la Lucha*, in which the stated goal is to empower Latinas to become agents of their own history: "One of the main goals of *mujerista* theology is to enhance the development of the moral agency of Hispanic Women."[105] The process of *conscientization*[106] in the work of Isasi-Díaz is characterized by four phases: (1) telling stories/personal testimony, (2) reflective analysis, (3) liturgy and celebration, and (4) political strategizing. The ultimate task is to further the holistic liberation of Latina women from psychological, socioeconomic, political, and religious oppression, which she recognizes as both a personal and social struggle:

> Liberation is a personal, self-actualizing struggle which each one must accept as one's own responsibility. Liberation is a struggle that lasts one's whole life. Personal responsibility is one of the elements at the core of the moral subject and, therefore, at the heart of moral agency. Liberation theologies insist that the poor and the oppressed must struggle consciously to be agents of our own history. They must move away from being mere objects acted upon by the oppressors and become active subjects: moral persons.[107]

Consequently, when considering Isasi-Díaz's contributions toward a theological understanding of *mestizaje*, it is important to highlight her emphasis on moral agency.

Like Virgilio Elizondo, Ada María Isasi-Díaz recognizes we live in a society polarized by race. Furthermore, she identifies the act of naming oneself as the most powerful act an individual can take.[108] If marginalization is understood as the systemic exclusion of a particular group from fully participating in society by naming that group undesirable or of little value to that society, then issues of self-identity and self-determination are at the heart of any praxis of liberation. By listening to and reflecting with Latina women about their lived experience in North American society, Isasi-Díaz identifies ethnicity, gender, and class as interrelated factors contributing to their marginalization and economic exploitation. To name oneself—that is, to recognize that one is a self-determining agent in history—is an important first step in the process of liberation. The process of self-naming for U.S. Latino/a theology began with Virgilio Elizondo's use of *mestizaje*; however, Isasi-Díaz argues that ethnicity is simply one of several factors to consider, and suggests Latino/a theologians need to embrace "difference" as a more inclusive category for reconceptualizing *mestizaje*.

Upon a cursory reading, Ada María Isasi-Díaz's conceptualization of *mestizaje* does not appear to differ significantly from Elizondo's original work:

> For us Hispanic Women, the creation of a new race is a very real part of our daily lives. *Mestizaje* is grounded in the fact that we live in-between, at the intersection of our countries of origin and the U.S.A. In the U.S.A. we are mostly marginalized people relegated to the outskirts of society, not really fully belonging. Regarding our countries of origin we know that even if or when we do return, it is never really possible to go back.[109]

In the work of both theologians, *mestizaje* describes a new way of life distinct from both parent cultures—belonging to both and neither—capable of empowering marginalized individuals with a liberating vision of personal and corporate identity. Thus, while Isasi-Díaz does not provide the same thorough biblical grounding for *mestizaje* articulated by Elizondo, she clearly accepts his argument and builds upon it. Isasi-Díaz even borrows Elizondo's language of *mestizaje* as the creation of a "new race": "*Mujerista* theologians affirm *mestizaje* as the coming together of different races and cultures in a creative way that necessarily precludes the subordination of one to another; we affirm it as the going forward of humankind."[110] Yet, while both theologians employ the language of "race" when describing *mestizaje,* Elizondo seems to emphasize the biological aspects of *mestizaje* more than Isasi-Díaz, who conceptualizes *mestizaje* as an existential decision—a new way of being in relationship with one another.

I do not want to reduce Elizondo's vital contributions to a one-dimensional conceptualization of *mestizaje* as primarily biological; however, the language utilized by Elizondo, even in his most recent writings, suggests a lack of theoretical reflection about race and racism. Unfortunately, in articulating what he means by this "third way" in which human cultures can relate one to another without one culture dominating and subjugating the other, Elizondo seems trapped by theoretical language that conceptualizes *mestizaje* as the creation of a new race—and by adopting the prevailing language of race he perpetuates an "us" versus "them" dichotomy that essentializes individual and corporate identity. Ada María Isasi-Díaz, by emphasizing the social creation of identity—especially our role as individual moral agents in determining our own identity—reconceptualizes *mestizaje* as a more fluid and changing reality. In reviewing her work on *mestizaje,* Isasi-Díaz comments, "I began to elaborate a non-exclusionary and non-oppositional perspective of differences and concluded by proposing the embracing of *mestizaje* as an ethical choice."[111] By grounding Latino/a social identity in the individual agent's act of solidarity (in the context of building community), Isasi-Díaz opens the door toward a transcultural understanding of *mestizaje,* since group identity no longer depends solely upon biological heritage but is the result of moral and political choice.

The strength of *mujerista* theology is its ability to provide a holistic framework for discussing the lived experience of Latina women in all its complexity without ignoring feminist, liberationist, cultural, or ecclesial concerns. The work of Isasi-Díaz is a clarion call for all people (although she speaks first to women) to struggle for self-determination and social transformation, in whatever social context they find themselves, in solidarity with all who are marginalized and exploited in obedience to the Gospel's vision of universal liberation. Nevertheless, certain conceptual weaknesses reveal themselves in *mujerista* theology as articulated by Isasi-Díaz. These include (1) an overwhelming emphasis upon extrascriptural sources (primarily cultural anthropology) without direct engagement of the biblical texts, (2) a tendency to focus on the lived experience of Roman Catholic Latina women,[112] and (3) an inadequate exploration of the role of doctrine in shaping a community's beliefs and practices. While the work of Isasi-Díaz contributes much to my own conceptualization of *mestizaje* as theological metaphor, these criticisms will be explored in later chapters, as I first deconstruct, and then reconstruct, *mestizaje* as a set of relationships rather than a static identity.

Luis G. Pedraja: From Ethnocentrism to Transculturalism

Cuban American Protestant theologian Luis G. Pedraja embodies the second wave of *mestizaje* described by both Virgilio Elizondo and Ada María Isasi-Díaz, in which the original *mestizo* culture resulting from the Spanish conquest of Latin America is undergoing a new *mestizaje* with the dominant North American culture as the result of twentieth-century Protestant missionary efforts, increased immigration, and intermarriage. While Latino/as in the United States continue to experience exclusion and marginalization on the basis of race, a sense of optimism accompanies their theological reflections on how *mestizaje* can serve as God's means for overcoming cultural differences and ending relationships of domination. However, while Elizondo's conceptualization of *mestizaje* emphasizes the creation of a new biological people whose mixed status will somehow contribute to the breakdown of long-standing prejudices, younger scholars like Pedraja conceptualize *mestizaje* as a process of dialogical communication that enables social transformation and liberation. Granted, multicultural communication is facilitated by the fact that Latino/as—because they embody a mixing of cultural, religious, *and* genetic identities—are better able to "appreciate the similarities and differences of the various cultures they embody, and as a result they create bridges between these cultures."[113] Nevertheless, by articulating a methodology that engenders social acceptance of the "other" and strives for greater transcontextuality, U.S. Latino/a theologians have built upon the groundbreaking work of Virgilio Elizondo in order to overcome some of the weaknesses of this earlier work.

As this marginalized community struggles to achieve a more holistic integration into all facets of North American society, its priority has changed from basic survival (manifest as ethnocentrism) to the need for more effective political engagement (manifest as increased discourse with other communities and toleration of cultural diversity within the community itself). Thus, while ethnic identity is the chief concern of Elizondo's *Galilean Journey* (and, to a lesser extent, of Isasi-Díaz's *En la Lucha/ In the Struggle*), U.S. Latino/a theologians have broadened the scope of their theological reflections. Luis G. Pedraja moves beyond the biological understanding of *mestizaje* in favor of a more cultural understanding by exploring ways in which *mestizaje* is constitutive of Christian identity and not merely ethnic identity. These ways include (1) the history of Christianity as a process of *mestizaje*,[114] (2) the "bilingual" theologian as a living bridge between cultures, languages, and perspectives, and (3) Christology as a *mestizaje* between the human and divine.[115]

Now that many Hispanic Christians in North America have embraced *mestizaje* as a unifying group identity, one of the challenges facing U.S. Latino/a theologians is the need to articulate a public theology that seeks discourse beyond the church's communal walls. Pedraja not only critically engages mainstream European and North American academic discourse, especially the theology of Paul Tillich and the philosophy of Alfred North Whitehead, but also integrates their insights into a distinctively Latino/a theology. This openness to other perspectives stems from a realization that Latino/a cultural and theological identity is not fixed. Recalling the language of Whitehead's process philosophy, Pedraja describes the evolving character of Latino/a identity:

> Hispanics are an organic reality. They are caught in a dynamic of change and becoming that prevents them from being defined by a singular abstraction. Instead, they continually create new communities and venues for becoming a people that defy static categories. Static definitions would deny their organic reality of growth, change, and redefinition.[116]

Concluding that the "dynamics of diversity and community found in the Hispanic communities of the United States should serve as a model for doing theology as an ongoing dialogue,"[117] Pedraja's approach moves beyond a narrow ethnocentrism and strives for genuine mutuality between cultures.

Luis Pedraja begins his theological reflections with an exploration of the reductionistic labels "Hispanic" and "Latino/a" used to describe our various peoples. Unlike other labels for ethnic group identity in North America, like Irish American or Italian American, the label "Hispanic" or "Latino/a" does not refer to a specific ethnic community or nationality but covers a multiplicity of racial, ethnic, national, and cultural backgrounds. Granted, while the first Hispanic communities that arose in this country tended to define themselves by national heritage—it is still possible to find Mexican, Puerto Rican, Dominican, or Cuban neighborhoods in major urban centers—when "faced with the task of confronting the bulk of U.S. society or when feeling isolated and alienated in non-Hispanic communities, a sense of commonality and community develops in spite of the diversity of the people in the community."[118] As a result of a common experience of marginalization based on ethnic otherness, Latino/as have embraced the descriptive terminology imposed upon them by the dominant North American culture, transforming it into a label of solidarity that allows them to foster a sense of community while preserving national, ethnic, and religious differences.[119]

However, in discussing Virgilio Elizondo's vision of *mestizaje* as a new people of God (in *The Future Is Mestizo*), Pedraja uncovers a tendency to ignore concrete differences for the sake of unity:

> Although the differences should not be denied, their synthesis and their promise for the betterment of all humanity indicate a tendency to blur distinctions and universalize. In synthesizing diversity we risk the dissolutions of distinctions that preserve a sense of respect for our otherness. Eradicating these tensions and dynamics that shape Hispanic identity and theological dialogue would only lead to a static paradigm.[120]

To avoid essentializing Latino/a cultural identity, Pedraja suggests a better use of the term *mestizaje* can be found in the theology of Ada María Isasi-Díaz, whom he quotes defining *mestizaje* "as the coming together of different races and cultures in a creative way that necessarily precludes the subordination of one to another."[121] Without denying the importance of ethnocentrism for empowering U.S. Latino/as in the struggle for liberation, Pedraja recognizes in Isasi-Díaz's use of *mestizaje* an approach that

> preserves the dynamic tension and particular differences to the resulting reality. Our reality is an organic, creative, evolving reality that preserves our differences in a creative tension. We need to stand in solidarity with one another without eradicating our differences. Thus, Hispanic theology must avoid language that may be construed as static and reductionistic.[122]

Pedraja offers an important response to those critics of contextual theologies who characterize contextual theologies as merely reflecting the horizons of the community in self-affirmation by defining that which unites the Latino/a community as an attitude of openness toward the "other" that is respectful of difference: "The common ground of the Hispanic community is the overlapping strands that enable dialogue within the community and outside of the community with the other groups with whom we also share overlapping traits."[123]

Accordingly, *mestizo* group identity is not limited to biological identity but encompasses many factors that are constantly negotiated by the *mestizo* in relation to both parent cultures. By defining Latino/a reality as a continuous "dialogic encounter," Luis Pedraja underscores the public and relational character of Latino/a contextual theologies, emphasizing the importance of seeking out "diverse and alien perspectives" in theologizing: "The dialogue begins in our present experience and moves to include others in its constant relational dynamic. As an ongoing dialogue, we recognize in humility that our voice is not the only one nor is it the last to have a say in the matter."[124] Seeking to describe that which unites U.S. Latino/a theologies while also preserving their differences, Pedraja rejects essentializing discourses, drawing upon the philosophy of Jacques Derrida and Emmanuel Lévinas to articulate a methodology that allows for "meaningful comparisons between these theologies without resorting to static abstractions"—an approach that blurs "rigid lines of demarcation between them while preserving distinctive identifying features necessary for a continuing mutual dialogue."[125]

Not surprisingly, the ability to navigate differences while building bridges is characteristic of many Protestant Latino/as who long for a shared Hispanic identity capable of transcending national and religious boundaries while at the same time undergoing a "slow withdrawal from the aspects of cultural and family life that are rooted in Catholicism."[126] This process is further complicated by what Pedraja describes as a "double marginalization," since Protestant Latino/as living in the United States are alienated from the Catholic faith and culture of their ancestors while experiencing marginalization within their "Anglo denominations and forced to conform to structures, rituals, and practices that are alien to their culture."[127] Consequently, he urges U.S. Latino/a theologians, regardless of confessional background, to work together by noting common sources, experiences, and goals. These shared experiences help to distinguish U.S. Latino/a theology as distinct "from other theologies while serving as points of comparison and contrast between Protestant and Catholic Hispanic theologies."[128] To facilitate the task of "mapping" North American Latino/a theology, Pedraja suggests three important markers along the way: (1) the creation of a unifying Hispanic ethnic identity, (2) the role of popular religious practices in the formation of Hispanic theology, and (3) a liberating reading of the Bible.

Like Ada María Isasi-Díaz, Pedraja embraces Virgilio Elizondo's notion of *mestizaje* as constitutive of Hispanic ethnic identity because this concept enables U.S. Latino/a theologians to bring together diverse Hispanic communities for the sake of political survival on the basis of their shared experiences of marginalization. Greatly influenced by Latin American liberation theology, U.S. Latino/a theologians have reinterpreted the preferential option for the poor by focusing on identity, since, in the North American context, those rejected by the dominant culture include the economically poor as well as those identified as ethnically (and gendered) other:

> The mestizo embodies those rejected by both cultures, those marginalized and impoverished physically, culturally, psychologically, and socioeconomically. God's preferential option for the poor becomes God's preferential option for those who are rejected by society and marginalized. The mestizaje of these people allows them to embody a diversity that creates a more inclusive notion of humanity, one that accepts, affirms, and celebrates "otherness." Similarly, their suffering and marginal status opens a new possibility for compassion and an affirmation of liberation.[129]

With the question of identity a central motif of U.S. Latino/a theological reflection, ethnocentrism becomes both a source of liberating praxis and a potential obstacle to transcultural discourse. Accordingly, Luis Pedraja makes use of postmodern notions of personal identity in order to emphasize the ethical demand toward the other *as* other while avoiding the tendency to essentialize Latino/a ethnic identity, which can further contribute to the marginalization of Hispanics by perpetuating the myth of incommensurability between different ethnic groups.[130] What is needed is a view of *mestizaje* that not only affirms diversity but also empowers individuals for transforming social praxis.

A second mark of Latino/a theological identity is the use of popular religious practices as a source of communal identity and political empowerment. While Pedraja acknowledges that popular religion has been a long-standing *locus theologicus* for Latino/a Roman Catholic theologies, because of the strong link to popular Catholicism there is much resistance within Latino/a Protestantism to the concept of popular religion.

Nonetheless, such practices are present in Protestant congregations. By defining popular religion as "a concrete expression of empowerment and resistance for marginalized communities," Pedraja concludes that popular religious practices exist in both Protestant and Catholic communities, but differ in expression.[131] For example, rather than finding expression in iconic symbols such as Nuestra Señora de Guadalupe or the Sacred Heart, Latino/a Protestants express their lived faith through public witness (*testimonios*) and popular songs (*coritos*). Furthermore, where "Catholics express their popular religion in concrete symbols, Protestants express it primarily through words," especially through the veneration of the written Word, which "takes the place of the icon in Catholic popular religion."[132]

This last aspect of Protestant Latino/a theological identity can lead to a form of Biblicism, but when this popular reverence for the Bible as sacred Word is coupled with a liberating reading of the Scriptures, Latino/a communities become empowered to take part in socially transformative action. Pedraja, influenced by first-generation Cuban-American theologian Justo L. González, undertakes to read the Bible "in Spanish"—not by mandating bilingualism as necessary for a proper "Latino/a" interpretation of the Christian tradition but in recognition that all theology is particular and contextualized.[133] While critics of contextual theologies argue that said theologies are irrelevant beyond their particular local contexts, Justo González counters that it is naïve to deny that every theology reflects the values and interests of a particular community of faith; thus he calls for a "non-innocent reading of history" that employs a hermeneutic of suspicion, challenges the power structures that beget oppression, and works to transform present reality.[134] At the same time González challenges Hispanic theologians by insisting that the task of doing theology from a Hispanic perspective does not preclude doing theology for the church at large.[135]

Like González, Pedraja envisions theology as a communal enterprise that embraces transcontextuality by overcoming obstacles to genuine discourse, such as the prejudices that exist between Protestants and Catholics or between marginalized groups and the dominant culture. The unifying identity of the various U.S. Latino/a theologies—whether Roman Catholic, mainline Protestant, or Pentecostal—rests in a liberating reading of Scripture that seeks to transcend the particularities of culture, race, and class. For Pedraja this multivalent identity necessitates a dialogical method in which, as "we listen to each other, we are challenged to broaden our theology to be more inclusive. Thus, we are able to contribute to other people's understanding of God while we also grow in our own."[136] None-theless, Pedraja's conceptualization of dialogic encounter depends upon, and originates with, "a common ground amidst diversity."[137] By champi-oning a notion of dialogue in which difference is an inherent aspect of the "other" with whom we dialogue, while "shared identity" enables mutual understanding by bridging differences between social groups, Pedraja's understanding of *mestizaje* has much in common with Elizondo's use of *mestizaje*—especially if the possibility for "bridging" differences depends upon the conversants having at least one ethnicity in common. Still, while the *mestizo* has a deeper appreciation for dialogic encounter—often born from necessity, since the *mestizo* is never fully at home in either parent culture— Pedraja's work transcends biological *mestizaje,* since the capac-ity to embrace and participate in dialogic encounter seems part of our common humanity. Pedraja defines theology as "an ongoing conversation between us and between us and God" that

> includes the people and . . . includes God. It includes our past and our future. As we continually enter into dialogue with diverse and alien per-spectives we address the voices of the other in our present actuality, as well as those voices that address us from the past in the same manner that we shall address those in our future. The dialogue begins in our present experience and moves to include others in its constant relational dynamic.[138]

Consequently, *mestizaje* not only is the source of U.S. Latino/a ethnic identity, but also can become a model for all liberating relationships.

U.S. Latino/a theologies are increasingly aware of the social construc-tion of personal and social identity—especially as regards race and eth-nicity. As evidenced by the works of Virgilio Elizondo, Ada María Isasi-Díaz, and Luis G. Pedraja, Hispanic theologians have long acknowledged that ethnic differences are used to objectify and marginalize people of color in North American society. However, more work needs to be done to develop a theological critique of North American racism that tran-scends and transforms the very boundaries perpetuating the structures of exclusion and exploitation. Certain rubrics in U.S. Latino/a theology hold much promise for deconstructing racism—especially *mestizaje* and God's preferential option for the poor and oppressed—but only insofar as these concepts are firmly planted in the soil of the community's lived faith. U.S. Latino/a theologians, while speaking from a particular perspective, need to engage the breadth of ecumenical Christianity in order to demonstrate how God's Word is always revealed by means of a particular word to a particular people.

Reconceptualizing Mestizaje *as a Transcultural Paradigm*

Given the open-ended and continually negotiated understanding of culture communicated by the concepts of hybridization, *mestizaje,* and transculturation, what are the more or less stable cultural forms indicative of a *mestizo* culture? In other words, what shared beliefs and practices give cultural formation to *mestizaje*? *Mestizaje* describes both individual and corporate identity; in fact, it is probably more accurate to speak about individual *mestizos* (as the children of two cultures) than to speak about a distinct *mestizo* culture. Nonetheless, U.S. Latino theology has attempted to articulate a unifying Hispanic cultural identity grounded in the shared experience of being *mestizo.* From the outset, we have recognized three distinct (if overlapping) uses of *mestizaje* within U.S. Latino/a theology: (1) the historical and biological reality of mixing between two or more human groups, (2) the complex interaction and mutual exchange between two or more cultures, and (3) a distinctly Christian theological anthropology grounded in Christ's own historical identity as *mestizo* that advocates a liberating vision of human equality distinguished by active resistance to various forms of cultural, political, and religious domination. In light of these three different uses of *mestizaje* present within U.S. Latino/a theology, we can make certain broad generalizations about what constitutes a distinctly *mestizo* cultural identity. *Mestizaje* involves (1) the coming together of two or more ethnic or cultural groupings (in a historical context where one group dominates the other) in one individual, (2) the experience of being marginalized by both parent cultures, (3) a desire to subvert the racist ideology that views the offspring of cross-cultural unions as "impure" by embracing *mestizo* identity (originally a racial slur) as politically empowering, and (4) liberating social praxis that seeks to transform relationships of domination into relationships of equality.

Having identified and rejected biologically essentialist and culturally essentialist tendencies within U.S. Latino/a theology, it is necessary to articulate a theory of cultural mixing that accounts for those communal practices that embody *mestizaje* as a source of group identity in nonessentialist ways. By emphasizing a moral-political act as the defining aspect of *mestizaje,* this work has tried to overcome some of these essentializing tendencies. On the other hand, focusing on the individual agent's decision increases the risk of reducing *mestizo* identity to the actions of the autonomous self while disregarding the role of collective identity and cultural particularity on the formation of individual identity. The goal is to avoid just such an atomistic view of the relationship between individual and group identity by reconstructing *mestizaje* as a set of relationships rather than a static identity, moving beyond a narrow ethnocentrism, and striving for genuine mutuality between cultures. Accordingly, group identity is not limited to either biological identity or a static view of culture, but is understood as something constantly negotiated by the *mestizo* in relation to both parent cultures. Thus, *mestizaje* is construed not just in terms of biological mixing (although it originates here), or just in terms of cultural mixing (perhaps the most common form of *mestizaje*), but also in terms of moral and political agency. By maintaining all three of these uses of *mestizaje* in constant tension—not allowing any one use to define what is meant by *mestizaje*—we can preserve the open-ended and interrelational aspect of cultural identity.

So while *mestizaje* is at its core the mixing of different cultures, its theological use entails a spiritual conversion from the old way of viewing human relationships as relationships of domination (the "us" versus "them" dichotomy) to a new, Christ-centered vision of human relationships as a "discipleship of equals" (Fiorenza) where "there is no longer Jew or Greek, there is no longer slave or free, there is no longer male or female" (Gal. 3:28, NRSV). The painful history of being both the oppressed and the oppressor that lies at the heart of any understanding of *mestizaje* can serve as a starting point for developing strategies of resistance and liberation. While the church has in the past contributed to the formation of racist ideologies, it has also given rise to social movements that seek to dismantle racism. U.S. Latino/a theology is united by a biblical vision of liberation and strives to work for political empowerment and positive social transformation within the church and in the broader society. *Mestizaje* can serve as a living reminder that God loves all of humanity in its great diversity and does not condone social stratification and relations of domination.

The second half of this book interprets *mestizaje* as the work of the Holy Spirit in order to articulate concrete liberating practices that must be embodied by the Christian community. Broadly, these include resistance to racism, sexism, and classism. More specifically, Christian practices that might constitute "marks" of the *mestizo* church include political action to resist racism and a new understanding of *ecclesia* defined as spiritual community wherever God's liberating work takes place. This vision of a prophetic Christian community emphasizes a liberative reading of Scripture in order to empower the church for positive social transformation while preserving a distinct theological identity that does not denigrate or exclude others.

3

The Public Relevance of Theology

The phrase "political theology," widely used to characterize diverse developments in Christian theology since the 1960s, encompasses post-Holocaust theologies in Cold War Europe, the turn toward Christian social ethics in North America, the rise of liberation theologies in Latin America and elsewhere, and, more recently, the articulation of explicitly "public" theologies.[1] One thing these various movements have in common is their use of political theory—especially Marxist analysis—to develop a critique of ideologies, including Marxism itself, in order to expose the extent to which Christianity has, throughout its history, uncritically embraced values that conflict with the Gospels. Jürgen Moltmann, writing about the European context during the Cold War, generalized that "anti-communism in the one camp and anti-capitalism in the other dominated the political ideologies and made any inward opposition impossible."[2] Therefore, the new "political theology" that he and colleagues like Johann Baptist Metz and Dorothee Sölle sought to articulate gathered together "very different things, though with a shared alignment" whose ultimate goal was "to make people who are the humiliated objects of the power and violence of others the free determining subjects of their own lives."[3] Accordingly, all such theologies can be subsumed under the heading of "liberation theology" whether they arise in the first world or the third world, since "the point is always liberation of the victims and criticism of the perpetrators."[4]

In the North American context, a religiously pluralistic society in which many diverse local/contextual theologies thrive, there has always existed a rich tradition of theological concern for the public life of the nation as demonstrated by the religious thought of such figures as Abraham Lincoln, the Reverend Martin Luther King Jr., Dorothy Day, and César Chávez. Contemporary liberationists in the United States—whether feminist, African American, Latino/a, and so forth—stand as heirs to this diverse tradition of publicly minded religious thinkers working for emancipatory social change on a national scale. Still, despite a long history of theological traditions that recognize the political implications of religious faith and affirm the role of religion in the public discourse, there is no single dominant paradigm for political theology in the United States. Recently, some theologians have called for more "public" theologies that transcend particular liberationist projects (without neglecting their importance or distinct contributions) in order "to address concerns of national public life with the resources of their specific religious traditions."[5] Recognizing that the term *public theology* embraces such disparate voices as Richard John Neuhaus and Victor Anderson,[6] it is important to identify some overarching characteristics that define a particular theological project as "public."

Parameters of a "Public" Theology

Public theology is a predominantly North American movement encompassing a broad range of theologians whose political views range from progressive to conservative but who share a commitment to transcend those sectarian tendencies within Christianity that undermine the possibility of a common moral discourse in favor of a vision of the Christian life that affirms the church's public voice and nurtures a sense of public responsibility in a pluralistic society. Max Stackhouse, whose theology is greatly indebted to that of Reinhold Niebuhr, even contends that Christianity is foundational to Western civilization and therefore publicly minded theologies are necessary for maintaining the well-being of Western liberal democracies.[7] Still, as theologian Mary Doak has argued, it is important to differentiate between "public theology" and "civil religion," since the latter "has come to be identified as the practice of invoking religious beliefs and symbols in *support* of a country's values and practices" whereas public theology moves beyond merely affirming a nation's interests "to engage in critical reflection on the nation's culture, plans, and actions."[8] In other words, while civil religion can easily deteriorate into an unreflective nationalism, public theology is methodologically committed to critical self-reflection in order to ensure that the public role of religion in a pluralistic society serves the betterment of the national public life and is not subverted in the pursuit of narrow sectarian or political goals.

Hispanic theologian Benjamin Valentin identifies three distinct yet interrelated projects that fall under the rubric of public theology in the

North American context: those theologies that seek to discern the role of the church in the public sphere, those theologies that defend the public character of theological discourse by articulating "common criteria of truth" that theology shares with other disciplines, and those theologies that "engage a wide public that transcends ecclesiastical boundaries" in order to address the most pressing social issues confronting the nation.[9] Valentin dismisses the first two approaches as too narrow in scope for a truly "public" theology, since the first type of theology more often than not limits itself to the language and internal concerns of the church community while the second type tends to exaggerate the public quality of explicitly theological discourse. Consequently, he prefers the third definition of public theology, since it works to achieve three equally important objectives: (1) to foster a publicly minded society, (2) to facilitate broad social coalitions across boundaries of belief, ethnicity, gender, and class in order to promote social justice, and (3) to develop an interdisciplinary discourse that can engage the broad range of perspectives within our pluralistic society. As a result, Valentin defines public theology as:

> a form of discourse that couples either the language, symbols, or background concepts of a religious tradition with an overarching, integrative, emancipatory sociopolitical perspective in such a way that it movingly captures the attention and moral conscience of a broad audience and promotes the cultivation of those modes of love, care, concern, and courage required both for individual fulfillment and for broad-based social activism.[10]

While I am sympathetic with Valentin's project, especially his desire to conceptualize theological traditions as discursive and open-ended, we differ on how theology should enter the public discourse.

There exists an underlying tension within Valentin's proposal for a public theology that on the one hand affirms, "If a theology is to be theological at all, it must in some way draw on the insights of a particular religious tradition," then argues on behalf of a "revisionist-constructive" approach[11] that characterizes dogmatic theology as necessarily authoritarian and exclusionary:

> The problem with a dogmatic theology is that it lends itself much too easily to forms of religious fanaticism, exclusive claims-making, narrow-minded discourse, rigid orthodoxies, and inconsiderate, authoritarian

impositions of values that can serve to short-circuit civil discourse and to engender divisions rather than rapport in the broader, pluralistic terrain of civil society. A dogmatic theology also runs the risk of having limited relevance, attracting the attention of those who share similar convictions and already stand within a theological circle but not beyond it.[12]

Valentin's attitude toward confessional theology is motivated by concerns about the marginalization of theology in the broader public discourse: "The reality is that theology rarely manages to have an impact or even be heard beyond its disciplinary, professional boundaries."[13] If, according to certain models of public theology, the only way for theology to participate in public discourse is to surrender much of what makes its discourse distinctly theological, can theology be both confessional and public?

Confessional Commitments and the Public Well-Being

This work has defined theology as a necessarily confessional undertaking that must nonetheless account for and converse with the plurality of beliefs existing both within the church and in the broader society. Therefore, as a theologian working in the context of a pluralistic and democratic society, I am committed to the three interrelated goals of public theology as defined by Benjamin Valentin yet remain cautious about models of public theology that justify theological commitments according to universal standards of rationality. Rather than articulating and defending a shared intellectual foundation that facilitates a common moral discourse, I opt for Jeffrey Stout's more modest definition of public theology: "If you express theological commitments in a reflective and sustained way, while addressing fellow citizens as citizens, you are 'doing theology' publicly—and in that sense doing public theology."[14] As a "public theologian," I am of course committed to the position that religious communities in a pluralistic and democratic society have both the right and the responsibility to influence public debate and democratic decision making. Furthermore, I do not hesitate to use explicitly religious premises when arguing in the public arena, since, as Stout convincingly argues, there is a long tradition of theologically committed political discourse in the United States:

> All democratic citizens should feel free, in my view, to express whatever premises actually serve as reasons for their claims. The respect for others

that civility requires is most fully displayed in the kind of exchange where each person's deepest commitments can be recognized for what they are and assessed accordingly. It is simply unrealistic to expect citizens to bracket such commitments when reasoning about fundamental political questions.[15]

Accordingly, my theological exploration of the problem of racism engages both the Christian community and the broader civil society, recognizing that expressing explicitly theological reasoning can sometimes stifle, even end, political debate, yet hopeful that by modeling an alternative understanding of public theology I can foster and nurture genuine conversation: "By this I mean an exchange of views in which the respective parties express their premises in as much detail as they see fit and in whatever idiom they wish, try to make sense of each other's perspectives, and expose their own commitments to the possibility of criticism."[16]

The dominant theologies in the North American context perpetuate a dualism between religious and secular models of reasoning. U.S. Latino/a theology—through its use of *mestizaje* as theological grounding for embracing a plurality of perspectives within the Christian tradition—offers an alternative approach to theology that transcends the current trend in popular culture to separate the Christian from the non-Christian. Having argued that *mestizaje* is not just a source of U.S. Latino/a group identity but also a powerful theological metaphor for liberation and solidarity, I contend that theology can successfully navigate various "publics" without having to choose sides in the dualistic "culture wars" that dominate contemporary political discourse. Furthermore, U.S. Latino/a theology—by bringing together issues of personal and cultural identity with concerns for political and economic liberation—embodies an alternative model of public theology that respects confessional commitments while positively transforming the public discourse on social justice.

Public theological discourse ought to reject a simple dichotomy between "traditional" and "contextual" approaches to theology. To borrow George Lindbeck's terminology, public theology seeks to allow for extrascriptural theological sources *without* subordinating Scripture and tradition to contemporary thought.[17] Without question, contemporary theology is best described as a plurality of competing perspectives. The challenge of theological pluralism is linked to the dramatic emergence around the world of local theologies resisting the hegemony of Western academic forms of theology and characterized by the realization that particular experiences, contexts, and traditions play a vital role in theological construction. Consequently, the "universalizing theologies of modernity have therefore now been forced to take seriously not only context and tradition, but to be open also to the possibility of seeing the Christian tradition itself as a series of local theologies."[18] However, if we define pluralism as mutual respect, understanding, and intersubjective communication between competing perspectives, then we must recognize that the postmodern emphasis on pluralism has often destroyed, rather than fostered, common discourse.

Alasdair MacIntyre describes the contemporary moment as one in which "disputed questions concerning justice and practical rationality are thus treated in the public realm, not as matter for rational enquiry, but rather for the assertion and counterassertion of alternative and incompatible sets of premises."[19] Frustrated by the cacophony of competing perspectives, MacIntyre concludes that "modern politics cannot be a matter of genuine moral consensus," but is instead "civil war carried out by other means."[20] While *After Virtue* offers some hope for the possibility of common moral discourse, the author pessimistically concludes that our culture is entering a new Dark Ages. In the end, the only hope for peaceful coexistence lies with a retreat into small intentional communities of shared belief "within which the moral life could be sustained so that both morality and civility and the intellectual moral life can be sustained."[21] Applying MacIntyre's analysis mutatis mutandis to the theological arena —that debate between competing perspectives rarely leads to consensus because these perspectives do not share the same conceptual frameworks —is it the case that rational discourse between competing traditions necessarily disintegrates into a struggle for power?

In spite of the current emphasis on pluralism, the North American theological landscape at the beginning of the twenty-first century appears to be dominated by two broad approaches: most theologies can be categorized as either narrative[22] or contextual.[23] What distinguishes one approach from the other is "the direction of interpretation" when engaging contemporary social realities. George Lindbeck, in *The Nature of Doctrine* (1984), argues that in order for systematic or dogmatic theology to remain faithful to its primary task of providing "a normative explication of the meaning a religion has for its adherents,"[24] it must allow Scripture to interpret culture and keep culture from determining the interpretive framework employed by theology. In other words, it is the text "which absorbs the world, rather than the world the text."[25] Contextual approaches, on the other hand, argue that contemporary situations necessarily inform and determine theological content, since every Christian theology is intrinsically linked to a particular historical situation and must therefore address those particularities or risk becoming irrelevant to the broader culture within which it is located. According to Stephen Bevans, whether or not a theology identifies itself as "contextual," it is nonetheless grounded in a particular human context. Furthermore, "if a theology is defensive and closed upon itself, not willing to be corrected, one can wonder whether such a theology can be an authentic expression of Christianity, even within its own context."[26] While conceptual models never adequately describe complex realities, it is important to underscore the dominance of these two distinct approaches within contemporary North American theology before exploring the possibility of an alternative model.

Kathryn Tanner, in *Theories of Culture: A New Agenda for Theology* (1997), has argued for an understanding of Christian cultural identity as a diverse "community of argument concerning the meaning of true discipleship," suggesting that ongoing disagreements over belief and practice are not harmful to Christian identity but in fact reveal something extremely important about the primacy of God's Word in relation to any human effort to interpret the Word.[27] According to Tanner, efforts at consensus or attempts to establish one "true" form of discipleship are actually destructive, "binding the freedom of theological interpretation to a human authority in that way actually threatens to interrupt the obedience of Christians to the Word."[28] The basic issue dividing the two dominant North American theological perspectives (narrative and contextual) is what Lindbeck has termed the "direction of interpretation." Does theology begin with Scripture and allow Scripture to shape our analysis of extrascriptural realities? Or does theology begin with the contemporary situation and allow extrascriptural realities to shape our interpretation of Scripture?

Kathryn Tanner argues that a "postmodern understanding of culture would of course dispute the sharp boundary between Christian and non-Christian cultures" that is often manifested by representatives of the narrative approach.[29] On the other hand, she is not happy with an "easy pluralism" that merely affirms diversity without addressing the seriousness of our theological differences. Tanner accepts that all Christians do not share the same beliefs and values yet argues that *Christians are united by a shared set of concerns*—concerns such as the status given to the Scriptures or the ordering of communal life around particular rituals. The second half of this work attempts to articulate what might constitute just such a shared set of concerns in the North American context by examining the contributions of U.S. Latino/a theology. This approach moves beyond the current methodological impasse, embracing the contributions of both narrative and contextual approaches without limiting Christian identity to one particular community's beliefs and practices, while at the same time arguing that a high degree of accountability to the theologian's particular tradition is a necessary ingredient of any theology; for without such accountability theology risks becoming, at best, a minor insular discourse within the academy.

It is my assumption that a theologian—as a particular tradition's caregiver—is necessarily a believer and practitioner of that tradition. However, this assumption is not always accepted within academic theology. Theologian Delwin Brown, while acknowledging that theology is rooted in communal practice, asserts that "such rootage does not necessarily mean that each theologian must be a believer in, or practitioner of, the tradition or traditions to which he or she gives care."[30] Brown then paints a picture of the "academic" theologian, in contradistinction to the "confessional" theologian, as someone capable of setting aside bias and making every effort to "give all relevant alternatives an equally open hearing"[31]—the obvious implication being that a theologian committed to the doctrinal claims of his or her faith is incapable of the same degree of detached objectivity. This characterization of the confessional theologian as "partisan" over against the academic theologian as "nonpartisan" hampers genuine public discourse by granting epistemic privilege to one perspective over another. It also illustrates how confessional perspectives are not always welcome in the public arena, even when theology enters the public discourse committed to making its confessional claims intelligible to all conversation partners on the basis of external and shared rational criteria.

Benjamin Valentin seems to foster similar attitudes about the superiority of "academic" theology over "confessional" approaches when he defines the public theologian, "unlike perhaps the systematic and/or practical church theologian, who speaks mainly to persons who already stand within his or her theological circle" as one who speaks "about the meaning of a religious tradition in terms that make sense to, and elicit response from, people who do not share his or her theological convictions."[32] This approach seems to privilege the norms of the secular academy as universally binding epistemological criteria for public discourse, and establishes the academic theologian as the authoritative interpreter of a tradition, suggesting that, while accountability to the community of faith is an important aspect of the intellectual's curatorial task, it is not *necessary* to the theological project. The current investigation counters this view by arguing that public theology is better served by adopting a model of tradition and canon that links the theologian's concrete praxis in the context of a particular community to his or her ability to properly interpret the tradition. As a theologian shaped by both the Reformed/Calvinist tradition and Latin American liberation theology, I bring these two perspectives together in order to recover vital, though often neglected, resources within the Christian theological tradition necessary for articulating a socially transformative public theology for a twenty-first-century church seeking cultural relevance in an increasingly pluralist and secularized society.

John Calvin's Theology as Model for Public Theology

The Reformed tradition, a diverse body emerging from the sixteenth-century union of Zwinglians and Calvinists, has long recognized that the church's social responsibility is an integral aspect of its spiritual mission.[33] While Calvinism is often identified with middle-class comfort and the political status quo, the theology of John Calvin (1509–64) can provide a useful model for developing a contemporary political theology. And even though Calvin represents a diachronically distant worldview, in which the work of civil government is seen as part of God's unfolding plan for salvation, a viable model of liberative praxis may be culled from Calvin's theology and pastoral praxis.

Critics of the Reformed theological tradition argue that it has often embraced "the cultural practices of ordered middle- to upper-class life, and in spite of all our announced concern and effort, U.S. Presbyterians tend to exclude from their midst the real presence of those who live within the lower ranges of economic and cultural life."[34] They also point to the victims of political oppression throughout the world who have failed to find a liberating voice in Calvinist theology as demonstrated by the rise of politically repressive fundamentalism within the Presbyterian Church of Brazil and the struggle of South Africa under apartheid where the Dutch Reformed church for years accepted the state's policy of "separate development."[35] While acknowledging the legitimacy of those who criticize John Calvin's emphasis on redemptive suffering as "world-repressive,"[36] this work argues that in light of his comments on civil government, his prophetic understanding of preaching, and his pastoral work with the victims of poverty and political persecution, Calvin's theology allows for the possibility of Christian political resistance. Given that Calvin's theology was conceived in exile and addressed the myriad social problems confronting sixteenth-century Geneva, such as population dislocation and urban poverty, a critical retrieval of John Calvin's theology will reveal its character as a public theology concerned with social transformation on behalf of the poor and oppressed.

Calvin on Civil Government

While John Calvin's views have had long-term effects for both church and society, he was not a political revolutionary. On the contrary, by repeatedly stressing upon Christians the duty of obedience to magistrates, Calvin appears a social conservative. According to Calvin, God's will is worked out in history to overcome the abuses of intolerable governments:

> The reason why we ought to be subject to magistrates is because they are constituted by God's ordination. For since it pleases God thus to govern the world, he who attempts to invert the order of God, and thus resist God himself, despises his power; since to despise the providence of him who is the founder of civil power, is to carry on war with him.[37]

He goes so far as to demand submission to the most tyrannical of human governments, cautioning the victims of political persecution that "if the correction of unbridled despotism is the Lord's to avenge, let us not at once think that it is entrusted to us, whom no command has been given except to obey and suffer."[38] Given that as subjects the people have neither the responsibility nor the duty to topple tyrants, "only this remains, to implore the Lord's help, in whose hand are the hearts of kings, and the changing of kingdoms."[39] John Calvin's counsel to the victims of political oppression—patience and prayer—amounts to the passive acceptance of an unjust situation, a view antithetical to liberationist and other political theologies that favor more active resistance to repression.

Nevertheless, before dismissing Calvin as a theological resource for liberation, it is important to have a better understanding of the historical context in which he gave this advice. The words quoted earlier from the *Institutes of the Christian Religion* reflect conditions in France at the time they were written (1535), when Protestants were "cruelly tormented by a savage prince," "greedily despoiled by one who is avaricious," and "vexed for piety's sake by one who is impious and sacrilegious."[40] These political circumstances need to be considered when reviewing Calvin's comments on civil government. His words imploring the victims of political persecution to persevere in their suffering and pray for divine intervention against human cruelty are not a justification for moral passivity; rather, this advice is given to "subjects" with little or no political power, so it is best understood as pastoral concern for the politically disenfranchised in a country where subjects lived under the absolute authority of a monarch who—in spite of political alliances with the Protestant Princes of Germany—persecuted as heretical the Reformed churches in France. In 1525 fewer than a dozen cities had held heresy trials, but by 1540 every region in France had conducted them, with the number of trials increasing steadily every decade through 1560. The intensification of visible persecution of Protestants during the latter half of the 1540s prompted the first of several waves of refugees fleeing to Geneva, and the writings of John Calvin were consistently the most cited in the French index of prohibited books.[41] Consequently, Calvin's advice to the Protestant subjects of Francis I was tempered by pastoral concern for their well-being in the midst of persecution, since political uprisings were quickly and violently quelled in the Sixteenth century.

On October 18, 1534, members of the Protestant minority publicly posted copies of a handbill containing crude attacks on the Catholic mass. The Affair of the Placards so angered Francis I (a copy of these articles had been posted on the door of the king's own bedchamber!), he proclaimed that anyone found concealing the person or persons responsible for posting the placards would be burned at the stake. Many were imprisoned and executed in the aftermath of this incident, and the king's attitude toward his Protestant subjects became decidedly hostile. The prefatory letter to Francis I of France found in the 1536 edition of the *Institutes* was written as an apologia on behalf of the persecuted French Protestant minority accused of heresy and sedition. Fearful that the Protestant cause would be discredited, especially after the brutal end to the 1535 Anabaptist revolution in Münster,[42] John Calvin pleads with the king for understanding: "So that no one may think we are wrongly complaining of these things, you can be our witness, most noble King, with how many lying slanders it is daily traduced in your presence."[43] Arguing that "falsehoods, subtleties, and slanders" have been spread by the enemies of French Evangelicals, Calvin demands toleration and official protection for the agents of ecclesial reform. It is not known whether Francis I ever read Calvin's letter (his policies toward Protestants did not change significantly), but it serves as a statement of the Reformed/Calvinist view of the relationship between church and state.

Much of what John Calvin says concerning civil government was written in polemical opposition either to Radical and Anabaptist reformers who advocated complete withdrawal from the unregenerate world or to the Roman Catholic establishment under which princes were subject to ecclesial authority. Also underlying this entire discussion is Calvin's agreement with the common Protestant view on "the priesthood of all believers" (1 Pet. 2:9), which gave higher status to princes than had been traditional in Roman Catholic theology while encouraging the leveling of all ranks in civil society. Nonetheless, in the prefatory letter to Francis I (written in 1536), it is the more radical wing of the Reformation that Calvin sees as undermining France's Protestant movement vis-à-vis the governing authorities.

The general position of Radical and Anabaptist reformers concerning church and state is encapsulated in the *Confession of Schleitheim,* whose fourth article reads: "We have been united concerning the separation that shall take place from the evil and wickedness which the devil has planted in the world . . . that we have no fellowship with them in the confusion of their abominations."[44] Article 6, concerning the state's use of coercive power, rejects any involvement in civil government for "it does not befit a Christian to be a magistrate: the rule of the government is according to the flesh, that of the Christian according to the spirit."[45] Thus, Calvin is quick to distance the French Evangelicals from the more radical reformers who advocated complete separation from—even disobedience to —the state:

> We are unjustly charged, too, with intentions of such a sort that we have never given the least suspicion of them. We are, I suppose, contriving the overthrow of kingdoms—we, from whom not one seditious word was ever heard; we, whose life when we lived under you was always acknowledged to be quiet and simple; we, who do not cease to pray for the full prosperity of yourself and your kingdom, although we are now fugitives from home![46]

Aside from the prefatory letter (which appeared in all editions of the *Institutes*), relevant discussions on civil government found in chapters 3.19 and 4.20 of the 1559 edition of the *Institutes* (as well as 4.11.1–5, in which Calvin discusses the power of the keys in Matt. 16:17–19) demarcate ecclesiastical and civil jurisdictions in marked contrast to the Roman church. The former chapter, "Christian Freedom" (*Institutes* 3.19), is concerned with the conscience of the individual believer while the latter, "Civil Government" (*Institutes* 4.20), deals primarily with the duties of citizens and magistrates. In the 1559 edition these two passages seem unrelated, yet in the 1536 edition they were closely linked, separated only by a section on ecclesiastical power. Given that the final edition of Calvin's *Institutes* is five times its original size, it is important to remember the original relation between these two chapters and to resist the temptation to read Calvin's discussion of civil government in the closing chapter of the final edition as an afterthought. Rather, responsible citizenship is an inherent part of Calvin's notion of the Christian life.

According to Calvin, in contrast to the Anabaptists, Christian theology must address the question of civil government, since it is God who founds the state and defines its jurisdiction and purpose:

> Civil government has as its appointed end, so long as we live among men, to cherish and protect the outward worship of God, to defend sound doctrine of piety and the position of the church, to adjust our life to the society of men, to form our social behavior to civil righteousness, to reconcile us with one another, and to promote general peace and tranquility. All of this I admit to be superfluous, if God's Kingdom, such as it is now among us, wipes out the present life. But if it is God's will that we go as pilgrims upon the earth while we aspire to the true fatherland, and if the pilgrimage requires such helps, those who take these from man deprive him of his very humanity. Our adversaries claim that there ought to be such great perfection in the church of God that its government should suffice for law. But they stupidly imagine such a perfection as can never be found in a community of men.[47]

Because of humanity's sinful and fallen state, God has ordained civil government to serve two purposes: "It provides that a public manifestation of religion may exist among Christians, and that humanity may be maintained among men."[48] To this end, temporal governments are granted the power of the sword, that is, the authority to use coercion to enforce its laws. In effect, God has ordained the secular order (the state) to maintain peace and justice in the world, by force if necessary, with the understanding that the spiritual government (the church) is "already initiating in us upon earth certain beginnings of the Heavenly Kingdom, and in this mortal and fleeting life affords a certain forecast of an immortal and incorruptible blessedness."[49]

According to Calvin, Christ himself declares "that there is no disagreement between his kingdom and political government or order."[50] Therefore, while throughout Calvin's discussion on civil government a distinction is maintained between the spiritual and temporal realms, they are two aspects of a single "twofold government." While the spiritual "resides in the soul or inner man and pertains to eternal life," and the temporal is concerned with the "establishment of civil justice and outward morality,"[51] there is no inherent conflict between them. Thus, unlike the modern separation of church and state, in Calvin's theology these two realms interpenetrate each other as manifestations of the one divine will. Beginning about 1560 and continuing over a thirty-year period, the Protestant Reformation in France gave rise to the wars of religion. While Protestants endured much at the hands of a Catholic government, Calvin did not support revolutionary activities; his theological writings reflect great care and effort to prevent social unrest and disorder. Consequently, each realm in Calvin's twofold government has clearly demarcated jurisdictions: the temporal government makes laws that maintain the social order while the spiritual government enforces discipline of church members. Not only is Calvin's position a contrast to Anabaptist separatism, it also opposes the sixteenth-century Roman Catholic view that the (visible) church is the highest authority. While recognizing a distinction between the spiritual and temporal realms, Calvin recognizes both jurisdictions as religious callings. In fact, the vocation of "magistrate" is for Calvin a holy calling, "not only holy and lawful before God, but also the most sacred and by far the most honorable of all callings in the whole life of mortal men."[52] Consequently, the question for Reformed/Calvinist theology is *not* whether the church has the right to enter the public arena or exert political influence. Rather, the question becomes, *How, and to what end?*

Governance is a high calling with great responsibility, and Calvin repeatedly stresses the responsibilities of rulers toward their subjects, while remaining steadfast about the obedience subjects owe their rulers, "whatever they may be like."[53] Conversely, magistrates—even absolute monarchs

—are subject to the teaching and discipline of the church as members of the one body.[54] Hence, Calvin exhorts magistrates to remain faithful to God's commands:

> For what great zeal for uprightness, for prudence, gentleness, self-control, and for innocence ought to be required of themselves by those who know that they have been ordained ministers of divine justice? How will they have the brazenness to admit injustice to their judgment seat, which they are told is the throne of the living God? How will they have the boldness to pronounce an unjust sentence, by that mouth which they know has been appointed an instrument of divine truth? With what conscience will they sign wicked decrees by that hand which they know has been appointed to record the acts of God? To sum up, if they remember that they are vicars of God, they should watch with all care, earnestness, and diligence, to represent in themselves to men some image of divine providence, protection, goodness, benevolence, and justice.[55]

Implicit in this warning is the belief that the second purpose of civil government is the use of its (God-given) power "to restrain the sinful tendencies of the strong to take advantage of the weak, and to secure a certain measure of social justice in human transactions,"[56] a point consonant with liberation theology's preferential option for the poor. However, given his emphasis on patient endurance, liberation theologians are correct to question whether or not Calvin's instruction is sympathetic to the task of enabling the historical transformation of an oppressive social order.

Considering the turbulent times in which he lived, and the atrocities committed against the French Protestant minority (Calvin himself fled France in 1536, never to return), the following passage from the 1536 edition of the *Institutes* accentuates the importance Calvin placed on subjects obeying their rulers:

> Therefore, if we are cruelly tormented by a savage prince, if we are greedily despoiled by one who is avaricious or wanton, if we are neglected by a slothful one, if finally we are vexed for piety's sake by one who is impious and sacrilegious, let us first be mindful of our own misdeeds, which without doubt are chastised by such whips of the Lord [cf. Dan. 9:7]. By this, humility will restrain our impatience. Let us then also recall this thought to mind, that it is not for us to remedy such evils; that only this remains,

to implore the Lord's help, in whose hand are the hearts of kings, and the changing of kingdoms [Prov. 21:1].[57]

While Calvin repeatedly stresses that Christians have the duty of obedience to magistrates as "vice-regents" of God—even demanding obedience to tyrannical rulers—there is for Calvin the possibility of legitimate Christian resistance to unjust states:

> But in that obedience which we have shown to be due the authority of rulers, *we are always to make this exception, indeed to observe it as primary, that such obedience is never to lead us away from obedience to him,* to whose will the desires of all kings ought to be subject, to whose decrees all their commands ought to yield, to whose majesty their scepters ought to be submitted. And how absurd would it be that in satisfying men you should incur the displeasure of him for whose sake you obey men themselves![58]

An apparent inconsistency runs through Calvin's understanding of church-state relations. On the one hand, it is not the role of subjects to overturn the rule of a tyrannical government, for God will vindicate, but on the other hand, it seems that Calvin does urge (some) resistance to the state when it contradicts the will of God, since "we must obey God rather than men" (Acts 5:29, NRSV).

How are faithful Christians to withstand the rule of impious despots? Calvin suggests different options are available to different Christians—depending on what role they serve in the social order. In the earlier passage Calvin is addressing "those who have been put under the power of others," yet in the section immediately following, Calvin acknowledges that God sometimes "raises up open avengers from among his servants, and arms them with his command to punish the wicked government and deliver his people, oppressed in unjust ways, from miserable calamity."[59] Calvin appears conflicted on this issue—desiring a stable social order (even at the cost of innocent suffering), yet affirming that God acts in history to overcome tyranny. A crucial hermeneutical key for understanding Calvin's statements on political resistance depends upon recognizing to whom his comments are directed. He is speaking to private individuals when he warns, "If the correction of unbridled despotism is the Lord's to avenge, let us not at once think that it is entrusted to us, to whom no command has been given except to obey and suffer."[60] However, when addressing the lawfully appointed magistrates of the people, Calvin burdens them with the duty of restraining the abuses of kings and tyrants:

> I am so far from forbidding them to withstand, in accordance with their duty, the fierce licentiousness of kings, that, if they wink at kings who violently fall upon and assault the lowly common folk, I declare that their dissimulation involves nefarious perfidy, because they dishonestly betray the freedom of the people, of which they know that they have been appointed protectors by God's ordinance.[61]

Calvin urges constitutional magistrates to protect the liberties of the people through political means. This controversial passage, along with the explicit warning in the closing paragraph of the *Institutes* that obedience to earthly rulers must not become disobedience to God, provides the Reformed tradition with the basic tools for political resistance. Calvin never condoned political revolution, but in his works we find the theological foundations for resisting injustice and oppression.

The Prophetic Role of the Pastor in Civil Society

If the majority of believers are called to be obedient subjects, with patience and prayer their only means of political resistance, and a smaller number are set above them as magistrates, responsible for the just administration of human society and granted corresponding power by God, then an even smaller number is called to wield the power that stands in judgment of all: the Word of God. John Calvin accords preaching an exalted place in the church's ministry, and from the pulpit, pastors exercise great power for shaping the life of church and society.

The *Institutes of the Christian Religion* begins with a philosophical statement of purpose: "Nearly all the wisdom we possess, that is to say, true and sound wisdom, consists of two parts: the knowledge of God and of ourselves."[62] Calvin concludes, "Man never achieves a clear knowledge of himself unless he has first looked upon God's face, and then descends from contemplating him to scrutinize himself."[63] Whatever knowledge of God we derive from nature is distorted by human sin; true knowledge of God is found only in the Scriptures, and always mediated by Christ, for we need God "to take away all cause for enmity and to reconcile us utterly to himself, he wipes out all evil in us by the expiation set forth in the death of Christ; that we, who were previously unclean and impure, may show ourselves righteous and holy in his sight."[64] It is in Scripture that we encounter the divine visage, and through the inward action of the Holy Spirit, receive salvific knowledge of God:

> Just as old or bleary-eyed men and those with weak vision, if you thrust before them a most beautiful volume, even if they recognize it to be some sort of writing, yet can scarcely construe two words, but with the aid of spectacles will begin to read distinctly; so Scripture, gathering up the otherwise confused knowledge of God in our minds, having dispersed our dullness, clearly shows us the true God. This, therefore, is a special gift, where God, to instruct the church, not merely uses mute teachers but also opens his own most hallowed lips.[65]

If, as the Scriptures disclose, the Word of God is revealed by preaching, we must acknowledge as God's will that today the Word is also heard in the same way, mediated through the human word in the church's proclamation.

Undoubtedly social, political, and cultural factors shaped Calvin's theology, yet his approach is generally described as a *biblical* theology insofar as he attempts a faithful exegesis of the whole of Scripture: "It is well known that Calvin shared the sixteenth-century Protestant determination to be a faithful teacher of scripture, eschewing all human invention."[66] Therefore, when Calvin's practical theology focuses on matters of social justice and economic equity, it can be assumed that in his judgment this theme is essential to the biblical message. In an extensive commentary on Psalm 82:3, Calvin's views on poverty resonate with liberation theology's demand that the church serve as an advocate on behalf of the poor and powerless with the powers that be:

> We are here briefly taught that a just and well-regulated government will be distinguished for maintaining the rights of the poor and afflicted. By the figure synecdoche, one part of equitable administration is put for the whole; for it cannot be doubted that rulers are bound to observe justice towards all men without distinction. But the prophet, with much propriety, represents them as appointed to be the defenders of the miserable and oppressed. . . . The end, therefore, for which judges bear the sword is to restrain the wicked, and thus to prevent violence from prevailing among men, who are so much disposed to become disorderly and outrageous. . . . From these remarks, it is very obvious why the cause of the poor and

needy is here chiefly commended to rulers; for those who are exposed as easy prey to the cruelty and wrongs of the rich have no less need of the assistance and protection of magistrates than the sick have of the aid of the physician. Were the truth deeply fixed in the minds of kings and other judges, that they are appointed to be the guardians of the poor, and that a special part of this duty lies in resisting the wrongs which are done to them, and in repressing all unrighteous violence, perfect righteousness would become triumphant through the whole world.[67]

Granted, there are crucial differences between liberation theology's "preferential option for the poor" and Calvin's biblical vision of "perfect righteousness"—perhaps the sixteenth and twenty-first centuries are working with vastly different notions of what constitutes a "just" human society —yet both share "common places," since their views of justice originate in the world of the Old and New Testaments.

Whereas liberation theology struggles against hierarchical social orders, Calvin accepts a rigid social hierarchy in which most are called to be obedient subjects while a select few are called to be benevolent rulers. And while some liberation theologies have gone so far as to advocate revolutionary violence to overcome oppression, Calvin offers little practical advice on what to do when the powerless suffer because rulers are unfaithful in their God-appointed duties. So perhaps Mark Taylor is correct in suggesting that there is "a deep-running fault beneath the mountainous range of Calvinist social piety" that equates social justice with "good order," thereby excluding those outside "the dominant order of things."[68] Still, it cannot be denied that Calvin placed the needs of the poor in sixteenth-century Geneva at the forefront of his efforts at ordering political and ecclesial life. While it is tempting to view systematic attempts at constructing and perpetuating certain social structures with postmodern suspicion, contemporary Reformed theology should be mindful of the fact that in spite of a single-minded "will-to-order," John Calvin does not avoid Scripture's demand to act for justice at great cost to ourselves. An analysis of how the Word of God—primarily through prophetic preaching—exhorts, judges, and continually reforms public life on behalf of the poor and powerless provides an antidote to the more "repressive" manifestations of the Reformed tradition.

John Calvin's understanding of the preaching office begins with thorough exegetical work of the Old Testament, focusing primarily on the prophets who speak with God's voice and authority: "The word goeth out of the mouth of God in such a manner that it likewise 'goeth out of the mouth' of men; for God does not speak openly from heaven, but employs men as his instruments, that by their agency he may make known his will."[69] Preaching is so vital for the church that "we ought to be so much affected by it, whenever he (God) speaks by his servants, as though he were nigh to us, face to face."[70] Furthermore, preaching serves a dual purpose, revealing God's will while providing an opportunity for believers to demonstrate their obedience:

> But as he did not entrust the ancient folk to angels but raised up teachers from the earth truly to perform the angelic office, so also today it is his will to teach us through human means. As he was of old not content with the law alone, but added priests as interpreters from whose lips the people might ask its true meaning [cf. Malachi 2:7], so today he not only desires us to be attentive to its reading, but also appoints instructors to help us by their effort. This is doubly useful. On the one hand, he proves our obedience by a very good test when we hear his ministers speaking just as if he himself spoke. On the other, he also provides for our weakness in that he prefers to address us in human fashion through interpreters in order to draw us to himself, rather than to thunder at us and drive us away.[71]

Central to Calvin's ecclesiology is the belief that we are called to live in community as the one body, nurtured by Mother Church through the preaching of the Word, in faithful obedience to those called to lead the church. While affirming the priesthood of all believers, Calvin nonetheless recognizes differing vocations within the body and emphasizes the importance of preaching. Yet, he is quick to admonish pastors—perhaps to keep them humble—that only by an act of the Holy Spirit does the word of the preacher become the Word of God (the same can be said for the receptiveness of the hearer), for "when God separates himself from his ministers, nothing remains in them."[72]

Thus, it is Christ who speaks through preaching, and preaching the means by which Christ rules the church. In the words of the apostle Paul,

> How are men to call upon him in whom they have not believed? And how are they to believe in him of whom they have never heard? And how are they to hear without a preacher? And how can men preach unless

they are sent? As it is written, "How beautiful are the feet of those who preach good news!" (Rom. 10:14–15, RSV)

Commenting on a line from the prophet Isaiah, "He made my mouth like a sharp sword" (Isa. 49:2, RSV), Calvin asserts that Christ has "been appointed by the Father, not to rule, after the manner of princes . . . but his whole authority consists in doctrine, in the preaching of which he wishes to be sought and acknowledged; for nowhere else will he be found."[73] Jesus Christ, through his ministers on this earth, exercises power and authority over the church and the world. However, "as to the Church collective, the sword now put into our hand is of another kind, that of the word and spirit."[74] Recalling Calvin's discussion of civil government, specifically his claim that the power of the sword is granted (by God) to temporal governments because of human sin, it follows that "the church does not have the power to coerce, and ought not to seek it (I am speaking of civil coercion), it is the duty of godly kings and princes to sustain religion by laws, edicts, and judgments."[75]

Christ's sword is the preached Word, his scepter the Gospel. Not surprisingly, preaching was at the center of Calvin's activities in Geneva, and his long and arduous relationship with the Council and Consistory of Geneva serves as a model for how the church wields the spiritual sword. From Calvin's successor in Geneva, Theodore Beza, we gain a sense of Calvin's tenure as pastor and teacher:

> Besides preaching every day from week to week, usually and as often as he could he preached twice every Sunday; he lectured three times a week on theology; he gave remonstrances in the consistory, and delivered as it were an entire lesson in the conference on Scripture that we call a congregation; and he so closely followed this program without interruption until his death that he never failed once during extreme illness.[76]

John Calvin served a parish much bigger than most modern churches with a far more demanding preaching schedule. Aside from preaching duties, Calvin also instituted weekly "congregations" for the other ministers in Geneva for the purpose of providing instruction in Scriptural exegesis and doctrine:

> It will be expedient that all the ministers, for conserving purity and concord of doctrine among themselves, meet together one certain day each

week, for discussion of the Scriptures; and none are to be exempt from this without legitimate excuse. . . . As for those who preach in the villages, throughout the Seigneury, they are to be exhorted to come as often as they are able.[77]

The fruits of his labor survive in the form of the *Institutes* in its various drafts, commentaries on almost every book of the Bible, numerous theological treatises, pastoral correspondence, and forty-four bound volumes of sermons. While Denis Raguenier, a professional scribe hired in 1549, recorded two thousand sermons in shorthand, scholars estimate that John Calvin preached more than four thousand sermons in his lifetime. During this long tenure, Calvin's preaching often challenged Geneva's politicians.

In fact, Calvin (along with associates Farel and Courault) was expelled from Geneva for mixing politics with religion. In March 1538 Calvin was reprimanded for calling the city council "a Council of the Devil," and he and Farel were warned "not to mix themselves in magistracy."[78] Throughout Calvin's career in Geneva his struggles with the Council centered on the issue of the church's independence from temporal government, specifically over the ban and readmission to the Lord's Supper. During his early years, prior to being exiled in 1538, Calvin was adamant about requiring all citizens of Geneva to swear a Confession of Faith written by Farel. The citizens refused, and the Council registry contains numerous mentions of efforts made to persuade the people to accept the Confession, until Calvin and his pastoral colleagues brought the matter to a climax in 1538 by announcing their intention to refuse the Lord's Supper to those who did not subscribe to the Confession. The Council was firm in denying the pastors the unilateral power to ban and then acted to impose liturgical reforms without informing Calvin, Farel, and Courault, requiring them to celebrate the sacrament on Easter morning according to this new order. And had the pastors refused, they would have been prohibited from preaching on Easter morning. Calvin and his colleagues did refuse and proceeded to preach on why administering the sacrament under these conditions would have profaned it, which led the Council to act immediately to dismiss the three preachers and order them to leave the city within three days.

Eventually, once the political climate changed, Calvin was called back to Geneva as preacher. In 1541 he returned to Geneva to continue his struggles for ecclesiastical and political reform unyielding on the conviction that the church alone has the right to excommunicate. His new *Ecclesiastical Ordinances* (1541) provided for the election of a Consistory composed of pastors and laypeople whose duties included maintaining the purity of the church:

> The elders, as already said, are to assemble once a week with the minis-
> ters, that is to say on Thursday morning, to see that there be no disor-
> der in the Church and to discuss together remedies as they are required.
> Because they have no compulsive authority or jurisdiction, may it please
> their Lordships, to give them one of their officials to summon those
> whom they wish to admonish. If anyone refuses with contempt to com-
> ply, their office will be to inform their Lordships, in order that remedy be
> applied.[79]

Still, the ordinances do not clarify who actually has the power of excom-
munication and readmission—the Consistory or the Council. Eventually,
Calvin gained approval for his church order, but not before important
changes were made to Calvin's text, including this additional article in-
serted after the above discussion on the Consistory's right to exercise the
ban:

> All this is to take place in such a way that *ministers have no civil jurisdic-
> tion, nor use anything but the spiritual sword of the Word of God*, as Paul
> commands them; nor is the Consistory to derogate from the authority
> of the Seigneury or ordinary justice. The civil power is to remain unim-
> paired. Even where there will be need to impose punishment or to con-
> strain parties, the ministers with the Consistory having heard the parties
> and used such remonstrances and admonitions as are good, are to report
> the whole matter to the Council, which in their turn will advise sentence
> and judgment according to the needs of the case.[80]

The power struggle over the right to readmit members to the Lord's Supper continued for many years. The Consistory would bar someone from
the Supper and send them to the Council for civil punishment where the
Council would hear the Consistory's report, declare a sentence and fine,
then assume that person would be admitted into full communion with the
church. Calvin and the other pastors disagreed, insisting that those who
were excommunicated had to appear before the Consistory yet again, in
order to establish their genuine repentance. Then, and only then, would
they be readmitted to the Supper, regardless of the decision reached by
the civil court.

John Calvin faced great opposition over the right to ban, and on this and other matters the Council questioned the content of his preaching on numerous occasions because "with great choler [he] preached that the magistracy permits many insolences. Ordered that he should be called before the Council in order to know why he has so preached, and that if there is some insolence in the city, the lieutenant should be commanded to look into it and to do justice concerning it."[81] Calvin's struggle to establish the church's independence from the Council provides a glimpse of how he used preaching as a means of advocating social reform. In his capacity as pastor and teacher, Calvin concedes that the church has certain obligations vis-à-vis the state. First, Christians ought to pray for the civil government and submit to its legitimate authority. Never, throughout his many disagreements with the Genevan civil authorities, does Calvin sanction rebellion. (Although, as has been demonstrated, Calvin allows for the remote possibility of legitimate rebellion against repressive governments, but only when such resistance is led by lesser magistrates constitutionally appointed to protect the individual liberties of the populace.) Second, the church has a duty to encourage the state to defend the poor and defenseless against the rich and powerful. The church in Geneva battled usury, unemployment, disease, and every manner of economic injustice, in great part because John Calvin preached the Gospel without diluting its message. Since magistrates, just like any member of the body of Christ, are subject to the teaching and discipline of the church, there is an expectation that their public policies will be criticized from the pulpit: "Oppression utters a sufficiently loud cry of itself; and if the judge, sitting on a high watch-tower, seems to take no notice of it, he is here plainly warned, that such connivance shall not escape with impunity."[82] Finally, the church is to admonish the state when it acts unjustly.

Drawing upon the prophet Amos (a favorite text among liberation theologians), who warns, "Hear this, you who trample upon the needy, and bring the poor of the land to an end. . . . The Lord has sworn by the pride of Jacob: 'Surely I will never forget any of their deeds'" (Amos 8:4, 7, RSV), Calvin comments:

> But as more guilt belongs always to leaders, this is the reason why the
> Prophets treated them with more sharpness and severity: for many of the
> common people go astray through thoughtlessness or ignorances or are
> led on by others, but they who govern, pervert what is just and right, and

then become the originators of all kinds of licentiousness. It is no wonder then that the Lord by his Prophets inveighed so sharply against them.[83]

The minister, as the "mouth of God," is duty bound to speak out against all injustice and to exhort magistrates to perform their God-ordained tasks with equity and mercy. Calvin thus demonstrates that he wanted a church free from the control of the state, not because he was a megalomaniac wanting to establish himself as "bishop of Geneva" (as some modern critics have suggested), but for the simple fact that—in order to maintain purity of doctrine—the church needs the freedom to preach the Word of God in prophetic criticism of the state. Calvin wielded the spiritual sword with great finesse, persuading political opponents by the truth and righteousness of the preached Word, all the while acting with the certainty that both church and state exist under the Lordship of Christ.

Calvin's Pastoral Praxis

All theological questions have an ethical dimension—that is, the theological question (who is God) is inseparable from the moral question (what ought we to do)—a point best articulated by Gustavo Gutiérrez, whose book *A Theology of Liberation* is considered the most important work of Latin American liberation theology. In this seminal work Gutiérrez asserts that theology (talk about God) is a "second moment," implying that there is a "first moment" antecedent to all theological formulation consisting of the silent language of Christian spirituality, prayer, worship, and moral action.[84] Methodologically, Latin American liberation theology seems worlds apart from Calvin's naïve attempt to exegete the text while "eschewing all human additions" (McKee), since Gutiérrez begins by acknowledging the cultural, political, and ecclesial commitment of the theologian and also draws upon the social sciences, as interpretations of reality, to provide theology with some of its "raw" material. However, just because theology employs extrascriptural tools of analysis does not make these methods the source or locus of theology; liberation theology is not Marxism, although at times it has employed Marxist social analysis. By the same token, the fact that Calvin was influenced by humanism and employed its methods in interpreting the Bible does not reduce his biblical and Christocentric theology to mere humanism.

The most important aspect of liberation theology is that it adopts the perspective of the poor and powerless as its starting point when formulating its theology. Liberation theologians do not come to the text with some abstract notion of a preferential option for the poor that they then read into the text; rather, they approach the text as the poor (or as pastors and theologians serving the poor) and find within the text good news for the poor (Luke 4:18). Liberation theology makes a preferential option on behalf of the poor and powerless because in the Scriptures God institutes this preferential option. Gutiérrez identifies three interrelated levels or dimensions of liberation: (1) liberation from oppressive socioeconomic structures, (2) liberation as personal transformation, and (3) liberation from sin. Ultimately, however, he recognizes that "only liberation from sin gets to the very source of social injustice and other forms of human oppression and reconciles us with God and our fellow human beings."[85] While Calvin does not expressly speak about liberation in the same sense as Gutiérrez, his social ethics emphasize the need for equity in all human relations. Furthermore, both approaches seek to bring about social transformation by means of pastoral care and instruction. For John Calvin and Gustavo Gutiérrez the local congregation is the nexus of moral action and education; from the grassroots level the church reaches out to the broader cultural context, seeking social change by modeling an alternate way of living in community. As Gutiérrez has always maintained, the church wields great power and influence in society and should not be afraid to use this power on behalf of the poor and oppressed.[86] John Calvin the pastor would agree.

In a sermon on 2 Samuel 8:9–18, Calvin charges all believers, not just Christian magistrates, "to take as strong a stand against evil as we can. This command is given to everyone not only to princes, magistrates, and officers of justice, but to all private persons as well."[87] Scripture is clear that as Christians we are called to suffer persecution for the sake of righteousness, and for Calvin such suffering even becomes a source of joy, for "we are too ungrateful if we do not willingly and cheerfully undergo these things at the Lord's hand."[88] Forbearance—especially in defense of the innocent—is an important virtue of the Christian life. In Calvin's Geneva, countless opportunities to suffer for the sake of righteousness presented themselves.

Geneva was a small city, with an estimated population of 10,000 in 1537, but surging as high as 21,400 in 1560. The first wave of immigration in 1542 (some 5,000 French refugees fleeing political persecution) generated increased poverty, crime, unemployment, and xenophobia. Not only did the ecclesiastical and civic leaders of Geneva face the consequences of breaking with the Roman church, but the deterioration of the medieval social order created new cultural, political, and economic realities that both church and state were ill prepared to confront.[89] Because Calvin's theology and preaching originate in a context of political persecution, extreme poverty, and innocent suffering—a social situation analogous to contemporary liberation efforts in Latin America—it is tempting to judge his praxis according to current standards of pastoral care. Yet, while Calvin's pastoral duties were extremely demanding, they consisted primarily of preaching and teaching. Calvin was not a social worker, political activist, or psychological counselor, roles which the contemporary pastor often dons, yet Calvin was very involved in reorganizing church order and liturgy, in reorganizing the city's social order properly to meet the needs of the poor and helpless, in defending the autonomy of the church against any infringement by the temporal government, and in maintaining the religious education and doctrinal purity of the faithful.

According to Calvin, aside from preaching and teaching, pastoral care is primarily defined as care for the poor and sick. To this end, the church in Geneva established several institutions and practices to provide for the well-being of the disabled and disadvantaged. First and foremost among these is the diaconate, established by Calvin as a permanent ministry of the church. Deacons provide the church's ministry to the suffering of the world; they are responsible for collecting and administering finances for this purpose, as well as for the actual care of the needy. In the *Ecclesiastical Ordinances* Calvin explains the division of labor within the diaconate: "There were always two kinds [of deacons] in the ancient Church, the one deputed to receive and hold goods for the poor, not only daily alms, but also possessions, rent and pensions; the other to tend and care for the sick and administer allowances to the poor."[90] Calvin's church order calls for a similar organization to be followed in the administration of public hospitals, with the installment of procurators and hospitallers, and he charges pastors to always inquire after the welfare of the citizenry. Should they find anyone lacking of anything, they are instructed to inform the Council so that appropriate action can be taken to remedy the situation.

Not only were the poor of Geneva provided for, but also in order to meet the needs of the constant stream of Protestant refugees from Roman Catholic regions, a welfare fund for poor foreigners known as the Bourse française was established.[91] While Geneva's welfare institutions were designed to help those who, through illness or disability, had no hope of becoming self-supporting, most aid was temporary and designed to help the recipient become independent:

> The goal of the deacons was apparently to get able-bodied refugees back on their feet as soon as possible, by providing temporary housing, short-term support, and job retraining when necessary. The deacons paid for tools to set up artisans in trade and provided some of them with raw materials. . . . Such relatively modest expenditures could make people financially independent with little outlay, and since loans were preferred to handouts, the deacons had an opportunity to recover some of their outlay.[92]

Aside from such immediate welfare needs, John Calvin also made primary education compulsory for boys and girls in Geneva, promoted secondary education for boys and girls, and founded what became the University of Geneva.

Nonetheless, contemporary liberationists still find fault with Calvin's social reforms. The section of the *Ecclesiastical Ordinances* dealing with the church's ministry to the poor ends with a warning against begging, "which is contrary to good order."[93] This emphasis on "good order" has raised the criticism that "the middle-class denominations add organization upon organization to meet the needs of the disordered and disinherited, but still the church at best reinforces the distance between the middle-class churches and the churches of the disinherited."[94] Granted, the social piety arising from Calvin's theology emphasizes good order, but not from a hidden desire to exclude or marginalize the "disinherited" as Taylor (and Wolterstorff) suggests. Rather, the rigid systematic approach to social welfare concerns demonstrated in Calvin's church order is the inescapable by-product of implementing voluminous social reforms in response to great social upheaval and immeasurable human suffering. A more thorough examination of Calvin's correspondence unmasks the human side of the "world-repressive" social engineer who struggled, often against great odds, to create stability and peace for Geneva.

Calvin's correspondence reveals a pastor who took time to write to political prisoners and refugees, offering comfort, material assistance, and practical advice, while interceding with governing authorities on their behalf. In 1545, when the French victims of royal persecution sought refuge in Geneva, John Calvin was instrumental in convincing the Genevan civil authorities not only to offer safe haven but also to provide the refugees with means of subsistence.[95] Further evidence of Calvin's political advocacy is found in a letter to Farel, dated May 4, 1545, in which Calvin writes for counsel on how to help the persecuted Protestants of Provence:

> One of them has returned to us with the melancholy intelligence that several villages have been consumed by fire, that most of the old men had been burned to death, that some had been put to the sword, others having been carried off to abide their doom; and that such was the savage cruelty of these persecutors, that neither young girls, nor pregnant women, nor infants, were spared. . . . On hearing of this dreadful tragedy, and considering what ought to be done, it seemed advisable to the brethren [ministers in Geneva] in the first place, that we should send a man to you with my letter which recommends the cause of all the Churches to the ministers; and in the next place we asked the advice of the [Genevan city] Council, because we were not so clear among ourselves what measures ought to be taken. It was the opinion of the Council that I should go in person to the Swiss Churches [as an ambassador for the people of Provence]. I shall therefore set out tomorrow on the journey. . . . As soon as I can, I shall urge the Senate to grant me an audience of the Council.[96]

Calvin's efforts to liberate political prisoners were not always successful, as in the case of the five theological students imprisoned in Lyons and burned at the stake in 1553, yet his pastoral letters were intended to not only provide comfort to the prisoners but also praise the witness of the Protestant martyrs. This is evidenced in a letter of encouragement addressed to Liner, a Protestant merchant who was working to free the five prisoners of Lyons:

> Reflect, moreover, how many worthy brethren there are who glorify God for what you are doing, who would be scandalized if you altered your course. As for the dangers which they set before you, I have no fear of their coming to pass, for the good brethren for whom you have done so much feel themselves so indebted to you that, were they at liberty, far from being cowardly enough to betray you, they would expose themselves to death for your sake. . . . Be of good courage therefore in this holy work, in which you serve not only God and His martyrs but also the whole church.[97]

From reading these letters it becomes evident that John Calvin's understanding of the Christian life does not promise freedom from turmoil and affliction. Rather, Christ's grace comes to us amid the trials of life, enabling us not only to persevere in faith in spite of our adversities but also to see God's providence in our sickness, imprisonment, and even death. Furthermore, according to Calvin, it is the vocation of all Christians to take up "the protection of the good and the innocent against the wrongs of the wicked," even at the cost of undergoing "the offenses and hatred of the world, which may imperil either our life, our fortunes, or our honor."[98]

It has been demonstrated how Calvin's theology and pastoral practice sought to create a just and equitable society founded upon his understanding of the Gospel of Jesus Christ. But Calvin's methods reflect the rigidly hierarchical society of late medieval/early modern Europe, so to modern eyes his efforts at caring for the poor and oppressed can appear paternalistic. Thankfully, not every aspect of Calvin's ordering of church life and society is essential to Reformed theology. What is essential is faithfulness to the Word of God when defining the church's ecclesiology and missiology. Historian Elsie Anne McKee highlights Calvin's greatest strength as his determination to be faithful to the sole authority of Scripture by allowing all of Scripture to instruct him without skipping inconvenient passages. The message Calvin finds in Scripture is akin to the fundamental affirmation of liberation theology—that God acts in the world in order to liberate the poor and oppressed, making historical liberation a necessary dimension of salvation—insofar as Calvin understands the Christian life as a call to suffer for the sake of righteousness (*Institutes* 3.8.7).

In sixteenth-century Geneva, Christ's call to minister to the poor, the sick, the orphan, the widow, the refugee, and the prisoner was purposefully integrated into the life of the church and legislated by civil law. In the twenty-first century, mainline Protestantism in North America can transform the character of global Christianity by helping pastors and laypeople alike rediscover the Reformed/Calvinist tradition's commitment to socially transformative praxis. Thus, while always conscious of the fact that the Reformed tradition has at times used its theology to legitimate oppression, a theology guided by this tradition should nonetheless tread bravely into the public arena, confident that Calvin has already walked that path and, more important, with the sure knowledge that Christ himself first marked the trail.

Jesus on Slavery: A Theological Framework for Engaging the Politics of Race

Translating Jesus' teachings across two thousand years of historical and cultural change raises many obstacles for contemporary theological reflection. The very fact that Jesus addressed the political realm indirectly —most often through the use of parables containing multiple layers of meaning requiring complex analysis and interpretation—means that discerning Jesus' ethical command in new situations entails a certain level of risk and open-endedness.[99] This investigation looks at the problematic of racism in theological construction, and enters the public discourse on race, from a Reformed and liberationist perspective. Nevertheless, the historical Jesus known primarily through the canonical Gospels stands as a principal source for articulating a transcultural theology of human liberation. Given this commitment to historical-critical methods, no subject creates greater hermeneutical frustration for contemporary emancipatory theologies than the Gospels' tacit acceptance of slavery. Risking glibness, one cannot help but ask, "What would Jesus do?"

A cursory reading of both the Old and New Testaments reveals no explicit condemnation of slavery. Following the liberation of Israel from slavery in Egypt, the Mosaic Law nonchalantly includes the commandment not to covet your neighbor's slaves (Exod. 20:17), an exhortation repeated almost word for word in Deuteronomy: "Neither shall you desire your neighbor's house, or field, or male or female slave, or ox, or donkey, or anything else that belongs to your neighbor" (5:21, NRSV). Slavery was foundational to the social organization of the ancient Mediterranean world, part and parcel of the Hebrew and Greco-Roman cultural matrix in which Jesus lived and the earliest Christian communities arose. While the Mosaic Law demonstrated a degree of compassion toward slaves, commanding that they, like the ox and ass, not profane the Sabbath by working on that day (Exod. 20:10; Deut. 5:15), ancient Israel was so completely a slaveholding society that its foundational sacred text, the Ten Commandments, unquestioningly lists human beings as one item among many in a long list of personal property.

The historical data do not provide a complete picture of the lives of slaves in the ancient world, but it is known that the majority of rural slaves were men while the majority of domestic slaves were women and children.[100] Economically, slaves were indispensable for running the farms that supplied the Roman legions. Furthermore, most slaves were aliens enslaved through military conquest and therefore vulnerable to exploitation in ways free citizens were not. For example, slaves were often rented out as prostitutes or simply taken by their owners for sexual gratification; at the same time, the law did not recognize marriages among slaves, so it was common for slave families to be broken up when slaves were sold. Under Roman law the sale of slaves was no different than the sale of animals, and Roman slave traders covered the ends of the known world from Gaul to the Caucasus, Germany to Africa, in order to meet the expanding needs of the empire. Robbing slaves of their cultural identity by renaming them and then transporting them far from their country of origin to where they had no familial ties and could not speak the language was also standard practice among Roman slave traders. Thus, even though in ancient Rome slavery had not become fully racialized (e.g., by equating blackness with slavery), and in spite of a law promising all slaves manumission at age thirty (there is little evidence this law was ever enforced), the cruel excesses of slavery in the ancient world rival the worst practices of slavery in the antebellum American South. This fact proved particularly problematic for nineteenth-century Christian abolitionists who, embarrassed by the acceptance of slavery in the Bible, sought to differentiate slavery in the ancient world from slavery in the American South. The Bible condoned slavery and the treatment of slaves as property to be bought and sold like cattle; no amount of hermeneutical gymnastics can conceal the historical evidence. In ancient Rome slaves were referred to as *instrumentum vocale,* "a talking tool," while the Torah declares it lawful to own aliens residing in Israel as well those enslaved through military conquest: "These you may treat as slaves, but as for your fellow Israelites, no one shall rule over the other with harshness" (Lev. 25:46, NRSV). By implication, even when the Torah provides some legal protections for slaves and resident aliens, they remain subject to "harsh" treatment no Israelite would ever tolerate. Nearer the time of Jesus, the book of Sirach includes practical advice for the treatment of slaves, suggesting a complete lack of theological resistance to the practice of slavery:

> Fodder and a stick and burdens for a donkey; bread and discipline and work for a slave. Set your slave to work, and you will find rest; leave his hands idle, and he will seek liberty. Yoke and thong will bow the neck, and for a wicked slave there are racks and tortures. Put him to work, in order that he may not be idle, for idleness teaches much evil. Set him to

work, as is fitting for him, and if he does not obey, make his fetters heavy.
(Sir. 33:25–30a, NRSV)

Consequently, it is not surprising that Jesus constantly employed the term
slave (doulos/doule) in his teaching—"No slave can serve two masters"
(Luke 16:13, NRSV)—and often illustrated his stories by making reference
to the institution of slavery (Luke 12:42–46; 14:16–24; 15:22), thereby revealing a more than passing familiarity with the everyday lives of slaves.

At the same time, none of the Gospel narratives ever depict Jesus in
conversation with slaves, even though he is shown transgressing other social boundaries by speaking to the Samaritan woman (John 4:7–30), the
Roman centurion (Matt. 8:5–13; Luke 7:2–10), tax collectors (Matt. 9:9–13;
Mark 2:13–17; Luke 19:1–10), lepers (Matt. 8:1–4; Mark 1:40–45; Luke 5:12–
15), and the woman caught in adultery (John 8:2–11). Considering that in
his teaching Jesus often made use of marginalized and excluded minorities to challenge and transform existing prejudices—the paradigm for this
use of parables as subversive speech is the parable of the Good Samaritan
in which Jesus contrasts the hypocritical actions of a priest and a Levite to
the selfless act of a Samaritan, a member of a hated ethnic and religious
minority (Luke 10:25–37)—why did Jesus never question the morality of
slavery? In the Gospel of Luke Jesus defines his mission in light of Isaiah's
prophecy, "to proclaim release to the captives" and "to let the oppressed
go free" (Luke 4:18, NRSV). Who is more oppressed than enslaved human
beings? Not only does Jesus remain silent about an institution that at its
core defaces the image of God in all humanity (Gen. 1:27), he then utilizes
slavery as the model for proper obedience to the Word of God:

> "Who among you would say to your slave who has just come in from
> plowing or tending sheep in the field, 'Come here at once and take your
> place at the table'? Would you not rather say to him, 'Prepare supper for
> me, put on your apron and serve me while I eat and drink; later you may
> eat and drink'? Do you thank the slave for doing what was commanded?
> So you also, when you have done all that you were ordered to do, say, 'We
> are worthless slaves; we have done only what we ought to have done!'"
> (Luke 17:7–10, NRSV)

The argument could be made that Jesus spoke metaphorically about fallen
humanity in general as "captive" to sin in much the same way that Matthew's version of the beatitudes takes Luke's "Blessed are you who are

poor" (Luke 6:20, NRSV) and reinterprets it spiritually: "Blessed are the poor in spirit" (Matt. 5:3, NRSV). Or, "Blessed are you who are hungry now" (Luke 6:21) becomes "Blessed are those who hunger and thirst for righteousness" (Matt. 5:6). However, looking at Luke's Gospel in its entirety reveals a consistent and coherent message in which Jesus understands his mission as bringing liberation to the captives, the poor, and the oppressed through a cataclysmic act of God that, in effect, brings to an end the existing unjust social order: "He has brought down the powerful from their thrones, and lifted up the lowly; he has filled the hungry with good things, and sent the rich away empty" (Luke 1:52–53, NRSV). The Gospel narratives are consistent: Jesus does not explicitly condemn slavery. Still, the fact that Jesus never speaks directly with slaves—even while making numerous references to slaves and slavery in his preaching —seems counterintuitive, especially when one considers that many of the earliest Christians were themselves slaves.[101]

Given the tenuous status of the early church within the Roman Empire, it could be argued that the Gospel writers excised such encounters from their narratives in order to allay accusations of political subversion. After all, the persecution of Christians was often justified with the argument that the Christian movement undermined political stability. Celsus, a second-century Hellenistic philosopher and critic of early Christianity, defended the absolute right of kings to rule while accusing Christians of overthrowing this doctrine: "If everyone were to do the same as you . . . earthly things would come into the power of the most lawless and savage barbarians, and nothing more would be heard among men either of your worship or of true wisdom."[102] Roman culture was generally tolerant of religious pluralism and only sought to regulate those cults that seemed to threaten the Roman state and the public order. The fact that Christians worshiped in private and were exclusive monotheists who refused to participate in the pagan religious observances of the state contributed to the suspicion that the Christian movement was an illegal and potentially dangerous (i.e., seditious) mystery religion. However, such polemical attacks merely reflect a general mistrust of Christianity by the general populace rather than political reality, since apostolic teaching on the relationship of the church to temporal powers encouraged obedience to the state as God's appointed means of maintaining civil order (Rom. 13:1–7), even in the face of persecution (1 Pet. 2:13–14; 4:12). Based on the evidence contained in the Gospels alone, perhaps it becomes necessary for contemporary liberation theologies to postulate that the evangelists (or later redactors) removed any and all language condemning the practice of slavery for fear of further persecution, which then necessitates hypothesizing a silenced tradition within early Christianity that opposed the practice of slavery. Thankfully, the Christian faith does not depend on the ossified nature of historical evidence to argue against the immorality of slavery. Whether or not the historical Jesus—the man, Jesus of Nazareth, born "in the time of King Herod" (Matt. 2:1, NRSV), whose public ministry began in "the fifteenth year of the reign of Emperor Tiberius" (Luke 3:1, NRSV), and who was executed under Pontius Pilate, governor of Judea (Matt. 27:15–26; Mark 15:6–15; Luke 23:13–25)—ever spoke a single word against the institution of slavery during his lifetime does not preclude Christian faith from asserting that Jesus, the Christ of God, opposes all forms of oppression, slavery included.

The Christian faith proclaims the risen Christ, not the reconstructed Jesus of historical criticism. Without minimizing the importance of historical criticism for Christian theology, it is important to remember this foundational belief and understand the full consequences entailed in believing that Christ guides the formation of Christian doctrine. Before his death Jesus prepared the disciples for the persecution to come by promising them divine guidance in the midst of their struggles: "But the Advocate, the Holy Spirit, whom the Father will send in my name, will teach you everything, and remind you of all that I have said to you" (John 14:25, NRSV). Consequently, "When the Spirit of truth comes, he will guide you into all the truth; for he will not speak on his own, but will speak whatever he hears, and he will declare to you the things that are to come" (John 16:13, NRSV). Thus, even when the Gospel narratives are silent on slavery, other books in the New Testament canon—not to mention numerous theological texts from the early church—address slavery directly and can guide our theological and ethical reflections on human liberation. Jesus, in spite of the (underdeveloped) message of liberation found in Luke's Gospel, never acted to abolish slavery. But neither did he legitimate it. In spite of violent slave uprisings, like the one led by Spartacus (c. 70 BCE) resulting in the eventual crucifixion of 6,600 of his followers along the Appian Way,[103] *no one* in the first century wrote abolitionist tracts or even questioned the legitimacy of slavery. The fact that slavery is a constant motif in Jesus' preaching (Matt. 13:24–30; 18:23–35; 22:1–14; 24:45–51; 25:14–30; Mark 12:1–12; Luke 14:15–24; 15:11–32; 20:9–19) is itself unique. Placed within the context of the Gospels' overall message, in which the Messiah is depicted as both slave (*doulos*) and Lord (*kyrios*), and in which this lordship is attained by becoming a slave (Phil. 2:5–11), a subversive view of slavery begins to coalesce.

When Jesus employs slavery as a metaphor for understanding our relationship to God, he is giving primacy to one relationship above all others: God makes an absolute and exclusive demand upon the life of each believer. As Jesus has taught, "No slave can serve two masters" (Luke 16:13, NRSV). Rather than legitimating the practice of slavery, the analogous use of slavery for understanding our relationship to God—when properly understood—radically transforms all other relationships. The slave image appears fifty times in the New Testament (in eighteen different books), so, in spite of the discomfort it causes modern sensitivities, we must accept the early church's communal self-understanding as a "band of slaves."[104] The apostle Paul builds on Jesus' image by reminding believers that "you are not your own" for "you were bought with a price" (1 Cor. 6:20, NRSV). Thus, all who follow Christ become slaves of Christ:

> Were you a slave when called? Do not be concerned about it. Even if you can gain your freedom, make use of your present condition now more than ever. For whoever was called in the Lord as a slave is a freed person belonging to the Lord, just as whoever was free when called is a slave of Christ. You were bought with a price; do not become slaves of human masters. In whatever condition you were called, brothers and sisters, there remain with God. (1 Cor. 7:24, NRSV)

Paul, like Jesus, does not explicitly condemn slavery or call for the abolition of slavery, yet his use of slavery as a metaphor for humankind's relationship to God builds upon Jesus' own in order to eliminate differences between free and slave within Christian communities. Given that Paul's understanding of divinity is grounded in the act of God becoming a slave for our sake (Phil. 2:6–7), he naturally envisions the Christian life in terms of becoming "a slave to all" (1 Cor. 9:19, NRSV). In Christ Jesus —that is, between fellow Christians—there is neither slave nor free (Gal. 3:27–28; 1 Col. 3:11). So, while slaves are told to "obey your earthly masters with fear and trembling, in singleness of heart, as you obey Christ" (Eph. 6:5, NRSV), masters are also cautioned to "do the same to them [slaves]. Stop threatening them, for you know that both of you have the same Master in heaven, and with him there is no partiality" (Eph. 6:9, NRSV). Paul's teaching on slavery, however, is not limited to the metaphoric. In the letter to Philemon, a friend and fellow convert, Paul returns Philemon's runaway slave, Onesimus (who has also converted to Christianity), with the following instruction:

> For this reason, though I am bold enough in Christ to command you to do your duty, yet I would rather appeal to you on the basis of love—and I, Paul, do this as an old man, and now also as a prisoner of Christ Jesus. I am appealing to you for my child, Onesimus, whose father I have become during my imprisonment. Formerly he was useless to you, but now he is indeed useful both to you and to me. I am sending him, that is, my own heart, back to you. I wanted to keep him with me, so that he might be of service to me in your place during my imprisonment for the gospel; but I preferred to do nothing without your consent, in order that your good deed might be voluntary and not something forced. Perhaps this is the reason he was separated from you for a while, so that you might have been back forever, no longer as a slave but more than a slave, a beloved brother—especially to me but how much more to you, both in the flesh and in the Lord. (Philem. 8–16, NRSV)

In this passage Paul explicitly distinguishes metaphoric from literal, exhorting Philemon to receive Onesimus as a beloved brother both in the "flesh" and "in the Lord," then drives the point home by writing, "Confident of your obedience, I am writing to you, knowing that you will do even more than I say" (Philem. 21, NRSV). That this letter survived, was duplicated, and widely dispersed—despite the pervasiveness of slavery in first-century Mediterranean culture—reflects its importance for the earliest Christian communities. That the virtues extolled in the letter clashed with the dominant cultural ethos is evidenced by the attitudes toward Christians in classical antiquity. The words of Celsus bring to light the scandal created by treating slaves as brothers and equals in Christ (without necessarily opposing the institution of slavery):

> The Christians make this offer, "Let no well-educated, wise, or great person come to us—such we consider bad. But if anyone is uneducated, foolish, and ignorant, let him take courage and come!" By maintaining that such people are of themselves worthy of their God, they prove that they desire and are able to win only the simple, the lowly, the foolish, the slaves, old women, and little children.[105]

Thus we find in early Christianity a worldview that stands over against the dominant culture, especially as regards notions of wealth, power, and happiness: "That we for the most part must be considered poor is no disgrace to us but an honor. A life of luxury weakens the spirit. Frugality makes it strong."[106] The anonymous *Letter to Diognetus,* dated as early as the second and as late as the early fourth century CE, illustrates well the countercultural aspects of the early Christian movement:

> Happiness does not consist in ruling over one's neighbors or in longing to have more than one's weaker fellowmen. Nor does it consist in being rich and in oppressing those lowlier than oneself. No one can imitate God by doing such things. They are alien to his sublimity. On the contrary, anyone who takes his neighbor's burden upon himself, who tries to help the weaker one in points where he has an advantage, who gives what he has received from God to those who need it, takes God's place, as it were, in the eyes of those who receive. He is an imitator of God. In this way, though living on earth, you will know with awe that there is a God who reigns in heaven, and you will begin to proclaim the mysteries of God. Then you will learn to love and admire those who are punished by death because they refuse to deny God. In this way you will despise the deception and error of the world.[107]

This emphasis on the Christian life of service/slavery to others was at times taken to literal extremes: "We know of many among our number who have given themselves up freewillingly to imprisonment so that they might bring freedom to others. Many have sold themselves into slavery to feed others with the money they received."[108] So in spite of representing a marginalized view within the dominant culture, this distinctly Christian practice of elevating slaves to equal status—even if only within the worship life of the church—survived into the fourth century as evidenced by the teaching of the Cappadocian Fathers, who emphasized the dignity of all human beings as the image of God. In fact, Gregory of Nyssa decried slavery as an affront to the *imago Dei,* voicing the strongest condemnation of slavery among the ancient church fathers by arguing that if we respected the image of God in one another, "poverty would no longer afflict humankind, slavery no longer debase it, shame would no longer distress it, for all things would be common to all."[109]

The Cappadocian Fathers—like Calvin in the sixteenth century—used the power of the pulpit to transform civil society, often directly chastising corrupt and tyrannical government officials, in order to direct the "power of the state to try to correct injustices and to improve the lot of the needy."[110] As these few examples demonstrate, traditions of theological resistance to political injustice have persisted throughout the history of Christian thought and are part and parcel of the biblical grand narrative of salvation history. Theology in the twentieth century struggled with the critical issues of social justice and human liberation by reclaiming aspects of the broad Christian tradition—like the Cappadocians or Calvin's reforms—consonant with the gestational liberation motif underlying Luke's Gospel. Arguably, emancipatory theologies continue to dominate theological discourse in the twenty-first century as the church looks forward with hope and backward with a critical eye in order to recover those strains within the tradition that emphasize life and liberation in the face of death and oppression. Latino/a theology enters the contemporary conversation as a movement that lives at both the center and the margins of theological discourse, whose people embody a *mestizaje* of the oppressed and their oppressors, and whose faith exhibits a genuine openness to the other's experience of divine mystery. Rather than representing something completely new on the theological landscape, U.S. Latino/a theology understands itself as a continuation of the liberating mission of Christ, made possible by the indwelling of the Holy Spirit, and perpetuated throughout the ages by various Christian communities. Yet, as a movement arising within the lived experience of a racially marginalized group, Hispanic theology takes the problem of racism very seriously and therefore critically revisits all aspects of Christian theology in order to better incarnate the oneness of the church in the midst of a world divided by race.

PART II

The Theological Response

4

Guadalupe
Imago Dei *Reconsidered*

César Chávez is arguably the most famous Latino public figure in U.S. history. Often compared to Martin Luther King Jr., Chávez is remembered by academics and activists as primarily a political organizer and charismatic leader, while the role of his Catholic faith in the struggle for justice has been largely ignored. Recent scholarship is working to counter this misconception by arguing that both the liberal intelligentsia and Chicano activists uncomfortable with the role of faith in public matters perpetuated the myth of a "secularized" Chávez.[1] This popular perception of Chávez as a secular activist survives despite the fact that protesting United Farm Workers often carried banners of Nuestra Señora de Guadalupe and despite his own words, which often described his cause in terms of *imitatio Christi* (imitation of Christ): "I am convinced that the truest act of courage, the strongest act of manliness is to sacrifice ourselves for others in a totally non-violent struggle for justice. To be a man is to suffer for others. God help us to be men!"[2] In fact, Chávez invoked the Old Testament prophet Micah in his first major speech after his 1988 hunger strike: "What does the Lord require of you, but to do justice, to love kindness, and to walk humbly with your God."[3]

Some Latino/a theologians maintain that at this point in history, U.S. Latino/a theology needs to move beyond the narrow walls of confessional theology in order to strive for a "wider sense of human solidarity across racial, cultural, and ideological lines."[4] At the same time, the prophetic witness of César Chávez and the ubiquitous presence of Guadalupe necessitate an analysis of Latino/a political activism that understands the role of religion—especially Roman Catholic popular religion—in the struggle for liberation. In this search for political solidarity Latino/a theologians have downplayed significant doctrinal differences between Protestants and Catholics for the sake of creating a unified movement. While U.S. Hispanic/Latino/a theology defines itself as an intentionally ecumenical movement, it is important to engage the beliefs and practices of particular communities of faith. Accordingly, when confronted by certain essentialist claims about ethnicity and theological identity from U.S. Latino/a theologians, it is important to question such claims or risk undermining the intellectual credibility of the movement. For example, Virgilio Elizondo projects a particularly Mexican American and Roman Catholic popular religiosity as normative for *all* Latino/a Christians when he writes, "I do not want to say that every Hispanic has to remain a member of the Roman Catholic Church in order to be a Hispanic, but I am saying that when a Hispanic ceases to be catholic (to participate in the religious-cultural expressions of our people), he or she ceases to be a Hispanic."[5] He thereby overlooks the many Hispanic Protestants who consider some aspects of popular Catholicism—especially the apparition of (and subsequent devotion to) Our Lady of Guadalupe—as superstitious and therefore antithetical to the Gospel of Jesus Christ.

In the spirit of the thirty-year history of cooperation across confessional boundaries, I am arguing that for U.S. Hispanic/Latino theology to mature as an emergent movement in North American theology, it must engage in critical self-analysis. This investigation develops a constructive approach for crossing the borders between Protestant and Catholic Latino/as by exploring the doctrinal significance of Guadalupan devotion. Specifically, I evaluate and critique Virgilio Elizondo's contribution to the Christian doctrine of Creation in *Guadalupe: Mother of the New Creation* (1997), in such a way that Reformed/Calvinist Protestants might come to appreciate the strong Christological focus and profound doctrinal insights of Elizondo's interpretation of the Guadalupe narrative.

In this second part of the book I posit *mestizaje* as a liberative metaphor that opposes racism and transcends ethnocentrism without neglecting ethnic and cultural differences through an exploration of the emancipatory dimension of traditional doctrines. Utilizing Guadalupe as a case study for the encounter between Christ and culture, this chapter (1) defends Elizondo's interpretation of the Guadalupe myth as a legitimate manifestation of Guadalupan devotion in light of Stafford Poole's historical critique; (2) traces the Reformed Protestant discomfort with and objections to Guadalupan devotion to iconoclastic tendencies among sixteenth-century Protestant Reformers and the strict Christocentric understanding of divine revelation in the theology of John Calvin; (3) recovers resources within the Reformed theological heritage that allow Protestants to approach Guadalupe as a vehicle of divine self-communication (i.e., a new cultural manifestation of the Gospel); (4) argues that the Guadalupan tradition is compatible with a Reformed Protestant Christocentric theology; and (5) suggests constructive directions for reconstructing the doctrine of Creation through the liberating lens of *mestizaje*. Recognizing the power of images to communicate sacred truth as well as foster ideological transformation, I employ Guadalupe in order to identify potentially harmful tendencies in Reformed doctrine while preserving the uniqueness and primacy of the Christ event for the Christian faith.

Why Guadalupe?

Further discussion is warranted among U.S. Latino/a theologians concerning the role of popular Catholicism, and in particular Guadalupan devotion, in the formation and preservation of U.S. Latino/a culture. Given the diversity of national origins among U.S. Latino/a theologians, the strong focus in the theological literature on Guadalupe is surprising, especially since the image of the blessed Virgin has manifested itself in similar ways in other Latino/a cultural contexts, such as Our Lady of Charity in Cuba and the Virgin of Monserrat in Puerto Rico.[6] Virgilio Elizondo, considered by many the progenitor of U.S. Hispanic/Latino/a theology, often treats Guadalupe as *the* generative event for *mestizo* identity and links the 1531 apparition of Our Lady of Guadalupe to the birth of Hispanic Christianity as "the beginning of a new creation, the mother of a new humanity, and the manifestation of the femininity of God—a figure offering unlimited possibilities for creative and liberating reflection."[7] For, unlike other Latin American Marian cults, Guadalupe is a wholly indigenous tradition in which the Virgin appeared in the traditional clothing of the region and her image resembled an Indian or *mestiza*. To understand Elizondo's claims about Guadalupe's centrality for Hispanic Christianity—an event he describes as "the indigenous account of the real new beginnings of the Americas"[8]—it is important to first understand Elizondo's methodological commitment to the study of popular religion as a privileged means of evangelization.

Guadalupe's Role in Latino/a Cultural Identity

Elizondo's interest in popular religion arose in the context of his pastoral work as a priest and educator in San Antonio, where he learned to value and respect popular forms of Catholicism. From his earliest works to the present, Elizondo, while recognizing its limitations, has viewed popular religion as a privileged source for theology; he does not seek to supplant "official" doctrine but is a tireless defender of the people's faith as authentically Catholic. Elizondo argues for the methodological incorporation of popular religion into the church's theological reflection because it is both a legitimate way of being Catholic (arguably the way in which the majority of the world's Catholics express their faith) and a way in which the "official" tradition may be positively transformed.[9] In other words, popular practices that do not originate in official church teaching and which thrive without the presence of clergy—often arising out of a communal desire to "supplement" or even "correct" official teaching—are in fact vessels through which God speaks to the church and the world. Thus, popular religion interprets and transforms received doctrine while also giving voice to religious experiences not yet articulated in doctrine.[10]

Elizondo not only views popular religion as the primary means of Christian evangelization but also understands popular Catholicism as a key element for preserving a distinctly Latino/a cultural identity—whether one is Catholic, mainline Protestant, Pentecostal, agnostic, or atheist—because of Catholicism's influence in the historical and cultural development of Latin America and Latino/a communities in the United States. It is with this understanding of the "Catholic" cultural context of Latino/a experience that I now consider Elizondo's theological reflections on Our Lady of Guadalupe. Interpreting the Guadalupe event "through the Mariological practices and theologies of the West will lead to misunderstanding and error. Such a process would impose a meaning that would not correspond to the true meaning it has for the people."[11] Accordingly, Elizondo demonstrates great pastoral sensitivity to both the community's lived faith and the broader Christian tradition by articulating a prophetic theology grounded in the popular beliefs and practices of Guadalupanos and Guadalupanas. Thus, *Guadalupe: Mother of the New Creation* is not just Elizondo's account of the theophany of the Virgin of Guadalupe at Tepeyac but also an exploration of its theological significance for contemporary ecumenical Christianity.

The importance of the Guadalupe event for *all* Latino/as is linked to the violent conquest of the Americas that resulted in the racial, ethnic, and cultural *mestizaje* of its people. Her symbolic power is attributed to (1) the appearance of the Virgin to a lowly Indian (or *mestizo*) laborer rather than a Spaniard ruler or church official, (2) the Virgin's physical appearance resembling an Indian or a *mestiza*,[12] and (3) the location of her apparition on Mount Tepeyac, the ancient site of Tonantzin worship, the mother goddess of the Aztecs. Ultimately, the Guadalupe event marks the cultural, biological, and religious union of the conqueror and the conquered, a *mestizaje* that symbolizes the birth of a new humanity. Therein lies the importance of the Guadalupe event as culturally and theologically significant for the people of Mexico, Mexican Americans, and other Latino/a Christians throughout the Americas.

Historical Critiques of Popular Guadalupan Devotion

In his classic text, *The Spiritual Conquest of Mexico* (1966), Robert Ricard argues that the cult of Guadalupe is an invention "born, and it matured and triumphed, under the active influence of the episcopate . . . in the midst of Dominican and Augustinian indifference, and despite the hostile anxiety of the Franciscans."[13] Elizondo acknowledges these suspicions and dismisses them by pointing out that (according to the earliest documentation) church officials tried to suppress Guadalupan devotion among the Indians as a threat to their own missionary and evangelical efforts.[14] Whether or not the roots of the Guadalupe myth lie in popular devotion or ecclesial manipulation, evidence of strong Franciscan opposition to the Guadalupan devotion among the indigenous population exists in the form of a 1556 sermon by a Franciscan friar denouncing the cult of Our Lady of Guadalupe as a "disguised idolatry."[15] If understanding and interpreting the social significance of Guadalupe for the formation of a distinctively Latino/a (specifically Mexican and Mexican-American) culture allows Elizondo to defend the role of popular religion as a locus for theological reflection, his unpacking of the Guadalupe narrative also allows him to interpret it as a symbol of liberation: "I do not know of any other event since Pentecost that has had such a revolutionary, profound, lasting, far reaching, healing, and liberating impact on Christianity."[16] While Virgilio Elizondo overstates the significance of this event within the history of ecumenical Christianity, such hyperbolic statements reveal his deep commitment to the Guadalupe narrative as the guiding myth for Latino/a self-understanding.

Still, in spite of the privileged role Elizondo grants Guadalupe as the hermeneutical key for understanding Latino/a theology and culture, any scholarly engagement of the Guadalupe event must address certain historical-critical questions. First and foremost, the historical verity of this event is still debated, with some critics dismissing the story as a fabrication of the criollo ruling class to foment nationalism in their struggle for independence from Spain.[17] Stafford Poole, who provides the most thorough critical historical analysis of the Guadalupe myth in the English language, concludes, in effect, that no historical foundation exists for authenticating the Guadalupan apparitions: "The fundamental question here is whether a sign or a symbol can exist apart from an underlying reality."[18] He contends that, as a Mexican national and religious symbol, Guadalupe was not "born" at Tepeyac in 1531 but was the result of a growing criollo independence movement that linked the indigenous apparition story to the birth of Christianity in the New World in order to eliminate the criollos' dependence on Catholic Spain. In other words, contra Elizondo, Poole contends that the cult of Guadalupe has its origin in Spanish/criollo interests, not within Indian or *mestizo* religiosity, and notes that "there is no evidence of mass conversion of the Indians after 1531" and "almost nothing is known about the devotion among the Indians in the seventeenth century."[19] Of course, when applying Poole's standards of historiography to the origins of Christianity, the same lack of evidence surrounds the Resurrection story, which for many is the central doctrine of the Christian faith and is accepted as a historical event in spite of a lack of evidence. So, rather than undertake a critical history of the Guadalupan devotion, or trace the origin and redaction of the Guadalupe narrative, I grant Stafford Poole's evaluation of Elizondo's interpretation of Guadalupe as historically inaccurate (according to certain canons of scholarship) yet important for understanding popular practices among Mexican Americans, since Elizondo "exemplifies a contemporary Catholic attitude toward Guadalupe."[20]

Flor y canto: The Postmodern Rediscovery of Mystery

Recognizing the complex history of the various interpretive controversies underlying the transmission of oral and written Guadalupe traditions, I choose to focus on Elizondo's interpretation of contemporary Guadalupan devotion because its contributions to Christian theology transcend its local context. Unlike Poole, who characterizes Elizondo as manipulating the Guadalupe myth for "the needs of contemporary agendas,"[21] I contend that such instances of Guadalupan devotion need not document their historical relationship to the first three centuries of Guadalupan devotion in order to be studied as legitimate manifestations of the Guadalupe myth.

The well-documented history of this sort of manipulation demonstrates the cultural importance of the Guadalupe myth. However, it is Poole's other critique—that Guadalupe has not been widely embraced as a symbol of liberation by liberation theologians—that most challenges Elizondo's reading of the Guadalupe tradition.[22]

As recently as 1987, Andrés Guerrerro recognized that historically, "with a few exceptions, the symbol of Guadalupe has not been proclaimed as a liberating symbol."[23] Whether or not Guadalupe has been or can become a symbol for liberation depends on the person defining Guadalupe. In the past, the institutional church has used Guadalupe "to placate the Indians and the Chicanos," but Guerrerro challenges these received traditions by asking, "How do we redefine Guadalupe as a symbol of liberation as opposed to a symbol of placation and passivity?"[24] Guerrerro exposes the manipulation of the Guadalupe myth by the church hierarchy as a means of social control in order to contrast it with popular devotion, especially among indigenous peoples and *mestizos,* for whom Guadalupe is often a source of dignity and group pride in the face of conquering powers. Contra Poole's generalization, not only Virgilio Elizondo in the North American context but also Latin American liberation theologian Leonardo Boff (writing on the eve of the quincentennial of the Spanish-Catholic conquest and evangelization of the Americas) has proffered the Guadalupe event as a model of evangelization, liberation, and cross-cultural interaction for the Latin American church.[25] Still, Poole dismisses precisely this kind of creative retrieval and reconstruction of the Guadalupe tradition because such approaches disregard historical accuracy in order to meet "the needs of contemporary agendas."[26] Is it possible to retrieve a liberating reading of the Guadalupe myth that remains true to the "facts" as Poole has presented them? Allan Figueroa Deck, in a review of Stafford Poole's work, asserts, "No ultimately satisfactory assessment of the Guadalupe phenomenon can be made outside the framework of the faith of the living community in dialogue with Scripture and the ongoing Christian tradition."[27] In other words, while the kind of thorough deconstructive analysis of tradition undertaken by Poole is important, religious worldviews cannot be reduced to a collection of historical facts. Accordingly, Deck commends David Tracy's postmodern theological project for its ability to hold "critical reason in tension with a profound sense of wonder and mystery."[28]

The disputed events at Tepeyac are central to Elizondo's interpretation of the Guadalupe myth, despite the brutal historical events that gave birth to *mestizaje* and during which the Virgin of Guadalupe appeared, because the birth of this new humanity is a source of hope—a new way for human beings to relate one with another that transcends relationships of domination. This last point is evidenced by Elizondo's emphasis on reconciliation throughout his analysis of the conquest of the Americas and attempts to understand, without completely condemning either, the cultural and historical factors that shaped both the Iberian conquerors and the various pre-Columbian indigenous peoples:

> Through faith, we are totally rehabilitated in our humanity as men and women. This new person will have no need of becoming like the victimizing conquistador (the ongoing curse of the creole and mestizo) but will be him/herself in a radically new way. This is redemptive birth. This is the beginning of the truly "new church" of the eventual new humanity of the New World, which was just beginning to dawn at Tepeyac.[29]

Granted, Elizondo does not wish to diminish the sinfulness of the genocidal atrocities committed by the Spanish conquerors (and tacitly condoned by the church), but his analysis also recognizes how several aspects of the indigenous cultures contributed to the Spanish takeover.

The Aztecs dominated other Nahuatl peoples by means of a strong military and a rigid aristocratic order; consequently, they were hated and feared by subjugated groups, especially for their religious obsession with human sacrifice. Elizondo does not condemn either culture, believing that each civilization "had its unique ways of approaching truth, expressing beauty, and communicating with ultimate reality."[30] The latter point—the genuine *mestizaje* of two very different theological perspectives—Elizondo finds most fascinating and instructive for the twenty-first-century church:

> Guadalupe brings about what even the best and most sensitive missioners would not have wanted or even suspected as salutary: the mutually enriching dialogue of the Christian notions of God with the Nahuatl notions of God. . . . The two religions need not kill one another and should come together as in the conjugal relation to produce a new offspring—in continuity with both yet transformative of both into something new.[31]

While according to Stafford Poole the Guadalupan devotion did not play a crucial role in the sixteenth-century evangelization of the Indians, Elizondo traces the origins of Latino/a Christianity to the unsubstantiated events of 1531. Why? Because he is committed to giving voice to the re-ligion of the people and believes, in the face of scant historical evidence, that the events at Tepeyac gave birth to a Guadalupe tradition that has survived in the popular collective consciousness in spite of official church resistance.

Notwithstanding the lack of historical evidence, the fact remains that as early as 1556 Franciscan friars were preaching against some form of popular Guadalupan devotion. While there is no historical evidence that the sixteenth-century Guadalupe tradition embraced both the apparitions at Tepeyac and the pre-Christian worship of Tonantzin, subsequent mani-festations of Guadalupan devotion incorporated both strands into one tradition with its spiritual nascence at Tepeyac (despite its suspect his-torical origins). Thus, in spite of Poole's concerns, Virgilio Elizondo gives voice to a form of popular Guadalupan devotion with legitimate links to the first three hundred years of Guadalupe history. This gap in standard historiographical evidence does not necessarily imply the manipulation of facts for the sake of a contemporary agenda; it can also point to the sup-pression of an alternative history—a history of resistance that Elizondo reclaims through his work on popular religion.

Reformed Protestant Engagement of Guadalupan Devotion

Elizondo's championing of Our Lady of Guadalupe may appear, from a classical Reformed perspective,[32] to undermine Christian doctrine given his proclaiming of her as "the beginning of a new creation, the mother of a new humanity, and the manifestation of the femininity of God."[33] The role we give to various cultural symbols (like Guadalupe) reveals much about our hermeneutical perspective. Is the Bible a record of the acts of God in human history that provides (somewhat) reliable knowledge about the character and nature of God, or is the Bible a collection of narratives from the collective human religious imagination that gives meaning to some (but not all) people's existence? For the most part, Reformed theology has always presumed that theological statements are possible because God first reveals God's self. God not only reveals God's self, but God is the only means by which humans can know God with any degree of reliability. Yet, while the event of revelation is at the heart of all our human talk about God, we have access only to interpretations of this event, not the event it-self. As the dominant forms of Christian theology (in this particular case

I am speaking specifically about the Reformed/Protestant perspective) encounter and critically engage popular and indigenous forms of religion, like the Guadalupan devotion, we must ask: Is our doctrine of the Word of God broad enough to include new theophanies? New revelations? Or is God's act of self-revelation circumscribed by the biblical witness?

Protestant Discomfort with Sacred Images

John W. de Gruchy, a South African liberation theologian rooted in the Reformed tradition, suggests Protestant discomfort with sacred images like Guadalupe is partially attributable to iconoclastic tendencies prevalent during the Reformation. The question of sacred images was only part of Protestantism's polemic on Rome: "The cult of the Virgin, prayers to the saints and pilgrimages to their relics, passion plays, the endowments of masses for the dead, indeed, the mass itself, along with the veneration of images, were, for the Reformers, all part of the same popish parcel."[34] Granted, John Calvin drew upon the ancient Iconoclastic Controversy in his own anti-idolatry polemic by linking the decline of early Christianity to the introduction of images.[35] Still, while forbidding the use of images in worship, Calvin affirms human creativity, including sculpture and painting, as a gift from God that can—in the proper context—give pleasure.[36] In fact, de Gruchy commends Calvin's exegetical principle of accommodation,[37] by which God bridges the gulf between creator and creature, as a possible avenue for Reformed theology to recover the aesthetic as theological locus.[38]

Christianity, Art and Transformation is de Gruchy's attempt to bring together social justice concerns with theological aesthetics by analyzing the role of art in social transformation. Specifically, de Gruchy explores the contributions of visual images in resisting apartheid (while acknowledging similar developments in Latin American Christianity) to argue that the arts may play prophetic and redemptive roles in the struggle for justice. Echoing Calvin's conviction that humankind is fallen and inevitably misuses God's gifts, de Gruchy recognizes that images both are extremely powerful and can be easily manipulated for oppression as well as liberation and cautions not to "confuse the glory and power of God with images that invariably reflect or reinforce our own interests, whether personal, national, ethnic or class. Iconoclasm in this regard is a necessary outworking of the prophetic trajectory in the biblical tradition."[39] Nevertheless, de Gruchy maintains that "recovery of aesthetic experience is of considerable importance for the renewal of the church and its mission in the world, and that its neglect has serious consequences to the contrary."[40] That theological aesthetics has become a pressing concern given the changing face of world Christianity is evidenced by the often-tragic history of European and American missionary encounters with "alien" cultures that have embraced sacred images.

While de Gruchy identifies the use of sacred images in non-Western cultures as the primary source of discomfort for Reformed/Protestant theology, I believe the strong Christocentric conception of divine revelation inherited from John Calvin presents a greater obstacle to cross-cultural understanding. Specifically, I contend that by focusing on the issue of images in worship and theological reflection Protestant theologians risk misrepresenting both Calvin's theology and the Guadalupe tradition. The central issue for sixteenth-century iconoclasm is the potential for idolatry when images created by human hands—that is, the product of human imagination—are used in the context of worship. Considering Calvin's principle of accommodation as an avenue for greater aesthetic appreciation, an honest interpretation of Calvin's theology recognizes that—even when Calvin identifies both the beauty of God's creation and the product of human creativity as vehicles of divine revelation—Scripture and the Incarnation are the only reliable instances of God's accommodating God's self to our human limitations (because of humanity's tendency toward idolatry). As Ford Lewis Battles concludes, "Surely the incarnation, to which (for the Christian) all this evidence points and from which it takes its meaning, must be the accommodating act par excellence of our divine Father, Teacher, Physician, Judge, and King," since, "after the Fall, there is no salvation apart from the Mediator."[41]

Guadalupanos and Guadalupanas do not view the image of Nuestra Señora de Guadalupe as the creation of human hands but as a direct and unmediated revelation from God. This raises a fundamental concern: *Does Christian theology allow for "new" revelations from God, or is "Christian" religious experience necessarily a remembering and retelling of the formative and unique Christ event?* From a systematic perspective, it is necessary to determine whether theophanies like Guadalupe are "new" revelations or culturally specific variations of the same Mariological event. As a Reformed theologian, when I consider Virgilio Elizondo's interpretation of popular Catholicism (a pastorally sensitive and accurate representation of his community's devotion to Guadalupe), I have to ask whether or not the theological commitments arising from this devotion—especially the belief that Guadalupe's image originates in an act of divine revelation—are harmonious with the broader Christian tradition. Granted, more research is needed to determine whether the typical Guadalupano/a understands Nuestra Señora de Guadalupe as something new—as a new church, a new revelation from God—or if the popular beliefs and practices of the people have stronger Mariological and/or Christological components than many Latino/a intellectuals are willing to acknowledge. Nonetheless, Elizondo's own claims about the uniqueness and "newness" of the Guadalupe event appear to stand as a barrier to mutual understanding between Protestants and Catholics. How (if at all) should Protestant and Pentecostal churches embrace the various cultural manifestations of the Virgin?

Overcoming Iconoclastic Objections

Although Elizondo does not seek to supplant official doctrine, his language suggests that the Guadalupe event is a new theophany—a new manifestation of the divine communicating a new revelation—and thus problematic to any understanding of Christian doctrine that grants the Christ event unique revelatory status. Is a Christocentric theology necessarily at odds with theologies receptive to new revelations from God *not* mediated by Christ, or is it the case that the Guadalupe event—while a new cultural expression of the divine—is nonetheless a manifestation of the Christ event? As I read Elizondo, the Guadalupe event is a new cultural manifestation of the Christ event, calling the church to repentance and conversion because the church has strayed from original Christianity. Hence, it is not a new revelation but a strong Christological critique of the dominant (European and Anglo-American) forms of the Christian religion rooted in the original Gospel witness yet incarnated in new and different ways.

There is an evolution in Elizondo's writings on Our Lady of Guadalupe, from Guadalupe as the foundational event of Mexican Catholicism, to Guadalupe the protector and liberator of the poor as evangelizer of the church and the Americas, and, most recently, Guadalupe as the beginning of a new creation and feminine manifestation of God.[42] Several key passages in his most recent book on the subject, *Guadalupe: Mother of the New Creation* (1997), reveal a move away from a Marian reading of Guadalupe to a more Christological interpretation, which bolsters my position that the Guadalupe theophany is not a new revelation from God but a different cultural manifestation of the central Christian revelation. By outlining the traits of the Guadalupe event that make it similar to, or continuous with, the Christ event—even while manifest in new cultural forms—I appeal to Elizondo's strong Christocentric interpretation of the Guadalupe theophany in order to counter Protestant objections to the use of Guadalupe as a source for Christian theology.

A Christological Reading of Guadalupan Devotion

According to Elizondo, the Lady announces "the reign of God that was the core of the life and message of Jesus. Guadalupe is thus a good Nahuatl translation of the New Testament reality of the reign of God as revealed by Jesus."[43] Consequently,

> Our Lady of Guadalupe is not just another Marian apparition. Guadalupe has to do with the very core of the gospel itself. It is nothing less than an original American Gospel. . . . In Our Lady of Guadalupe at Tepeyac, God pitched a tent and came to dwell among us. The Word became flesh in the Americas through Our Lady of Guadalupe and dwells among us truly as one of us.[44]

Without question, Elizondo understands the events of 1531 on Mount Tepeyac as a genuine manifestation of the one God—God incarnate as Indian or *mestiza*—and not a competing revelation. Rather, Guadalupe properly understood is a call to repentance and a return to the original Gospel witness. Still, Elizondo is aware there is much resistance within the broader Christian tradition to embrace Guadalupe as a Christological theophany:

> Because the gospel through Guadalupe was such a powerful force in the creation and formulation of the national consciousness and identity of the people as expressed, understood, and celebrated through their art, music, poetry, religious expression, preaching, political discourse, and cultural-religious celebrations, its original meaning—that is, the original gospel of Jesus expressed in and through native Mexican terms—has become eclipsed. This has led some modern-day Christians—especially those whose Christianity is expressed through U.S. cultural terms—to see Guadalupe as pagan or as something opposed to the gospel.[45]

A careful reading of the parallels between Elizondo's interpretation of the Guadalupan event (as recorded in the *Nican mopohua*)[46] and the Gospel narrative will underscore its Christological content and perhaps challenge those Protestant Christians who dismiss Guadalupe as pagan to come to terms with their prejudices.

Elizondo's reading of the New Testament witness identifies several key themes: (1) God's preferential option for the poor and oppressed, (2) a new inclusive vision of community where all people—including *mestizo/ as* and other outcast and marginalized persons—are valued as *imago Dei*, and (3) the ongoing incarnation of the Christian Gospel in new cultural contexts. The early Christian movement embraced the poor and disenfranchised because Christ himself ministered to those on the margins of society: "The Spirit of the Lord is upon me, because he has anointed me to bring good news to the poor. He has sent me to proclaim release to the captives and recovery of sight to the blind, to let the oppressed go free, to proclaim the year of the Lord's favor" (Luke 4:18–19, NRSV). Jesus preached to the poor and outcast, and in his words they discovered their place as children of God made in the image of God (Gen. 1:27). His parables confronted the dominant culture and challenged listeners to question and reevaluate their most basic beliefs, as in the case of the Good Samaritan—a member of a despised ethnic minority whom Jesus praises for his actions in contrast to the religious hypocrisy of the priest and Levite (Luke 10:25–37). In *Galilean Journey*, Virgilio Elizondo compares the Galilean context of Jesus' earthly ministry and subsequent crucifixion to the cultural situation during the Christianization and conquest of the Americas by identifying the *mestizo* peoples born from violent rape with the earliest converts to the way of Jesus. In fact, Jesus himself is identified as culturally *mestizo*:

> The God of Jesus cannot be known unless Jesus is known . . . yet we cannot really know Jesus of Nazareth unless we know him in the context of the historical and cultural situation of his human group. Jesus was not just a Jew, he was a Galilean Jew and throughout his life he and his disciples were identified as Galileans. In order to know Jesus, efforts must be made to know the Galileans of his day. It is only in their identity that the identity of the Word of God, made flesh, is to be found.[47]

Recalling the history of the region—Galilee was a land route connecting great empires like the Assyrians, Babylonians, Persians, and Egyptians whose people had been conquered numerous times—Elizondo concludes that Galilee was a land of mixed peoples and that the image of the Galilean Jew in the minds of the Jerusalem Jew is comparable to the image of the *mestizos* in the minds of the Spanish conquerors. And—according to the Guadalupan devotion—just as God became the flesh-and-blood Jesus of Nazareth in first-century Galilee, God became manifest in Our Lady of Guadalupe, a *mestiza,* in sixteenth-century America.

According to Elizondo, the text of the *Nican mopohua,* like the Gospel, first takes root among the poor and marginalized: "First she allowed herself to be seen by a poor and dignified person whose name is Juan Diego."[48] He also suggests that the author of the Guadalupe narrative situates the events during a time when the brutal reality of the Spanish conquest was not just a distant memory but a still bleeding wound ten years after the conquest of the city of Mexico. Elizondo comments that it "was very much like St. Luke wanting to situate the birth of the Savior of the world at the very precise moment of the census ordered by Caesar Augustus."[49] However, before commencing the historical narrative of Juan Diego's encounter with Our Lady, the author presents a brief and highly symbolic Creation narrative—overtly linking the cosmic creation at the dawn of time to the liberating events at Tepeyac:

> But when Juan Diego arrives at Tepeyac, there is a radical new beginning —from the darkness of nothingness to the darkness of expectation. Juan Diego leaves his home "when it was still night" but arrives at Tepeyac while "it was already beginning to dawn" (v. 8). Tepeyac will be the site of the new creation. It is here that a new humanity will begin. This will not be a new conquest but a new creation.[50]

A similar strategy was employed during the earliest period of Christian theology when the affirmation that God is one—Creator and Redeemer —became the first article of "orthodox" faith. For example, the second-century Christology of Irenaeus reconciled the radical monotheism of the Hebrew Scriptures with the bi-theism implied by the salvific work of Jesus Christ by articulating a doctrine of recapitulation in which the Redeemer is the Creator. Correcting the teachings of Arius—who argued that no creature can redeem another, and since Jesus is a creature, Jesus cannot redeem humanity—Athanasius (c. 296–373 CE) affirms that Jesus is God incarnate. Therefore, since only God can save, and we know from Scripture (and from personal experience of grace) that Jesus Christ saves, we must conclude that Jesus Christ is God (making the act of Redemption inseparable from the act of Creation).

The author of the *Nican mopohua* defends the theological "orthodoxy" of the narrative by identifying the theophany at Guadalupe with "the Ever-Virgin Holy Mary, Mother of God" (v. 1). Still, this raises questions about the origins of this written narrative, which according to scholarly consensus dates to the seventeenth century, and which, even if attributable to an indigenous sixteenth-century oral tradition, has been indelibly shaped by Miguel Sánchez and other criollo theologians advancing their own nationalistic agendas. Without minimizing the importance of historical criticism, I suggest that Elizondo—who is well acquainted with the breadth of Guadalupe scholarship—is attempting to explicate the text for the purposes of the reader's edification, not historical accuracy. Furthermore, regardless of the complex history of Spanish evangelization, coerced acculturation of the indigenous populations, or how many redactions the *Nican mopohua* (and its underlying oral tradition) has undergone, the fact remains that today the Guadalupe event is embraced by millions of people as a genuine Christian revelation.[51]

Thus, when Tonantzin/Guadalupe introduces herself to the Indian peasant Juan Diego, saying, "I am the Ever-Virgin Holy Mary, Mother of the God of Great Truth, Téotl, of the One through Whom We Live, the Creator of Persons, the Owner of What Is Near and Together, of the Lord of Heaven and Earth" (v. 22), she is not the manifestation of some competing divine pantheon but the action of the one God in a new cultural context. By introducing herself as the Mother of the true God (Téotl), she subsumes the God of the Nahuatls into the triune God of Western Christianity.

As the translation of Christ's Gospel into a new cultural and historical context, Our Lady of Guadalupe represents for many millions "the temple in whom and through whom Christ's saving presence is continually incarnated in the soil of the Americas."[52] It is through Guadalupe's mediation that Latino/a people come to know God's liberating message previously communicated in the Magnificat of Mary: "He has shown strength with his arm; he has scattered the proud in the thoughts of their hearts. He has brought down the powerful from their thrones, and lifted up the lowly; he has filled the hungry with good things, and sent the rich away empty" (Luke 1:51–52, NRSV). Ultimately, the Guadalupan epiphany points away from itself to the liberating work of Christ through whom we come to know the true God. Thus, in spite of the historical development of the

Guadalupan devotion into a national and cultural symbol, it is first and foremost a witness to the person and work of Jesus Christ.

Elizondo points out that the Lady names herself "the Mother of God" but never explicitly identifies herself as the mother of Jesus. Rather, it is Juan Diego who recognizes her as Mary the mother of Jesus and so names her in his conversation with the bishop (v. 53). This detail is significant because it demonstrates affinity between the Gospel taught by Spanish missionaries and the Gospel proclaimed at Tepeyac: "Juan Diego combines what he has heard from the friars about Jesus Christ with what he has heard and seen at Tepeyac and deduces that she is the mother of our Lord and Savior Jesus Christ."[53] Yet, it is the Lady's actions that fully confirm her divine mission, by restoring to health Juan Diego's dying uncle. Furthermore, her gift of healing is accompanied by the miraculous transformation of Creation, confirming that the truth of God is at hand: "All over the place there were all kinds of exquisite flowers from Castile, open and flowering. It was not a place for flowers, and likewise it was the time when the ice hardens upon the earth" (v. 81).

In his concluding reflections to *Guadalupe: Mother of the New Creation*, Elizondo identifies five theological loci he associates with the Guadalupe event: (1) it is about ultimate truth, (2) it is about evangelization and faith, (3) it is about God, (4) it is about Christ and the New Humanity, and (5) it is about the triune God. He confirms that the Guadalupe theophany "is not something totally new, for it is simply the ideal of the kingdom of God as lived and proclaimed by Jesus," the same good news "that is recorded in the Gospels and lived and celebrated by Christians, especially in the Eucharist."[54] Nonetheless, there is something unique and new about Guadalupe. As the *mestizaje* of the Nahuatl cosmic religion with the Christianity of the Spaniards, Guadalupan devotion "introduces us to a more comprehensive and open-ended concept of God—a mestizo God."[55] While Guadalupe points beyond itself back to the original Christian Gospel, it can also become an impediment to faith for Christians from other—sometimes vastly different—traditions. Elizondo attributes much of this resistance to certain views of human rationality that dominate Western theological reflection: "Guadalupe is not an isolated abstract, doctrinal truth; neither is it legal or moralistic truth."[56]

Guadalupe, as the *mestizaje* of Western and Nahuatl perspectives, "merges the two into a new metaphysics that recognizes the interconnectedness and interdependence of all creation while equally recognizing the uniqueness and value of the individual within the cosmic."[57] At its core, Guadalupan devotion is grounded in the ecstatic experience of the religious believer in mystic communion with God. Without dismissing the need for doctrine, catechetical instruction, and critical reflection, Elizondo nonetheless challenges the church to experience the divine in ways that have long been ignored or marginalized within the Western tradition. The truth revealed by Guadalupe "cannot be obtained or arrived at through observation, rational analysis, and argumentation alone, but can only be fully grasped through the beauty of sight and sound followed by critical questioning."[58] Accordingly, he challenges the church to embrace mystical experience as a legitimate source of theological reflection, since "Dreams and visions are as much a part of the process of discovering and knowing as critical observation and analysis of reality."[59] However, not every believer knows and experiences God in this manner. If Elizondo's theology is going to "convert" the ecumenical church to the Lady's beautiful vision of universal *mestizaje,* in which all the world's people are welcomed and included and the dehumanizing actions of racism, sexism, and classism are reversed, then U.S. Latino/a theologians must articulate this vision not just in terms of mystical participation but also in terms of a theology of the Word.[60]

Mestizo *Theological Reconstruction: The Creation*

Having demonstrated the strong Christological focus of Virgilio Elizondo's interpretation of the Guadalupe encounter, I argue that dominant theological traditions can benefit from an open and receptive encounter with different, even apparently incompatible, perspectives. Theological reflection about the Guadalupan understanding of Creation teaches us to (1) view the whole Creation as interconnected and interdependent, (2) affirm an inclusive theological anthropology that views all human beings—but especially the marginalized and oppressed—as *imago Dei,* and (3) incorporate historical liberation into our understanding of divine providence. Contextual theologies originate within a local community but are relevant to the whole of Christianity. While each and every Christian community does not share all the same beliefs and practices, a major task of theology has always been to preserve the diachronic and synchronic unity of the church in the face of such pluralism by identifying those doctrines and practices without which a tradition cannot name itself Christian. In this continuing theological conversation, the task of marginalized perspectives is often to correct historical errors by emphasizing neglected or silenced aspects of doctrine—not to supplant one perspective with the other but in order to articulate a richer, more authentic comprehension of divine mystery. Thus, while not every Christian community need embrace the Guadalupan devotion, every Christian community can broaden its understanding of God by listening to what Guadalupe teaches us about Creation and liberation.

The Interconnectedness of All Creation

By identifying Guadalupe as the "Mother of the New Creation" Elizondo highlights several important, often neglected, aspects of the doctrine of Creation. First, by embracing the Nahuatl metaphysical perspective that sees the Creation as an interconnected and interdependent organic system, Elizondo seeks to counterbalance the dominant Western theological perspective, which has tended to focus almost exclusively on humanity as the pinnacle of the Creation. While the worldwide ecological crisis has caused the Western church to reconsider traditional understandings of the doctrine of Creation,[61] European and North American culture since the Enlightenment has tended to view the earth and its resources as objects for human manipulation and control instead of as gifts from God to be faithfully nurtured and protected. Guadalupe calls the church back to the original Gospel of Jesus Christ, in which the whole Creation is mysteriously involved in the work of Redemption. According to the biblical witness, both humanity and the nonhuman world are included in God's promises. In fact, the earliest covenant between God and humanity—the divine covenant with Noah—includes all of Creation in God's promise of redemption: "As for me, I am establishing my covenant with you and your descendants after you, and with every living creature that is with you" (Gen. 9:9–10, NRSV). Nahum M. Sarna's commentary on Genesis notes that numerous elements in the Noah story "are artful echoes of the Creation narrative. . . . Noah's ark is the matrix of a new creation, and, like Adam in the Garden of Eden, he [Noah] lives in harmony with the animals."[62] In much the same way that the Genesis account attributes the undoing of God's Creation via the flood to human sinfulness and the renewal of the Creation to God's covenant with Noah, the Guadalupe event inaugurates a new Creation: "Her presence begins to reverse the devastation of the conquest."[63] Biblical religion has always acknowledged that evil has disrupted the natural order of Creation and envisions

God's redemption in terms that transcend a personal notion of salvation to encompass all of Creation: "Then I saw a new heaven and a new earth; for the first heaven and the first earth has passed away, and the sea was no more. . . . And the one who was seated on the throne said, 'See, I am making all things new'" (Rev. 21:1,5, NRSV). Hopefully, greater emphasis on the cosmic dimension of the doctrine of Creation will allow Christian theology to embrace the radical interdependence of all life by embracing Creation's absolute dependence on God as Creator.

Imago Dei and Radical Inclusion

Second, by having Guadalupe appear as a *mestiza*, God utilized the Guadalupan event to reverse the dominant theological anthropology of the time. No longer can the racially "other" be viewed as less than human given the Virgin's "introduction of the new paradigm of partnership" in which the Indian Mother sends the *mestizo* child (Juan Diego) to call the European Christian father (the bishop) to conversion: "The integrity of the Mother, the rebirth of the conquered Indian, and the repentance of the conquering bishop . . . will be the basis of mestizo spirituality: openness to everyone without exception."[64] Consequently, a central aspect of the New Creation is a conception of the *imago Dei* that embraces and values *mestizaje*. Furthermore, as a feminine manifestation of the divine, Guadalupe challenges the church to embrace the full humanity of women: "It is a declaration that the women will no longer remain silent, passive, and subject to abuse."[65] As liberation theology broadens its scope to consider all forms of social oppression, Latinas continue to expose the gender bias underlying our patriarchal culture and reinterpret the Bible in ways that reveal the inherent dignity of women as men's equals: "So God created humankind in his image, in the image of God he created them; male and female he created them" (Gen. 1:27, NRSV). As Christians with a firm belief in a benevolent and omnipotent God, Hispanic theologians attempt to understand the intolerable realities of poverty, racism, and sexism in our society. Accordingly, any discussion of liberation must come to terms with the fact that the greatest challenge facing U.S. Latino/a theology today is the sexism ingrained in our culture. Nonetheless, many in the church still have a difficult time accepting that women are not subordinate to men, but share equally in the *imago Dei*. In the contemporary social context one of the ways in which our faithfulness to the covenant with God can, and must, be measured is the way in which women are treated in our society.[66]

Thus, Guadalupe reminds the church that contemporary conceptions of the *imago Dei* must contend with the realities of racism and sexism within the church and offer society an alternative model of community. Traditional reflections on the *imago Dei* provide us with tools to resist relationships of domination by emphasizing that (1) we are created in God's image insofar as we possess rationality, (2) we are created in God's image insofar as we have the freedom and capacity to transform the world through our work, (3) we are created in God's image insofar as we share in the capacity for self-transcendence, and (4) we are created in God's image insofar as we share in the capacity to care for others. The biblical witness understands Creation as an act of divine grace and values humanity by virtue of the fact that we are created to live in covenant with God. As an act of grace, the gift of life is unmerited, and our value as God's creatures independent of our moral choices, our physical and mental abilities, or our social status. Theologically speaking, the value and dignity given to us as a gift in the act of Creation can never be lost or taken away. Granted, the *imago Dei* is distorted by sin, yet our faith rests on the promise that through Jesus Christ, God will redeem us. Therefore, our inherent dignity as creatures in the image of God does not depend upon our moral worth, and this fact prescribes how we must treat others and how we can expect others to treat us.

Simply put, there are ways of relating to others that violate the covenant between God and God's creation, since the value and dignity we possess as God's creatures entitle each and every human being to be recognized as the image of God and treated with the appropriate respect and care. Hence, a theological anthropology informed by the Guadalupe myth (echoing a biblical understanding of Creation) reminds the church that our identity as creatures made in the image of God necessarily includes the "other" historically marginalized because of race or gender. Elizondo writes:

In the events of Tepeyac, the process of unjust and dehumanizing segregation by sex, race, class, and ethnicity is totally reversed not by providing a finished humanity but by initiating a new process by which a truly new humanity recognizing the legitimacy, beauty, and dignity of each and every human group might gradually develop and come to be. Within the new process, *mestizaje* will be transformed from a source of shame and dislocation to a source of belonging and pride.[67]

Theological reflections that consider the Guadalupan event seriously must strive to find doctrinal support for multicultural diversity and a liberating praxis of inclusion that breaks down historical barriers between human groups.

From *imago Dei* to *imago Christi*

Finally, the doctrine of Creation interpreted through a Guadalupan lens must incorporate human liberation into the unfolding of God's plans. Christian theology has always recognized the purposive character of Creation—that is, there is an order and a goal to the Creation toward which all things point, and this purpose is revealed to us in the person and work of Jesus Christ: "He is the image of the invisible God, the firstborn of all creation; for in him all things in heaven and on earth were created, things visible and invisible, whether thrones or dominions or rulers or powers —all things have been created through him and for him. He himself is before all things, and in him all things hold together" (Col. 1:15–17, NRSV). And just as through Christ God first ordered Creation, so through Christ God promises to redeem Creation. The messianic promise of the Gospel is that of a new Creation in which injustice and suffering are replaced with fellowship and celebration: "See, the home of God is among mortals. He will dwell with them; they will be his peoples, and God himself will be with them; he will wipe every tear from their eyes. Death will be no more; mourning and crying and pain will be no more, for the first things have passed away" (Rev. 21:3–4, NRSV). In much the same way, Guadalupe restored the sick to health and transformed broken relationships into Christian fellowship. Comparing and contrasting the evangelization of the Native peoples by the Spaniards to the new evangelization embodied in Guadalupe, Elizondo writes, "Our Lady prefers to offer us a foretaste of heaven. This is the new method, which is actually the method of Jesus and which is supposed to be lived out in the Eucharist."[68] Although grounded in a mystical experience that is difficult to express through language, this foretaste of heaven leads to concrete emancipatory praxis: "Her presence is to have immediate results, and the people are to experience her saving powers in their very flesh."[69] Consequently, a doctrine of Creation that embraces the interdependence of all of God's creatures by definition desires the liberation of Creation from sin and death. Led by the Holy Spirit, we are called to be God's partners (1 Cor. 3:9) in liberation (understood holistically to include spiritual salvation and historical liberation) by continuing the ministry of reconciliation begun by Christ—a ministry that clearly involves the transformation of unjust social structures (Luke 4:18–19).

I have argued that at its core the Guadalupe event is a Christological critique of dominant forms of Christianity that have strayed from the original liberating ministry and message of Jesus Christ—that, in spite of Protestant discomfort, Latino/a popular Catholicism stands well within the orthodox Christian tradition while articulating a culturally unique witness to the person and work of Christ. Theological reflection is "Christian" insofar as it acknowledges the centrality of Jesus Christ in God's plan for salvation. Christ's saving work, properly understood through the lens of *mestizaje,* embraces all of humanity and resists racist theologies and ideologies. In order to gain a deeper understanding of the work of Christ manifest in the social realities of *mestizaje,* the next chapter engages the doctrine of Christ in order to affirm that we cannot know who God is or what it means to be human apart from God's activity in Christ. Accordingly, that which is salvific about Jesus Christ is not his static essence (his Jewishness, his maleness, etc.) but his complete obedience to God's will in completing the work of liberation and reconciliation, even when such obedience meant certain death.

5

The *Mestizo* Christ

This investigation defends the concept of *mestizaje* as a liberating theological metaphor through a critical retrieval of Christian doctrines. In the previous chapter, I analyzed Virgilio Elizondo's interpretation of the Guadalupe theophany as an instance of *mestizaje* often associated with Mexican nationalism that nonetheless contains valuable resources for a theology of liberation. Drawing upon certain Creation themes emphasized in the Guadalupan devotion, I examined the doctrine of *imago Dei* through the lens of *mestizaje* in order to articulate a more inclusive theological anthropology that embraces the racially and ethnically "other." In this chapter, I explore *mestizaje* as a Christological metaphor that allows us to see how in Jesus of Nazareth God became incarnate as *mestizo*. Working within the framework of Chalcedonian Christology, this work affirms Jesus as both Lord (*kyrios*) and Savior (*soter*), emphasizing the centrality of the Incarnation through which "both humanity and divinity come together to create a new reality that includes both while preserving their differences."[1] At the same time, recognizing the limitations of the static metaphysical language of Nicaea (325 CE) and Chalcedon (451 CE), special effort is made to understand the saving work of Christ in light of the earthly life and ministry of Jesus. Therefore, since Jesus himself identifies with the racialized other—God becoming incarnate as a marginalized Galilean—the church should affirm and actively struggle to preserve the full humanity of those marginalized and oppressed because of race or ethnicity.

The metaphor of *mestizaje* provides valuable insights for understanding the person and work of Christ. If, as Virgilio Elizondo contends, Jesus of Nazareth was biologically and culturally a *mestizo*, then it is important to come to terms with the racially mixed status of the historical Jesus in order to fully understand the Incarnation. Nonetheless, in linking Jesus' biological heritage to his saving work, we risk granting ethnicity soteriological status, hence the importance of recalling that what is salvific about

Jesus Christ is not his static essence (his Jewishness, his maleness, etc.) but his praxis (in complete obedience to God's will). Consequently, embracing *mestizaje* as a liberating theological metaphor demands our reconceptualizing *mestizaje* as fluid and open-ended—a personal and communal identity constantly negotiated at the boundaries of cultural interaction. When this revitalized metaphor is applied to the person and work of Christ, it yields a Trinitarian Christology that focuses on the nature of Jesus' relationships with his neighbors, his relationship to God, and his relationship to the dominant religious and civil authorities.[2]

Those U.S. Latino/a theologies employing *mestizaje* to transcend ethnic and cultural exclusion understand the main work of Christ as liberation. By emphasizing the ethical dimension implicit in the act of embracing *mestizo* identity, then relating Jesus' Galilean identity to the contemporary situation, we can move toward an understanding of Christology in terms of God's activity in the world. The result is a uniquely Christian theological use of *mestizaje* as a concrete liberating praxis grounded in the doctrine of the Incarnation that provides a valuable framework for discussing the relationship between divine revelation and human culture. Accordingly, a *mestizo* reinterpretation of the doctrine of the Incarnation affirms that God is incarnate here and now in our own work for liberation—that is, incarnate in human cultures—by empowering believers to combat injustices like racism within the church and in the broader society.

The Centrality of Christological Questions

Christology is a subdiscipline of theology that reflects systematically on the person and work of Jesus Christ in light of the Word of God, Christian praxis, and Christian worship. While Christian theology cannot be reduced to Christology, understanding the person and work of Jesus the Christ provides the focal point from which to understand all other doctrines. In other words, what makes Christian theological reflection "Christian" is the centrality given to the saving work of Christ in God's plans for humankind. Recalling the words of Jesus to his disciples, the principal task of Christian theology is to answer the question, "But who do you say that I am?" (Matt. 16:15; Mark 8:31; Luke 9:20). At times it seems there are as many answers to this question as there are Christian believers. For some scholars the answer lies in rediscovering the "historical Jesus" by piecing together fragments known about Jesus from noncanonical sources, while for other scholars knowledge of Jesus is limited to the witness of the synoptic Gospels. Either way, the Jesus of history is divorced from the Jesus of faith. Meanwhile, for many churchgoing Christians, Jesus is an amalgam of what they have learned in church combined with what they have gleaned from popular culture—like Mel Gibson's recent film *The Passion of the Christ* (2004) or devotional literature like Rick Warren's *The Purpose Driven Life* (2002)—to create a private and personal Christ. In response to this veritable Babel of interpretations, Christology is the attempt to say, "God is . . . ," by affirming God's ultimate self-revelation in the Christ.

Since its earliest days, the church has debated how to interpret this revelatory event and what it communicates to us about God. This debate has yet to be satisfactorily resolved. Often, Christological reflection begins with the dogmatic formula of the Council of Chalcedon (451 CE) that Christ is fully human and fully divine: "two natures without confusion, without change, without division, without separation—the difference of the natures being by no means taken away because of the union, but rather the distinctive character of each nature being preserved."[3] However, dissatisfaction with ancient philosophical conceptualizations of Christ's nature has generated a plurality of alternative, often incongruous, Christological formulations.[4] One very influential example is Jon Sobrino's liberating Christ: "In traditional Catholic theology it has been customary to start with the dogmatic formulation of the Council of Chalcedon . . . but it hardly seems suitable or adequate as a point of departure."[5] Sobrino opts to begin with the "historical Jesus," by which he means "the person, teaching, attitudes, and deeds of Jesus of Nazareth insofar as they are accessible, in a more or less general way, to historical and exegetical investigation."[6] Emphasizing the life and ministry of Jesus, not just the cross and resurrection, Sobrino seeks a "satisfactory midway point between two extremes: turning Christ into an abstraction on the one hand, or putting him to direct and immediate ideological uses on the other."[7] By beginning with the earthly ministry of Jesus rather than the abstract formulations of the first four ecumenical councils, Sobrino places the historical liberation of the poor and oppressed at the center of any understanding of the salvific work of Christ.[8]

So while the Chalcedonian definition states the problem correctly and establishes the limits of a Christian understanding of the Christ/Messiah, it does not bring us any closer to understanding *how* the Incarnation achieves salvation. Still, there is general agreement among theologians that in the person of Jesus (called the Christ) we learn most fully what it means to be both divine and human. Every Christology makes reference to the historical person Jesus of Nazareth and attempts to explain the nature of the relationship between this particular human being and the eternal God. While different Christological traditions have interpreted this special relationship in a variety of ways, they all relate the person Jesus of Nazareth to God's plan for salvation. The earliest creedal formulations found in Scripture use titles to refer to Jesus such as "Jesus is Lord" (1 Cor. 12:3) and "Messiah" (Mark 8:29) that necessarily link him to soteriological concerns. Consequently, it "is taken to be indisputable that, according to the New Testament pattern of events, the life span designated as 'Jesus Christ,' whether interpreted primarily 'from above' or 'from below' in its space-time juxtapositions, has to do with a *coming* into the world and with an *overcoming* of the world."[9] In other words, speaking of Jesus as the Christ of God is a foundational theological statement that orients theology toward matters of liberation.

Jesus and Politics

Political theologian Jürgen Moltmann asserts that wherever "Jesus is acknowledged as the Christ of God, Christian faith is to be found,"[10] begging the question, how do Christians understand the title "Christ"? Jesus of Nazareth is identified in the New Testament by the Greek term *ho christos,* the Christ, from the Hebrew (*ha-*) *mashiah,* the Messiah, meaning an anointed person or the anointed one. In the centuries prior to the life of Jesus, various messianic expectations coexisted within Judaism, many directly traceable to the Old Testament itself, but reaching a fever pitch during the Second Temple period (c. 352 BCE–68 CE), especially after the death of Julius Caesar (44 BCE) when several Jewish groups reasoned that political instability in the Roman Republic would facilitate a successful rebellion in Jerusalem.[11] Within early Christian theological reflection the conviction that Jesus was the Christ, the Messiah expected by Israel, led to an understanding of the Old Testament term *anointed* as referring to a future agent of divine deliverance. However, recent scholarly consensus argues that to understand the term *messiah* as denoting only one specific figure distorts the broad range of messianic expectations that thrived within Judaism between 200 BCE and 100 CE. These scholars contend that this conception of messianism is marginal to the dominant forms of Judaism at the time, appearing only infrequently in the Old Testament and Jewish writings of the intertestamental period; some even maintain that messianism is tangential to Jesus' own ministry and the development of New Testament Christology.[12] More recently, biblical scholar William Horbury has offered a contrasting interpretation of messianism, arguing not only that messianism played a more centralized role in Second Temple Judaism but also that the flourishing messianism of the Herodian period directly contributed to the formation of the Christian cult of Christ.[13]

Still, despite this diversity of messianic views, one aspect of first-century messianism remains constant: whatever else one understands by the term *messiah*, it is always used in reference to God's chosen leaders—be they prophet, priest, or king. Considering that for first-century Jews there was no hard-and-fast distinction between religion and politics, sacred and secular, the various expected messianic figures—whether a messianic king from the house of David, an eschatological prophet, a messianic priest from the house of Aaron, the Righteous Teacher of the Qumran community, or the messianic movements described by the historian Josephus —share the prevalent Jewish mind-set that discerns the will of God in all aspects of life. Consequently, some Jewish messianisms focused intensely on the affairs of government while others regarded temporal governments as contrary to God's will, yet all subsumed the political under the theological insofar as there is no part of life that stands outside religion. In other words, there are political consequences to messianic faith, so unraveling and interpreting the interrelation of theology and politics becomes a necessary task of Christian theology.

Accordingly, two separate but interconnected arguments contribute to an understanding of how Jesus engaged the political sphere of life by embracing, rejecting, or transforming aspects of first-century Jewish messianic expectations. First, a historical inquiry into the word *messiah* confirms the claim that the title messiah cannot be interpreted apolitically. Second, a look at the historical development of Christology—under the influence of Hellenistic philosophical conceptions of God and divinity— reveals that the political dimension was gradually eroded from the Christian understanding of Messiah. This work seeks to recover Jesus' own self understanding of *messiah* as God's anointed ruler in order to identify the concrete political consequences of acknowledging Jesus as "the Christ of God" (Moltmann) for contemporary Christian faith.

Toward a "Political" Messiah

The historical origins of Israel's messianic hopes are traceable to the Davidic monarchy in the Old Testament. In the New Testament this nationalistic hope underlies Zechariah's vision at the birth of his son John (the Baptist):

> Blessed be the Lord God of Israel, for he has looked favorably on his people and redeemed them. He has raised up a mighty savior for us in the house of his servant David, as he spoke through the mouth of his holy prophets from of old, that we would be saved from our enemies and from the hand of all who hate us. (Luke 1:68–71, NRSV)

Here the evangelist locates the life of Jesus of Nazareth within a messianic theological framework in which the hope of the people of Israel is linked to an anointed political leader from the Davidic line—perhaps hinting at the reestablishment of the old monarchy—while suggesting that this "mighty savior" comes not to vanquish old enemies with an iron fist but to "guide our feet into the way of peace" (Luke 1:79, NRSV). While there existed a plurality of messianic expectations within first-century Judaism, it cannot be denied that the notion of a singular figure anointed by God to restore the nationalistic hopes of Israel was among the accepted interpretations thriving within the various Jewish sects.

God anoints (*mashiah*) kings, priests, and prophets throughout the Old Testament, yet it is David's anointing in favor of Saul that indissolubly unites the notion of divine deliverance with Israel's national interests. While the expectation of national divine deliverance originates in the Exodus narrative in which Moses acts as God's chosen agent of liberation, the Israelites' identity is primarily theological, since they are described as the people who worship the God of Abraham, the God of Isaac, and the God of Jacob (Exod. 3:6; 3:15). Yet when David becomes "messiah," it is in response to the nation's rebellion against the divinely established political order for an inherited monarchy that projects a powerful image to the rest of the world: "We are determined to have a king over us, so that we may be like other nations, and that our king may govern us and go out before us and fight our battles" (1 Sam. 8:19–20, NRSV). Consequently, while Moses was God's anointed prophet whose primary task was liberating the Israelites from slavery, David was God's anointed king burdened with preserving Israel's political independence and coalescing its national identity over against the imperialist aggression of its geographic neighbors. Granted, there is a theological dimension to God's favoring David in place of Saul, who had disobeyed God's commandments and "rejected the word of the Lord," so consequently the Lord rejected his kingship (1 Sam. 15:26, NRSV); nevertheless, the focus of David's mission was to unite all the tribes of Israel and rule over them for thirty-three years, thereby establishing the pattern for all Israelite monarchs to come (2 Sam. 5:1–5). Not surprisingly, one finds prophecies throughout the Old Testament concerning future Davidic kings who will return the nation to its former greatness.

The prophet Micah identifies Bethlehem, David's birthplace, as the source of "one who is to rule in Israel, whose origin is from of old, from ancient days" (v. 2); the prophet Amos condemned Israel's political division between northern and southern kingdoms and wanted a unified nation under the rule of a Davidic king (Amos 9:11); during the Babylonian exile the prophet Ezekiel envisions a new covenant between God and Israel in which the lost sheep of Israel return to their land and the Davidic dynasty is restored: "I will set up over them one shepherd, my servant David, and he shall feed them: he shall feed them and be their shepherd" (Ezek. 34:23, NRSV); the restitution of the Temple in Jerusalem—facilitated by the Persian empire's more tolerant policies under Cyrus (identified by the prophet Isaiah as a "Messiah")—returned to prominence certain Israelite traditions, exemplified by the Zion and Davidic motifs: "Rejoice greatly, O daughter Zion! Shout aloud, O daughter Jerusalem! Lo, your king comes to you" (Zech. 9:9, NRSV); "And the house of David shall be like God, like the angel of the Lord, at their head" (Zech. 12:8, NRSV). However, it is with the prophecies of Daniel during the Babylonian exile that Israel's tenuous political existence gave rise to eschatologically oriented interpretations of God's Anointed ruler to whom will be "given dominion and glory and kingship, that all peoples, nations, and languages should serve him. His dominion is an everlasting dominion that shall not pass away, and his kingship is one that shall never be destroyed" (Dan. 7:14, NRSV).

In postexilic times, various messianic texts in the Old Testament apocryphal and pseudepigraphical writings attest to a shared expectation of a divinely promised ruler who will restore Israel politically and theologically, linking national deliverance to the reestablishment of governance according to the Word of God (Torah). The book of 1 Enoch contains a longing for the Messiah who will bring judgment and save the people of Israel from all who assail them: "I kept seeing till the Lord of the sheep came unto them and took in his hand the rod of his wrath and smote the earth. . . . Then I kept seeing till a throne was erected in a pleasant land."[14] In the Psalms of Solomon, the political restoration of the Davidic dynasty is inseparable from the theological longing for divine deliverance: "See, Lord, and raise up for them their king, the son of David, to rule over your servant Israel in the time known to you, O God. . . . At his warning the nations will flee from his presence; and he will condemn sinners by the thoughts of their hearts."[15] Furthermore, after the Jewish rebellion against the Syrians (c. 164 BCE), the restoration of Temple worship in Jerusalem contributed to a strong nationalism laced with expectations of God's anointed Warrior-Deliverer who would restore authentic cultic worship according to the Mosaic Law and return Israel to its ancient glory. The book of 1 Maccabees sought to legitimize the Hasmonean dynasty—which controlled both the Temple priesthood and the monarchy until the time of Herod the Great—because many pious Jews questioned their right to rule. Still, in spite of such pragmatic political maneuvering, Mattathias's armed resistance against the Syrian king also appears motivated by "zeal for the law" (1 Macc. 2:26–27), suggesting that messianic expectations were deeply woven into both the national and the religious consciousness of first-century Jews and thus ought never to be interpreted apolitically. According to Josephus and Philo, even the ascetic Essenes—a politically passive party—fought in the war against the Romans (66–70 CE). While our present knowledge of the Essenes is scant and unreliable, most sources agree that they were known for both their ascetic practices and their commitment to pacifism (Essenes were not allowed to make or carry weapons of war except for a walking staff for personal defense when traveling).[16] In fact, the notion that God will liberate the community from its enemies is preserved within the Qumran prophecies:

> The King of Glory is with us and the host of His spirits is with our steps. . . . Rise up, O Hero, Take your captives, O Glorious One, and take Your plunder, O You Who do valiantly. Lay your hand upon the neck of Your enemies, and Your foot upon the backs of the slain. Crush the nations, Your adversaries, and let Your sword devour flesh. Fill Your land with glory, and Your inheritance with blessing. An abundance of cattle is in Your fields, silver and gold in Your palaces. O Zion, rejoice greatly, and rejoice, all you cities of Judah.[17]

Contrary to scholarship that defines first-century messianic expectations of a promised deliverer as marginal to the dominant Jewish traditions, it is evident that a consistent messianic theme runs through the Old Testament that easily lent itself to a variety of interpretations, as preserved in such diverse Jewish literature as the intertestamental Judeo-Hellenistic literature, the Septuagint, the Targums, and the Qumran fragments.

Whether the Messiah is understood as a single individual—an anointed king, priest, or prophet—or collectively as God's chosen people Israel, the prevailing view of "messiah" during the time of Jesus has profound political implications. The expected Messiah is God's chosen leader in a tradition of interpretation dating back to the formative texts of Israelite national identity in which Moses delivered the Israelites from captivity in Egypt and David preserved the nation from Philistine control. Thus, in the Christian Gospels we find evidence that the people of Israel were awaiting some sign that would identify God's chosen savior who would bring about the longed-for national deliverance:

> Now there was a man in Jerusalem whose name was Simeon; this man was righteous and devout, looking forward to the consolation of Israel, and the Holy Spirit rested on him. It had been revealed to him by the Holy Spirit that he would not see death before he had seen the Lord's Messiah. Guided by the Spirit, Simeon came into the temple; and when the parents brought in the child Jesus, to do for him what was customary under the law, Simeon took him in his arms and praised God, saying: "Master, now you are dismissing your servant in peace, according to your word; for my eyes have seen your salvation, which you have prepared in the presence of all peoples, a light for revelation to the Gentiles and for glory to your people Israel." (Luke 2:25–32, NRSV)

Although Jesus did not fulfill the political expectations of those who expected a national savior, a political dimension persisted throughout early Christian literature that not only acknowledged Jesus as anointed with the Spirit (Isa. 61:1–2; Luke 4:18; Acts 4:25–27; 10:38), but also proclaimed him "Christ" and "Lord" (Luke 2:12; Acts 2:36). Furthermore, as Christ/Messiah, Jesus is identified as "Son of David," "king of Israel," and "King of the Jews" (Luke 1:32; 2:4, 11; 3:31; Mark 12:35–37; 14:61–62; 15:1–32).

The letters of Paul, representing the chronologically earliest Christian literature, also identify Jesus as the Christ ("Messiah") of God, quoting the prophet Isaiah: "And again Isaiah says, 'The root of Jesse shall come, the one who rises to rule the Gentiles; in him the Gentiles shall hope" (Rom. 15:12, NRSV). In the seven letters regarded as genuine, Paul does not utilize *christos* as a general term but always as a title reserved exclusively for only one person, Jesus. Undoubtedly, Paul and his readers were familiar with contemporary Jewish messianic expectations, yet Paul's letters never explicitly argue that Jesus is the long-expected *christos* of Israel. Rather, they define the very concept of divine anointing in terms of the life, ministry, death, and resurrection of Jesus, the *one* Christ of God. While Paul does identify Jesus as descended from David (Rom. 1:3–4), presuming some knowledge of Israel's nationalistic messianic hopes, his use of the title "Christ" always refers to Jesus' soteriological mission rather than any temporal political agenda. Paul consistently emphasizes that Jesus Christ died on the cross (1 Cor. 1:13, 17–18; 2:2, 8; 2 Cor. 13:4; Gal. 3:1; 6:12, 14; Phil. 2:8; 3:18), demonstrating that for Paul and the earliest Christian communities the title "Messiah" became intimately linked with the death and resurrection of Jesus for the eternal salvation of all humankind. At the same time, the fact that Paul employed such a politically and theologically loaded term to describe Jesus' divine mission implies an attempt to build upon common messianic expectations even while radically transforming them. Although Paul does not explicitly link Jesus' role as "the Christ" to any particular first-century Jewish conception of Messiah, it is clear that for early Christians (who were themselves Jewish), the life, ministry, death, and resurrection of Jesus of Nazareth were interpreted in terms of Old Testament prophecies about an anointed figure proclaiming God's sovereignty over all of humankind. Thus we find that in the book of Acts Paul articulates a distinctly Jewish understanding of "messiah" while translating the term for the Gentile world:

> And Paul went in, as was his custom, and on three Sabbath days argued with them from the scriptures, explaining and proving that it was necessary for the Messiah to suffer and to rise from the dead, and saying, "This is the Messiah, Jesus whom I am proclaiming to you." Some of them [the Jews in the synagogue] were persuaded and joined Paul and Silas, as did a great many of the devout Jews and not a few of the leading women. (Acts 17:2–4)

That is to say, Paul is here convincing fellow Jews that the one whom the Christians are proclaiming as Messiah is the Messiah of Israel, but contrary to first-century Warrior-Deliverer expectations, "it was necessary for the Messiah to suffer and to rise from the dead" (v. 3). Accordingly, we must assume that in spite of the Hellenistic context of Paul's apostolic mission, his understanding of messiah preserves some of the political implications present in various first-century Judaisms. Admittedly, Paul expands the meaning of the Messiah's rule to encompass the Gentiles, but here Paul stands well within an accepted prophetic tradition found in Amos, Isaiah, and other Old Testament prophets who affirm the sovereignty of the one true God by calling all nations to obedience and salvation.

The various first-century political players each had their own interpretation of the role and power of the Messiah, yet all shared in the hope and expectation of a messianic figure. The earliest Christian communities embraced these expectations as a framework for understanding the life, ministry, and death of Jesus of Nazareth, who is universally acknowledged in first-century Christian literature as the Christ (*ho christos*). Still, the question remains whether Jesus' own understanding of messiah preserves the political dimension so prevalent in first-century Judaism.

Jesus Transforms Messianic Expectations

Our knowledge of the earthly life and work of Jesus the Christ comes primarily from the canonical Gospels (Matthew, Mark, Luke, and John), texts that reflect the beliefs and concerns of particular Christian communities yet—in spite of differences and inconsistencies—reveal a consistent narrative at the heart of early Christian literature. Typically, scholars view the synoptics (Mark, Matthew, and Luke) as more representational of historical fact and the Gospel of John as muting the historical details of Jesus' life in order to emphasize the eternally preexistent Word of God (John 1:14; 8:58; 17:1, 5, 24). Nevertheless, it is inaccurate to presume that the synoptic Gospels portray Jesus as a human teacher of wisdom while John's Gospel presents Jesus as a divine miracle worker, since there exists within the synoptics an implicit high Christology in which Jesus understands himself as greater than the Old Testament prophets (Mark 2:21–28; Matt. 16:13–20; Luke 11:29–32) and speaks with divine authority (Mark 1:21–28; Matt. 5:21–48; 7:13–29), while John's Gospel explores the human dimension of Jesus' earthly life (John 2:1–12; 4:6; 5:2–18; 11:33–35) to reveal someone who feels compassion, thirsts and hungers, and is even moved to tears. Furthermore, certain themes remain constant throughout the various Jesus narratives: Jesus proclaimed the imminent kingdom of God (Matt. 12:28; Mark 1:15; Luke 11:20); Jesus worked miracles that were signs of God's impending reign (Mark 3:22–30; John 10:31–38); Jesus embraced his Davidic descent (Mark 11:1–11; Matt. 21:1–11; Luke 19:28–40; John 12:12–19); and Jesus accepted his mission as the Messiah of God empowered by the Spirit to bring good news to an afflicted people (Isa. 61:1–3; Mark 8:27–30; Luke 6:20–21; 9:18–21; Matt. 5:3–12; 16:13–20; John 4:25–26). Given the political aspect of many first-century Jewish notions of the Messiah, Jesus' own self-understanding as Son of David and Messiah created political consequences for the earliest (Jewish) Christians, who were nurtured and formed by these messianic expectations. At the same time, Jesus rejected many such expectations and radically reinterpreted them in light of his obedience "to the point of death—even death on a cross" (Phil. 2:8, NRSV).

A political theology guided by the teachings of Jesus understands "politics" in its broadest sense as the social organization of human communities and not just the machinations of particular parties or states. Still, if Jesus of Nazareth is the promised messiah of Israel, then the historical actuality is far removed from most first-century expectations. Jesus made no claims to any temporal kingdom but understood himself as the Christ— God's promised deliverer—whose kingdom is God's own independent of and above all human political structures, yet embodied in human political structures. Accordingly, Jesus transforms the understanding of messiah as God's anointed ruler (prophet, priest, king) by modeling a radically different form of leadership. Therefore, those who claim Jesus as "the Christ of God" (Moltmann) are placing themselves under his rule, declaring God's self-revelation in Jesus the Christ the standard by which all human political projects are judged and evaluated.

The title "Christ" carries the meaning "one anointed to rule," yet the life and ministry of Jesus of Nazareth, universally acknowledged by early Christians to be the Christ, can be interpreted as a rejection of precisely those political expectations in which the Messiah comes to overthrow Israel's oppressors and reestablish a temporal order under the Word of God. Standing before Pilate, the embodiment of temporal political power in first-century Jerusalem, Jesus was accused of political sedition for claiming to be "King of the Jews":

> Then Pilate entered the headquarters again, summoned Jesus, and asked him, "Are you the King of the Jews?" Jesus answered, "Do you ask this on your own, or did others tell you about me?" Pilate replied, "I am not a Jew, am I? Your own nation and the chief priests have handed you over

to me. What have you done?" Jesus answered, "My kingdom is not from this world. If my kingdom were from this world, my followers would be fighting to keep me from being handed over to the Jews. But as it is, my kingdom is not from here." (John 18:33–36, NRSV)

Pilate then asks, "So you are a king?" to which Jesus replies, "You say that I am a king. For this I was born, and for this I came into the world, to testify to the truth. Everyone who belongs to the truth listens to my voice" (v. 37). Conversely, just because Jesus defines his kingdom as "not from this world" does not mean that followers of Jesus ought to disengage from the concerns of this world, as demonstrated by the consistent themes of Jesus' preaching: poverty (Matt. 23:14; Mark 10:17–27; Luke 6:20–25), taxation (Matt. 9:10; 17:24–27; 22:15–22; Mark 12:13–17), leadership (Matt. 20:24–28; Luke 22:24–30; John 13:1–5, 12–14; 15:12–17), wealth (Matt. 19:16–26; Luke 16:10–13; 18:18–27).

Jesus' own self-understanding references Isaiah's suffering servant while expressing hope in terms of resurrection: "Then he began to teach them that the Son of Man must undergo great suffering, and be rejected by the elders, the chief priests, and the scribes, and be killed, and after three days rise again" (Mark 8:31, NRSV). While the notion that the righteous will suffer for the sake of righteousness is well established in first-century Jewish thought (Isa. 53:10–11; Daniel 7; Wisdom 5:1–5; 2 Maccabees 7:23), Christ interprets his suffering—and the suffering his followers will likely endure—in terms of God's impending reign: "The time is fulfilled, and the kingdom of God has come near; repent, and believe in the good news" (Mark 1:15, NRSV). In other words, there are serious "political" consequences for those who choose to follow Jesus:

> Then he said to them, "Nation will rise against nation, and kingdom against kingdom; there will be great earthquakes, and in various places famines and plagues; and there will be dreadful portents and great signs from heaven.
>
> "But before all this occurs, they will arrest you and persecute you; they will hand you over to the synagogues and prisons, and you will be brought before kings and governors because of my name. This will give you an opportunity to testify. So make up your minds not to prepare your defense in advance; for I will give you words and a wisdom that none of your opponents will be able to withstand or contradict. You will

be betrayed even by parents and brothers, by relatives and friends; and they will put some of you to death. You will be hated by all because of my name. But not a hair of your head will perish. By your endurance you will gain your souls. (Luke 21:10–19, NRSV)

However, this suffering is alleviated by the risen Christ's imminent return:

"When you see Jerusalem surrounded by armies, then know that its desolation has come near. . . . For there will be great distress on the earth and wrath against this people; they will fall by the edge of the words and be taken away as captives among all nations; and Jerusalem will be trampled on by the Gentiles, until the times of the Gentiles are fulfilled.

"There will be signs in the sun, the moon, and the stars, and on the earth distress among nations confused by the roaring of the sea and the waves. People will faint from fear and foreboding of what is coming upon the world, for the powers of the heavens will be shaken. Then they will see 'the Son of Man coming in a cloud' with power and great glory. Now when these things begin to take place, stand up and raise your heads, because your redemption is drawing near." (Luke 21:20, 23b–28, NRSV)

Not surprisingly, the first Christians interpreted the fall of Jerusalem (c. 70 CE) as the sign of the Parousia, or Second Coming (Matt. 24:3–8; Mark 13:24–27; Luke 21:25–28; Acts 1:11), yet once it became evident to succeeding generations of Christians that Christ's return was not imminent, there followed a shift in emphasis in Christian thought. The delay of the Parousia proved a major concern during the apostolic era but ultimately did not undermine Christian faith, as evidenced by Peter's teachings on the subject:

First of all you must understand this, that in the last days scoffers will come, scoffing and indulging their own lusts and saying, "Where is the promise of his coming? For ever since our ancestors died, all things continue as they were from the beginning of creation!" They deliberately ignore this fact, that by the Word of God heavens existed long ago and an earth was formed out of water and by means of water, through which the world of that time was deluged with water and perished. But by the same word the present heavens and earth have been reserved for fire, being kept until the day of judgment and destruction of the godless.

But do not ignore this one fact, beloved, that with the Lord one day is like a thousand years, and a thousand years are like one day. The Lord is not slow about his promise, as some think of slowness, but is patient with you, not wanting any to perish, but all to come to repentance. But the day of the Lord will come like a thief, and then the heavens will pass away with a loud noise, and the elements will be dissolved with fire, and the earth and everything that is done on it will be disclosed. (2 Pet. 3:3–7, NRSV)

It is more important that believers be prepared for Christ's return (Luke 21:34–36) than worry about the specific time frame of the Parousia, for not even Jesus knows God's will on this matter: "But about that day and hour no one knows, neither the angels of heaven nor the Son, but only the Father" (Matt. 24:36, NRSV). Here the apostolic teaching is consistent with Jesus' own: "Keep awake therefore, for you do not know on what day your Lord is coming. . . . Therefore you also must be ready, for the Son of Man is coming at an unexpected hour" (Matt. 24:42, 44, NRSV). The consequence for the development of Christian doctrine was a move away from preoccupation with eschatology toward a preoccupation with the present, in which the church is understood collectively as the body of Christ (1 Cor. 12:12–31) through which God brings about reconciliation (2 Cor. 5:11–21). This identification of the *ecclesia* with the risen Christ (Eph. 1:20–23; 3:5–10) understands the present age as a foretaste of the kingdom of God—delayed but still expected—in which the church, by the power of the Holy Spirit, participates in the messianic mission of Jesus Christ to reconcile sinful humanity with God. In other words, the delay of the Parousia does not call into question the promises of Christ but is evidence of God's extreme grace in Christ, "not wanting any to perish, but all to come to repentance" (2 Pet. 3:9, NRSV), for "through him God was pleased to reconcile to himself all things, whether on earth or in heaven, by making peace through the blood of his cross" (Col. 1:20, NRSV). Thus, as Jürgen Moltmann contends, Christian self-understanding is grounded in the messianic mission of the earthly Jesus, "which was neglected in the christological dogma of Nicaea," and which provides the foundation for a Trinitarian Christology that transcends the doctrinal language of two-natures Christology so that Jesus cannot be reduced to a mere human preacher nor elevated to the status of the Docetic Christ.[18]

In light of Jesus' messianic self-understanding, it is appropriate for Christian theology to look to the teachings of Jesus for guidance in the realm of social ethics. Yet, what we find is that rather than taking the path of direct political engagement—for example, by linking his proclamation of God's impending kingdom to an existing political movement—Jesus chooses the path of renunciation: "The choice that he made in rejecting the crown and accepting the cross was the commitment to such a degree of faithfulness to the character of the divine love that he was willing for its sake to sacrifice 'effectiveness.'"[19] Thus, it is not surprising that as Christian doctrine developed, the political/social dimension of Jesus' ministry became more muted, since Jesus himself reminds us, "My kingdom is not from this world" (John 18:36, NRSV). All the same, the New Testament retains vestiges of a strong social ethic centered on the act of taking up the cross (Mark 8:34–38; Matt. 16:24–27; Luke 9:23–26), which saw its maturation in the costly political stance of the early Christian martyrs. Theologian Zaida Maldonado Pérez argues that martyrdom is "a subversive act against the state and the dominant pagan culture,"[20] with strong Old Testament precursors but whose paradigmatic example is the martyrdom of Stephen in Acts 7:54–60. Just before his death, Stephen experiences a vision of Jesus exalted "at the right hand of God" (Acts 7:56, NRSV), challenging and undermining the dominant Jewish view that Jesus was a justly executed blasphemer. Stephen's martyrdom is a reaffirmation of the power of the cross through which God challenges dominant notions of power. Temporal powers led Jesus to the criminal's cross, but God's power raised Jesus from death and glorified him at the right hand of the Father; temporal powers tried to take the life of the early church martyrs, yet God raised them to eternal life; temporal powers continue to legislate life and death today, but Jesus' teaching still stands as the ultimate countercultural force: "For those who want to save their life will lose it, and those who lose their life for my sake, and for the sake of the gospel, will save it" (Mark 8:35, NRSV); "No one has greater love than this, to lay down one's life for one's friends" (John 15:13, NRSV); "Let the same mind be in you that was in Christ Jesus, who, though he was in the form of God, did not regard equality with God as something to be exploited" (Phil. 2:5–6, NRSV). Accordingly, while the New Testament presents a range of ethical instruction, it also contains a consistent unifying narrative grounded in the view that things are not as they ought to be and only Jesus Christ brings genuine liberation from every kind of bondage.

The culture of Jesus' time expected a political messiah, yet Jesus stands outside these messianic expectations insofar as his own self-understanding as the Messiah of God rejected the Warrior-Deliverer pattern. Instead, Jesus interprets his own mission as Messiah primarily through the lens of the Suffering Servant portions of the book of Isaiah. Not only is John the Baptist ("the voice of one crying in the wilderness") linked to Isaiah 40 (Luke 3:4–6), Jesus lays the path for his entire ministry by reading Isaiah 61 ("The Spirit of the Lord is upon me, because he has anointed me to bring good news to the poor"), then proclaims, "Today this scripture has been fulfilled in your hearing" (Luke 4:21, NRSV). The Gospel of Matthew also interprets Jesus' earthly mission in terms of Isaiah 42:1–4:

> This was to fulfill what had been spoken through the prophet Isaiah: "Here is my servant, whom I have chosen, my beloved, with whom my soul is well pleased. I will put my Spirit upon him, and he will proclaim justice to the Gentiles. He will not wrangle or cry aloud, nor will anyone hear his voice in the streets. He will not break a bruised reed or quench a smoldering wick until he brings justice to victory. And in his name the Gentiles will hope." (Matt. 12:17–21, NRSV)

By choosing to follow the paradigm of Isaiah's Messiah—the King (Isaiah 1–37), the Suffering Servant (Isaiah 38–55), and the Anointed Conqueror (Isaiah 56–66)—Jesus understood his own ministry in terms that were at least partly political, affirming in his own words the calling and anointing of God to bring justice and liberation. Nevertheless, by interpreting kingship in terms of the Suffering Servant, Jesus subverts dominant views that expected God's anointed leader to bring about change by means of political rule. Jesus discards the false god called the state in recognition of the absolute sovereignty of God over all nations and empires through a radical reevaluation of values in which divine rule is embodied in the suffering servant who was oppressed and afflicted "like a lamb that is led to the slaughter" (Isa. 53:7, NRSV). Accordingly, we find in Jesus' life and ministry broad guidelines for our political life together under the Word of God, not in terms of a particular political agenda but as a general orientation toward what any temporal government needs to be and do in order to be a just and righteous government in the eyes of God. As a result, any theology guided by Jesus' messianic mission is necessarily adversarial and willing to take a costly stance in which martyrdom is often the consequence of following Christ.[21]

Some Conclusions about Person and Work of Christ

In answering questions about the person of Christ, a Christology "from below" begins its theological reflection with Jesus' history as presented in the synoptic Gospels and tends to emphasize the humanity of Christ. In the fifth century CE, the Antiochene school associated with Nestorius embodied this approach when it emphasized the "indwelling" of the man Jesus by the eternal Logos for the sake of our salvation, preserving the full humanity of Jesus at the expense of genuine incarnation.[22] By contrast, a Christology "from above" begins by reflecting on the preexistent Logos of John's Gospel (John 1:14) who descends into the world and takes on human flesh. The Alexandrian School, associated with Cyril of Alexandria in the fifth century but with roots in the third-century theologies of Clement and Origen, emphasizes the divinity of Christ without denying the reality of the Incarnation while remaining vague about what, if anything, the humanity of Jesus contributes to salvation.[23] The greatest value of the Chalcedonian definition for Christological reflection is that, by insisting upon the union of the human and the divine in the person of Jesus Christ for the sake of our salvation, it rejects any view that diminishes the humanity, the divinity, or their union. Thus, it avoids the shortcomings of both Alexandrian and Antiochene christologies by refusing to allow the divinity in Christ to overwhelm the humanity (Alexandrian), or the humanity in Christ to be preserved at the cost of denying its genuine union with the divine (Antiochene).

In order to make adequate sense of the entirety of the New Testament witness, approaches from below and from above need to complement each other. Thus, Jon Sobrino's liberation Christology "from below" also affirms Jesus' identity as the eternal Logos:

> Instead of beginning with the doxological affirmation of the incarnation of the eternal Son in Jesus of Nazareth (the theology of *descent*), it ends up with the doxological statement that this Jesus of Nazareth is the eternal Son. . . . The advantage of my approach here over that of the traditional Christology of descent is that it regards the history of Jesus as basic and essential to the dogmatic assertion that Christ is the eternal Son.[24]

Sobrino's bold claims do not deny the divinity of Christ; rather, they locate political human liberation within the divine Trinitarian life. Thus, in spite of Vatican criticism to the contrary, his approach adheres to the dogmatic formulation of Chalcedon while offering a new way of understanding the personal unity of humanity and divinity in Jesus by proclaiming a holistic view of salvation that is not limited to economic and political liberation, yet cannot be realized without them.

"High" and "low" Christologies, while similar to those from above and below, form a distinct grouping of Christological approaches. A high Christology acknowledges the divinity of Christ and in some instances, as in Docetism, denies the full humanity of Jesus. Low christologies, on the other hand, one-sidedly emphasize the human life of Christ and ignore or undermine the full divinity of Christ. "Adoptionism" is a form of low Christology characterized by the belief that the man Jesus of Nazareth was not the incarnation of the preexistent Logos, but merely a man who was "adopted" as son by God through the power of the Holy Spirit. While some scholars argue adoptionism is the diachronically earliest Christological formulation in the New Testament (Mark 1:9–11; Rom. 1:4; Acts 2:22–24, 32–36), predating the doctrine of preexistence and incarnation (John 1:14; Heb. 1:1–14), both low and high christologies find justification in the various biblical titles for Jesus. High titles like "Word of God" or "Son of God" emphasize the eternal, divine nature of Christ, while low titles like "Son of David" and "Messiah" point to the historical and human aspect of Christ's mission. Nevertheless, the church's Christological consensus eventually rejected adoptionist views because they undermine God's sovereignty and blur the distinction between Jesus' true Sonship and the adoption of Christian believers into the life of Christ.[25] The converse is also true: low titles that refer to the earthly mission of the Christ (what Karl Barth names the humiliation of the Lord as servant in *Church Dogmatics* IV/1, §59) need not exclude Christ's divine nature. Hispanic theologies in the United States embrace Jon Sobrino's methodological commitment to a Christology "from below" while affirming a "high" Christology that understands the Incarnation as a divine act of solidarity with humankind. For emancipatory theologies emerging from culturally marginalized and economically exploited communities, the Chalcedonian definition remains significant because it concretizes the work of Christ in the world by embracing humanity in all its frailness and rejecting spiritual escapism in all its forms.

A general principle of modern Christology—best embodied in the theology of Karl Barth—states that theological reflection about the relationship between Jesus of Nazareth and the eternal God is incomplete without reference to the work of salvation. Traditionally, Christian theology has discussed the work of Christ under the rubric of atonement. While making distinctions between the person and work of Christ facilitates systematic discussion of the topic, it is important to remember that we cannot make sense of the life, ministry, and passion of Jesus apart from our understanding of the resurrection, and vice versa. In other words, a Christology that promises eternal life without addressing human suffering here and now is as vacant as a Christology promising historical liberation without also overcoming sin and death. This investigation affirms the earthly life and liberating ministry of Jesus as crucial to his saving work without minimizing the centrality of his death and resurrection for understanding God's plan for reconciliation. The cross is the focal point of most doctrines of the Atonement in Western theology, so clearly the power of the cross is essential to salvation and necessary for understanding the Christian faith. Yet *how* the cross achieves salvation is much debated.

Unlike the Christological definition of Chalcedon, there is no recognized ecumenical consensus on Soteriology, only several models of atonement that have more or less withstood the test of time. The following typology, while far from comprehensive, identifies key themes. One of the earliest explanations for the Atonement, the "ontological theory," views the Christ event as something unique that redeems the fallen Creation (including human nature) and makes possible a new way of life. This view of salvation is often associated with the Patristic theologies of Irenaeus and Athanasius and can be characterized as a union with God achieved by Christ that—unlike many modern understandings that view salvation as something personal and private—transforms the whole of Creation. Patristic scholar J. N. D. Kelly briefly summarizes Irenaeus's theory of redemption as an expansion of the apostle Paul's doctrine of recapitulation in Romans 5:12–21 that identifies Christ as the "second Adam":

> The conclusion to which his argument leads is that humanity, which as we have seen was seminally present in Adam, has been given the opportunity of making a new start in Christ, the second Adam, through incorporation in His mystical body. The original Adam, by his disobedience, introduced the principle of sin and death, but Christ by His obedience has reintroduced the principle of life and immortality. Because He is identified with the human race at every phase of its existence, He restores fellowship with God to all, "perfecting man according to God's image and likeness." And because He is a real man, born of a woman, He is able to vanquish the Devil, into whose power mankind had fallen.[26]

In this approach the genuine humanity of Christ is necessary for salvation; the Incarnation is the means of reconciling fallen humanity with God. What we lost in Adam—the image and likeness of God—we recover in Christ Jesus. Christ did what we cannot do for ourselves.

A later, more influential, theory of atonement is the "satisfaction" theory associated with medieval theologian Anselm of Canterbury. According to Anselm, humanity's disobedience dishonors God and—just as in the feudal social order—when a lord's honor is offended, proper satisfaction must be given. Applying the analogy that the relationship between Creator and creature is similar to the relationship between feudal lords and their vassals, Anselm concludes that due to the greatness of our offense we are unable to provide adequate satisfaction. Nevertheless, since humanity committed the offense, humanity must provide satisfaction. Consequently, God becomes human in Christ for the redemption of humankind, exemplifying perfect obedience—even unto death—thereby eliminating the need for our punishment while also restoring God's honor.

While Anselm's doctrinal formulations reflect a medieval worldview that unduly influenced his notions of honor, offense, and satisfaction, the sacrificial interpretation of Christ's death is firmly grounded in the New Testament, which itself reinterpreted Old Testament images of sacrifice and redemption. Most telling is Paul's description of the uniqueness of Christ's saving works

> since all have sinned and fall short of the glory of God; they are now justified by his grace as a gift, through the redemption that is in Christ Jesus, whom God put forward as a sacrifice of atonement by his blood, effective through faith. He did this to show his righteousness, because in his divine forbearance he passed over the sins previously committed. (Rom. 3:23–25, NRSV)

Accordingly, contemporary theological reconstruction cannot ignore the theme of the cross as sacrifice—in spite of politically repressive manipulation of sacrificial imagery—without losing something distinctive about the Christian view of salvation.

A third approach to the doctrine of Atonement has been named the "moral influence" theory. Unlike the more "objective" ontological and satisfaction theories of atonement, the moral influence theory is considered "subjective," since in the former God's work of salvation is done by

Christ *extra nos* and once-for-all—implying that the work of salvation is complete and independent of the participation of those who are saved—whereas in the latter, salvation is understood as the human response in thanksgiving to God's example of self-sacrificing love. The contemporary appeal of this theory (Jon Sobrino's theory of atonement can be classified as moral influence) rests with the fact that it emphasizes both God's love and the role of human moral agency. Twelfth-century theologian Peter Abelard pioneered the moral influence theory of atonement as an alternative to what he saw as Anselm's cruel and to some extent sadistic satisfaction theory: "Indeed, how cruel and wicked it seems that anyone should demand the blood of an innocent person as the price for anything, or that it should in any way please him that an innocent man should be slain —still less that God should consider the death of his Son so agreeable that by it he should be reconciled to the whole world."[27] Instead, Abelard emphasizes the role of our faith in response to the greatness of God's love for us:

> By the faith which we hold concerning Christ love is increased in us, by virtue of the conviction that God in Christ has united our human nature to himself and, by suffering in that same nature, has demonstrated to us that perfection of love of which he himself says: "Greater love than this no man hath" (John 15:13), etc. So we, through his grace, are joined to him as closely as to our neighbor by an indissoluble bond of affection.[28]

Like the other two models for understanding the Atonement, the moral influence theory also finds scriptural support in the New Testament: "In Christ God was reconciling the world to himself, not counting their trespasses against them, and entrusting the message of reconciliation to us. So we are ambassadors for Christ, since God is making his appeal through us" (2 Cor. 5:19–20, NRSV).

However, though Abelard has stressed the role of our moral response in understanding the events of the cross, he does not reduce salvation to the subjective (as some critics contend): "That is to say that through this righteousness—which is love—we may gain remission of our sins. . . . I say remission is granted, yes, even for past sins, 'through the forbearance of God' (Rom. 3:26)—because of the long-suffering of God, who does not summarily punish the guilty and condemn sinners, but waits a long time for them to return in penitence, and cease from sin, and so obtain forgiveness."[29] Clearly, the work of forgiveness is Christ's alone, since, through his self-sacrifice on the cross, Christ obtains for us something we ourselves cannot attain without his help: "that is, that he may both will to fulfill in Christ what he had promised concerning our redemption or justification. . . . Namely, of him who believes him to be Jesus, that is, Saviour, by virtue of what Christ actually is—God and man."[30] The moral influence theory rejects both the notion that salvation is a cosmic battle independent of our role as "ambassadors for Christ" (ontological theory) and the notion that salvation depends on a "legal" transaction that satisfies God's wrath (satisfaction theory). Rather, the moral influence theory seeks to understand the cross in terms of what it reveals about God and the sanctified life.

That is why Jon Sobrino, in articulating a liberation Christology, emphasizes that Jesus' crucifixion was the historical consequence of his life.[31] He argues that theories like Anselm's become theological abstractions by removing the events of the cross from the historical context of Jesus' life, defining redemption in terms of this once-for-all event without accounting fully for the consequences of a properly Chalcedonian Christology that seeks to understand God's plan for salvation "in terms of the real, authentic incarnation of God."[32] Accordingly, Jesus' crucifixion is the direct result of the startling truths about God revealed by the Incarnation:

> To say that Jesus dies according to God's design is, in my opinion, to say much too little. We do much better to say that Jesus dies because he chose to bear faithful witness to God right to the end in a situation where people really wanted a very different type of God. Their condemnation of Jesus indicates that they clearly saw the option he was posing to them. They would have to choose between the God of their religion and the God of Jesus, between the temple and human beings, between the security provided by their own good works and the insecurity of God's gratuitous coming in grace.
>
> Jesus' cross is no accident. It flows directly from the self-justifying efforts of the "religious" person who tries to manipulate God rather than letting God remain a mystery. . . . Paradoxical as it may seem, it was "religion" that killed the Son. So we are left with the question as to why the Father allowed his death. Is it possible that he accepted Jesus' death on the cross so that he might overcome the old religious schema once and for all, so that he might show that he is a completely different sort of God who serves as the basis for a completely new kind of human existence?[33]

God became incarnate as Jesus of Nazareth. The "scandal of particularity" demands that we take seriously every aspect of the humanity of God —his death included—for it is in the history of this particular person (a marginalized Galilean who transgressed social boundaries to bring good news to the poor and oppressed) that God is known. Jesus' crucifixion is a direct result of the life he lived not because he was a criminal but for the reason that as the Christ of God he challenged the dominant values of the religious and governing authorities of his day. In other words, a truly messianic Christianity understands the work of the Christ as adversarial politics: God's preferential option for the poor and oppressed of history demands that the church, as the body of Christ, choose sides.

In the Chalcedonian definition the ecumenical church has made several, very important, theological claims about the person Jesus of Nazareth: Jesus is fully human, Jesus is fully divine, and Jesus is fully human and fully divine in perfect unity. These three affirmations have implications for contemporary Christology: (1) Jesus is the norm for humanity— humanity redeemed and in proper relationship to God; (2) Jesus is God's self-revelation—therefore, a Christian doctrine of God defines God in terms of what the life, death, and resurrection of Jesus reveal about God's character; and (3) the union of true God and true humanity in the Incarnation must be understood in light of God's triune identity—Father, Son, and Holy Spirit eternally bound in a relationship of self-giving mutuality and fellowship. Thus, while the language of the ecumenical creeds might appear mired in the static categories of classical Greek metaphysics, the Chalcedonian definition can also point us toward a more relational and socially engaged Christian praxis grounded in Trinitarian theology.[34]

The descriptive typology employed earlier in this discussion does not view the various atonement theories as mutually exclusive. Granted, at different times in the history of the church one or another has been emphasized to the exclusion of the others, but the fact remains that the ecumenical church has never singled out any one theory of atonement as authoritatively binding. Rather, the church (to paraphrase Jon Sobrino) has chosen not to manipulate God, allowing God's self-revelation on the cross to remain a mystery. Contemporary theologians should trust the collective wisdom of the church and resist absolutizing any one theory of atonement. Sobrino's emphasis on Christ's redemptive suffering on the cross differentiates him from North American liberation theologians like Mark L. Taylor who deny that the cross itself is salvific.[35] Addressing Taylor's concerns about atonement, U.S. Latino/a theology affirms the redemptive suffering of the Christ by emphasizing the following assertions: (1) There is something unique about the work of Christ "for us" that no other human being can accomplish; (2) the work of salvation is inextricably linked to the Incarnation; (3) salvation is both spiritual and historical, involving a human moral response to the work of God in Christ; (4) salvation is both personal and corporate, shaping our moral response in socially transformative ways; and (5) salvation is not limited to Christ's death on the cross but incorporates what Mark Taylor terms the "whole way of the cross"—that is, the life, ministry, and preaching of Jesus of Nazareth and the various Christian movements that to this day continue his work of reconciliation (2 Cor. 5:19–20).[36]

Mestizo *Theological Reconstruction: The Christ*

Latino theologian Luis Pedraja begins his Christological reflections by pondering how in Spanish the name of "Jesus the Christ" runs together into one word, "Jesucristo." For Pedraja, this particularity of the Spanish language points to something extremely important about Christology—namely, that the person of Christ cannot be divided from his work:

> It is almost as if in that one phrase the entire christological problem is encapsulated and resolved. Jesus, the human being born of Mary into a particular history, context, and culture, comes together with the title, the Christ, the Messiah, the anointed of God. The words seem to convey an innate understanding that we cannot take one without the other —that we cannot understand who Jesus is apart from Jesus' work as the Christ. . . . *Jesucristo* expresses, in a sense, the very essence of Christology, the coming together of humanity and divinity in a way never before encountered.[37]

Pedraja's Christological musings stand well within the long and rich tradition of Western Christianity reviewed earlier. Yet, as representative of a culturally and politically marginalized group, Hispanic theologies also provide an alternative to dominant theological models by utilizing "the lenses of bilingualism and biculturalism to examine Christology from a Hispanic perspective" in order to bring to light "new christological insights and paradigms that might otherwise have gone unnoticed."[38] Justo L. González, in his introduction to Pedraja's book-length Christology,

Jesus Is My Uncle (1999), writes that the most important contribution of this book is the insight "that when we look at Jesus through different cultural eyes, our image of Jesus is enriched."[39] Still, Pedraja's contributions —even at their most critical—are offered for the betterment of the whole Christian tradition and the positive transformation of civil society. In *Jesus Is My Uncle*, Pedraja identifies several important tensions Christology needs to resolve. Concerning the doctrine of the Incarnation, Pedraja affirms that Christ is incarnate *historically* in the person Jesus of Nazareth and incarnate *in the present* through our acts of love:

> God's incarnational power cannot be limited to a single historical event. God also works within humanity in all ages through God's love for us, empowering us to do God's will and receive God's revelation. Thus, through the power of the Holy Spirit, God's love can become concretely incarnate through us, acting in us to reach others.[40]

Affirming that Christ is incarnate "through us" poses a challenge to more traditional understandings of the person of Christ that emphasize the uniqueness of the Incarnation, so Pedraja reinterprets the doctrine by arguing that humanity encounters God in the midst of humanity—Christ revealed *through* culture.

Concerning the doctrine of Atonement (the work of salvation), Pedraja argues that Latino/as cling to the salvific aspect of Christ's death as a source of hope: "In Jesus' suffering, they also see the promise of the resurrection and vindication for which they long."[41] Yet Pedraja is very aware that by limiting our understanding of salvation to the cross there is a danger of fetishizing death and "redemptive" suffering, since focusing "on tragedy can easily become a way to idealizing martyrdom, passivity, and resignation to powerlessness. This tragic fatalism can resign us to suffering in this world while we long for deliverance in the next."[42] Nonetheless, one of the insights of the Latino/a Christian experience is the gift of recognizing "that in the face of suffering, in the struggle of life and death, God is present with us. Just as God is present sacramentally in the Eucharist, God is present in the lives of those who suffer and agonize."[43] Hence, by emphasizing the Incarnation, theology can (1) overcome the tendency to "spiritualize" God's command to love our neighbor, (2) interpret God on the cross as suffering "with us" in solidarity and not just vicariously "for us," and (3) focus on the *whole* life of Jesus in order to articulate a moral influence theory of atonement that emphasizes God's love and rejects the view that divine power is coercive. In the Christ event the world witnesses a reversal of the world's values, coming to know God's power as self-sacrificing love instead of as might and domination. Jon Sobrino's influence on U.S. Latino/a theology, especially the notion that the Incarnation is essential for understanding salvation, allows us to see how Jesus was crucified because he challenged the dominant theological perspectives of his day and threatened the political and cultural domination of the established powers. Accordingly, keeping "Christology enmeshed in the flesh-and-blood existence of human life"[44] requires appropriating the Galilean identity of Jesus.

The Contemporary Relevance of Jesus' Galilean Identity

Building upon recent biblical scholarship[45] and the contributions of Latino/a theologian Virgilio Elizondo,[46] Mark Taylor argues for a vision of Christian cultural engagement as adversarial politics grounded in Jesus' Galilean identity as a member of a marginalized minority population organized to resist imperial domination:

> In sum, Jesus' struggle in a Galilee repressed by client-king Herod, by imperial Rome, and by a religious elite centered in Jerusalem who reinforced both was a struggle that anticipated and can inform our own today. This struggle is the way of one who was executed by state power. Those who follow his way now may also suffer the way of some execution, but because it is the way of the executed God, we may expect some flourishing.[47]

While Taylor has directed these insights toward dismantling the abuses of the U.S. penal system and its indiscriminate use of capital punishment, he also recognizes the importance of Jesus' Galilean identity as a theological resource for resisting racism in Elizondo's work. Given Jesus' identity as racially marginalized other, Latino/a Christological reflections employ the Incarnation as the lens through which to view both humanity and divinity:

> The overwhelming originality of Christianity is the basic belief of our faith that not only did the Son of God become a *human being*, but he became *Jesus of Nazareth*. Like every other man and woman, he was culturally situated and conditioned by the time and space in which he lived.

The God of Jesus cannot be known unless Jesus is known (John 12:44–45, 14:9). And we cannot really know Jesus of Nazareth unless we know him in the context of the historical and cultural situation of his people. Jesus was not simply a Jew, he was a Galilean Jew; throughout his life and his disciples were identified as Galileans.[48]

A key difference between Taylor's understanding of the adversarial politics arising from Jesus' Galilean identity and how Virgilio Elizondo and other Latino/a theologians employ Jesus' Galilean identity concerns the role given to the cross and crucifixion in understanding Christ's liberating work. Taylor strongly rejects traditional views of Christ's crucifixion as salvific because there is a "deep-running propensity in our culture, and also other cultures, to displace the faults and violence spread throughout the entire body politic onto a few bodies,"[49] and most often in our society these "scapegoats" are people of color. In spite of such objections, U.S. Latino/a theology affirms the cross as a locus of liberation—fully aware of the dangers of scapegoating—yet convinced that in the cross of Christ the "crucified peoples" of the world find hope and strength for their struggles.[50]

Luis Pedraja's Christology retains the salvific power of the cross while arguing that this power is not linked to a substitutionary atonement for our transgressions. Instead, he articulates views that echo Abelard's moral influence theory:

> To see God as exacting such a price from humanity or from Jesus is to paint a sadistic picture of God's justice as one that can be satisfied only by inflicting pain and suffering. . . . The salvific power of the cross resides in its power to reveal the depth of God's love for us—a love that is willing to endure humiliation, suffering, and death at our hands—and the depth of our sin.[51]

Answering the question "Who is Jesus Christ for us?" Pedraja makes the following theological affirmations: (1) Jesus reveals God's nature is love: "The content of Jesus' revelation is the extent and nature of God's love for humanity and all of creation";[52] (2) Jesus reveals God in the midst of humanity; and (3) Jesus reveals where and when God is present—namely, "God is present in those who act justly and compassionately out of their love for others."[53] Aptly, the contemporary relevance of Jesus' Galilean identity stems from a view of the Incarnation that does not limit itself to the earthly life and ministry of Jesus but dares to identify the risen Christ as incarnate in the lives of the marginalized and rejected of the world. The logical consequence is a view that not only privileges the experience of the poor and oppressed in understanding the work of salvation but also understands liberation as integral to the Trinitarian life of God.

Understanding "Christ through Culture"

Pedraja brings Christology and praxis together, affirming the methodology of Gustavo Gutiérrez, who writes: "For liberation theologians orthodoxy (right belief) is coupled with orthopraxis (right action) so that the former is judged by the latter."[54] Consequently, Pedraja concludes that "God's love reveals itself through concrete action."[55] Driven by a commitment to understand the Incarnation as a present reality and not just a past historical event, Pedraja contends Hispanic christologies begin not with abstract speculation but with the concrete experiences of Latino/as and argues that "anyone who takes the Incarnation seriously truly" cannot separate "Christ or Christianity from its cultural and historical matrix."[56] Thus, it is vital that theology adequately understands the intersection of faith and culture, and comes to terms with the role of culture in theological construction. To this end, Pedraja appeals to H. Richard Niebuhr's five paradigms for understanding Christ's relationship to culture, and offers his own paradigm: Christ through culture.[57]

Niebuhr would categorize most Latino/a understandings of the Christ under the "Christ of culture" paradigm that views Christ as "part of culture in the sense that he himself is part of the social heritage that must be transmitted and converted."[58] Without disregarding the value of Niebuhr's paradigms for understanding the relationship of Christianity to culture, Pedraja rejects the "Christ of culture" paradigm in favor of his own formulation, "Christ through culture," because we cannot reduce Christianity to culture.[59] Still, "we must agree with Niebuhr's fifth paradigm, Christ transforming culture. We do want Christ and Christianity to exert a prophetic voice in culture in the hopes of a transformation. Liberation theologies, in their eschatological aim for the reign of God on earth, work toward the transformation of culture."[60] Pedraja's major critique of Niebuhr's paradigms concerns the inadequacy of Niebuhr's "high" view of culture because it ignores everyday life and popular religion, important sources for U.S. Latino/a theological reflection yet practices often ignored as "low" and unimportant in the academic study of culture: "Culture is what cultivates and cares for the human spirit, civilization, and society along with all the things that emerge out of that process of cultivation, including language and technology, making the term more inclusive in nature."[61] The implication of claiming that all aspects of human experience are embedded in particular cultural matrices is that both divine revelation and theological reflection occur within culture.

Understanding "Christ through culture" presumes two things: (1) Jesus is not a mere creation of culture, though born into a particular culture, and (2) God's revelation never occurs separate from culture (i.e., there is no unmediated experience of the divine). Given this understanding, the theologian's task is not to abstract Christ from culture in order to attain some kernel of transcendent truth free from cultural distortions, but to discern how Christ is known in and through particular cultures. To this end, Pedraja adopts Paul Tillich's correlational method in order to interpret the New Testament witness as a model and guide for discerning "how Christ comes to us through our cultures and our experiences."[62] By observing how the life and ministry of Jesus of Nazareth correlate to our situation, we "are called to discern who Jesus is and what he means to us. At the same time, we must also be able to discern how and where Jesus comes through culture to meet us."[63]

Encountering Christ through culture, Pedraja navigates the distinction between the transcendence and immanence of God while affirming both:

> In love, God's transcendence does not negate God's immanence in any respect. Most Hispanics believe in an immanent God who is accessible to them and who stands with them. But they also believe in a transcendent God who can empower them. The God of the Incarnation is also the God of the Resurrection and of the Ascension.[64]

Rather than focusing on the epistemological issues surrounding God's self-revelation in Christ—as with much modern theology after Immanuel Kant that posits a false choice between divine revelation and human experience—Pedraja opts to "understand who God is by what God does,"[65] placing the emphasis of Christology on Jesus' activity rather than his abstract divinity, "thereby uniting two of the traditional christological questions: the work and the person of Jesus."[66] Pedraja labels this approach a *theological ontopraxis*—understanding God's being in terms of God's actions. Reflecting both Gutiérrez's methodological concerns and Eberhard Jüngel's efforts to transcend static metaphysical categories in order to better understand God's presence in human history as God "for us,"[67] Pedraja argues that "theology and Christology will have to move beyond traditional ontological concerns, with their quest for being and its structures, towards ontopraxis—active being."[68] The most radical implication of theological ontopraxis is the requirement "that theology today be done not just by being attentive to where we once encountered God's work—the Exodus, the Incarnation, the cross, and the Resurrection—but also by being attentive to where God continues to work today."[69]

Pedraja's reconstruction of Christology from a Hispanic perspective has much in common with Mark Taylor's understanding of the "way of the cross," arguing that the church needs to articulate a broader conceptualization of the Incarnation that embraces the risen Christ's ongoing work in the world:

> Through those who suffer at the hands of others, God becomes incarnate as the object and recipient of the very real consequences of our sin. Through those who struggle on behalf of life, who act out of love and compassion for others, God becomes incarnate as a subjective agent of history, working to transform human history into God's kingdom, where love and justice reign.[70]

A view of Christ incarnate wherever the work of liberation is present challenges the church to embrace public theology: "It requires the church to pay close attention to the active presence of God in human history and society . . . the church must be willing to discern God's presence in the world and to follow to wherever God leads, for there is where the church truly should be."[71] While advocating a moral influence theory of atonement, Pedraja nonetheless remains faithful to the notion that the work of salvation is inextricably linked to the Incarnation. Given this investigation's methodological commitment to preserving the uniqueness of the Incarnation—that there is something about the work of Christ "for us" that no other human being can accomplish—how do we make sense of Pedraja's more inclusive understanding of the Incarnation?

Christian Praxis as the "Way of the Cross"

Understanding "Christ through culture" does not negate the reality of divine revelation. Rather, it forces theology to become fully incarnational by accepting culture as a central source of theological reflection, since "our experience of God and our interpretation of that experience occur within this cultural matrix."[72] In other words, there are no revelations from God that are not highly contextualized, so that when we encounter God it is always within a particular historical and cultural context. Not only do theologians have to work hard to discern the meaning of theological symbols in their original sociocultural context—for example, by locating the life and ministry of Jesus of Nazareth within the context of first-century Israel—they also have to interpret and translate these symbols for their contemporary context.

A guiding principle of Pedraja's theological method is the realization that all human beings "live at the intersections of cultures."[73] Not surprisingly, *mestizaje* is an important, multifaceted concept of central importance to his theology because

> the very definition of culture is in itself fluid and transitional, caught up in generalities, definitions, and discourses. . . . there is a sense in which culture defies a given definition. . . . ultimately, culture, like context, is not a singular reality, but a plurality of realities containing our creations and artifacts—creations that sustain, form, and transform us as we continually transform them. Culture cultivates us as we cultivate it.[74]

Consequently, the metaphor of *mestizaje*—grounded in the Hispanic experience of embodying two different cultures—provides valuable insights for analyzing the relationship between divine revelation and culture. However, while it seems almost tautological to claim that in today's pluralistic society most people live at the intersection of two or more cultures, U.S. Latino/a theologians like Luis Pedraja intentionally embrace *mestizaje*—rather than the more universal (also more abstract) paradigm of hybridity—because they want to make a specific criticism about the dominant understanding of cultural interaction. It is not enough to affirm pluralism; theology needs to also address the complexities of power, politics, and domination by employing a hermeneutics of suspicion. U.S. Latino/a theologians embrace *mestizaje* as a theological metaphor because it brings to mind (1) the long and painful history of the European conquest of the Americas, (2) the continuing U.S. policies that threaten the sovereignty of Latin America and the Caribbean, (3) the stratification of society according to racial/ethnic difference that accompanied that conquest, and (4) the fact that Euro-American culture still perpetuates white cultural and political domination through the economic exploitation of the racially "other."

Ultimately, the metaphor of *mestizaje*—in spite of its multivalent character and potential to essentialize racial differences—remains a strongly liberative paradigm for analyzing and transforming North American society.

Luis Pedraja embraces the eschatological hope proclaimed in Virgilio Elizondo's groundbreaking *Galilean Journey* (1984), arguing that, as different races and cultures intermarry and become embodied in *mestizo* peoples, old biases are harder to maintain: "Despite those who advocate preserving racial purity, we are inevitably headed to a global *mestizaje* and *mulatez*."[75]

On this point, Pedraja is vulnerable to the same critique I made of Elizondo in chapter 2, that there is no guarantee that *mestizos*—in spite of having experienced marginalization and oppression at the hands of both parent cultures—will embrace the work of political liberation. In fact, as demonstrated by Cornel West's genealogy of racism, one of the greatest tragedies of racism is its power to entrap the very victims of racist social structures into perpetuating racism, as in the case of racial minority groups who create social hierarchies among themselves based on skin color. However, whereas I criticized Elizondo for not adequately articulating how those who are oppressed and marginalized—and not just their oppressors—can come to experience a conversion to God's preferential option for the poor and oppressed, Luis Pedraja's reflections on the Incarnation offer a means of empowering the faith community to combat racism within the church and in the broader society.

Incarnating Christ Today: "The Story Does Not End at the Cross . . ."

In *Jesus Is My Uncle*, Pedraja claims that the Incarnation is the "ultimate" *mestizaje* because "the Incarnation joins human and divine natures without dissolving the uniqueness of their differences."[76] Beyond Jesus' Galilean identity as culturally and ethnically mixed, Christ is *mestizo* because in the Incarnation, "God has a human face of flesh and blood" and "is also incorporated into humanity."[77] Accordingly, just as the reality of biological *mestizaje* can contribute to the dissolution of racial and cultural barriers (Elizondo), the Incarnation dissolves the radical discontinuity between humanity and God characteristic of many Christological approaches. Consequently, if a theology is to remain faithful to the principle of Incarnation—that God is revealed in the midst of human life—then it must account for how God is incarnate here and now, and not just during the lifetime of Jesus of Nazareth.

U.S. Latino/a theology is unabashedly a liberation theology. In articulating a liberation Christology, Latino/a theologians begin their theological reflection with the popular beliefs and practices of Latino/a peoples. Therefore, while there might be some cognitive dissonance among some Latino/a believers who want to more strongly affirm the uniqueness of Christ's Incarnation, there is also widespread support for an understanding of the Incarnation as manifest in our works of love. Scripturally, the latter perspective is grounded in a favorite Gospel text of liberation theologians:

> "For I was hungry and you gave me food, I was thirsty and you gave me something to drink, I was a stranger and you welcomed me, I was naked and you gave me clothing, I was sick and you took care of me, I was in prison and you visited me." Then the righteous will answer him, "Lord, when was it that we saw you hungry and gave you food, or thirsty and gave you something to drink? And when was it that we saw you a stranger and welcomed you, or naked and gave you clothing? And when was it that we saw you sick or in prison and visited you?" And the king will answer them, "Truly I tell you, just as you did it to one of the least of these who are members of my family, you did it to me." (Matt. 25:35–40, NRSV)

As Luis Pedraja continually reminds us, "the story does not end at the cross."[78] He argues that the Resurrection, like the Incarnation, affirms our material existence and empowers us to engage in socially transformative praxis: "Taken together, the cross and the resurrection promise us that life and love will triumph over death and hatred by confronting them and enduring in spite of them. . . . The promise of life in spite of death emboldens and empowers us to live and to confront evil."[79] One of these new possibilities is Virgilio Elizondo's vision of a universal *mestizaje,* in which God takes that which the world has rejected—the racially mixed "other" —and through this particular cultural reality reveals a new way of living together that strives to overcome relationships of domination and other exclusionary practices.

Pedraja fully embraces Elizondo's beautiful eschatological vision and weaves it into his understanding of Christian doctrine, so that when he reflects on the consequences of Christ's saving work he can conclude, "Our salvation comes through our reconciliation with God and through the restoration of proper relationship with God and creation, making possible the creation of new forms of community."[80] The closing chapter of Pedraja's *Jesus Is My Uncle,* entitled "Love Enacted," draws upon the miracle of Pentecost (Acts 2:1–11) to elaborate upon this new way of being community. Pedraja interprets Pentecost as the undoing of the punishment meted out at Babel (Gen. 11:1–9) because the "people attempted to build a community through a common language."[81] By contrast, at Pentecost a new way of being community—a *mestizo* community—is inaugurated by the power of the Holy Spirit, in which "God affirms our diverse languages and cultures, without the imposition of one language upon everyone. . . . The miracle of Pentecost is that everyone is able to hear God's word in their own tongue."[82] Rather than coercing a false sense of community through domination and social control, or simply breaking off into small enclaves of like-minded others, the new community born from Christ's saving work embraces difference and strives to build bridges between different cultures because in Christ we find an all-inclusive common ground that does not dissolve our cultural particularities. It bears repeating: at Pentecost everyone heard the Word of God in his or her own language. In other words, in Christ and through the Spirit we find a genuine *mestizaje.*

This inclusive community created by God at Pentecost not only celebrates cultural diversity but also struggles for social justice. As recorded in the book of Acts, the Christian community in Jerusalem "not only shared communion through the Eucharist but also shared their meals and property as needed (Acts 2:44–47). Pentecost formed a community that broke through not just the barriers of language and culture but also the barriers of wealth and social class."[83] This latter point, what Virgilio Elizondo terms the "Jerusalem principle," makes it clear that a vital aspect for understanding Christ's saving work is the importance of transgressing borders for the sake of a more equitable social order. It is not enough to self-identify as a marginalized minority group and then unite as an isolated ethnic community for political survival; genuine *mestizo* identity seeks to overturn the very process of social, political, and cultural marginalization in order to establish a society that recognizes the full humanity of all God's children. Given this understanding, *mestizo* identity cannot be reduced to either biology or culture; rather, *mestizaje* is the embodiment of a spiritual reality—"Let the same mind be in you that was in Christ Jesus"

(Phil. 2:5, NRSV). Accordingly, it is not merely a static identity but one characterized by a concrete liberating praxis best described as the continuation of Christ's saving work.

Understanding the person and work of Christ helps us to see how humanity is reconciled to God; understanding the work of the Holy Spirit will help us see how humanity is reconciled with one another. In the next chapter, I discuss the work of the Holy Spirit in founding and empowering the community of faith, arguing that moral agency is a crucial dimension of *mestizaje*—one that requires continuous effort to sustain. Interpreting the account of Pentecost in Acts 2 through the lens of U.S. Hispanic experience demonstrates how the unity of the eschatological community rests upon a spirit of solidarity made possible by both God's initiative and humanity's faithful response. Genuine, long-lasting solidarity is made possible by the power of the Holy Spirit because it is only in the Spirit that we can overcome the differences that divide us without negating each other's particularities.

6

The Spirit of Community

This theological investigation of *mestizaje* as a paradigm for resisting racism began by affirming the Christian belief that God is the Creator of heaven and earth who made humanity in all its great diversity the very image of God. In critical conversation with Virgilio Elizondo's theological reflections on Our Lady of Guadalupe, chapter 4 articulated a more inclusive doctrine of Creation that fully incorporates the reality of *mestizaje* into the *imago Dei*. Then, by engaging Latino/a contributions to Christology that reconceptualize *mestizaje* as a liberating praxis grounded in the doctrine of Incarnation, the previous chapter affirmed that Christ is incarnate wherever the work of liberation is manifest—that is, *mestizaje* understood as the embodied continuation of Christ's saving work. Accordingly, this chapter undertakes a discussion of the work of the Holy Spirit in founding and empowering the new community in Christ.

Christian systematic theology has traditionally discussed the church's life together under the doctrine of the Holy Spirit. By affirming faith in the Holy Spirit, who empowers humanity for the ministry of reconciliation, our understanding of *mestizaje* as theological metaphor is enriched. Given those traditional understandings of justification and sanctification that stress the Christian life begins with conversion, and that conversion is made possible by the indwelling of the Holy Spirit, the following pneumatological reflections accentuate solidarity with the poor and oppressed as an important mark of spiritual conversion. In discussing the theophany at Guadalupe, I considered whether or not a Christocentric theology allows for "new" revelations from God independent of the Christ event and concluded that events like Guadalupe are "Christian" only insofar as they bear witness to the central Christian revelation. However, I also contend that Christian theology needs to broaden its conception of revelation to include new cultural manifestations of the Gospel; hence the need to advocate for a more inclusive understanding of Incarnation that recognizes God's action in the world *wherever* we find the work of liberation.

Focusing theological reflection upon the work of the Holy Spirit enables the church to embrace God's presence in human cultures as well as God's presence beyond the Christian community. Thus, I begin by raising a question implied but never adequately stated in both chapter 4, on the doctrine of Creation, and chapter 5, on the person and work of Christ: *Does the church community exclusively mediate reliable knowledge of God? Or is reliable knowledge of God available independent of the teachings of the one, holy, catholic and apostolic church?*

Arguing that solidarity is a gift of the Holy Spirit, I defend the position that God's presence is manifest in concrete liberating praxis, which is often found outside the faith community, then respond to critics of liberation theology who say that liberationists have reduced the knowledge of God to liberating praxis. Theologian Eugene F. Rogers Jr. describes the problematic as follows:

> A thesis about the knowledge of God and the community, however, raises a number of challenges. Some of them are questions about knowledge of God apparently outside the church. If the knowledge of God belongs with the practices of the community, or if the practices of God yield the community's knowledge, what does that mean about apparent knowledge of God outside the community? Does God address the community from without? Does God address the community through those who dissent from its teaching? . . . To put it in trendier terms, what of the knowledge of God that is other to the community? Or in more biblical terms, what of the knowledge of God of the stranger?[1]

Luis Pedraja's paradigm for knowing "Christ through culture" illumines the work of the Holy Spirit in the world, especially when the Spirit is located outside "traditional" understandings of Christian community. Theology should not only attend "to where we once encountered God's work —the Exodus, the Incarnation, the cross, and the Resurrection—but also by being attentive to where God continues to work today."[2] Seeking the same degree of attentiveness to the ongoing work of Christ in the world, Mark Taylor proposes the metaphor of "tracking spirit" for understanding "spirit in culture":

> We can highlight the following features, then, of a theology that is tracking spirit, and doing so as a form of cultural critique in the United States today. First: if we envision a tracking person or group that seeks another

person or group, the latter being lost in a woods or at a distance but leaving tracks, then we know that tracking entails searching and investigation. We can begin with the already-noted feature of the metaphor, and recall that *theology is a searching and investigating reflection, attempting to discern the tracks of spirit.* It searches for tracks left, for example, by liminal dwellers and spinners (as labyrinthine as these may be!), by integrative visionaries, and by those fighting and hoping for liberation.[3]

Given that U.S. Latino/a theology names "liberation" its most critical marker for tracking spirit in culture, the work of Ada María Isasi-Díaz —with its emphasis on community and solidarity (defined as mutuality striving for "radical structural change")[4]—orients this discussion of the work of the Holy Spirit in transforming church and society:

> Given the network of oppressive structures in our world today that so control and dominate the vast majority of human beings, the only way we can continue to claim the centrality of love of neighbor for Christians is to redefine what it means and what it demands of us. Solidarity, then, becomes the new way of understanding and living out this commandment of the gospel.[5]

Consequently, "solidarity can and should be considered the *sine qua non* of salvation."[6] This chapter explores the praxis of solidarity in order to conceptualize the work of the Holy Spirit as building community through transformative social action. Given the prevalence of privatized forms of spirituality in North American society, it is important to identify those traditional themes and resources that allow for a more liberative—and politically engaged—reconstruction of the doctrine of the Holy Spirit.

Some Pneumatological Assumptions

Many theologians lament that Western theological reflection has long neglected the doctrine of the Holy Spirit. Even a theological giant like Karl Barth, whose *Church Dogmatics* signaled a renewal in Trinitarian theology, has been accused of "apparent binitarianism" for writing book IV/3, §72, on the Holy Spirit and the mission of the church, "entirely without mention of the Spirit."[7] Many times in the past, the church has been suspicious of the work of the Holy Spirit, as evidenced by ecclesial opposition to Spirit-driven renewal movements like the radical reformers in sixteenth-century Europe or the Latin American base communities of the 1970s and 1980s. In fact, this distrust dates back to the second century CE with the condemnation of the Montanists, which set the pattern for all future ecclesiastical responses to Spirit movements. The current historical moment, with the rise of Pentecostalism, charismatic movements within Roman Catholicism and mainline Protestantism, and the renewed dialogue between Eastern and Western Christianity, has moved the Holy Spirit to the forefront of contemporary theology.[8] For example, Orthodox theologian John D. Zizioulas, in *Being as Communion* (1985), argues that the church is "the image of the Triune God," therefore humankind "can approach God only through the Son and in the Holy Spirit."[9] According to Zizioulas, ever since the Eastern and Western churches parted over the *filioque* controversy, both traditions have tended to emphasize potentially harmful extremes:

> Orthodox theology runs the danger of historically disincarnating the Church; by contrast, the West risks tying it primarily to history, either in the form of an extreme Christocentrism—an *imitatio Christi*—lacking the essential influence of pneumatology or in the form of a social activism or moralism which tries to play in the Church the role of the image of God. Consequently, the two theologies, Eastern and Western, need to meet in depth, to recover the authentic patristic synthesis which will protect them from the above dangers.[10]

Hopefully, the current resurgence in Pneumatology and Christian spirituality will contribute to a creative reconstruction of the doctrine of the Holy Spirit that recognizes and values the presence of God beyond the narrow confines of past theological formulations.

There is credence to the charge that Western theology has a deficient or underdeveloped Pneumatology. In developing a liberative doctrine of the Holy Spirit, three conceptual steps help heighten the distinct agency of the Holy Spirit, thus overcoming the charge of subordinationism without severing the work of the Spirit from God's plan for salvation in Christ. First, it is important that Christian theology not speak of just any spirit, but of the Holy Spirit who is truly God in perfect communion with the Father and the Son and therefore an agent of God's salvific work. Consequently, Christian theology needs reliable criteria for identifying and accurately naming the spirits: "Beloved, do not believe every spirit, but test the spirits to see whether they are from God; for many false prophets have gone out into the world. By this you know the Spirit of God: every spirit that confesses that Jesus Christ has come in the flesh is from God, and every spirit that does not confess Jesus is not from God" (1 John 4:1–3, NRSV). Clearly, not every spirit that claims to be from God is from God. For this reason—in spite of the danger that Christocentrism can deteriorate into Christomonism—Western theology defends the addition of the *filioque* clause to the Nicene Creed as a means of testing the spirits. By declaring the work of the Spirit inseparable from the work of Christ, the Western church affirms that the Christ event is the definitive and normative revelation of God.[11] As demonstrated in the previous chapter, when we speak about the person and work of Christ, we speak about God's work for liberation in human history and not just the eschatological hope of eternal salvation. Hence, an emancipatory Pneumatology uses the term *Holy* to identify the Spirit that comes from God as that Spirit distinguished from other spirits by its unwavering critique of moral evil and social injustice. Therefore, among our criteria for testing the spirits, the work of liberation takes precedence: "Now the Lord is the Spirit, and where the Spirit of the Lord is, there is freedom" (2 Cor. 3:17, NRSV).

Second, having linked (though not limited) the work of the Spirit to the work of liberation, it is important to account for the various ways the New Testament describes the Holy Spirit. John's Gospel proclaims, "God is spirit" (John 4:24); Matthew identifies the Holy Spirit as the Father's spirit (Matt. 10:20), while the apostle Paul refers to "the Spirit of his Son" (Gal. 4:6); elsewhere in the New Testament, the Spirit is called "the Spirit of grace" (Heb. 10:29), the "Spirit of truth" (John 14:17), and "God's gift" (Acts 8:20). Regardless of the specific nuances emphasized by each of these titles given to the Spirit, they all affirm that the work of the Holy Spirit, while a distinct agent in salvation history, is inseparable from what God has done "for us" in Christ. Sixteenth-century Reformer John Calvin is often praised for the thoroughness of his theological reflection on the work of the Holy Spirit. In Calvin we find a clear understanding of how we participate in the life of Christ and receive the benefits of the Incarnation and Atonement:

First, we must understand that as long as Christ remains outside of us, and we are separated from him, all that he has suffered and done for the salvation of the human race remains useless and of no value to us. Therefore, to share with us what he has received from the Father, he had to become ours and to dwell within us. . . . Yet since we see that not all indiscriminately embrace that communion with Christ which is offered through the gospel, reason itself teaches us to climb higher and to examine into the secret energy of the Spirit, by which we come to enjoy Christ and all his benefits. . . . To sum up, the Holy Spirit is the bond by which Christ effectually unites us to himself.[12]

While Calvin's doctrine of the Holy Spirit has been criticized for focusing too much on the inner testimony of the Holy Spirit in transforming the individual believer to the detriment of our understanding of the Spirit's role in fostering the intersubjective bonds of the renewed community, such criticism ignores the fact that Calvin locates the individual believer's subjective appropriation of Christ's redemption in the context of the Christian community. In fact, Calvin stressed the authority of the visible, earthly church as *necessary* for salvation, following Cyprian in describing the church as the "mother" of all believers:

For there is no other way to enter into life unless this mother conceive us in her womb, give us birth, nourish us at her breast, and lastly, unless she keep us under her care and guidance until, putting off mortal flesh, we become like the angels. Our weakness does not allow us to be dismissed from her school until we have been pupils all our lives. Furthermore, away from her bosom one cannot hope for any forgiveness of sins or any salvation, as Isaiah [Isa. 37:32] and Joel [Joel 2:32] testify.[13]

Accordingly, we should read Calvin's treatment of the Christian life in book III of the *Institutes* alongside book IV on the church and sacraments, which is titled, "On the External Means or Helps by which God invites us into the Society of Christ and keeps us in it." So while union with Christ is brought about by the inner work of the Holy Spirit, the Spirit uses earthly means—that is, the church—to effect this union.

Emphasizing the work of the Holy Spirit within the believer, Calvin does not juxtapose the individual over against the church; rather, he locates the work of the Holy Spirit primarily within the community of faith, recognizing the Spirit's role in creating and preserving this community. Calvin even counsels believers that, "whatever a godly man can do he ought to be able to do for his brothers, providing for himself in no way other than to have his mind intent upon the common upbuilding of the church."[14] Thus, it is important that a contemporary reconstruction of the doctrine of the Holy Spirit account for how believers *both* subjectively appropriate *and* communally embody the reality of salvation in Christ, or risk alienating those who hunger for a deeper relationship with God yet feel church structures stifle genuine spirituality. In practice, and in marked contrast to Calvin's "high" ecclesiology, this might mean finding the community of the Holy Spirit outside the confines of traditional definitions of "church."

Finally, given this understanding of the gifts of the Spirit as possessing an inherently communal dimension, a contemporary Pneumatology should view the Christian life as a process of spiritual growth characterized by increased solidarity with our "neighbors"—especially the poor and marginalized (Matt. 25:31–46; Luke 10:25–37). In Christ, by the power of the Holy Spirit, humanity is reconciled with God and with one another, united as one community regardless of nationality, race, gender, or class (Gal. 3:28), and made members of one body, interdependent on one another (1 Cor. 12:12–31). The central affirmations of a Trinitarian theology are faith in God the Creator, whose image and likeness each and every human being bears, faith in Christ through whom we are reconciled to God, and faith in the Holy Spirit, who transforms and empowers us to participate in Christ's ministry of reconciliation. An inescapable consequence of our belief in a Trinitarian God whose very nature is community is the belief that humankind was created to live in lasting communion with God and with one another. Consequently, questions about the nature of the church and its mission cannot be avoided.

The church, while a flawed human institution always in need of reformation and renewal, is nonetheless the kingdom of God in our midst, or in more pragmatic political terms, an alternative community that stands in contrast to the world in order to model a new way of being community grounded in relationships of inclusion, mutuality, and reconciliation. Among the many biblical images of the church (*ecclesia*), a liberating theology emphasizes the image of the church as (1) the body of Christ (1 Cor. 12:12–31), in which all members are interdependent and work together to carry out Christ's mission in the world, (2) God's servant people (Mark 10:45; 2 Cor. 4:5; Matt. 20:26–28) who serve God through both worship and love of neighbor, and (3) the community of the Spirit (Acts 2; Joel 2:28–29) empowered and guided by the Holy Spirit to transform the world through the ministry of reconciliation and thus serving as a visible sign of God's salvation here and now. However, traditional understandings of the nature and mission of the church—even when grounded in biblical images of servanthood—have rarely done justice to the radical call of the Gospel that affirms Christ's presence among the poor, the hungry, the sick, and the imprisoned (Matt. 25:31–46). As a result, the church is called to be more present among the poor, the hungry, the sick, and the imprisoned.

To this end, the Spirit regenerates us to the life God originally intended—as persons meant to live in communion with God and with one another—by overcoming existing relationships of exclusion and domination through the praxis of solidarity in relationships of mutuality. Jürgen Moltmann identifies fellowship (*koinonia*) as the special gift of the Holy Spirit:

> "The fellowship of the Holy Spirit be with you all," runs an ancient Christian benedictory formulary (II Cor. 13.13). Why is the special gift of the Spirit seen to be its fellowship (*koinonia*), whereas grace is ascribed to Christ, and love to the Father? In his "fellowship" the Spirit evidently gives himself. He himself enters into the fellowship with believers, and draws them into *his* fellowship. . . . Fellowship means opening ourselves for one another, giving one another a share in ourselves. It creates respect for one another. Fellowship lives in reciprocal participation and from mutual recognition. Fellowship comes into being when people who are different have something in common, and when what is in common is shared by different people.[15]

Jesus proclaimed that the greatest commandment is to love God with all your heart, with all your soul, and with all your mind, and to love your neighbor as yourself (Matt. 22:34–40; Mark 12:28–31; Luke 10:25–28), affirming that "God is experienced not merely individually. . . . He is experienced socially too, in the encounter with others."[16] Hence, the new community founded by the power of the Holy Spirit (Acts 2) is distinguished by solidarity. Latina theologian Ada María Isasi-Díaz, who has written extensively on liberation praxis and advocates a paradigm shift in Christian ethics from an emphasis on charity toward an emphasis on solidarity, contributes an appreciation for the social consequences of the Spirit's indwelling in a *mestizo* reconstruction of Pneumatology.[17] While Isasi-Díaz does not articulate an explicit doctrine of the Holy Spirit, she does link the unfolding of the "kin-dom" with the work of the Holy Spirit. The Spirit's presence is also recognized in her affirmation of the Catholic doctrine of *sensus fidelium*.[18]

Indwelling and Solidarity

Reformed theologian Karl Barth describes the work of the Holy Spirit in part as the "subjective realisation of the atonement," since atonement "is both a divine act and offer and also an active human participation in it."[19] Accordingly, the Christian community is itself the work of the Holy Spirit "in the form of a human activity" with a definite history:

> To describe its being we must abandon the usual distinctions between being and act, status and dynamic, essence and existence. Its act is its being, its status is dynamic, is essence its existence. The Church *is* when it takes place that God lets certain men live as His servants, His friends, His children, the witnesses of the reconciliation of the world with Himself as it has taken place in Jesus Christ.[20]

While this embodied manifestation of the Holy Spirit has a particular form, it cannot be reduced to the historical church, since we can neither control nor limit the work of the Holy Spirit. Nevertheless, in order to avoid "ecclesiastical Docetism," the invisible church must be made visible as a distinctive public presence in human culture: "For the work of the Holy Spirit as the awakening power of Jesus Christ would not take place at all if the invisible did not become visible, if the Christian community did not take on and have an earthly-historical form."[21] Barth goes so far as to proclaim that the church, as the body of Christ, is "the earthly-historical form of existence of Jesus Christ Himself."[22] In other words, faith in Jesus Christ—made possible by the power of the Holy Spirit—is intimately linked to faith in the church ("We believe in one holy catholic and apostolic Church"): "Because He is, it is; it is, because He is."[23]

Thus, if the community of faith is the locus of God's work for liberation, and the work of the Holy Spirit creates and sustains this spiritual community, then an emancipatory reconstruction of Pneumatology must account for the interrelation of the Spirit's indwelling with the historical possibility of genuine solidarity. U.S. Latino/a theology employs *mestizaje* as a theological paradigm for transforming the community of faith into a community committed to economic, political, and cultural liberation. However, with the emancipatory potential of *mestizaje* also comes the risk of essentializing Latino/a cultural identity. Ada María Isasi-Díaz (along with other *mujerista* theologians) cautions against idealizing *mestizo/a* identity, since glossing over vital cultural and political differences undermines the community's goal of embodying an inclusive and socially transformative praxis. Rather than emphasizing the inherited aspects of *mestizaje*—biology and culture—Isasi-Díaz argues for an understanding of *mestizaje* as a political decision:

> First, there is a need for an in-depth analysis not only of differences among Hispanics, but of the way we deal with differences, because if we do not embrace differences there is no possibility of *mestizaje*. Second, we acknowledge that because ethnicity is a social construct, a heuristic device that includes not only biological and cultural characteristics but also social and economic elements of the Hispanic community in the U.S.A., Hispanics have a choice: we must choose to be or not to be Hispanics, and this includes choosing *mestizaje* as a way of understanding and interpreting ourselves.[24]

Simply put, Hispanics in the United States represent a diversity of nationalities, political perspectives, and religious traditions. Most Latino/as describe themselves according to their country of origin (even when born and raised in the United States!), saying, "I am Puerto Rican" or "I am Colombian," rather than saying, "I am Latino/a" or "I am Hispanic." Therefore, to self-identify as "Latino/a" or "Hispanic" is an act of political solidarity—recognition that in the North American context Latino/as, regardless of skin color or country of origin, are subjected to cultural and political marginalization[25]—that reveals a commitment to the political empowerment of all Hispanics.

In this context, *mestizaje* becomes a paradigm for Christian ethics that both respects difference and offers resistance to all forms of domination. While recognizing the similarities that bind U.S. Latino/as together, Isasi-Díaz also appreciates that "the insistence on particularity and specificity is not antithetical to *mestizaje*, but, on the contrary, is required for *mestizaje* to exist."[26] In fact, a recurring *mujerista* critique of Euro-American feminist theology concerns the latter's notion of racial justice as the elimination of group difference (e.g., through the establishment of a "color-blind" society): "To them this is what justice is about. In doing this, however, they are espousing a model of assimilation that excludes diversity and specificity and allows 'norms expressing the point of view and experience of the privileged groups to appear neutral and universal,' and ultimately, normative."[27]

In response to the myth of a color-blind utopia, Isasi-Díaz urges La-tino/a communities to embrace the experience of being considered "to-tally other" by the dominant culture as a means of first understanding and then rejecting domination. The goal of this painful process of self-examination is for Latino/as to come to terms with their own racism, classism, and sexism:

> That we are looked upon as all being the same, as a homogeneous group, can become an opportunity for us to make a conscious choice of what it does mean that we are Hispanics living in the U.S.A. as well as the role we want to have in society. In a word, we have the opportunity of defin-ing ourselves, of opting to be *mestizos*, opting to be *for* Hispanics, opting to be Hispanics.[28]

It is clear that for Isasi-Díaz, *mestizaje*—whatever else it might entail—necessarily includes a political decision in favor of a particular social jus-tice advocacy stance. She makes a direct link between *mestizaje* and the "preferential option for the poor" affirmed by the Latin American Bish-ops at the 1979 Puebla Conference, arguing for a broader understanding of "preferential option" that includes cultural marginalization. In fact, in a revealing footnote, Isasi-Díaz acknowledges that while *mestizaje* origi-nally referred to the mixing of Spanish and Amerindian blood, she uses the term to mean "embracing all sorts of diversity among Hispanics as an intrinsic element of our struggle for liberation."[29] Thus she can argue that, since the bishops grounded their defense of the preferential option for the poor on the assertion that "poverty dims and defiles the image of God," the option for *mestizaje* can likewise be defended: "Because Hispanic Women embody a diversity of races and cultures, of socio-economic strata and political ideologies, failure to affirm our *mestizaje* will defi-nitely dim and defile the image and likeness of God in us."[30] Isasi-Díaz concludes that only by opting for *mestizaje*—by choosing to become a *mestizo* community that embraces and affirms difference—can the church hope to positively transform society: "We must choose an integrating liberation that demands changes of structures rather than participation in present oppressive structures. For us to choose *mestizaje* means that as Hispanic Women we have to be committed to making our *proyecto histórico* a reality."[31]

This *proyecto histórico* (literally, "historical project") refers to the his-torical specifics that contribute to and bring about liberation for an oppressed community. While such a project must not be viewed as a rigid blueprint or specific political platform, it does entail concrete moral choices that will involve the community of faith in adversarial politics. James H. Cone, reflecting on the vocation of a theologian, writes about the consequences of our theological commitments:

> We must never forget that when we do theology for God's church and not just for the United Methodist Church, not just for the Presbyterian, AME Baptist, Pentecostal Church, but for God's church, then we are going to create some enemies because Christian theology is conflictual language; it is conflictual language because it makes a preferential option for the poor.[32]

Jesus as encountered in the Gospels can be interpreted as claiming that conflict is inevitable when we make theological stances: "Do not think that I have come to bring peace to the earth; I have not come to bring peace, but a sword . . . and whoever does not take up the cross and follow me is not worthy of me. Those who find their life will lose it, and those who lose their life will find it" (Matt. 10:34–39; Mark 8:34–35; Luke 12:51–53; 14:26–27; 17:33). At the same time, caution must be taken not to reduce our understanding of God's work of salvation to human historical efforts. According to Ada María Isasi-Díaz,

> [Our] *proyecto histórico* is based on an understanding of salvation and liberation as two aspects of one process. This is grounded in the belief that there is but one human history that has at its very heart the history of salvation. By "history of salvation" we refer to what we believe are divine actions—creation, incarnation, redemption—as well as our human responses to them, whether positive or negative. For us Latinas, salvation refers to having a relationship with God, a relationship that does not exist if we do not love our neighbor.[33]

In the theology of Ada María Isasi-Díaz, the divine actions of salvation history are inseparable from the repentance and conversion that lead to making a preferential option for the poor and oppressed. The faith community's liberation efforts can thus be understood as the unfolding of God's will and thus as the work of the Holy Spirit. Accordingly, it is appropriate to discuss what Isasi-Díaz means by liberation, and the type of community created by opting for *mestizaje,* in terms of the work of the

Holy Spirit, who brings enlightenment that yields repentance, which in turn creates a conversion to God's preferential option and results in liberating praxis.

If liberation is the concrete historical manifestation of God's salvation history, then the community of faith is the embodiment of the new community inaugurated by the Holy Spirit on Pentecost:

> At the center of the unfolding of the kin-dom is the salvific act of God. Salvation and liberation are interconnected. Salvation is gratuitously given by God: it flows from the very essence of God: love. Salvation is worked out through the love between God and each human being and among human beings. This love relationship is the goal of all life—it constitutes the fullness of humanity. Therefore, love sets in motion and sustains the ongoing act of God's salvation in which each person necessarily participates, since love requires, *per se,* active involvement of those who are in relationship.[34]

Augustine of Hippo (354–430 CE) is credited with articulating what is perhaps the most dominant conceptualization of the work of the Holy Spirit in Western theology in which the Holy Spirit is understood as the bond of love between the Father and the Son: "Scripture teaches us that he is the Spirit neither of the Father alone nor of the Son alone, but of both; and so his being suggests to us that mutual charity whereby the Father and the Son love one another" (*The Trinity,* 15.27).[35] It is this same love that then fills us and empowers us to participate in the Trinitarian life of God: "Thus the love which is of God and is God is specially the Holy Spirit, through whom is spread abroad in our hearts the charity of God by which the whole Trinity makes its habitation within us" (15.32).[36] More to the point, it is this indwelling of the Holy Spirit that enables us to participate in the ongoing work of salvation "we refer to as liberation."[37]

Isasi-Díaz states that the traditional understanding of Christian love as charity (Latin, *caritas*; Greek, *agape*) needs to be replaced with an understanding of Christian ethical behavior as solidarity. By "charity" she means love of neighbor manifest primarily as "a one-sided giving, a donation, almost always, of what we have in abundance," whereas by "solidarity" Isasi-Díaz means love of neighbor embodied in the ongoing process of liberation.[38] Specifically, solidarity is the creation of a community united in the work of positively transforming the world, better understood as "the unfolding of the 'kin-dom' of God."[39] Drawing upon her experience as a missionary in Peru, Isasi-Díaz recalls a conversation she had with one of the men in the impoverished community she served who said to her, "Remember, you can always leave this place; we can't."[40] This experience helped her to realize that we cannot understand Christian love as "a doing for others" in the typical sense of charity as a handout but must work hard to embody "a being with others": "The goal is not to be like the poor and the oppressed (an impossibility), but rather to be in solidarity with them."[41] In other words, solidarity entails a conscious moral and political decision *by the oppressors* to identify with the poor and oppressed in liberating praxis in order to transform the structures that perpetuate poverty and oppression, and by *the oppressed* to become moral agents in their own historical process of liberation (in great part by speaking truth to power). Accordingly, this praxis of solidarity is characterized as a conversation across lines of class, ethnicity, and gender, resulting in a raised awareness (*conscientization*) of (1) the factors that contribute to oppression, (2) each party's involvement in perpetuating oppressive structures, and (3) the need for joint action in order to liberate both the oppressor and the oppressed. The end result is the establishment of a more just and egalitarian society that can properly be identified as *mestizo* because it values difference and fosters genuine mutuality.

While I value Isasi-Díaz's emphasis on solidarity in understanding the process of liberation, I believe she makes a strategic mistake by rejecting the biblical language of charity (*agape/caritas*). If we take a closer look at the biblical understanding of love, we discover that *agape/caritas* does in fact bear the connotation of solidarity desired by Isasi-Díaz. Consequently, I defend "charity" as a distinctly Christian understanding of love, albeit one in need of much clarification. In Roman Catholic moral theology "charity" refers to the love of God and of neighbor mandated by Jesus in his summary of the law (Matt. 22:34–40; Mark 12:28–31; Luke 10:25–28); it is also one of the three theological virtues—faith, hope, and love (or charity)—described by the apostle Paul as the chief gifts of the Holy Spirit (1 Cor. 13:13). Over the course of history, charity became identified with almsgiving as the church's chief means of providing regular aid to the poor. Unfortunately, the practice of almsgiving contributes to three misunderstandings of Christian love: (1) it perpetuates legalistic thinking by quantifying virtue, (2) it perpetuates a stratified social order in which an ever-present underclass depends upon the generosity of the ruling class for its very survival, and (3) it undermines the moral agency of the underclass by encouraging this dependency. However, if we look at

Paul's reflections on the Spirit's gift of love (charity), we find no mention of almsgiving. In fact, what we find is a primer on the praxis of solidarity: "Love is patient; love is kind; love is not envious or boastful or arrogant or rude. It does not insist on its own way; it is not irritable or resentful; it does not rejoice in wrongdoing, but rejoices in the truth. It bears all things, believes all things, hopes all things, endures all things" (1 Cor. 13:4–7, NRSV).

According to Paul, love is the greatest of the Spirit's gifts (1 Cor. 13:13) because it builds up the Christian community. The community's unity depends upon both our acceptance of each other's differences and our recognition of our interdependence as many members of the one body (1 Cor. 12:12–31). Thus, when "one member suffers, all suffer together with it" (1 Cor. 12:26, NRSV). Paul describes the work of the Holy Spirit as the building of community in much the same terms Isasi-Díaz describes the praxis of solidarity:

> I therefore, the prisoner in the Lord, beg you to lead a life worthy of the calling to which you have been called, with all humility and gentleness, with patience, bearing with one another in love, making every effort to maintain the unity of the Spirit in the bond of peace. There is one body and one Spirit, just as you were called to the one hope of your calling, one Lord, one faith, one baptism, one God and Father of all, who is above all and through all and in all. (Eph. 4:1–6, NRSV)

Paul also states, "Above all, clothe yourselves with love, which binds everything together in perfect harmony" (Col. 3:14, NRSV). So while almsgiving can be considered a virtuous act under Paul's understanding of Christian love, we cannot reduce love to mere almsgiving (or any other single act). Rather, Christian theology must strive to embody Paul's view of love as the building of community, or, in the language of Isasi-Díaz, "Salvation is worked out through the love between God and each human being and among human beings."[42] By replacing the language of charity with the language of solidarity, Isasi-Díaz confronts the church's failure to actualize the liberating vision found in the Scriptures. Yet, as I have argued in chapter 3 (on the public relevance of theology), rather than forcing a new paradigm upon the faith community, a more successful strategy is to retrieve liberating themes from within the church's tradition. In other words, a major task of a prophetic and liberating theology is to critique the church for not embodying its beliefs through its praxis by appealing to

its distinctly Christian discourse. Such an approach recognizes the eschatological character of biblical language—it does not describe the church
as it is but as it ought to be—thereby serving as a symbol of our future
hope, empowering and motivating our present work to bring about God's
kin-dom.

Human Cultures and the Sensus Fidelium

While Ada María Isasi-Díaz does not always explicitly embrace biblical
language—especially pneumatological language—to describe the praxis of
solidarity, her comments on the *sensus fidelium* reveal that she is speaking about the work of the Holy Spirit when she talks about the church's
conversion to the preferential option for the poor and oppressed or when
she describes the creation of the new community. In Catholic belief the
sensus fidelium refers to the prophetic office of the faithful (clergy and
laity) who are anointed by the Holy Spirit and therefore "cannot err in
matters of belief" (Dogmatic Constitution *Lumen Gentium* [1964], chap.
II, par. 12). According to Isasi-Díaz, this emphasis upon the prophetic task
of the faithful "does not assert the inerrancy of the faithful apart from
the hierarchy. Nor does it provide, I believe, for the inerrancy of the hierarchy apart from the faithful unless the hierarchy considers itself as
separate from the People of God."[43] Accordingly, this recognition by the
church hierarchy that the gifts of the Spirit are manifest among all the
people supports the use of popular religion as a *locus theologicus* for U.S.
Latino/a theology. Orlando Espín, who has written at length on popular
religion, defines *sensus fidelium* as "faith-full" intuition: "Christian people
sense that something is true or not vis-à-vis the gospel, or that someone is
acting in accordance with the Christian gospel or not, or that something
important for Christianity is not being heard."[44] In other words, since the
source of the *sensus fidelium* is the Holy Spirit, the people's religion can be
considered "infallible" insofar as it is preserved from error by the power
of the Holy Spirit. In practice, this means that not only are the Scriptures
and Church tradition recognized as reliable sources of revelation, but also
the popular beliefs and practices of the laity. Hence, the laity serves a prophetic role in correcting perceived errors in official church doctrine and
practice—not by replacing the church hierarchy but by serving as its collective conscience. Isasi-Díaz recounts an exchange with an archbishop
of the Roman Catholic Church who argued that the faithful could never

disagree with the teaching of the magisterium. Pressing him to further articulate his understanding of the *sensus fidelium,* Isasi-Díaz countered that a proper understanding of *sensus fidelium* does not "provide space for the hierarchy to disagree with what was a generalized belief among the laity and a significant segment of the hierarchy."[45] Unfortunately, the archbishop "would only assert what it did not mean" without offering a positive definition.[46]

Recognizing that the *sensus fidelium* is always expressed through human cultures, and that all human cultures are capable of misunderstanding God's revelation, Orlando Espín identifies three "confrontations" for evaluating the faithfulness of popular religion. That which claims to be Christian revelation must (1) exhibit fundamental coherence with the Scriptures; (2) be in basic agreement with the normative decisions embodied in the creeds, doctrines, and general traditions of the "official" church; and (3) regardless of its cultural location, embody certain indispensable aspects of Christian praxis (i.e., the proclamation and practice of justice, peace, liberation, reconciliation).[47] Ultimately, these dialogical practices between hierarchy and laity (and between dominant and marginalized perspectives) identified by Espín can, by the power of the Holy Spirit, communicate a fuller understanding of the mystery of God. Furthermore, by understanding popular beliefs and practices as the work of the Holy Spirit, theology can embrace God's revelation beyond the walls of the church:

> Though Jesus Christ is the final and definitive revelation of God—*the* revelation in the strict sense of the term—nowhere is it affirmed that *only* through Christ has God revealed Godself. As a matter of fact, the exact opposite has been a constant in orthodox Christian Tradition. What one must affirm with the Tradition is the uniqueness and finality of the revelation in and through Christ, and the impossibility of its being repeated. But these affirmations do not exclude other means of revelation, only that these must never appear to compete with or add something *new* to the fullness of Christ's revelation.[48]

Admittedly, *mujerista* theology is not as church-centered as Orlando Espín's articulation of the *sensus fidelium.* In fact, for *mujerista* theology only those aspects of the canon and the tradition that contribute to (women's) liberation "are accepted as revealed truth."[49] Nevertheless, *mujerista* theology affirms the importance of a Spirit-led, two-way critical conversation between the magisterium and the people implied by the doctrine of *sensus fidelium*. Consequently, Isasi-Díaz's implicit Pneumatology yields an understanding of the work of the Holy Spirit similar to Luis G. Pedraja's view of the Incarnation: *wherever we find the work of liberation there we find the presence of the Holy Spirit.*

Mestizo *Theological Reconstruction: The Holy Spirit*

A *mestizo* reconstruction of the doctrine of the Holy Spirit considers concrete practices that yield an emancipatory vision of the church's "life together." Bringing U.S. Latino/a theological insights about the Christian life into conversation with Barth and Calvin demonstrates how political liberation is not alien to the Christian tradition, but is in fact a recurring theme in both Scripture and traditional formulations of doctrine. The end result is a view of the work of the Holy Spirit that transcends traditional notions of *ecclesia* yet is manifest in community.

Justification, Sanctification, Vocation

The Christian life can and should be viewed as a journey toward a particular goal. More to the point, the Christian life is a gradual process of transformation into the image and likeness of Christ (1) initiated by God's grace in the work of *justification*, (2) characterized as growth in Christian love in the work of *sanctification*, and (3) manifest as a divine calling (*vocation*) to a distinctly Christian praxis.[50] Justification is understood as God's act of free grace and forgiveness in Christ: "He did this to show his righteousness, because in his divine forbearance he had passed over the sins previously committed; it was to prove at the present time that he himself is righteous and that he justifies the one who has faith in Jesus" (Rom. 3:25–26, NRSV). However, care must be taken not to confuse faith as the human act by which we merit salvation. Rather, our very act of faith is the work of the Holy Spirit in us: "Now we shall possess a right definition of faith if we call it a firm and certain knowledge of God's benevolence toward us, founded upon the truth of the freely given promise in Christ, both revealed in our minds and sealed upon our hearts through the Holy Spirit."[51] Thus, prior to justification and sanctification there is regeneration (the indwelling of the Holy Spirit), since we cannot acknowledge God's work of justification and sanctification without the foundation of God's grace through the Holy Spirit. Nevertheless, in spite of being initiated by God and made possible by the transforming power of the Holy Spirit, faith remains a human *response* to God's act of justification.

Sanctification is then understood as the ongoing work of the Holy Spirit to make us holy. If faith is the proper response to justification, Christian love (both love of God and love of neighbor) is the proper response to sanctification. Isasi-Díaz characterizes the Christian life as a praxis of solidarity and mutuality; however, as demonstrated earlier in this discussion, what she means by solidarity is very close to what the New Testament refers to as *agape/caritas* (charity)—a gift of the Holy Spirit that begins with a conversion process leading us away from self-love (characterized by perpetuating oppressive structures that benefit us) toward love of God and neighbor (characterized by an other-regarding love that seeks to eliminate oppressive structures, often at great personal sacrifice). Growth in the Christian life is neither a natural process nor a strict calculus of legalistic and easily identifiable acts, but is best understood as an intimate relationship with God made possible by the fellowship of the Holy Spirit and characterized by a continuous dying (mortification) of the old life and rising (vivification) to a new way of life.[52] As long as we live, sanctification is a journey without end but with a clear-cut goal: "Be perfect, therefore, as your heavenly Father is perfect" (Matt. 5:48, NRSV). By the power of the Holy Spirit we become new creatures and are now free to respond to God's grace in obedience.

Human beings are "saved" for the purpose of becoming coworkers with God in the mission of liberation and reconciliation (2 Cor. 5:16–21), and we are expected to bear much fruit (John 15:16). Consequently, we also need a deeper understanding of Christian vocation. There is a tendency in North American spirituality to reduce the work of the Holy Spirit "in us" to the sphere of the private and personal without adequate recognition of the public aspects of sanctification. By relegating spirituality to the domain of private religious experience, the Christian faith has undermined its place in the public arena as well as its ability to make a positive impact on society. The doctrine of vocation recognizes that while the Christian life is a personal journey of renewal, spiritual growth also entails a turning away from self-love toward love of neighbor. In other words, the vocation (or calling) of each and every Christian is to continue the ministry of reconciliation, which as we have seen, consists of building a new community grounded in Christ's work for liberation and empowered by the Holy Spirit who unites us in fellowship (*koinonia*) in spite of our differences.

Karl Barth writes that the vocation to be a Christian is communal in nature: "To be a Christian means vocation or calling into Christendom or the Church, i.e., into the living community of the living Lord Jesus Christ. . . . There is no *vocatio,* and therefore no *unio cum Christo,* which does not as such lead directly into the communion of saints, i.e., the *communio vocatorum.*"[53]

Accordingly, Christian discipleship consists of concrete praxis that builds community and struggles against injustice. In other words, love of God is expressed through love of neighbor (Matt. 22:34–40; Mark 12:28–31; Luke 10:25–28). This leitmotif of liberation theology is echoed in John Calvin's social ethics. Commenting on Micah 6:6–8, Calvin writes:

> He then says, that God had shown by his Law *what is good;* and then he adds what it is, *to do justice, to love mercy,* or kindness, *and to be humbled before God.* It is evident that, in the first two particulars, he refers to the second table of the law; that is, *to do justice, and to love mercy.* Nor is it a matter of wonder that the Prophet begins with the duties of love; for though in order the worship of God precedes these duties, and ought rightly to be so regarded, yet justice, which is to be exercised towards men, is the real evidence of true religion.[54]

Calvin does not reduce Christian spirituality to love of neighbor—in fact, he identifies proper worship of God as the central aspect of the Christian life—but argues that since "hypocrites can make a show of great zeal and of great solicitude in the outward worship of God, the Prophets try the conduct of men in another way, by inquiring whether they act justly and kindly towards one another, whether they are free from all fraud and violence, whether they observe justice and show mercy."[55] The resultant view of the Christian life is that of a communal spiritual journey marked by increased solidarity with our neighbor, whom Christ explicitly identifies as the poor and marginalized "other" (Matt. 25:31–46; Luke 10:25–37).

The Christian Life as Conversion to God's Preferential Option

I find that Isasi-Díaz's highly communal understanding of the work of the Holy Spirit—drawing upon Gutiérrez's understanding of integral liberation—does not try to replace the prevenience of grace; rather, it integrates the spiritual and communal loci. Recalling Gustavo Gutiérrez's notion of integral liberation, liberation is an essential part of a Christian understanding of salvation. In other words, we cannot speak about salvation without speaking about liberation, and more radically, we cannot speak about liberation work that is not necessarily salvific. A liberation understanding of the Christian life presupposes an integral connection between salvation and our response to God's saving grace as liberation. Consequently, liberation spirituality remains critical of those spiritual traditions that divorce the subjective "religious" experience of grace from the objective "historical" love of neighbor. Here liberation theology does not break new ground but simply reminds the church of the prophetic Old Testament tradition that Calvin has called the test of true religion: "He has told you, O mortal, what is good; and what does the Lord require of you but to do justice, and to love kindness, and to walk humbly with your God" (Mic. 6:8, NRSV). Spirituality, understood as a concrete manner of living the Gospel (vocation), means reordering our individual and communal life under the guidance of the Holy Spirit. What liberationists like Isasi-Díaz are attempting to do is not "conflate" salvation into liberation but rather inseparably link historical liberation to Christian theology's understanding of salvation. To this end, Isasi-Díaz incorporates Gustavo Gutiérrez's threefold understanding of liberation as (1) liberation from oppressive social structures, (2) personal transformation, and (3) liberation from sin.[56]

While spirituality has always been part of Latin American liberation theology, liberationists continue to defend themselves from accusations of a monistic commitment to historical liberation to the detriment of other aspects of the Christian life. Yet such accusations are unwarranted insofar as liberation theology grounds the Christian life in the radical transformation of the self and society enacted by God's grace, since only the Holy Spirit can produce the radical "conversion to the neighbor" that makes liberation a historical possibility in the first place. Isasi-Díaz writes, "To struggle against oppression, against alienation, is a matter of an ongoing personal conversion that involves effective attempts to change alienating societal structures. This personal conversion cannot happen apart from solidarity with the oppressed."[57] More to the point, our participation in the praxis of solidarity is part of our participation in God's salvation history and is "gratuitously given by God."[58] Clodovis Boff responds to this same criticism by insisting that theology must always maintain the tension between liberation and salvation: "Even when theology is done on behalf of the poor, all dimensions of faith must always be addressed: personal, social, and eschatological. Christianity is not only social *transformation*, it is individual *conversion*, and it is *resurrection* of the dead, as well."[59]

In *We Drink from Our Own Wells* (1984), Gustavo Gutiérrez evaluates Christian spirituality's authenticity by its ability to integrate worship and prayer with social responsibility. Far from "historicizing" spirituality, Gutiérrez stands well within the rich tradition of Western spiritualities that seek to balance contemplation with action (specifically Ignatian spirituality) while emphasizing the communal nature of the life of Christian discipleship. The author discusses five marks of the spiritual journey: (1) *conversion*, which is initiated by God and experienced as a radical break with the past and the beginning of a new life; (2) *gratuitousness*, the awareness that God's gracious love is the source of all good things, including our own ability to love God and neighbor; (3) *joy* in the realization that through the death and resurrection of Christ God has defeated suffering, sin, oppression, and death (it should be noted that by emphasizing joy Gutiérrez does not minimize the reality of human suffering but refers to a deep joy grounded in God's eternal promises: "It is not the superficial kind of rejoicing . . . but the joy born of the conviction that unjust mistreatment and suffering will be overcome");[60] (4) *spiritual childhood*, referring to the humility described in the Gospels as being "poor in spirit" (Matt. 5:3) and described by Gutiérrez as "the ready disposition of one who hopes for everything from the Lord";[61] and (5) *community*, which is the intentional choice by the convert to live in solidarity with the poor. While not unique to liberation spirituality, this last point is indispensable for a liberationist understanding of the Christian life.

However, to equate this continuous emphasis on the practical moral consequences of sanctification by the Holy Spirit to a reduction of the work of salvation to human history is to ignore much of what liberation theology says. At the core of liberating praxis lies a radical conversion experience: "Evangelical conversion is indeed the touchstone of all spirituality. Conversion means a radical transformation of ourselves; it means thinking, feeling, and living as Christ—present in exploited and alienated persons."[62] As a consequence of this conversion, our lives are transformed by the Holy Spirit and we are called to "a definitive way of living 'before the Lord,' in solidarity with all human beings, 'with the Lord,' and before human beings. It arises from an intense spiritual experience which is later explicated and witnessed to."[63] Thus, in articulating a doctrine of the Holy Spirit, liberation theology insists that the church not ignore the communal aspects of our new sanctified life and—more important—questions past understandings of community and challenges the church to welcome those whom we have labeled as "other" into the community of the Spirit. Exegeting the parable of the Good Samaritan, Gutiérrez provides an important marker for tracking the Spirit in our world: "The neighbor was the Samaritan who approached the wounded man and made him his neighbor. The neighbor, as has been said, is not the one whom I find in my path, but rather the one in whose path I place myself, the one whom I approach and actively seek."[64] So, *Who is my neighbor?* The community of the Holy Spirit is found wherever the work of liberation takes place, for it is by going out of his way, by taking a personal risk, and by sacrificing his own wealth and comfort that the Samaritan acts as a neighbor to the injured man.

The Community of the Holy Spirit

Ada María Isasi-Díaz uses the metaphor of *mestizaje* to describe Christian theology's urgent need to embrace difference in establishing just communities. After a litany of statistics that describe the plight of the poor and oppressed in the world, Isasi-Díaz concludes that the "unwillingness or perhaps (perhaps?!) the incapacity to see the misery of such a large percentage of the human race is grounded, I believe, in the refusal to recognize that these vast numbers of suffering humanity are our sisters and brothers—people to whom and for whom we are responsible."[65] She then gives two main reasons for why we do not accept the poor, oppressed, and marginalized as our responsibility: either it is a matter of selfishness or it is the result of prejudice. That is, either we recognize that our wealth and comfort exist at the expense of the poverty and suffering of others (and we will therefore do what it takes to protect the status quo), or we adhere to certain (most likely irrational) beliefs that the poor and oppressed are poor and oppressed because they are lazy and inferior. In reconstructing Christian doctrine in ways that allow dominant groups to view those on the underside of society differently, we can embrace a theological anthropology rooted in *mestizaje* as a means of breaking down the false barriers that create division and prevent us from seeing all human beings as our brothers and sisters. Such a move requires a reconceptualized ecclesiology that recognizes the church's role in resisting racism.

Given that the church is not identical with the "kin-dom" of God but serves as a witness to and foretaste of the eschatological community, it is important for theology to identify criteria for recognizing the "true" church. According to the Nicene Creed, the classical "marks" of the church are unity, holiness, catholicity, and apostolicity. During the Reformation, Martin Luther and John Calvin tested the church's adherence to the Nicene formula with the addition of two complementary marks: "Whenever we see the Word of God purely preached and heard, and the sacraments administered according to Christ's institution, there, it is not to be doubted, a church of God exists."[66] If, as I have argued in this chapter, one of the criteria for recognizing Christian community is the presence of the Holy Spirit manifest in liberating work, and given that liberation and solidarity are gifts of the Spirit long recognized by both the biblical and Christian doctrinal tradition, then we must avoid defining church in terms that continue to separate worship from social ethics.

The paradigm of *mestizaje* as descriptive of the work of the Holy Spirit thus yields concrete liberating practices that must be embodied by the Christian community. Broadly, these "marks" of a *mestizo* church include resistance to racism, sexism, and classism. Recalling Cornel West's typology of resistance in *Prophesy Deliverance! An Afro-American Revolutionary Christianity* (1982), I urge U.S. Latino/a theology to develop inclusive communal practices and effective strategies of political resistance. Such a prophetic Christian community would emphasize (1) a liberative reading of Scripture that empowers the church to engage in positive social transformation, (2) a distinctly Latino/a cultural identity that does not denigrate or exclude other cultures, and (3) the need to continuously struggle against the tendency to essentialize group cultural identity at the expense of dissenting perspectives.

Conclusion

Toward a Mestizo *Church*

Perhaps a good starting point is to ponder the very possibility of an ecumenical ecclesiology. Given the visible divisions within Christianity, is it possible to reach unity on the doctrine of the church? U.S. Latino/a theology has distinguished itself by advocating a communal methodology called *teología en conjunto* that incorporates insights from pastors, laypersons, and academic theologians across confessional boundaries. The stated goal is a theology accountable to the community of faith that reflects the popular beliefs of Latino/as while offering a prophetic critique of the dominant theological perspectives. The challenge of ecumenical ecclesiology in the twenty-first century is to acknowledge the particularity of our different confessions while still confessing one, holy, catholic, and apostolic church. Given its commitment to *teología en conjunto*, U.S. Latino/a theology has much to contribute to the ecumenical conversation on the doctrine of the church. At the same time, one of the underlying tensions within U.S. Latino/a theology has been the reluctance to address doctrinal differences in order to preserve a unified movement, which might explain why there are no sustained ecclesiological reflections in the work of U.S. Latino/a theologians. This investigation challenges the romanticized vision of U.S. Latino/a theology as a homogeneous movement by arguing that downplaying significant differences in doctrine, liturgy, and political commitments does not preserve Latino/a unity and can hamper the movement's emancipatory objectives. U.S. Latino/a theology risks becoming an insular academic discipline, a top-down intellectual movement devoid of grassroots grounding, unless it nurtures greater accountability to concrete faith communities. This need for greater accountability to particular confessional traditions requires that we confront doctrinal obstacles to an ecumenical ecclesiology.

Despite major works by such figures as Justo L. González, Virgilio Elizondo, Ada María Isasi-Díaz, and Roberto S. Goizueta, U.S. Latino/a theology has yielded little systematic reflection on the doctrine of the church. Commenting on the dearth of Protestant Latino/a contributions to ecclesiology, Justo González attributes this to the fact that, "as Protestant Latinos and Latinas we have inherited a theology in which ecclesiology plays a very secondary role."[1] The roots of this antichurch attitude are traceable to the forms of nineteenth-century missionary Protestantism exported to Latin America from the United States that emphasized individual salvation to the detriment of communal life, coupled with the strong bias against highly organized hierarchical church governance often exhibited by Roman Catholic converts to Protestantism. Still, González finds this absence of an explicit ecclesiology a boon that opens the door for "all sorts of cooperative ventures" among Latino/a churches "that would be quite difficult in the old-line white denominations."[2]

While Hispanic Protestantism (with minor exceptions) has a brief hundred-year history in the United States, generations of Hispanic Catholics have populated California, Texas, and other parts of the American Southwest. Yet, looking at the issue from a Roman Catholic perspective, Gary Riebe-Estrella also concludes, "Little sustained reflection on ecclesiology has been done in U.S. Latino Catholic theology."[3] A major contributing factor is that in spite of constituting an estimated 39 percent of U.S. Catholics (according to the U.S. Conference of Catholic Bishops), Latino/as remain underrepresented and marginalized within ecclesial structures. Consequently, Latino/a theologians have characterized the life of Latino/as within the Catholic Church as a popular religious movement existing alongside official church governance thriving independently of the institutional church and arising in communities where clergy and the Eucharist are not always available.[4] Nevertheless, Riebe-Estrella portrays the U.S. Latino/a experience of marginalization within North American Catholicism as an opportunity to challenge dominant ecclesiologies by exploring the notion of church as People of God highlighted in *Lumen Gentium,* the Dogmatic Constitution of the Church of Vatican II.[5] While numerous ecclesiological insights pervade the scholarly contributions of U.S. Latino/a theologians, no one has yet to explicitly articulate an ecclesiology from a U.S. Latino/a perspective. This concluding chapter outlines a possible direction for future ecclesiological reflection by focusing on certain aspects of our *mestizo* experience that contribute to the development of an ecumenical twenty-first-century ecclesiology while simultaneously identifying obstacles within Protestantism and Catholicism that impede the establishment of a genuinely *mestizo* church.

This book's exploration of major Christian doctrines through the lens of U.S. Latino/a experience has yielded an understanding of *mestizaje* as a set of communal practices distinguished by a moral choice to recognize the inherent dignity of all human beings in political solidarity. The logical next step is to draw upon these doctrinal reconstructions to articulate an emancipatory doctrine of the church. From the beginning this book has articulated an alternative model of theology that engages political discourse from an openly confessional stance such that the theologian bears the double responsibility of articulating a political theology rooted in the distinct sources and traditions of the faith while also conversing with those who do not share the same confessional commitments, the underlying assumption being that the most effective means of transforming the faith community's praxis—and thereby the world—is by retrieving liberation themes from within the community's own rich heritage. By this view, both biblical narratives and church doctrines become valuable sources for liberation; to argue otherwise is to suggest that liberation is an extrascriptural and therefore unnecessary aspect of the Christian faith.

The use of particular biblical texts and repeated appeals to certain themes within the Reformed theological tradition might raise concerns that this work has uncritically embraced a "canon within a canon" in its reconstructive efforts. These apprehensions are assuaged in part by consistently employing a "hermeneutics of suspicion" that questions and challenges received traditions and frameworks of interpretation, repeatedly demonstrating the unconscious motivations, socioeconomic interests, political ideologies, and cultural biases that shape all interpretations of history, science, philosophy, and theology. Accordingly, I have articulated a consistent theological critique of racism in both church and society in order to transform both church and society. In spite of a long and painful history of passively condoning, and at times actively participating in, racial domination, the Christian church possesses rich resources for overcoming the problem of race in contemporary society. A *mestizo* reconstruction of the doctrine of the church invites the ecumenical church to look at the Latino/a experience not as a marginalized perspective that ought to be tolerated or as just another multicultural diversity that ought to be celebrated but as a present-day incarnation of the risen Christ. More to the point, as one instantiation of the body of Christ, the Latino/a church speaks with divine authority.

It has been demonstrated that there exists a long tradition of publicly engaged theologies that speak authoritatively as Word of God because as church—a community gathered and empowered by the Holy Spirit—they represent the risen Christ in the world. At the same time, great care has been taken not to absolutize the identification of any particular historical entity called church with Christ. In other words, that the church is the historical embodiment of the risen Christ remains a divine mystery, since we can neither fully comprehend nor control it. The doctrine of the church, ecclesiology, guides our life together by providing *notae ecclesia,* that is, distinct "marks" without which our faith communities cannot name themselves "church." The ecumenical Nicene Creed identifies holiness, catholicity, unity, and apostolicity as the major marks of the church; the Reformation emphasized a proper understanding of the preaching of the Word and the administration of the sacraments; today liberation theologies have added God's preferential option for the poor and oppressed.

A *mestizo* theological reconstruction of ecclesiology offers its own distinct "notes" for assessing the faithfulness of the Christian church in the world today. These *notae ecclesia* are not intended to replace the classical marks of the church but are offered as a supplement to the ecumenical confessions because the wisdom of the Latino/a church—guided and nurtured by the Holy Spirit—teaches us that the dominant traditions have not fully realized their vocation as body of Christ. Some members of the body have been neglected, excluded, even persecuted, but by appealing to historically marginalized prophetic perspectives that endure within Christianity in spite of great neglect or intentional suppression, the *mestizo* church offers its own distinct marks that need to be embodied in the public life of the church. In light of the theological reconstructions of the doctrines of *imago Dei,* Christ, and the Holy Spirit articulated in this work, specific Christian practices that constitute "marks" of the *mestizo* church include (1) engaging in political activism to resist racism grounded in a belief that the racially and ethnically "other" shares in the *imago Dei,* (2) continuing Christ's ministry of reconciliation by embodying the "way of the cross" as adversarial politics, (3) broadening our definition of community to recognize God's liberating work *wherever* it occurs, and (4) demonstrating a willingness to work together with new manifestations of spiritual community located outside traditional understandings of *ecclesia.*

Catholic theologian Susan K. Wood identifies "communion ecclesiology" as the dominant approach for conceptualizing church within Roman Catholic circles and also the leading paradigm for future ecumenical conversation.[6] Grounded in the images of the church put forth in the documents of Vatican II and affirmed in the June 1992 letter issued by the

Congregation for the Doctrine of the Faith to the bishops of the Catholic Church, "Some Aspects of the Church Understood as Communion," communion ecclesiology draws upon the biblical image of the church as the body of Christ (1 Cor. 12; Rom. 12:4–8; Eph. 2:11–3:6; Col. 1:18, 24) in order to confirm our participation in the life of Christ via mystical union. At the same time, these Pauline texts emphasize the distinction between the church and Christ by naming Christ the head of the body, thereby "assuring that the church always remains subordinate to its head, Christ."[7] Of particular interest for Catholic ecclesiology is Paul's grounding of the community as body of Christ in the Lord's Supper (1 Cor. 10:16–22, 11:17–34), which leads Wood to conclude, "Where the Eucharist is, there is church."[8] The resulting ecclesiology, building upon a Trinitarian understanding of God as a divine communion (*perichoresis*), affirms the sacramental real presence of Christ without reducing the church to the Eucharist, yet understands the very possibility of human communion with Christ and with one another as indissoluble from the "elements of grace and sacrament that ultimately identify ecclesial communities in terms of their relationship to Christ."[9]

One of the most important documents for reaching ecumenical consensus on ecclesiology, *Baptism, Eucharist and Ministry* (*BEM*), issued in 1982 by the Commission on Faith and Order of the World Council of Churches, brings together insights from various Christian traditions in order to affirm the predominance of the sacraments in the life of the church.[10] *BEM* stands as a historical landmark in ecumenical rapprochement that serves to underscore the appeal of and obstacles to communion ecclesiology for the contemporary situation. Protestant—particularly Evangelical—criticism of *BEM* centers on the document's assertion that the Lord's Supper is "the central act of the Church's worship"[11] rather than affirming the Reformation principle that the central act of God's self-revelation in Jesus Christ is manifest through *both* Word and sacrament. Equally objectionable is *BEM*'s insistence that episcopal succession is a necessary mark of apostolicity—though by no means the only mark —required for achieving full Christian unity. Many Protestant traditions contend that apostolic succession is preserved by fidelity to the proclamation and practice of the apostles rather than by means of a monarchical episcopate.

Still, in spite of its emphasis on the doctrine of the real presence, Catholic theologians view communion ecclesiology as a vital resource for ecumenical reconciliation, even while acknowledging the difficulty of achieving "full ecclesiastical communion" with those whom the Vatican has named "not Churches in the proper sense" (*Dominus Iesus*, IV.17). As interpreted by some Catholic theologians, communion ecclesiology focuses primarily on the church's sacramental life—particularly participation in the Eucharist—and consequently creates a doctrinal barrier with those churches that do not affirm a "common and mutual recognition of faith, sacramental practice, and ministry."[12]

Susan K. Wood engages Protestant theologian Robert Jenson as a conversation partner in order to advocate for communion ecclesiology as the preferred model for ecumenical reconciliation and finds his approach "neither singularly Protestant nor exclusively Roman Catholic."[13] Recognizing the profoundly ecumenical character of Jenson's ecclesiology, Wood emphasizes his affinity with Roman Catholic ecclesiology without denying his Reformation roots. According to Wood, Jenson's treatment of the church as the body of Christ "identifies the church as a fourth dramatic person in the biblical narrative" and "tends to place the church on the same plane" as the three persons of the Trinity.[14] If Wood's assessment of Jenson's ecclesiology is accurate, he risks creating a Quaternity, or at the very least, identifying the work of the Holy Spirit with the concrete historical church. By elevating the church beyond "creaturely" status Jenson distances himself from the Lutheran tradition and intentionally embraces a more Roman Catholic view of the church. However, as Wood concludes, Jenson's one-to-one correlation between the historical church and the body of Christ exceeds the claims of Roman Catholic ecclesiology: "As deeply sympathetic as I am with Jenson's identification of the church as the risen body of Christ, I fear that he often makes this identification too directly."[15] Wood proposes the church as sacrament as a model that allows for a clearer distinction between the church and Christ, since too "close an identification between Christ and the church ignores the fact that the church has not fully arrived at the eschaton."[16]

What does it mean that the church is the body of Christ (1 Cor. 12:12–31)? For Jenson this implies that the risen Christ must be embodied, occupying space and time, and that the "bread and the cup in the congregation's midst is the very same body of Christ."[17] While Jenson's Catholic critics agree there is an identity between the risen Christ *as* the Eucharistic body and the community of believers, for Jenson the church becomes Christ's "objective self." Rather than pursuing this direct identification of the risen Christ with the historical church, conceptualizing the church as sacrament provides a clearer distinction between the church as a human institution and the church as mystical communion. Given the church's eschatological character, it is a foretaste of the kingdom but not identical with the kingdom, the category of sacramental presence seems more adequate, since sacraments "point to a reality and contain a reality beyond themselves."[18] When understood sacramentally, Jenson's Protestant conceptualization of the body of Christ as embodied presence provides "a valuable contribution to Roman Catholic ecclesiology."[19]

Jenson's discussion of *ecclesia* as the body of Christ recalls Karl Barth's understanding in which the church is a community called by God's electing grace as "the earthly-historical form of existence of Jesus Christ Himself,"[20] as well as Dietrich Bonhoeffer's challenge to the Confessing Church movement that "the body of Christ takes up physical space here on earth."[21] While Jenson cautions "we may not so identify the risen Christ with the church as to be unable to refer to the one and then to the other,"[22] he struggles to maintain the necessary distinction between Jesus and the church:

> Sacrament and church are *truly* Christ's body for us. . . . The subject that the risen Christ is, is the subject who comes to word in the gospel. The object—the body—that the risen Christ is, is the body in the world to which this word calls our intention, the church around her sacraments. He needs no other body to be a risen man, body and soul.[23]

Still, he avoids the temptation of triumphalism by differentiating between the church as *association*—a gathering of individuals sharing common beliefs and/or goals, and the church as *communion*—the church gathered and united by the Holy Spirit. While Jenson locates the authority of the teaching office in the latter—the community, empowered by the Holy Spirit, as interpreter of Scripture, transcending the particular representatives ordained to the teaching office—when the church's "communal spirit is identically the Spirit that the personal God is and has,"[24] the result, intentional or not, is a complete identification of the work of the Holy Spirit with the person holding the teaching office. Thus, when the penitent asks for the assurance of pardon, Jenson concludes that the confessor's reply *must* be, "You know because I am about to absolve you, and my doing that *is* God's eternal act of decision about you."[25]

On the matter of church order and governance Robert Jenson's ecclesiology moves away from its Lutheran roots toward Roman Catholicism through an explicit identification of the officeholder with the grace being mediated. According to Jenson, canon, liturgy, and creed cannot exist apart from the ecclesial authority that legitimates them. In fact, Jenson argues for the necessity of a magisterium identified with a personal office: "Succession in office is the *personal* aspect of the church's institutional self-identity through time."[26] Reformed ecclesiology, while lacking episcopal succession, nonetheless preserves an "episcopate" in its representative form of governance. In a surprising move—surprising from a Reformed theological perspective, anyway—Jenson affirms the Roman Catholic definition of apostolic succession as located in the historical monarchical episcopate and agrees with then cardinal Joseph Ratzinger's description in *Dominus Iesus* of churches lacking episcopal succession as "wounded."[27] While acknowledging that Jenson also challenges Roman Catholics to reform their ecclesiology, Wood grants that "Lutherans must concede more to his theology than must Roman Catholics."[28] Jenson faces an almost insurmountable challenge in convincing fellow Protestants of his position given widespread belief that nonhierarchical church governance can fulfill the function of the bishop's office just as well as a monarchical episcopate.[29] Isn't this, after all, still a form of "embodied" presence? While Jenson is correct that some Reformed ecclesiologies tend to devalue church unity, his generalizations diminish the contributions of the mainline Protestant churches at the forefront of ecumenical unification efforts in the mid–twentieth century.

According to Jenson, the historical self-identity of the church is preserved by the church's teaching office, a point further heightened by the distinction between the church's *synchronic* and *diachronic* unity. The church is one, holy, catholic, and apostolic. Therefore, a necessary task of theology is to account for the church's diversity diachronically (differences due to the passage of time) and synchronically (differences existing in the same time arising from contextual changes—social, political, cultural, gender, etc.). Theology is both gatekeeper and barrier for Jenson. Responding to criticism that such a strong identification of the work of the church with the work of the Spirit might hamper the church's ability to reform itself, Jenson asserts that the very possibility of churchly reform demands an ontological identification of the church with the risen body of Christ. Just as the individual person disciplines his or her own body, Jesus disciplines his body, the church: "If there is to be churchly reform, the Spirit must do it; it must be done by the triune person who frees the church to be the own body of Christ."[30] Unfortunately, Jenson fails to say how the teaching office, Christ's reforming agent as the arbiter of dogma, is itself reformed.

Jenson's choice to focus on the church's diachronic unity is driven by ecumenical concerns to heal deep historical rifts in the church. Unfortunately, he says very little about the church's synchronic unity—other than to remind the teaching office of its duty to maintain one communion—leaving the impression that confessional traditions are internally monolithic and free from dissent. Perhaps the greatest weakness in Jenson's two-volume systematic theology is its inability to address and properly account for the contemporary church's synchronic unity. Specifically, there is no direct engagement of theological voices from the third world or the perspective of women and ethnic minorities within the dominant European and North American cultures. Diachronically his theology is strong; synchronically it is weak. A *mestizo* ecumenical ecclesiology strives for inclusion at both the diachronic and synchronic levels.

Still, Jenson's treatment of the church's diachronic unity is very rich, drawing upon a variety of confessional traditions throughout the history of the church. His hope is that, by equating the church's self-identity through time with the teaching office in apostolic succession, contemporary divisions will become superfluous:

> At bottom, the chief thing to be done about the integrity of the church across time is to pray that *God* will indeed use the church's structures of historical continuity to establish and preserve it, and to believe that he answers this prayer. Much futile polemical theology will be spared on all sides when this is recognized without qualification.[31]

Jenson stands firm on his view that the historical church—and specifically the episcopal hierarchy—speaks with divine authority because it is the earthly embodiment of the risen Christ.

Diachronic unity preserves the historical self-identity of the church, assuring us that the church of the present is in continuity with the teaching of the apostles, and will continue into the future being one and the same church, while synchronic unity seeks to preserve the church's self-identity in different contemporary contexts. Comparing diachronic to synchronic is like comparing a telescope to a microscope: when the historical unity of the church is observed from afar, petty details are glossed over and consensus seems within reach; observed up close, the smallest differences are greatly magnified and seem unavoidably divisive. Jenson's inability to address the church's synchronic reality is particularly noticeable in his lack of dialogue with Pentecostalism—the fastest-growing branch of Protestantism in the Western Hemisphere (if not the world)—in spite of his emphasis on Pentecost and the role of the Holy Spirit in founding the church. Sadly, by characterizing the Free Church movement as "free-floating spiritualism,"[32] Jenson risks closing the door to any future dialogue with these churches. To use Jenson's own words, it is as if certain confessional traditions—or marginalized voices within a tradition—have been judged to be "not church."

One strand of Roman Catholic theology—Latin American liberation theology—presents a model of communion ecclesiology that holds much promise for articulating a *mestizo* view of the church. Liberation theologians challenge the church to look beyond its liturgical celebrations and recognize the sacramental dimension of the work of historical liberation as a means of extending Christ's redemptive work to all humankind. The vision of Christian community resulting from the apostle Paul's reflections on "the body of Christ" articulated in Vatican II and embraced by the Second General Conference of the Latin American Episcopate in 1968 at Medellín, Colombia, affirms a diversity of ministries that challenge traditional ecclesiologies to move beyond clericalism, recognizes the need to transcend existing boundaries (such as the ordination of women) that limit the full expression of spiritual gifts, and affirms the need to work toward full Eucharistic unity as members of the one body: "For in the one Spirit we were all baptized into one body—Jews or Greeks, slaves or free —and we were all made to drink of one Spirit" (12:13). By conceptualizing the church as a sacrament of God's salvific work—with an emphasis on human historical liberation—theologians like Gustavo Gutiérrez and Leonardo Boff build on Vatican II's "body of Christ" ecclesiology while transcending traditional understandings of the church as a sacramental community.[33] By linking the church's liturgical practice to its social ethics, liberation theologies broaden the Catholic view of church as mystical communion to include concrete political action without compromising sacramental realism (a primary Catholic concern) while embodying an alternative model of "communion" that does not privilege a particular organizational model (a chief Protestant objection), since the "notion of sacrament enables us to think of the Church within the horizon of the salvific work and in terms radically different from those of the ecclesiocentric emphasis."[34] In other words, while drawing inspiration from the

"new ecclesiological perspective" of Vatican II,[35] Latin American liberation theology has articulated one of the strongest criticisms of the hierarchical church, thus providing contemporary theology with a paradigm
for evaluating the inherited ecclesiologies of both Roman Catholic and
Protestant traditions.

Although the "church as sacrament" model conceptualized by Gustavo
Gutiérrez has been highly influential among Latino/a theologians in the
United States—especially among Roman Catholics, as evidenced by the
theology of accompaniment articulated by Roberto S. Goizueta[36]—*mestizo* theology still faces its greatest challenge: articulating a distinctive ecclesiology. True to its *mestizo* identity, Latino/a Christianity in the United
States ought to persevere in navigating borderlands—not just between
cultures but also between confessional traditions. In practice, however,
dormant confessional commitments often rise to the surface over questions of ecclesiology, as evidenced by the ongoing ecumenical debate and
discussion on *BEM*. Still, since U.S. Latino/a theology already occupies
the borderlands between official church structures and popular practices,
and given that Latino/a churches either survive at the periphery of major
denominations or become "free churches" that empower local congregations and nurture "home-grown" leadership but still remain marginalized
within the broader society, U.S. Latino/a theology ought to embrace its
unique social location to push the boundaries of our inherited ecclesiologies. As a movement, U.S. Latino/a theology has avoided serious doctrinal
conversation about those ecclesiological commitments that divide Catholics, Protestants, and Pentecostals, namely, very different understandings
of the Lord's Supper (with some Protestant and Pentecostal traditions lacking the very concept of sacrament) and long-standing historical divisions
about the interpretation of apostolic succession. Pushing the theological
metaphor of *mestizaje* to its logical consequence demands a willingness to
transcend received ecclesiological traditions, however sacred, in order to
construct a doctrine of the church consistent with the liberative and inclusive vision found in the Scriptures and embraced by the Roman Catholic Church in the documents of the Second Vatican Council.

Allusions to the church as "the body of Christ" can be found scattered
throughout the New Testament (Mark 14:22 and parallels; John 2:19–21;
Heb. 10:5, 10; 13:3, 11–12; 1 Pet. 2:24), but only the Pauline letters use the
image explicitly to describe the church. Without minimizing existing
doctrinal divisions, *mestizo* theology needs to revisit these complex biblical images at the heart of communion ecclesiology and, guided by the

emancipatory concerns highlighted in this book, delineate what level of ecumenical consensus can be achieved. While there are many images for the church in the New Testament, communion ecclesiology—especially as articulated by Latin American liberation theologians—employs the Pauline phrase "the body of Christ" in order to highlight human participation in the triune life of Christ while acknowledging that human community is not possible without the spiritual transformation effected by Jesus Christ.

In the letter to the Romans, chapters 5 through 8, Paul develops an argument about redemption from the "body of death" (7:24) through the body of Christ in which a bifurcation between death and life becomes obvious, and life is possible only through mystical union with Christ:

> For if we have been united with him in a death like his, we will certainly be united with him in a resurrection like his. We know that our old self was crucified with him so that the body of sin might be destroyed, and we might no longer be enslaved to sin. For whoever has died is freed from sin. But if we have died with Christ, we believe that we will also live with him. We know that Christ, being raised from the dead, will never die again; death no longer has dominion over him. The death he died, he died to sin, once for all; but the life he lives, he lives to God. So you also must consider yourselves dead to sin and alive to God in Christ Jesus. (Rom. 6:5–11, NRSV)

Throughout the letter Paul is addressing the church—the spiritual community of those who have died with Christ through faith and have risen to new life—of whom now much is expected: "You have died to the law through the body of Christ, so that you may belong to another, to him who has been raised from the dead in order that we may bear fruit for God" (Rom. 7:4, NRSV). While life in the Spirit is described as a form of bondage—slaves to Christ as opposed to slaves to sin (Rom. 8:15)—we are slaves "in the new life of the Spirit" (Rom. 7:6, NRSV), which brings freedom. According to Paul, all of humanity is subject to the law of sin and death; the only other option available to humanity is life in Christ. One way of understanding the church as a spiritual community in Christ is through this mystical participation in the death and resurrection of Christ.

The community of believers—the "saints"—is made up of individuals who belong to Christ and to one another. By employing this image of a body composed of many members (1 Cor. 12:12) with Christ as its head,

Paul underscores the importance of individual moral responsibility for the preservation of community: "For you were bought with a price; therefore glorify God in your body" (1 Cor. 6:20, NRSV). Accordingly, enforcing community discipline is one of the Pauline marks of the new spiritual community in Christ, since our bodies belong to Christ as members of his body and that which we do with our bodies either profanes or glorifies him. But who is included as "members" of the "body of Christ"? Those who through faith have received grace and have been incorporated into the new spiritual community inaugurated by Christ's death on the cross. Yet, even though Paul divides the world into those who are enslaved to sin and those who have taken on the yoke of discipleship, he does not envision the church as an exclusive community. In fact, in the Pauline literature, the very notion of Christ as our "head" (*kephale*) stresses the vastness of Christ's self-sacrifice: "For in him the whole fullness of deity dwells bodily, and you have come to fullness in him, who is the head of every ruler and authority" (Col. 2:9–10, NRSV). In other words, Christ is the "head" of each and every human being whether or not he is acknowledged as such by unbelievers. Consequently, since Christ is the ruler of all, his reconciliation extends to all: "For in him all the fullness of God was pleased to dwell, and through him God was pleased to reconcile himself to all things, whether on earth or in heaven, by making peace through the blood of the cross" (Col. 1:19–20, NRSV). That Christ seeks to reconcile with all of humanity (and all of Creation), and not just with those who self-identify as "members" of the one body, resonates with the *mestizo* understanding of spiritual community as wherever God's work for liberation takes place, and also undermines the exclusive tendencies of our inherited ecclesiologies.

In spite of the universal scope of Christ's lordship, unity remains one of the desired characteristics of the new spiritual community described by Paul. In Corinth we find a community divided over the Eucharistic meal, and Paul's words to that community provide a strong challenge to those traditions that do not affirm a real sacramental presence in the celebration of the Lord's Supper, and to all who persist in accepting doctrinal divisions without working toward a historical unity: "The cup of blessing that we bless, is it not a sharing in the blood of Christ? The bread that we break, is it not a sharing in the body of Christ? Because there is one bread, we who are many are one body, for we all partake of the one bread" (1 Cor. 10:16–17, NRSV). Paul distinguishes between a shared common meal and the Eucharistic fellowship, arguing that for a meal to be the Lord's Supper there needs to be a unity of spirit embodied in solidarity and characterized by the sharing of common resources for the well-being of all. This dying of self-interest and living for others—"Do not seek your own advantage, but that of the other" (10:24)—is essential for a genuine celebration of the Eucharistic meal in which the many become one in Spirit with the risen Christ. Consequently, Paul warns, "Whoever, therefore, eats the bread or drinks the cup of the Lord in an unworthy manner will be answerable for the body and blood of the Lord. Examine yourselves, and only then eat of the bread and drink of the cup" (11:27–28). An ecumenical ecclesiology ought to strive for genuine unity, not only of belief, but also of praxis. As Gutiérrez has argued, the spiritual reality of conversion and solidarity in community celebrated in the Eucharist becomes an "empty action" when it is celebrated without "a real commitment against exploitation and alienation and for a society of solidarity and justice."[37] Still, while liberative action provides a concrete marker for identifying those practices that constitute the church, we are able to celebrate our unity in the Eucharist because we are mystically one body in faith through Christ. Paul's emphasis on self-examination prior to receiving the bread and the cup elevates the importance of what happens in the Lord's Supper above mere memorialization to include some notion of a real sacramental presence, challenging many Protestant communions to revisit their sacramentology.

At the same time, a biblical understanding of church as "the body of Christ" reveals a diversity of ministries within the one body that challenges some of the more rigid hierarchical aspects of Roman Catholic ecclesiology. Paul recognizes and affirms a multiplicity of *charisms,* or spiritual gifts, without privileging one over the other: "Now there are varieties of gifts but the same Spirit; and there are varieties of services, but the same Lord; and there are varieties of activities, but it is the same God who activates all of them in every one" (1 Cor. 12:4–6, NRSV). Nevertheless, the test of whether or not a spiritual gift is genuine is if it proclaims, "Jesus is Lord" (12:3), and whether or not it builds up the "common good" (12:7). Paul recognizes that the church contains many forms of ministry and argues that making exclusive claims about the superiority of one over the others—even such revered offices as apostle, prophet, and teachers—contradicts God's purpose for these various spiritual gifts, that is, the edification of the spiritual community, "so that the church may be built up" (14:5). In fact, Paul goes on to argue that none of these gifts have value aside from the spiritual gift of love: "If I have all faith, so as to move mountains, but do not have love, I am nothing" (13:2). In chapter 13 Paul focuses on the actions of love, affirming that the spiritual reality of new life in Christ yields concrete praxis—we participate in the death and resurrection of Christ both Eucharistically and through our individual and communal actions, for if "one member suffers, all suffer together with it" (12:26).

Looking to the future reminds us that our inherited ecclesiologies often prove inadequate in the face of secularization, globalization, and pluralism. Furthermore, this plurality of perspectives represents the fullness of the Christian heritage rather than the advent of a new reality. From the beginning the Christian community has embodied *mestizaje,* since Christian identity has always involved the continuous interaction of multiple cultural, theological, and political perspectives, whether we look to the Jerusalem church in its struggle to integrate Gentile believers, the Patristic church and its efforts to accommodate Greco-Roman culture, or the effects of globalization and immigration upon North American Christianity over the last twenty years. If Christianity has reached a point in its history where we can no longer simply label the other as "not church" (Jenson), then we must strive to live in mutual interrelation. The experience and wisdom of the Latino/a church say we must learn to appreciate the richness of our diverse religious history rather than fall back upon inherited ecclesiologies that seek to erect new barriers where now we find porous borders. As *ecclesia,* a gathered mystical communion empowered by the Spirit for historical action, we embody the risen Christ when we welcome the stranger among us, take an adversarial stance in the face of injustice, and create community in the midst of division and strife. The experience of *mestizaje* as a privileged location for theological reflection is one that Latino/as share with the whole church because, aside from being our own story of immigration and acculturation, it is also the Gospel's story of inclusion and reconciliation.

Notes

NOTES TO THE INTRODUCTION

1. While in North America racial stratification resulted in the practice of identifying all mixed-race black/white persons as black, Latin America *mestizaje* often recognized the European ancestry of persons of mixed (*mestizo*/mulatto) background, thereby allowing them a place in the dominant society at the expense of their ethnicity.

2. Frederick Douglass, "What to the Slave Is the Fourth of July? An Address Delivered in Rochester, New York, on 5 July 1852," in *The Norton Anthology of African American Literature,* ed. Henry Louis Gates Jr. (New York: Norton, 1997), 388–89.

3. See Randall Balmer, "Casting Aside the Ballast of History and Tradition: White Protestants and the Bible in the Antebellum Period," in *African Americans and the Bible: Sacred Texts and Social Textures,* ed. Vincent L. Wimbush (New York: Continuum, 2001), 193–200.

4. See Eric Williams, *Capitalism and Slavery* (Chapel Hill: University of North Carolina Press, 1944).

5. See James H. Sweet, "The Iberian Roots of American Racist Thought," *William and Mary Quarterly,* 3rd ser., 54, no. 1 (Jan. 1997): 143–66.

6. A note on language: throughout the text every effort is made to use gender-inclusive language, but quotations are left exact in order to preserve the author's original intent or bias. The terms *Latino/a* and *U.S. Latino/a* used throughout this work are accepted gender-inclusive self-referential terms for the peoples, traditions, and theologies sharing a common Iberian (Spanish/Portuguese) linguistic and cultural heritage whose social location is the United States.

7. See H. Richard Niebuhr, *Christ and Culture* (New York: Harper Torchbooks, 1956). In spite of its simplicity, Niebuhr's paradigm provides a general framework for discussing the relation of theology to culture; in chapters 2 and 3 I articulate a more complex conceptualization of the relationship of Christ to culture in conversation with Kathryn Tanner's work *Theories of Culture: A New Agenda for Theology* (Minneapolis, MN: Fortress Press, 1997).

8. My use of certain descriptive categories for discussing the role of tradition on the formation of identity is indebted to the work of Paul Ricoeur and

Hans-Georg Gadamer. See Paul Ricoeur, *Figuring the Sacred: Religion, Narrative, and Imagination,* trans. David Pellauer, ed. Mark I. Wallace (Minneapolis, MN: Fortress Press, 1995); and Hans-Georg Gadamer, *Truth and Method,* 2nd rev. ed., trans. Joel Weinsheimer and Donald G. Marshall (New York: Continuum, 2000).

9. See John Calvin, *Institutes of the Christian Religion,* trans. Ford Lewis Battles, ed. John T. McNeill, 2 vols. (Philadelphia: Westminster Press, 1960), 296ff. (1.6.1). According to Calvin, Scripture "clearly shows us the true God" and presents us with new knowledge about God not given in nature.

10. See Karl Barth, *Church Dogmatics* I/2, ed. G. W. Bromiley and T. F. Torrance (Edinburgh: T & T Clark, 1956), §§23–24. Barth's insights on dogmatics as a function of the "hearing" and "teaching" church highlight the provisional nature of theological statements. Genuine obedience to the Word of God demands the proper churchly attitude whereby the church continually submits its teaching (the human word) to the judgment and guidance of the divine Word.

11. For an introduction to the issue of the contextual character of theology, see Stephen B. Bevans, *Models of Contextual Theology* (Maryknoll, NY: Orbis Books, 1992), 11–22; and Robert J. Schreiter, *Constructing Local Theologies* (Maryknoll, NY: Orbis Books, 1985), 1–21, 75–94.

12. See *The Kairos Document: Challenge to the Church: A Theological Comment on the Political Crisis in South Africa* (Grand Rapids, MI: Eerdmans, 1986); and Robert McAfee Brown, ed., *Three Prophetic Challenges to the Church* (Grand Rapids, MI: Eerdmans, 1990). The New Testament Greek term *kairos,* meaning "time," is employed by the writers of this confessional statement in a similar sense to Paul Tillich's use of the term to refer to a particular moment in history in which God confronts humanity, offering both judgment and grace, and challenges us to respond in a spiritually informed and politically engaged manner.

13. *Status confessionis,* meaning a "confessional situation," refers to those rare instances in the history of the Christian church when Christians are faced with a clear-cut "either-or" decision in which it is possible to say that something is or is not Christian. The most notable modern instance of a *status confessionis* was the decision of the Confessing Church in Germany to affirm—in "The Barmen Declaration" (1934)—that it was no longer possible for Christians to support Hitler and still call themselves "Christian" because the totalitarian demand of complete obedience to the Nazi state amounted to a false doctrine in which the state usurped Christ's role as the only Lord and Savior.

14. David Tracy has argued for the public character of theology, identifying three "publics" (society, the academy, and the church) that all theologians must engage critically or risk cultural irrelevance. Tracy's model of theology as conversation informs my own search for cross-cultural understanding in theological interpretation. See *The Analogical Imagination: Christian Theology and the Culture of Pluralism* (New York: Crossroad, 1981), 1–28, 99–135.

15. The prototypical example of this approach is the constructive theological project espoused by Gordon D. Kaufman. See *An Essay on Theological Method* (Atlanta, GA: Scholars Press, 1979) and *In Face of Mystery: A Constructive Theology* (Cambridge, MA: Harvard University Press, 1993). In my opinion, Kaufman's theological project is not grounded in the lived faith of a particular community and as such is not an adequate representative of confessional perspectives in the public discourse.

16. See Alister E. McGrath, *The Genesis of Doctrine: A Study in the Foundation of Doctrinal Criticism* (Grand Rapids, MI: Eerdmans, 1990), 35–80. According to McGrath, one of the primary tasks of theology is to maintain and preserve the historical self-identity of the Christian church over time.

17. See Jeffrey Stout, *Democracy and Tradition* (Princeton, NJ: Princeton University Press, 2004). I embrace Stout's modest definition of public theology: "If you express theological commitments in a reflective and sustained way, while addressing fellow citizens as citizens, you are 'doing theology' publicly—and in that sense doing public theology" (113).

18. Mark Kline Taylor, *Remembering Esperanza: A Cultural-Political Theology for North American Praxis* (Maryknoll, NY: Orbis Books, 1990), 23–75.

19. See Clifford Geertz, "Thick Description: Toward an Interpretive Theory of Culture," and "Religion as a Cultural System," in *The Interpretation of Cultures*, rev. ed. (New York: Basic Books, 2000), 3–30, 87–125. Geertz offers a vision of human self-description as a complex, multilayered reality best characterized as an ongoing conversation within culture and with other cultures. Accordingly, cultural analysis is "intrinsically incomplete" and "essentially contestable": "The essential vocation of interpretive anthropology is not to answer our deepest questions, but to make available to us answers that others, guarding other sheep in other valleys, have given, and thus to include them in the consultable record of what man has said" (30).

20. Taylor, *Remembering Esperanza*, 23.

21. See Esther Kaplan, ed., *With God on Their Side: How Christian Fundamentalists Trampled Science, Policy, and Democracy in George W. Bush's White House* (New York: New Press, 2004); Anatol Lieven, *America Right or Wrong: An Anatomy of American Nationalism* (Princeton, NJ: Princeton University Press, 2004); Jean Bethke-Elshtain, *Just War against Terror: The Burden of American Power in a Violent World* (New York: Basic Books, 2003); Mark L. Taylor, *Religion, Politics, and the Christian Right: Post-9/11 Powers and American Empire* (Minneapolis, MN: Fortress Press, 2005). The latter book equates both of these fundamentalisms as "militant faiths," Islamists operating through deadly terrorist networks and the U.S. Christian Right combining "a Christian nationalism with the lethal systems of violence purveyed by U.S. military forces" (ix).

22. See Jim Wallis, *God's Politics: Why the Right Gets It Wrong and the Left Doesn't Get It* (San Francisco: HarperSanFrancisco, 2005).

23. See Samuel P. Huntington, *Who Are We? The Challenges to America's National Identity* (New York: Simon and Schuster, 2004). Huntington defines "Hispanization" as the drive toward a distinct Latino/Hispanic culture within the United States, resulting in a "culturally bifurcated Anglo-Hispanic society with two national languages" (221).

24. Miguel H. Díaz, *On Being Human: U.S. Hispanic and Rahnerian Perspectives* (Maryknoll, NY: Orbis Books, 2001), xvi.

25. See Richard Rodriguez, *Brown: The Last Discovery of America* (New York: Viking, 2002). The author argues that North America was "brown" long before it was "white," critiques the American preoccupation with race solely in terms of "black-and-white," and writes "about race in America in hopes of undermining the notion of race in America" (xi). Rodriguez has struggled with the history of *mestizaje* as a history of conflict embodied in the people of Latin America but also celebrates the "browning of America" as the "reunion of peoples" in which "rival cultures and creeds conspire with Spring to create children of beauty, perhaps of harmony, previously unknown" (xiii).

26. See Roger Sanjek, "The Enduring Inequalities of Race," in *Race,* ed. Steven Gregory and Roger Sanjek (New Brunswick, NJ: Rutgers University Press, 1994), 1–17.

NOTES TO CHAPTER 1

1. See Ellis Cashmore, ed., *Dictionary of Race and Ethnic Relations,* 3rd ed. (London: Routledge, 1994); Kwame Anthony Appiah, "Race," in *Critical Terms for Literary Study,* 2nd ed., ed. Frank Lentricchia and Thomas McLaughlin (Chicago: University of Chicago Press, 1995), 274–87; Werner Sollors, "Ethnicity," in Lentricchia and McLaughlin, *Critical Terms for Literary Study,* 288–305; Les Back and John Solomos, eds., *Theories of Race and Racism: A Reader* (London: Routledge, 2000).

2. For examples of this view, see Joe Feagin and Hernan Vera, *White Racism* (New York: Routledge, 1995); Paula Rothenberg, *Racism and Sexism: An Integrated Study* (New York: St. Martin's Press, 1988); and Joseph Barndt, *Dismantling Racism: The Continuing Challenge to White America* (Minneapolis, MN: Fortress/Augsburg Press, 1991).

3. See Averil Cameron, *Christianity and the Rhetoric of Empire: The Development of Christian Discourse* (Berkeley: University of California Press, 1991). See also Michael Hardt and Antonio Negri, *Empire* (Cambridge, MA: Harvard University Press, 2000).

4. See Gay L. Byron, *Symbolic Blackness and Ethnic Difference in Early Christian Literature* (New York: Routledge, 2002), 1–6. Byron defines "ethno-political rhetorics" as discursive uses of ethnicity (or "otherness") in classical literature that add to our understanding of the complex power relations within Greco-Roman

society, especially when describing the relationship between distinct groups of people.

5. See Frank Snowden, *Before Color Prejudice: The Ancient View of Blacks* (Cambridge, MA: Harvard University Press, 1983), 82–87. See also Dominique Zahan, "White, Red and Black: Colour Symbolism in Black Africa," in *The Realms of Colour,* ed. A. Portman and R. Ritsema (Leiden: Brill, 1972), 365–96.

6. Lloyd Thompson, *Romans and Blacks* (Norman: University of Oklahoma Press, 1989); Frank Snowden, *Blacks in Antiquity: Ethiopians in the Graeco-Roman Experience* (Cambridge, MA: Belknap Press of Harvard University Press, 1970), and *Before Color Prejudice.* Snowden and Thompson document the belief (widespread in antiquity) that differences in physical appearance (skin color, hair texture, etc.) are caused by weather extremes (hot/cold) at the geographic extremes (south/north) of the known world. This Scythian-Ethiopian polarity is common in ancient Greco-Roman and Near East literature to signify not only geographic but also cultural and racial extremes. See also David Goldenberg, "Scythian-Barbarian: The Permutations of a Classical Topos in Jewish and Christian Texts of Late Antiquity," *Journal for Jewish Studies* 49 (1998): 87–102.

7. See Cornel West, *Prophesy Deliverance! An Afro-American Revolutionary Christianity* (Louisville, KY: Westminster John Knox Press, 2002), 47–65.

8. See Thompson, *Romans and Blacks,* 42–43, 49–55. Thompson criticizes Snowden for ignoring irrational Roman attitudes about blackness and the effect such views might have on the reality of black-white social relations in Roman society. Nevertheless, while recognizing the presence of irrational color prejudice and antipathy based on color, Thompson denies classical antiquity was racist as defined by modern social scientists. See also Morton Smith, "Book Review of Blacks in Antiquity," *American Historical Review* 76 (1971): 139–40. Smith notes Snowden neglected to include many texts from Greco-Roman antiquity that referenced "grotesque Negroid figures."

9. See David M. Goldenberg, *The Curse of Ham: Race and Slavery in Early Judaism, Christianity, and Islam* (Princeton, NJ: Princeton University Press, 2003), 26–40.

10. Ibid., 45.

11. Ibid., 74.

12. The metaphoric use of Ethiopian/Kushites as symbols for the unbaptized/Gentile church predates Origen (see Irenaeus of Lyon, in *Against Heresies* 4.20.12, who interprets Moses' marriage to an Ethiopian as symbolizing the acceptance of Gentiles into the Christian faith), yet, judging by the number of Patristic commentators who cite him, Origen's exegetical framework for understanding blackness in the Bible had greater influence. See Snowden, *Before Color Prejudice,* 101, 114.

13. Goldenberg, *The Curse of Ham,* 49. See also Snowden, *Before Color Prejudice,* 82ff.; and Thompson, *Romans and Blacks,* 40, 110–13.

14. Origen interprets the line "black but beautiful" to mean that the Ethiopian maiden is beautiful in spite of her blackness because "through faith in Jesus and conversion to Christianity" her blackness "diminishes and she 'becomes white and fair' (based on a reading of Song 8:5 found in the Old Greek translation: 'Who is she that comes up having been made white?'" (48). See also Byron, *Symbolic Blackness and Ethnic Difference in Early Christian Literature*, 55–76, in which the author cites Jerome (348–420 CE): "At one time we were Ethiopians in our vices and sins . . . who have been transformed from blackness to whiteness" (55).

15. See Raoul Lonis, "Les trois approches de l'Ethiopien par l'opinion gréco-romaine," *Ktema* 6 (1981): 81.

16. Snowden, *Blacks in Antiquity*, 196.

17. Byron, *Symbolic Blackness and Ethnic Difference in Early Christian Literature*, 115.

18. Ibid., 118.

19. Thompson, *Romans and Blacks*, 139.

20. Byron, *Symbolic Blackness and Ethnic Difference in Early Christian Literature*, 118.

21. Ibid., 121.

22. This does not imply that all blacks were slaves, rather that outside of sub-Saharan Africa most blacks encountered by Europeans were likely to be slaves.

23. Sweet, "The Iberian Roots of American Racist Thought," 146.

24. Ibid., 145.

25. Ibid., 147.

26. See Antonio Gramsci, *Selections from the Prison Notebooks*, ed. and trans. Quintin Hoare and Geoffrey Nowell Smith (New York: International Publishers, 1971). Gramsci defines *hegemony* as "a conception of the world that is implicitly manifest in art, in law, in economic activity and in all manifestations of individual and collective life" (328). Accordingly, culture and ideology are inextricably bound together so that those things described as "culture"—the values, norms, beliefs, and institutions that express a shared conception of the world—are manifest in a sociopolitical unity enforced by the dominant social group. See also *An Antonio Gramsci Reader: Selected Writings 1916–1935*, ed. David Forgacs (New York: Schocken Books, 1988).

27. James A. Sloan, *The Great Question Answered; or, Is Slavery a Sin in Itself (Per Se) Answered According to the Teaching of the Scriptures* (Memphis, TN: Hutton, Gallaway, 1857), 75, 78, 80 (emphases in the original).

28. St. Augustine, *Concerning the City of God against the Pagans*, trans. Henry Bettenson (New York: Penguin Books, 1984), 874 (book XIX, chap. 15).

29. Ibid., 875.

30. Stephen R. Haynes, *Noah's Curse: The Biblical Justification of American Slavery* (Oxford: Oxford University Press, 2002), 7.

31. Sweet, "The Iberian Roots of American Racist Thought," 148–49, quoting

the tenth-century Persian historian Tabari from *Ta'rih ar-rusal wa'l-muluk,* ed. J. De Goeje (Leiden, 1879), 223.

32. Haynes, *Noah's Curse,* 82.

33. Ibid., 80–81.

34. Frederick Douglass, "Narrative of the Life of Frederick Douglass," in *The Norton Anthology of African American Literature,* ed. Henry Louis Gates Jr. (New York: Norton, 1997), 311–12.

35. Vincent L. Wimbush, *The Bible and African Americans: A Brief History* (Minneapolis, MN: Fortress Press, 2003), 38.

36. Ibid., 41–42.

37. Ibid., 37–38.

38. Judith M. Lieu, *Neither Jew Nor Greek? Constructing Early Christianity* (London: T & T Clark, 2002), 1–8.

39. Elisabeth Schüssler Fiorenza, "Feminist Theology as a Critical Theology of Liberation," in her *Discipleship of Equals: A Critical Feminist Ekklesia-logy of Liberation* (New York: Crossroad, 1993), 68.

40. Ibid., 69.

41. Elisabeth Schüssler Fiorenza, "The Twelve and the Discipleship of Equals," in *Discipleship of Equals,* 105. Also Fiorenza, *In Memory of Her: A Feminist Theological Reconstruction of Christian Origins* (New York: Crossroad, 1983), 205–41, 343–51.

42. Robin Scroggs, *Paul for a New Day* (Philadelphia: Fortress Press, 1977), 44.

43. See James H. Evans Jr., *We Have Been Believers: An African-American Systematic Theology* (Minneapolis, MN: Fortress Press, 1992), 35–40. According to Evans, proslavery writers used this epistle as support for the Fugitive Slave Law of 1850.

44. See Robert J. C. Young, *Colonial Desire: Hybridity in Theory, Culture and Race* (London: Routledge, 1995), 118–41, for a critical review of the development of craniometry and scientific racism in nineteenth-century America.

45. Stephen Jay Gould, *The Mismeasure of Man* (New York: Norton, 1981), 72. While theological justifications of racism have survived within the more conservative Biblicist traditions, Protestant liberalism became the dominant theological voice in North America in the late nineteenth and early twentieth centuries in great part because it embraced the secular scientific worldview. A question that needs further exploration—but lies beyond the scope of this investigation—is whether or not Protestant liberalism offered a critical voice of resistance against scientific racism.

46. See George M. Fredrickson, *Racism: A Short History* (Princeton, NJ: Princeton University Press, 2002), 43–45, 51–52. Fredrickson writes that "the orthodox Christian belief in the unity of mankind, based on the Bible's account of Adam and Eve as the progenitors of all humans, was a powerful obstacle to the development of a coherent and persuasive ideological racism" (52).

47. *Race, Science and Society,* rev. and ed. with an introduction by Leo Kuper (New York: Columbia University Press, 1975), 343; first published as *The Race Question in Modern Science* (Geneva: UNESCO, 1956).

48. Ibid., 360.

49. Ibid., 362.

50. Gould, *The Mismeasure of Man,* 323.

51. "AAPA Statement on Biological Aspects of Race," *American Journal of Physical Anthropology* 101 (1996): 569–70 (emphasis added).

52. "Statement on 'Race' and Intelligence," American Anthropological Association Web site, December 1994 (http://www.aaanet.org/stmts/race.htm).

53. Peter T. Nash, *Reading Race, Reading the Bible* (Minneapolis, MN: Fortress Press, 2003), 57.

54. Richard J. Herrnstein and Charles Murray, *The Bell Curve: Intelligence and Class Structure in American Life* (New York: Free Press Paperbacks, 1994), xxi.

55. Ibid., 553.

56. Ibid., 552.

57. Ibid., 297–98.

58. Ibid., 550 (emphasis added).

59. Ibid., 313.

60. West, *Prophesy Deliverance!* 5.

61. Ibid., 6.

62. Cornel West, "The Dilemma of the Black Intellectual," in *The Cornel West Reader* (New York: Basic Civitas Books, 1999), 311.

63. West, *Prophesy Deliverance!* 49.

64. David Harvey, *The Condition of Postmodernity: An Enquiry into the Origins of Cultural Change* (Cambridge: Blackwell, 1990), 44.

65. Michel Foucault, "Space, Knowledge, and Power," in *The Foucault Reader,* ed. Paul Rabinow (New York: Pantheon Books, 1984), 245 (emphasis in the original).

66. Ibid., 249.

67. Cornel West, "On Prophetic Pragmatism," in *The Cornel West Reader,* 163.

68. Ibid., 164.

69. West, *Prophesy Deliverance!* 53.

70. Ibid., 64.

71. Ibid., 54.

72. Cornel West, "Race and Social Theory," in *The Cornel West Reader,* 264.

73. West, *Prophesy Deliverance!* 69.

74. Ibid., 78.

75. Ibid., 79.

76. Ibid., 80.

77. Ibid., 82.

78. Ibid., 83.

79. Ibid., 89–90.

80. Ibid., 90.

81. See Benjamin Valentin, *Mapping Public Theology: Beyond Culture, Identity, and Difference* (Harrisburg, PA: Trinity Press International, 2002). Valentin's central thesis argues that U.S. Latino/a theology is obsessed with matters of cultural and personal identity to the detriment of political and economic liberation and therefore is not an adequate model of public theology. Valentin embraces Cornel West's "prophetic pragmatism" as a model for public theology yet downplays West's emphasis on individual and cultural identity as inseparable from economic and political liberation.

82. West, *Prophesy Deliverance!* 35.

83. Ibid.

84. Ibid., 36.

85. Kimberlé Crenshaw, Neil Gotanda, Garry Peller, Kendall Thomas, and Cornel West, *Critical Race Theory: The Key Writings That Formed the Movement* (New York: New Press, 1995), xxix.

86. Girardeau A. Spann, "Pure Politics," in *Critical Race Theory: The Cutting Edge,* ed. Richard Delgado (Philadelphia: Temple University Press, 1995), 22.

87. Ibid., 31.

88. Joseph Tilden Rhea, *Race Pride and the American Identity* (Cambridge, MA: Harvard University Press, 1997), 1.

89. Ibid., 2.

90. Ibid., 125.

91. Anthony E. Cook, "Beyond Critical Legal Studies: The Reconstructive Theology of Dr. Martin Luther King, Jr.," in Crenshaw, et al., *Critical Race Theory,* 101.

92. *Mujerista* theology, specifically the work of Ada María Isasi-Díaz, emphasizes storytelling and self-naming as a vital first step toward holistic liberation. Critical race theory is also distinguished by its use of storytelling, counterstorytelling, and analysis of narrative in order to reconstruct the history of racism and resistance to racism, as exemplified by the work of Derrick Bell, who is considered the founder of this movement. As discussed earlier, Cornel West's genealogy of racism is a deconstruction and reconstruction of intellectual history in order to give voice to previously ignored (by the academic mainstream) discourses. While West focuses primarily on intellectual history, *mujerista* theology gives voice to the popular religious practices of marginalized Latinas, and CRT has increased scholarly interest in slave narratives and other "lost" perspectives, all three approaches seek a more complete history of racism in which the victims of racism are recognized as active agents with rich cultural resources with which to resist racism.

93. Roberto S. Goizueta, "Rediscovering Praxis: The Significance of U.S. His-

panic Experience for Theological Method," in *We Are a People! Initiatives in Hispanic American Theology,* ed. Roberto S. Goizueta (Minneapolis, MN: Fortress Press, 1992), 52–53 (emphasis added).

94. G. W. F. Hegel, *Phenomenology of Spirit,* trans. A. V. Miller (Oxford: Oxford University Press, 1977), 111–19.

95. Ibid., 111.

96. It is important to note that the use of *mestizaje* as a source of Latin American cultural and political identity can be traced to the late nineteenth-century and early twentieth-century philosophy of José Vasconcelos. However, the work of Virgilio Elizondo is considerably more influential for the formation of U.S. Latino/a theology, since, in my estimation, most U.S. Latino/a theologians have only a passing familiarity with Vasconcelos, yet all of them have read *Galilean Journey.* See the bilingual edition of *The Cosmic Race/La raza Cósmica* (Baltimore: John Hopkins University Press, 1997) by Vasconcelos, along with Roberto Goizueta's critique of Vasconcelos in *Caminemos con Jésus* (Maryknoll, NY: Orbis Books, 1995), 89–131, in which Goizueta faults Vasconcelos for emphasizing *mestizaje* as an aesthetic category to the detriment of its emancipatory potential. Specifically, Vasconcelos traces the origin of Latin American *mestizaje* to an "abundance of love" by the Spanish conquerors toward indigenous women, ignoring the brutal and violent rapes that are the true origin of Spanish and Amerindian mixing. For a thorough history of the violent and forced *mestizaje* of Mesoamerica's Indian population at the hands of their Spanish conquerors, see Luis N. Rivera, *A Violent Evangelism: The Political and Religious Conquest of the Americas* (Louisville, KY: Westminster/John Knox Press, 1992), and Tzvetan Todorov, *The Conquest of America,* trans. Richard Howard (New York: Harper and Row, 1984). I opt to begin my discussion of *mestizaje* with the work of Virgilio Elizondo because he explicitly links this concept to human liberation without ignoring or romanticizing the tragic reality of *mestizaje.*

NOTES TO CHAPTER 2

1. See Roland Robertson, "Globalization and the Future of 'Traditional Religion,'" in *God and Globalization,* vol. 1, *Religion and the Powers of the Common Life,* ed. Max L. Stackhouse with Peter J. Paris (Harrisburg, PA: Trinity Press International, 2000), 53–68. Robertson, while recognizing the long and complex history of globalizing forces, defines globalization "simply as the compression of the world" (53). Accordingly, whether one views globalization with optimism as the promise of a common culture, currency, and community, or skeptically as the encroachment upon local cultures and national sovereignty by economic hegemony, Robertson's definition accurately identifies the role of increasingly affordable access to global telecommunications as central to any understanding of

globalization. For an introduction to hybridity as a conceptual paradigm in contemporary cultural theory, see Robert J. C. Young, *Colonial Desire: Hybridity in Theory, Culture and Race* (London: Routledge, 1995).

2. Nikos Papastergiadis, "Tracing Hybridity in Theory," in *Debating Cultural Hybridity*, ed. Pnina Werbner and Tariq Modood (London: Zed Books, 1997), 261.

3. See Dick Hebdige, *Cut 'n' mix: Culture, Identity and Caribbean Music* (New York: Methuen, 1987); also Alan Warde, "Eating Globally: Cultural Flows and the Spread of Ethnic Restaurants," in *The Ends of Globalization: Bringing Society Back In*, ed. D. Kalb, M. Van Der Land, R. Staring, B. Van Steenbergen, and N. Wilterdink (Lanham, MD: Rowman and Littlefield, 2000), 299–316.

4. Rasheed Araeen, "A New Beginning: Beyond Postcolonial Cultural Theory and Identity Politics," *Third Text*, no. 50 (2000):15.

5. Andrew Irvine, "Mestizaje and the Problem of Authority," *Journal of Hispanic/Latino Theology* 8, no. 1 (August 2000): 23.

6. John P. Rossing, "Mestizaje and Marginality: A Hispanic American Theology," *Theology Today* 45, no. 3 (1988): 304.

7. See Benjamin Valentin, *Mapping Public Theology: Beyond Culture, Identity, and Difference* (Harrisburg, PA: Trinity Press International, 2002).

8. While this notion of *mestizaje* deserves rigorous and comprehensive treatment, it is beyond the scope of the current work. For an insightful analysis of the perpetuation of racial hierarchies in spite of racial mixing and an accompanying ideology of a new Puerto Rican "race," see Magali Roy-Féquière, *Women, Creole Identity, and Intellectual Life in Early Twentieth-Century Puerto Rico* (Philadelphia: Temple University Press, 2004); for an introduction to the Caribbean notion of *mestizaje*, see Bienvenida Mendoza B., "La mujer negra caribeña y el racismo," and Ninfa Patiño Sánchez, "Mestizaje, racismo e identidad étnica," in *Los problemas raciales en la República Dominicana y el Caribe* (Santo Domingo, Dominican Republic: Editora Collado, 1998), 155–72, 173–89; and for an exploration of racial and cultural identity in Puerto Rico, see José Luis González, *El país de cuatro pesos y otros ensayos* (Río Piedras, Puerto Rico: Ediciones Huracán, 1989).

9. See Virgilio Elizondo, *Galilean Journey: The Mexican-American Promise*, 2nd ed., revised and enlarged edition (Maryknoll, NY: Orbis Books, 2000), 36; and Elizondo, *The Future Is Mestizo: Life Where Cultures Meet,* rev. ed. (Boulder: University Press of Colorado, 2000), 125ff.

10. Luis G. Pedraja, *Jesus Is My Uncle: Christology from a Hispanic Perspective* (Nashville, TN: Abingdon Press, 1999), 37.

11. Fernando Ortiz, *Cuban Counterpoint: Tobacco and Sugar,* trans. Harriet de Onís (Durham, NC: Duke University Press, [1940] 1995), 97–103.

12. Ibid., 102.

13. Ibid., 98.

14. Ibid., 103.

15. See Walter D. Mignolo, *Local Histories/Global Designs: Coloniality, Subaltern Knowledges, and Border Thinking* (Princeton, NJ: Princeton University Press, 2000), 3–16.

16. Orlando O. Espín, "Toward the Construction of an Intercultural Theology of Tradition," *Journal of Hispanic/Latino Theology* 9, no. 3 (February 2002): 57.

17. See Raúl Fornet-Betancourt, ed., *Theologie im III. Millennium—quo vadis? Antworten der Theologen; Dokumentation einer Weltumfrage* / Raul Fornet-Betancourt (Hrsg.); im Auftrag des Missionswissenschaftlichen Instituts Missio e.V. (Frankfurt/M: IKO/Verlag für Interkulturelle Kommunikation, 2000), and Verändert der Glaube die Wirtschaft?: Theologie und Ökonomie in Lateinamerika (Freiburg im Breisgau: Herder, 1991).

18. Espín, "Toward the Construction of an Intercultural Theology of Tradition," 26.

19. Ibid.

20. Mignolo, *Local Histories/Global Designs,* 14.

21. Espín, "Toward the Construction of an Intercultural Theology of Tradition," 40.

22. Mignolo, *Local Histories/Global Designs,* 168.

23. Ibid., 170.

24. Kathryn Tanner, *Theories of Culture: A New Agenda for Theology* (Minneapolis, MN: Fortress Press, 1997), 38.

25. Ibid.

26. Ibid., 57.

27. Ibid., 57–58.

28. Ibid., 58.

29. Jan Nederveen Pieterse, *Globalization and Culture: Global Mélange* (Lanham, MD: Rowman and Littlefield, 2004), 82.

30. Literally, "discourse about last things," eschatology refers broadly to the fulfillment of God's plans for humanity in the coming of Christ. Given numerous New Testament references to the Second Coming of Christ (Parousia), Christian thought is characterized by an "already–not yet" quality in which the first coming of Christ inaugurated the kingdom of God, but its full realization remains a future event.

31. Positivism, a philosophical movement founded by Auguste Comte, declared false and meaningless all problems, concepts, and propositions of traditional philosophy that could not be solved or verified by empirical evidence.

32. José Vasconcelos, *The Cosmic Race/La raza cósmica,* trans. Didier T. Jaén (Baltimore: Johns Hopkins University Press, 1997), 3.

33. Ibid., 31.

34. Ibid., 18–19.

35. See Andrés Gonzales Guerrero, *A Chicano Theology* (Maryknoll, NY: Orbis Books, 1987).

36. In a conversation that took place at Princeton Theological Seminary on January 17, 2007, with Timothy Matovina, a friend and colleague of Elizondo at the University of Notre Dame, he confirmed my suspicions concerning what role (if any) Vasconcelos played in the formation of Elizondo's conceptualization of *mestizaje*. When Matovina put the question to Elizondo directly, he confirmed that the Mexican American popular religious practices of his childhood—and not *La raza cósmica*—led him to employ *mestizaje* as *locus theologicus*.

37. Roberto Goizueta, *Caminemos con Jesús: Toward a Hispanic/Latino Theology of Accompaniment* (Maryknoll, NY: Orbis Books, 1995), 89–131. Goizueta's critical analysis of the philosophy of José Vaconcelos recognizes the possibility of turning *mestizaje* into an oppressive ideology while arguing for its universal significance as a hermeneutical and theological category.

38. Andrew Irvine, "Mestizaje and the Problem of Authority," *Journal of Hispanic/Latino Theology* 8, no. 1 (August 2000): 7.

39. Ibid., 6.

40. Ibid., 7.

41. Ibid.

42. Ibid., 10–21.

43. Ibid., 30.

44. Valentin, *Mapping Public Theology*, 4–5.

45. Ibid., 76.

46. Ibid., 67.

47. Ibid., 69.

48. Benjamin Valentin, "Strangers No More: An Introduction to, and an Interpretation of, U.S. Hispanic/Latino/a Theology," in *The Ties That Bind: African American and Hispanic American/Latino/a Theologies in Dialogue*, ed. Anthony B. Pinn and Benjamin Valentin (New York: Continuum, 2001), 51–53.

49. Benjamin Valentin's proposal for how Latino/a theology should enter the public discourse is methodologically indebted to the constructive theological project articulated by Gordon D. Kaufman, which in my opinion is not an adequate representative of confessional perspectives in the public discourse. His commitment to certain aspects of Kaufman's theological project—while creating greater acceptance within certain narrow "publics" (especially within the academy and to a lesser degree among political progressives)—hampers the reception of Valentin's proposal within many Latino/a churches, especially when he describes their discourse as narrowly ecclesiocentric. Accordingly, chapter 3 evaluates Benjamin Valentin's proposal for an emancipatory public theology by defending the public relevance of "confessional" theology over against accusations of "dogmatic intolerance."

50. Valentin, *Mapping Public Theology*, 42n1.

51. Ibid., 43.

52. The phrase *en conjunto* means "all together"; however, *conjunto* is also a

musical term describing an ensemble of musicians playing distinct yet complementary parts to make a unified whole, which in my opinion is a highly appropriate metaphor for theological discourse. This movement was born through the
collaborative efforts of U.S. Latino/a theologians in professional organizations like
La Communidad of Hispanic American Scholars of Theology and Religion and
the Academy of Catholic Hispanic Theologians in the United States (ACHTUS).
Teología en conjunto (also called *teología de conjunto*) was the theme of a major
conference sponsored by ACHTUS called "Somos un Pueblo" ("We Are a People") and held at Emory University in June 1990, resulting in the publication of
a highly influential collection of essays, *We Are a People!,* edited by Roberto S.
Goizueta. In 1995 a group of Latino/a theologians, pastors, teachers, and students
gathered at Princeton Theological Seminary to put *teología en conjunto* into practice; the fruits of this conference were published in the volume *Teología en Conjunto: A Collaborative Hispanic Protestant Theology,* ed. José David Rodríguez and
Loida I. Martell-Otero (Louisville, KY: Westminster John Knox Press, 1997). For a
concise introduction to and history of this theological movement, see Eduardo C.
Fernández, *La Cosecha: Harvesting Contemporary United States Hispanic Theology
(1972–1998)* (Collegeville, MN: Liturgical Press, 2000).

    53. The liberation theology movement began in Latin America in the late
1960s and early 1970s with parallel African American liberation movements in
the United States, followed by the articulation of feminist and other autochtho-
nous liberation theologies throughout the world. No single event marks the birth
of liberation theology; however, the Second Vatican Council (1962–65) stands as
an important landmark. Latin American liberation theology argues that Christians are called to make a preferential option for the poor because in the Scriptures God acts on behalf of the weak and abused of human history; this reading
of Scripture leads the church to make political commitments in solidarity with
the oppressed, seeking the historical transformation of oppressive situations and
social orders.

    54. Anthony C. Thiselton, *New Horizons in Hermeneutics: The Theory and
Practice of Transforming Biblical Reading* (Grand Rapids, MI: Zondervan, 1992),
410.

    55. Justo L. González, "Scripture, Tradition, Experience, and Imagination:
A Reflection," in *The Ties That Bind: African American and Hispanic American/
Latino/a Theologies in Dialogue,* ed. Anthony B. Pinn and Benjamin Valentin
(New York: Continuum, 2001), 64.

    56. Benjamin Valentin, "Nuevos Odres para el Vino: A Critical Contribution
to Latino/a Theological Construction," *Journal of Hispanic/Latino Theology* 5, no.
4 (May 1998): 44.

    57. While Elizondo dates the origins of the second wave of *mestizaje* to the
nineteenth-century U.S. conquest of Mexico (driven by the ideology of "manifest destiny"), this category also encompasses current mixing of the (primarily

Catholic) Mexican American mestizo culture with the dominant (primarily Protestant) North American culture. Elizondo's analysis of the Mexican American situation is applicable to all Latino/as in general, as he himself suggests when discussing "universal mestizaje" in *The Future Is Mestizo*, 87–111.

58. Elizondo, *Galilean Journey*, 5.

59. Ibid., 16.

60. Ibid., 17.

61. Ibid.

62. Ibid., 18.

63. Ibid., 47.

64. Ibid. (emphasis in original).

65. Ibid.

66. Ibid., 49 (emphasis in original).

67. Ibid., 91 (emphasis in original).

68. Ibid.

69. Ibid., 102.

70. Ibid., 103.

71. Ibid., 107 (emphasis in original).

72. Ibid., 117 (emphasis added).

73. Ibid., 124.

74. Ibid., 125.

75. Virgilio Elizondo, in the foreword to Justo L. González, *Mañana: Christian Theology from a Hispanic Perspective* (Nashville, TN: Abingdon Press, 1990), 16.

76. Elizondo, *Galilean Journey*, 32–46.

77. Ibid., 43.

78. Virgilio Elizondo, "Mestizaje and the Future of Humanity," in *Beyond Borders: Writings of Virgilio Elizondo and Friends*, ed. Timothy Matovina (Maryknoll, NY: Orbis Books, 2000), 180.

79. Gustavo Gutiérrez, "Foreword: Virgil Elizondo's Vision as a Hermeneutics of Hope," in Matovina, *Beyond Borders*, vii–xii.

80. Elizondo, *The Future Is Mestizo*, 87.

81. Virgilio Elizondo, "The New Humanity in the Americas," in Matovina, *Beyond Borders*, 273.

82. Arturo J. Bañuelas, "U.S. Hispanic Theology: An Initial Assessment," in *Mestizo Christianity: Theology from the Latino Perspective*, ed. Arturo J. Bañuelas (Maryknoll, NY: Orbis Books, 1995), 58.

83. Elizondo, *The Future Is Mestizo*, 89.

84. Gustavo Gutiérrez, *We Drink from Our Own Wells: The Spiritual Journey of a People*, trans. Matthew J. O'Connell (Maryknoll, NY: Orbis Books, 1984), 96.

85. Ibid., 106.

86. See Alejandro García-Rivera, "Crossing Theological Borders: Virgilio Elizondo's Place among Theologians of Culture," in Matovina, *Beyond Borders*, 246–

56. García-Rivera recounts his first meeting with Virgilio Elizondo at the Hispanic Summer Institute, where he discovered they had much in common: "One reason for this spontaneous camaraderie (outside of Virgilio's magnetic personality) became clear during our first conversation. We both shared a common background in the natural sciences. . . . Virgilio was delighted with the subject and we had a wonderful conversation over the role of the natural sciences in theological reflection" (254). García-Rivera states that for Elizondo the mestizo becomes a "new phylum of humanity" and describes Elizondo's theology as both a theology of culture and an evolutionary cosmology. Perhaps Elizondo's science background and personal fascination with evolutionary theory contribute to the tendency I have identified in his theology to "biologize" mestizo identity.

87. See Richard J. Herrnstein and Charles Murray, *The Bell Curve: Intelligence and Class Structure in American Life* (New York: Free Press Paperbacks, 1994). In the afterword Charles Murray summarizes the controversy created by this book and categorizes the variety of critical responses to their conclusions about the determining role of genetics in accounting for race differences in intelligence. Chapter 1 of this investigation analyzes what many have labeled the "new scientific racism" inaugurated by this landmark study in relation to U.S. Latino/a theology's emphasis on biological *mestizaje* as a defining trait of Latino/a cultural identity. My position, like that of Herrnstein and Murray, is that both environment and genes determine human characteristics in unknown proportions. Unlike Herrnstein and Murray, I am reluctant to attribute differences between ethnic groups, such as differences in test scores and socioeconomic achievement, to genetic causes because doing so fosters and legitimizes old racist attitudes. Perhaps most troubling is Murray's defense of J. Philippe Rushton's theory of race that divides humanity into Negroid, Caucasoid, and Mongoloid when explaining differences in intelligence (563–64). Prior to *The Bell Curve,* biological theories of race had been challenged and discredited within academic discourse, especially by Stephen Jay Gould's landmark text, *The Mismeasure of Man* (New York: Norton, 1981). Other recent scholarship has defended biological theories of race and accused the academy of uncritically accepting Gould's position. See M. Snyderman and Stanley Rothman, *The IQ Controversy: The Media and Public Policy* (New Brunswick, NJ: Transaction Books, 1988).

88. Elizondo, *The Future Is Mestizo,* 95.

89. Ibid., 99.

90. Ibid.

91. Ibid., 125.

92. Ibid., 130.

93. Elizondo, foreword to *Mañana,* 16.

94. See my discussion of Benjamin Valentin's recent work, *Mapping Public Theology: Beyond Culture, Identity, and Difference* (Harrisburg, PA: Trinity Press

International, 2002), earlier in this chapter. See also the work of Teresa Chavez Sauceda, "Love in the Crossroads: Stepping-Stones to a Doctrine of God in Hispanic/Latino Theology," in *Teología en Conjunto: A Collaborative Hispanic Protestant Theology*, ed. José David Rodríguez and Loida I. Martell-Otero (Louisville, KY: Westminster John Knox Press, 1997), 22–32. While Sauceda does not advocate abandoning *mestizaje*, she recognizes the risk of using "the metaphor of mestizaje" (30).

95. Elizondo, "Mestizaje and the Future of Humanity," 182.

96. *Mujerista* theology has much in common with North American feminist theology, yet like the womanist movement among African American feminists, *mujerista* theology recognizes that the experience of Latina women is mired within patterns of poverty, racism, and sexism that Anglo feminists may fail to recognize. Isasi-Díaz describes *mujerista* theology as a Hispanic women's liberation theology that, while acknowledging the influence of its intellectual and spiritual forebears, critiques both Latin American liberation theology and North American feminist liberation theology for not properly considering the perspectives of persons marginalized according to race as well as gender.

97. Fernando F. Segovia, "Two Places and No Place on Which to Stand," in *Mestizo Christianity: Theology from the Latino Perspective*, ed. Arturo J. Bañuelas (Maryknoll, NY: Orbis Books, 1995), 29–42.

98. Ada María Isasi-Díaz, "A New *Mestizaje/Mulatez*: Reconceptualizing Difference," in *A Dream Unfinished: Theological Reflections on America from the Margins*, ed. Eleazar S. Fernandez and Fernando F. Segovia (Maryknoll, NY: Orbis Books, 2001), 203.

99. Ada María Isasi-Díaz, *En la Lucha/In the Struggle: Elaborating a Mujerista Theology*, 2nd ed. (Minneapolis, MN: Fortress Press, 2004), 201.

100. Ada María Isasi-Díaz, "Preoccupations, Themes, and Proposals of Mujerista Theology," in *The Ties That Bind: African American and Hispanic American/Latino/a Theologies in Dialogue*, ed. Anthony B. Pinn and Benjamin Valentin (New York: Continuum, 2001), 137–38.

101. Ibid., 141.

102. *Lo cotidiano*, literally "the everyday," refers to the community's ability to experience the salvific presence of God in their daily struggles for a better quality of life and for greater social justice. This focus on everyday life by *mujerista* theology gives rise to a shared practical wisdom about how to order and interpret reality that is validated by the collective experience of the community. For Isasi-Díaz the category of popular religiosity is important for exploring and articulating the community's "practical wisdom" in the struggle for self-identity and self-determination.

103. Isasi-Díaz, "Preoccupations, Themes, and Proposals of Mujerista Theology," 137–42. Isasi-Díaz recognizes a fifth theme, namely, the need to elaborate a

distinctly *mujerista* Christology; however, given the fact that Latina theologians have only just begun to elaborate this Christology, and that this Christology is subsumed under the more central theme of liberation ("we cannot say anything about Christ that does not contribute to justice and peace" [142]), I choose to focus on those themes most central to the work of Isasi-Díaz.

104. See Harold Garfinkel, *Studies in Ethnomethodology* (Cambridge: Polity Press, 1984), for an introduction to this methodology.

105. Isasi-Díaz, *En la Lucha/In the Struggle*, 150.

106. This concept originates in the work of Brazilian educator Paulo Freire, *Pedagogy of the Oppressed*, rev. ed., trans. Myra Bergman (New York: Continuum, 1998), 68–105. *Conscientization* refers to the process by which the oppressed in society link theory with praxis in order to develop a "critical awareness" of their social reality and commit themselves to the positive transformation of their situation.

107. Isasi-Díaz, *En la Lucha/In the Struggle*, 176.

108. Ibid., 22–23.

109. Ibid., 33.

110. Ibid.

111. Isasi-Díaz, "A New *Mestizaje/Mulatez*," 208.

112. While Isasi-Díaz makes an effort to include a diversity of cultural backgrounds among the women she interviews (she records testimonies from Mexican American, Puerto Rican, and Cuban women), she recognizes in footnote 13, page 85, of *En la Lucha* that no concerted effort was made to recruit women for her sociological research from outside her own Roman Catholic circles. At the same time, she notes that her more recent academic work has been in ecumenical settings where she has had meaningful contact with Latina women from mainline Protestant and Pentecostal backgrounds.

113. Luis G. Pedraja, *Jesus Is My Uncle: Christology from a Hispanic Perspective* (Nashville, TN: Abingdon Press, 1999), 36.

114. The New Testament church can serve as a paradigm of *mestizaje* (cultural mixing) insofar as Christianity originated as a Semitic religious sect that spread quickly throughout the Greco-Roman world. Given that the Christian Gospel has been successfully "translated" into many cultures suggests that cultural mixing is indispensable for understanding the biblical narrative.

115. Pedraja, *Jesus Is My Uncle*, 34–38. Like Isasi-Díaz, Pedraja opts for the hyphenated *mestizaje-mulatez* as a more inclusive term for Latino/a ethnic identity. Please see the previous discussion in this chapter regarding why this work continues to use the term *mestizaje* as inclusive of all the ethnic mixings found within Latino/a culture. Pedraja acknowledges that both words refer to racial mixture, but chooses to add *mulatez* (from the Arabic) to acknowledge the mixture of Iberians and Africans that existed even before the Spanish conquest of America.

116. Luis G. Pedraja, "Doing Theology as Dialogue in the Hispanic Community," *Journal of Hispanic/Latino Theology* 5, no. 3 (February 1998): 39.

117. Ibid.

118. Ibid.

119. The experience of being categorized and labeled as a homogeneous "other" by the dominant culture is not unique to U.S. Latino/a cultural history. For example, the label "Asian American" has been imposed upon Korean, Japanese, Chinese, Indian, and various other peoples each with their own distinct cultures and traditions.

120. Pedraja, "Doing Theology as Dialogue in the Hispanic Community," 46.

121. Ibid., 47 (citing Isasi-Díaz, *En la Lucha*, 33).

122. Ibid.

123. Ibid.

124. Ibid., 49.

125. Luis G. Pedraja, "Guideposts along the Journey: Mapping North American Hispanic Theology," in *Protestantes/Protestants: Hispanic Christianity within Mainline Traditions*, ed. David Maldonado Jr. (Nashville, TN: Abingdon Press, 1999), 123.

126. Ibid., 131.

127. Ibid.

128. Ibid., 127.

129. Ibid., 130–31.

130. Pedraja cautions that, while postmodernism embraces pluralism by celebrating diversity, this emphasis on tolerance can result in a moral relativism capable of undermining justice as a guiding paradigm.

131. Pedraja, "Guideposts along the Journey," 133.

132. Ibid., 134.

133. If Virgilio Elizondo is the "father" of Roman Catholic Hispanic theology in the United States, then Justo L. González is the progenitor of Protestant Latino/a theology. Allan Figueroa Deck, in the introduction to *Frontiers of Hispanic Theology in the United States* (Maryknoll, NY: Orbis Books, 1992), has described González's theological corpus as "the most cogent statement yet on what, why and wherefore of a U.S. Hispanic theology" (xvi). Luis Pedraja engages Justo González's systematic presentation of Christian doctrines, *Mañana: Christian Theology from a Hispanic Perspective* (Nashville, TN: Abingdon Press, 1990), in the first chapter of *Jesus Is My Uncle*, in order to "thoughtfully consider the challenges and perspectives that Hispanics bring to the biblical text" (18).

134. González, *Mañana*, 38–41.

135. Ibid., 75.

136. Pedraja, *Jesus Is My Uncle*, 22.

137. Pedraja, "Guideposts along the Journey," 47.

138. Ibid., 48–49

NOTES TO CHAPTER 3

1. See, for example, Johann Baptist Metz, *Faith in History and Society*, trans. David Smith (New York: Seabury Press, 1980); Dorothee Sölle, *Political Theology*, trans. John Shelley (Philadelphia: Fortress Press, 1974); Jürgen Moltmann, *Theology of Hope: On the Grounds and the Implications of a Christian Eschatology*, trans. James Leitch (New York: Harper and Row, 1967), and *The Trinity and the Kingdom: The Doctrine of God*, trans. Margaret Kohl (Minneapolis, MN: Fortress Press, 1993); Reinhold Niebuhr, *Moral Man and Immoral Society* (New York: Scribner, 1960), and *The Children of Light and the Children of Darkness: A Vindication of Democracy and a Critique of Its Traditional Defence* (New York: Scribner, 1960); Stanley Hauerwas, *A Community of Character: Toward a Constructive Christian Social Ethic* (Notre Dame, IN: Notre Dame University Press, 1981), and *In Good Company: The Church as Polis* (Notre Dame, IN: Notre Dame University Press, 1995); John Howard Yoder, *The Christian Witness to the State* (Newton, KS: Faith and Life Press, 1964), and *For the Nations: Essays Evangelical and Public* (Grand Rapids, MI: Eerdmans, 1997); Gustavo Gutiérrez, *A Theology of Liberation: History, Politics, and Salvation*, rev. ed., trans. and ed. Sister Caridad India and John Eagleson (Maryknoll, NY: Orbis Books, 1988); Ignacio Ellacuría, *Teología política* (San Salvador: Ediciones del Secretariado Social Interdiocesano, 1973); Juan Luis Segundo, S.J., *Liberation of Theology*, trans. John Drury (Maryknoll, NY: Orbis Books, 1976); Martin E. Marty, "Two Kinds of Civil Religion," in *American Civil Religion*, ed. Russell E. Richey and Donald G. Jones (New York: Harper and Row, 1974), 139–57; Linell Elizabeth Cady, *Religion, Theology, and American Public Life* (Albany: State University of New York Press, 1993); Parker Palmer, *The Company of Strangers* (New York: Crossroads, 1983); Max Stackhouse, *Public Theology and Political Economy: Christian Stewardship in Modern Society* (Grand Rapids, MI: Eerdmans, 1987); Ronald F. Thiemann, *Constructing a Public Theology: The Church in a Pluralistic Culture* (Louisville, KY: Westminster John Knox Press, 1991).

2. Jürgen Moltmann, *God for a Secular Society: The Public Relevance of Theology*, trans. Margaret Kohl (Minneapolis, MN: Fortress Press, 1999), 48.

3. Ibid., 51, 58.

4. Ibid., 58.

5. Mary Doak, *Reclaiming Narrative for Public Theology* (Albany: State University of New York Press, 2004), 6.

6. See Richard J. Neuhaus, *The Naked Public Square: Religion and Democracy in America* (Grand Rapids, MI: Eerdmans, 1984); Victor Anderson, *Pragmatic Theology: Negotiating the Intersections of an American Philosophy of Religion and Public Theology* (Albany: State University of New York Press, 1998).

7. See Max L. Stackhouse, *Creeds, Society, and Human Rights* (Grand Rapids, MI: Eerdmans, 1984).

8. Doak, *Reclaiming Narrative for Public Theology*, 6.

9. Benjamin Valentin, *Mapping Public Theology: Beyond Culture, Identity, and Difference* (Harrisburg, PA: Trinity Press International, 2002), 85.

10. Ibid., 87.

11. Ibid., 110.

12. Ibid., 111.

13. Ibid., 80.

14. Jeffrey Stout, *Democracy and Tradition* (Princeton, NJ: Princeton University Press, 2004), 113.

15. Ibid., 10.

16. Ibid., 10–11.

17. See George Lindbeck, *The Nature of Doctrine: Religion and Theology in a Postliberal Age* (Philadelphia: Westminster Press, 1984), 113–24.

18. J. Wentzel van Huyssteen, *The Shaping of Rationality: Toward Interdisciplinarity in Theology and Science* (Grand Rapids, MI: Eerdmans, 1999), 241.

19. Alasdair MacIntyre, *Whose Justice? Which Rationality?* (Notre Dame, IN: University of Notre Dame Press, 1988), 6.

20. Alasdair MacIntyre, *After Virtue: A Study in Moral Theory,* 2nd ed. (Notre Dame, IN: University of Notre Dame Press, 1984), 253.

21. Ibid., 263.

22. The term *narrative theology* refers to a twentieth-century theological movement associated with Yale theologians George Lindbeck and Hans Frei (both heavily influenced by Karl Barth) that views (1) the task of theology as "Christian self-description," (2) doctrines as "rules" for articulating said self-description, and (3) the Bible's language and narrative as the primary formative and normative source of theology. I choose to categorize any theological approach as "narrative" that, like Lindbeck, understands theology's proper relationship to contemporary situations in such a way that Scripture defines "being, truth, goodness, and beauty. . . . Intratextual theology redescribes reality within the scriptural framework rather than translating Scripture into extrascriptural categories" (*The Nature of Doctrine,* 118).

23. For the purposes of this investigation I use *contextual* as an umbrella term for various twentieth-century theological movements that "take culture and cultural change seriously" (Bevans, *Models of Contextual Theology,* 22). Under this rubric I choose to include theologies that employ a method of correlation (e.g., David Tracy, Gordon D. Kaufman, Sallie McFague), as well as liberation theologies (e.g., Gustavo Gutiérrez, James H. Cone, Rosemary Radford Ruether), since, in spite of substantive differences, they are similar in their approach. In contradistinction to Lindbeck's narrative approach, contextual theologies begin with human experience and allow extrascriptural realities to shape theological content.

24. Lindbeck, *The Nature of Doctrine,* 113.

25. Ibid., 118.

26. Bevans, *Models of Contextual Theology,* 19.

27. Kathryn Tanner, *Theories of Culture: A New Agenda for Theology* (Minneapolis, MN: Fortress Press, 1997), 156–75.

28. Ibid., 163.

29. Ibid., 157.

30. Delwin Brown, *Boundaries of Our Habitations: Tradition and Theological Construction* (Albany: State University of New York Press, 1994), 146.

31. Delwin Brown, "Public Theology, Academic Theology: Wentzel van Huyssteen and the Nature of Theological Rationality," *American Journal of Theology and Philosophy* 22, no. 1 (January 2001): 96–101.

32. Valentin, *Mapping Public Theology*, 111.

33. For a general history of the Reformed/Calvinist tradition, from its sixteenth-century origins to the height of scholastic orthodoxy, see John T. McNeill, *The History and Character of Calvinism* (New York: Oxford University Press, 1954); and Philip Benedict, *Christ's Churches Purely Reformed: A Social History of Calvinism* (New Haven, CT: Yale University Press, 2002). For an examination of Calvinist social ethics, see John H. Leith, *John Calvin's Doctrine of the Christian Life* (Louisville, KY: Westminster/John Knox Press, 1989); and W. Fred Graham, *The Constructive Revolutionary: John Calvin and His Socio-economic Impact* (Richmond, VA: John Knox Press, 1971).

34. Mark K. Taylor, "Immanental and Prophetic: Shaping Reformed Theology for Late Twentieth-Century Struggle," in *Christian Ethics in Ecumenical Context: Theology, Culture, and Politics in Dialogue*, ed. Shin Chiba, George R. Hunsberger, and Lester Edwin J. Ruiz (Grand Rapids, MI: Eerdmans, 1999), 156.

35. See Rubem Alves, *Protestantism and Repression: A Brazilian Case Study*, trans. John Drury and Jaime Wright (Maryknoll, NY: Orbis Books, 1985); and John W. de Gruchy (with Steve de Gruchy), *The Church Struggle in South Africa: 25th Anniversary Edition* (Minneapolis, MN: Fortress Press, 2005).

36. Taylor, "Immanental and Prophetic," 154. In this article Taylor focuses on John Calvin's *Ecclesiastical Ordinances* (1541) in order to expand a thesis developed by Nicholas Wolterstorff that the Calvinist Reformed tradition suffers from two failings: (1) an understanding of a just social order that barely tolerates opposing viewpoints, and (2) a recurrent triumphalism that imposes its worldview upon others. See Wolterstorff, *Until Justice and Peace Embrace* (Grand Rapids, MI: Eerdmans, 1983).

37. John Calvin, *Calvin's Commentaries*, vol. XIX, reprint of the Edinburgh Edition, various editors and translators (Grand Rapids, MI: Baker Book House, 2003), 478–79 (Rom. 13:1). A note on language: throughout the text every effort is made to use gender-inclusive language, but quotations are left exact in order to preserve the author's original intent or bias.

38. John Calvin, *Institutes of the Christian Religion*, 2 vols., ed. John T. McNeill, trans. *Ford Lewis Battles* (Philadelphia: Westminster Press, 1960), 4.20.31.

39. Ibid., 4.20.29.

40. Ibid.

41. For a concise history of the clandestine Reformed churches in France, see Philip Benedict's discussion of the construction and defense of a minority church in *Christ's Churches Purely Reformed*, 127–48.

42. See Benedict, *Christ's Churches Purely Reformed*, 66–67; Williston Walker, Richard Norris, David W. Lotz, and Robert Handy, *A History of the Christian Church*, 4th ed. (New York: Scribner's, 1985), 455–65; also Jaroslav Pelikan, *The Christian Tradition: Reformation of the Church and Dogma (1300–1700)* (Chicago: University of Chicago Press, 1984), 313–22.

43. Calvin, "Prefatory Address to King Francis," in *Institutes*, 10.

44. Michael Sattler, "Brotherly Union of a Number of Children of God Concerning Seven Articles," in *The Legacy of Michael Sattler*, trans. and ed. John H. Yoder (Scottdale, PA: Herald Press, 1973), 37–38.

45. Ibid., 40.

46. Calvin, "Prefatory Address to King Francis," 30.

47. Calvin, *Institutes* 4.20.2.

48. Ibid., 4.20.3.

49. Ibid., 4.20.2.

50. Calvin, *Calvin's Commentaries*, vol. XVIII., 209 (John 18:36).

51. Calvin, *Institutes* 4.20.1.

52. Ibid., 4.20.2.

53. Ibid., 4.20.29.

54. See David Willis-Watkins, "Calvin's Prophetic Reinterpretation of Kingship," in *Probing the Reformed Tradition: Historical Studies in Honor of Edward A. Dowey, Jr.*, ed. Elsie Anne McKee and Brian G. Armstrong (Louisville, KY: Westminster/John Knox Press, 1989), 116–34, for an investigation of Calvin's mature understanding of the office of king focusing on sermons on 2 Samuel. Willis-Watkins argues that Calvin preached on David as king in order to present a prophetic reinterpretation of kingship in which no earthly king can be viewed as legitimate who hampers the preaching of the Word; such a king would be overthrown by God and replaced by one who "hears and obeys the prophetic Word" (125).

55. Calvin, *Institutes*, 4.20.6.

56. Guenther H. Haas, *The Concept of Equity in Calvin's Ethics* (Waterloo, Ontario: Wilfrid Laurier University Press, 1997), 108.

57. Calvin, *Institutes* 4.20.29.

58. Ibid., 4.20.32 (emphasis added).

59. Ibid., 4.20.30.

60. Ibid., 4.20.31.

61. Ibid.

62. Ibid., 1.1.1.

63. Ibid., 1.1.2.

64. Ibid., 2.16.3.

65. Ibid., 1.6.1.

66. Elsie Anne McKee, "Exegesis, Theology, and Development in Calvin's In-stitutio: A Methodological Suggestion," in *Probing the Reformed Tradition: Historical Studies in Honor of Edward A. Dowey, Jr.*, ed. Elsie Anne McKee and Brian G. Armstrong (Louisville, KY: Westminster/John Knox Press, 1989), 155.

67. Calvin, *Calvin's Commentaries*, vol. V, 332 (Ps. 82:3).

68. Taylor, "Immanental and Prophetic," 155–56.

69. Calvin, *Calvin's Commentaries*, vol. VIII, 172 (Isaiah 55:11).

70. Calvin's *Commentaries*, vol. XV, 343 (Haggai 1:12).

71. Calvin, *Institutes* 4.1.5.

72. Calvin, *Calvin's Commentaries*, vol. XV, 630 (Malachi 4:6).

73. Ibid., vol. VIII, 9 (Isaiah 49:2).

74. Ibid., vol. VI, 316 (Ps. 149:9).

75. Calvin, *Institutes* 4.11.16.

76. T. Beza, *L'historie de la vie et mort de Calvin* (1565), OC 21, col. 33, quoted in Cottret, *Calvin: A Biography*, 288–9.

77. John Calvin, "Draft Ecclesiastical Ordinances (1541)," in *John Calvin: Selections from His Writings*, ed. John Dillenberger (Missoula, MT: Scholars Press, 1975), 231. This practice was first codified in 1541 and preserved in the ordinances of 1561.

78. Amédée Roget, *Historie du people de Genève*, 7 vols. (Geneva: J. Jullien, 1870–83), vol. 1, 86–94, cited by W. Fred Graham in *The Constructive Revolutionary: John Calvin and His Socio-economic Impact* (Richmond, VA: John Knox Press, 1971), 60, as an accurate account of the circumstances leading up to the exile of Farel and Calvin taken directly from the Council registry.

79. Calvin, "Draft Ecclesiastical Ordinances (1541)," 241.

80. Ibid., 242n21 (emphasis added).

81. Ibid., quoting the *Registres du Conseil*, May 21, 1548.

82. Calvin, *Calvin's Commentaries*, vol. V, 332 (Ps. 82:3).

83. Ibid., vol. XIV, 363–64 (Amos 8:4).

84. See Gustavo Gutiérrez, *A Theology of Liberation: History, Politics, and Salvation*, rev. ed., trans. and ed. Sister Caridad Inda and John Eagleson (Maryknoll, NY: Orbis Books, 1988), 3–12.

85. Ibid., xxxviii.

86. Ibid., 76.

87. John Calvin, *Sermons on 2 Samuel: Chapters 1–13*, trans. Douglas Kelly (Carlisle, PA: Banner of Truth Trust, 1992), 419.

88. Calvin, *Institutes* 3.8.8.

89. For a fuller accounting of the social situation in sixteenth-century Geneva, see Graham, *The Constructive Revolutionary*, 97–115; Cottret, *Calvin*, 157–81; Benedict, *Christ's Churches Purely Reformed*, 93–109; and Elsie Ann McKee,

Diakonia in the Classical Reformed Tradition and Today (Grand Rapids, MI: Eerdmans, 1989), 47–60.

90. Calvin, "Draft Ecclesiastical Ordinances (1541)," 235–36.

91. See Jeannine E. Olson, *Calvin and Social Welfare: Deacons and the Bourse française* (Cranbury, NJ: Associated University Presses, 1989), for a thorough study of this institution and its relation to the rest of the social welfare system in Calvin's Geneva. The author notes that the Bourse française is not mentioned in the *Ecclesiastical Ordinances* of 1541, since the large influx of refugees began shortly thereafter, but the records indicate that sometime in the mid-1540s the need for an alternate welfare program for refugees became apparent, and by September 30, 1550, the fund had been officially established.

92. Ibid., 39.

93. Calvin, "Draft Ecclesiastical Ordinances (1541)," 237.

94. Taylor, "Immanental and Prophetic," 156.

95. For an overview of Calvin's advocacy on behalf of French refugees, see Graham, *The Constructive Revolutionary*, 97–115; and Olson, *Calvin and Social Welfare*, 29–36. For translations of Calvin's pastoral correspondence and advocacy for justice for the victims of political persecution, see John Calvin, *Writings on Pastoral Piety*, ed. and trans. Elsie Anne McKee (New York: Paulist Press, 2001), 315–32.

96. Calvin, *Writings on Pastoral Piety*, 317–18.

97. Ibid., 323.

98. Calvin, *Institutes*, 3.8.7.

99. See Sallie McFague, *Speaking in Parables: A Study in Metaphor and Theology* (Philadelphia: Fortress Press, 1975); William R. Herzog II, *Parables as Subversive Speech: Jesus as Pedagogue of the Oppressed* (Louisville, KY: Westminster/John Knox Press, 1994); and John Drury, *The Parables in the Gospels: History and Allegory* (New York: Crossroad, 1989). McFague reminds us that theology is "always hermeneutical, always concerned with how the gospel can be 'translated' or understood—grasped—by people. . . . Such hearing and acceptance in the parables takes place through imaginative participation when an old word or story or event is suddenly seen in a new setting, an insight with implications for one's belief and life" (7).

100. See Geoffrey De Ste Croix, "Early Christian Attitudes to Property and Slavery," in *Studies in Church History, 12: Church Society and Politics*, ed. Derek Baker (Oxford: Ecclesiastical History Society, 1975), 1–38; Dale B. Martin, "Slavery and the Ancient Jewish Family," in *The Jewish Family in Antiquity*, ed. Shaye J. D. Cohen (Atlanta, GA: Scholars Press, 1988), 113–29; W. E. Heitland, *Agricola: A Study of Agriculture and Rustic Life in the Graeco-Roman World from the Point of View of Labour* (Cambridge: Cambridge University Press, 1927).

101. See Wayne A. Meeks, *The First Urban Christians*, 2nd ed. (New Haven, CT: Yale University Press, 2003), 21, 63–64.

102. Cited by Origen in *Contra Celsum,* trans. Henry Chadwick (Cambridge: Cambridge University Press, 1965), 504.

103. Keith R. Bradley, *Slavery and Rebellion in the Roman World, 140 B.C.–70 B.C.* (Bloomington: Indiana University Press, 1989), 83–101.

104. See Paul S. Minear, *Images of the Church in the New Testament* (Louisville, KY: Westminster/John Knox Press, 2004), 156–61.

105. Celsus, cited by Origen in *Contra Celsum,* 62.

106. Minucius Felix, early Christian apologist, cited in Eberhard Arnold, *The Early Christians in Their Own Words,* 4th ed., trans. and ed. by the Society of Brothers (Farmington, PA: Plough Publishing House, 1997), 107.

107. *Letter to Diognetus,* paragraph 10, cited in Arnold, *The Early Christians in Their Own Words,* 108.

108. First Letter of Clement to the Corinthians, cited in Arnold, *The Early Christians in Their Own Words,* 211.

109. Gregory of Nyssa, *Homilies on the Beatitudes,* cited in Justo L. González, *Faith and Wealth: A History of Early Christian Ideas on the Origin, Significance, and Use of Money* (San Francisco: Harper and Row, 1990), 178.

110. González, *Faith and Wealth,* 181. The author argues that the Cappadocians "lacked a comprehensive vision or theory of the matter in which government policies enrich some and impoverish others, and therefore one does not find in their writings grand schemes of social reform like those of more recent times. Yet they repeatedly saw the impact of specific government action on individuals and even on entire towns, and they tried to correct the injustices they perceived."

NOTES TO CHAPTER 4

1. See Frederick John Dalton, *The Moral Vision of César Chávez* (Maryknoll, NY: Orbis Books, 2003); Stephen R. Lloyd-Moffett, "The Mysticism and Social Action of César Chávez," in *Latino Religions and Civic Activism in the United States,* ed. Gastón Espinosa, Virgilio Elizondo, and Jesse Miranda (New York: Oxford University Press, 2005), 35–51; and Luís D. Leon, "César Chávez and Mexican American Civil Religion," in *Latino Religions and Civic Activism in the United States,* ed. Gastón Espinosa, Virgilio Elizondo, and Jesse Miranda (New York: Oxford University Press, 2005), 53–64.

2. Jacques E. Levy, *César Chávez: Autobiography of La Causa* (New York: Norton, 1975), 286.

3. Lloyd-Moffett, "The Mysticism and Social Action of César Chávez," 40.

4. Benjamin Valentin, "Nuevos Odres para el Vino: A Critical Contribution to Latino/a Theological Construction," *Journal of Hispanic/Latino Theology* 5, no. 4 (May 1998): 44.

5. Virgilio Elizondo, foreword to Justo L. González, *Mañana: Christian Theology from a Hispanic Perspective* (Nashville, TN: Abingdon Press, 1990), 17.

6. See Miguel H. Díaz, "Dime con quién andas y te dire quién eres: We Walk with Our Lady of Charity," in *From the Heart of Our People: Latino/a Explorations in Catholic Systematic Theology,* ed. Orlando O. Espín and Miguel H. Díaz (Maryknoll, NY: Orbis Books, 1999), 153–71.

7. Virgilio Elizondo, *Guadalupe: Mother of the New Creation* (Maryknoll, NY: Orbis Books, 1997), xi.

8. Ibid., xviii.

9. While Elizondo speaks primarily about popular Catholicism, his insights are applicable to any form of Christianity that thrives in popular belief and practice though not always recognized by official doctrine. A proper understanding of tradition cannot ignore the role of popular beliefs and practices in the formation of official doctrine, as evidenced by the Trinitarian and Christological controversies of the early church. See J. N. D. Kelly, *Early Christian Doctrines,* 5th rev. ed. (New York: Harper and Row, 1978); Aloys Grillmeier, *Christ in Christian Tradition,* 2nd ed., trans. J. Bowden (Atlanta, GA: John Knox Press, 1975); and Jaroslav Pelikan, *The Christian Tradition: The Emergence of the Catholic Tradition (100–600)* (Chicago: University of Chicago Press, 1971).

10. This synopsis of how Virgilio Elizondo understands and employs popular religion is gleaned from various works, especially *Galilean Journey: The Mexican-American Promise* (Maryknoll, NY: Orbis Books, 1984); *Religious Practices of the Mexican American and Catechesis* (San Antonio, TX: Mexican American Cultural Center Press, 1974); *Christianity and Culture: An Introduction to Pastoral Theology and Ministry for the Bicultural Community* (Huntington, IN: Our Sunday Visitor, 1975); and his doctoral dissertation, published in English as *Mestizaje: The Dialectic of Cultural Birth and the Gospel* (San Antonio, TX: Mexican American Cultural Center Press, 1978).

11. Virgilio Elizondo, "Mary and the Poor: A Model of Evangelizing Ecumenism," in *Mary in the Churches,* ed. Hans Küng and Jürgen Moltmann (New York: Seabury Press, 1983), 59.

12. In Elizondo's works there remains an ambiguity as to whether Guadalupe is *mestiza* or an indigenous woman. The Guadalupe tradition has long identified Guadalupe and Juan Diego as indigenous persons, yet in Elizondo's various writings he sometimes refers to Guadalupe as Indian and other times as *mestiza*. Of greater importance for understanding Elizondo is that Juan Diego, while biologically an Indian, nonetheless embodies cultural *mestizaje*. Accordingly, throughout this discussion I refer to both Guadalupe and Juan Diego as *mestizos* insofar as they represent for Elizondo the genesis of a new humanity that transforms the history of conquest into salvation history.

13. See Robert Ricard, *The Spiritual Conquest of Mexico—An Essay on the*

Apostolate and the Evangelizing Methods of the Mendicant Orders in New Spain: 1523–1572 (Berkeley: University of California Press, 1966), 302 (also see 35–38, 188–91).

14. Elizondo, *Guadalupe*, 84.

15. Ricard, *The Spiritual Conquest of Mexico*, 189.

16. Elizondo, *Guadalupe*, xi.

17. Miguel Sánchez, author of *Imagen de la Virgen María, Madre de Dios de Guadalupe. Milagrosamente aparecida en la ciudad de México. Celebrada en su historia, con la profecía del capítulo doce del Apocalipsis* (Mexico, 1648), is considered by many critics the "inventor" of the criollo Guadalupe myth, in which he compares the Mexican Guadalupe to the European Our Lady of Remedios by employing the typology of Naomi and Ruth (Guadalupe is the native-born Naomi while Remedios is the foreign-born Ruth). David Brading's exhaustive history of the Guadalupe tradition, *Mexican Phoenix. Our Lady of Guadalupe: Image and Tradition across Five Centuries* (Cambridge: Cambridge University Press, 2001), challenges Poole's conclusion that the Guadalupe myth was a criollo creation of the seventeenth century by proposing the thesis that there are two distinct yet interrelated Guadalupe traditions—one indigenous dating back to the sixteenth century, the other criollo and linked to Miguel Sánchez's 1648 publication. Still, Brading argues that even if Sánchez did not initiate the Guadalupan devotion, this first published account of the apparition at Tepeyac determined the direction of both traditions, eventually converging into today's recognizable devotion.

18. Stafford Poole, *Our Lady of Guadalupe: The Origins and Sources of a Mexican National Symbol, 1531–1797* (Tucson: University of Arizona Press, 1995), 214.

19. Ibid., 216–17.

20. Ibid., 13.

21. Ibid.

22. Ibid., 13–14.

23. Andrés G. Guerrerro, *A Chicano Theology* (Maryknoll, NY: Orbis Books, 1987), 115.

24. Ibid., 116.

25. For examples of Guadalupe as a liberating symbol other than the work of Virgilio Elizondo, see Leonardo Boff, "The Amerindian Gospel: The Liberating Method of Our Lady of Guadalupe," *SEDOS Bulletin* 23, no. 2 (February 1991): 42–45; Susan D. Buell, "Our Lady of Guadalupe: A Feminine Mythology for the New World," *Historical Magazine of the Protestant Episcopal Church* 51, no. 4 (December 1982): 399–404; and Nora O. Lozano-Díaz, "Ignored Virgin or Unaware Women: A Mexican-American Protestant Reflection on the Virgin of Guadalupe," in *A Reader in Latina Feminist Theology: Religion and Justice,* ed. María Pilar Aquino, Daisy L. Machado, and Jeanette Rodríguez (Austin: University of Texas Press, 2002)204–16; and Jeanette Rodríguez, *Our Lady of Guadalupe: Faith*

and Empowerment among Mexican-American Women (Austin: University of Texas Press, 1993).

26. Poole, *Our Lady of Guadalupe,* 13.

27. Allan Figueroa Deck, S.J., review of Stafford Poole, *Our Lady of Guadalupe: The Origins and Sources of a Mexican National Symbol, 1531–1797, Journal of Hispanic/Latino Theology* 3, no. 3 (February 1996): 64.

28. Ibid., 65.

29. Elizondo, *Guadalupe: Mother of the New Creation,* 121.

30. Ibid., xiv.

31. Ibid., 127.

32. See Daniel Migliore, "Woman of Faith: Toward a Reformed Understanding of Mary," in *Blessed One: Protestant Perspectives on Mary,* ed. Beverly Roberts Gaventa and Cynthia L. Rigby (Louisville, KY: Westminster John Knox Press, 2002), 117–30, for a brief overview of John Calvin's views on Mary's role in Christian devotion. I also want to thank Timothy Matovina for introducing me to the work of Maxwell E. Johnson, *The Virgin of Guadalupe: Theological Reflections of an Anglo-Lutheran Liturgist* (Lanham, MD: Rowman and Littlefield, 2002), which to my knowledge is the only book-length theological reflection on Guadalupe from a Protestant perspective. Johnson describes his project as "a Protestant-Catholic Mestizaje, a synthesis of popular Guadalupanismo and Protestant theological convictions" (174). It is in the same spirit that I offer these reflections on Guadalupe, complementing Johnson's Lutheran emphasis upon justification by grace alone through faith with a Reformed/Calvinist Christocentric theology that also emphasizes the freedom of God to act in new ways.

33. Elizondo, *Guadalupe,* xi.

34. John W. de Gruchy, *Christianity, Art and Transformation: Theological Aesthetics in the Struggle for Justice* (Cambridge: Cambridge University Press, 2001), 37.

35. John Calvin, *Institutes of the Christian Religion,* 2 vols., trans. Ford Lewis Battles, ed. John T. McNeill (Philadelphia: Westminster Press, 1960), 112–14 (1.11.13).

36. Ibid., 1.2.12; 2.2.16.

37. See Ford Lewis Battles, "God Was Accommodating Himself to Human Capacity," *Interpretation* 31 (January 1977): 19–38.

38. Still, de Gruchy concludes the chief contribution of Calvinism "has been in the field of music, hymnody and poetry, that is the arts that appeal to the ear and add enrichment to the Word," not the visual arts (*Christianity, Art and Transformation,* 44).

39. Ibid., 243.

40. Ibid., 254.

41. Battles, "God Was Accommodating Himself to Human Capacity," 36, 38.

42. See Jeanette Rodríguez, "The Common Womb of the Americas: Virgilio Elizondo's Theological Reflection on Our Lady of Guadalupe," in *Beyond Borders: Writings of Virgilio Elizondo and Friends,* ed. Timothy Matovina (Maryknoll, NY: Orbis Books, 2000), 109–17.

43. Elizondo, *Guadalupe,* 129.

44. Ibid., 134–35.

45. Ibid., 113–14.

46. Ibid., 3–4. I am relying upon Elizondo's own English translation of the Spanish translation of Siller Acuña's text of the *Nican mopohua,* fully aware of the controversy over the origins of this text (first published in 1649, more than one hundred years after the events at Tepeyac) given that popular devotion claims that the *Nican mopohua* dates back to the sixteenth century.

47. Elizondo, *Galilean Journey,* 49.

48. Elizondo, *Guadalupe,* 5.

49. Ibid., 25.

50. Ibid., 33.

51. J. Lafaye, *Quetzalcóatl and Guadalupe: The Formation of Mexican National Consciousness, 1531–1813* (Chicago: University of Chicago Press, 1976), 238–300. Lafaye points out that Guadalupe became the central religious symbol of the poor centuries before it became the symbol of Mexican independence.

52. Virgilio Elizondo, "Our Lady of Guadalupe as a Cultural Symbol," in *Beyond Borders: Writings of Virgilio Elizondo and Friends,* ed. Timothy Matovina (Maryknoll, NY: Orbis Books, 2000), 124.

53. Elizondo, *Guadalupe,* 68.

54. Ibid., 115.

55. Ibid., 124.

56. Ibid., 116.

57. Ibid., 117.

58. Ibid.

59. Ibid.

60. For a discussion of the two prevalent forms of religious expression, "manifestation" and "proclamation," see David Tracy, *The Analogical Imagination: Christian Theology and the Culture of Pluralism* (New York: Crossroad, 1981), 202–18. The author argues that the Catholic and Orthodox forms of Christianity emphasize sacramental participation in divine manifestation, whereas Protestant Christianity is distinguished by its emphasis on word and "a sense of radical non-participation" in the divine life (203). In other words, a theology of proclamation is one in which God is understood as radically transcendent and knowledge of God an act of God's grace to overcome the "infinite qualitative difference" between God and the Creation.

61. See Jürgen Moltmann, *God in Creation: A New Theology of Creation and the Spirit of God,* trans. Margaret Kohl (San Francisco: Harper and Row, 1985);

and Kathryn Tanner, *God and Creation in Christian Theology: Tyranny or Empowerment?* (New York: Basil Blackwell, 1988).

62. Nahum M. Sarna, *The JPS Torah Commentary: Genesis* (New York: Jewish Publication Society, 5749/1989), 49–50.

63. Elizondo, *Guadalupe: Mother of the New Creation*, 74.

64. Ibid., 107. See note 12 for a discussion of Elizondo's ambiguous use of *mestizaje* in reference to Guadalupe and Juan Diego.

65. Ibid.

66. Sadly, Elizondo remains silent on a pressing issue of gender discrimination within the Catholic Church: the prohibition on ordaining women to the priesthood. In my opinion, Guadalupe as a female incarnation of God counters arguments that the priesthood must remain exclusively male because of the doctrine of *in persona Christi*.

67. Elizondo, *Guadalupe*, 113.

68. Ibid., 119.

69. Ibid., 90–91.

NOTES TO CHAPTER 5

1. Luis G. Pedraja, *Jesus Is My Uncle: Christology from a Hispanic Perspective* (Nashville, TN: Abingdon Press, 1999), 83.

2. See Jürgen Moltmann, "The Trinitarian History of God," in *The Future of Creation*, trans. Margaret Kohl (Philadelphia: Fortress Press, 1979), 80–96; Moltmann, *The Way of Jesus Christ: Christology in Messianic Dimensions* (San Francisco: HarperSanFrancisco, 1990), 73–150. Moltmann articulates a Spirit Christology that seeks to overcome the christomonism typical of two-natures Christology in order to locate the saving work of Christ within the "trinitarian history of God" (*The Way of Jesus Christ*, 74).

3. Edward R. Handy, ed., *Christology of the Later Fathers* (Philadelphia: Westminster Press, 1954), 373.

4. See Jürgen Moltmann, *The Crucified God: The Cross of Christ as the Foundation and Criticism of Christian Theology*, trans. R. A. Wilson and John Bowden (Minneapolis, MN: Fortress Press, 1993), 82–111; Robert W. Jenson, *Systematic Theology*, vol. 1, *The Triune God* (Oxford: Oxford University Press, 1997), 125–45; Wolfhart Pannenberg, *Jesus: God and Man*, trans. Lewis L. Wilkins and Duane A. Priebe (Philadelphia: Westminster Press, 1977); John Macquarrie, *Christology Revisited* (Harrisburg, PA: Trinity Press International, 1998).

5. Jon Sobrino, *Christology at the Crossroads*, trans. Cesar Jerez (Maryknoll, NY: Orbis Books, 1978), 3.

6. Ibid.

7. Ibid., 10.

8. See Jon Sobrino, *Jesus the Liberator: A Historical-Theological View*, trans.

Paul Burns and Francis McDonagh (Maryknoll, NY: Orbis Books, 1993), 40–44. Not surprisingly, Sobrino has come under examination by the Congregation for the Doctrine of the Faith over several aspects of his Christology, including his methodological decision to begin Christological reflection with the "Church of the poor" rather than the Chalcedonian formula, and his statements that "the New Testament does not clearly affirm the divinity of Jesus" ("NOTIFICATION on the works of Father Jon Sobrino, SJ: *Jesucristo liberador. Lectura histórico-teológica de Jesús de Nazaret* [Madrid, 1991] and *La fe en Jesucristo. Ensayo desde las víctimas* [San Salvador, 1999]," posted on the Vatican Web site, http://www.vatican.va/roman_curia/congregations/cfaith/documents/rc_con_cfaith_doc_20061126_notification-sobrino_en.html).

9. Christopher Morse, *Not Every Spirit: A Dogmatics of Christian Disbelief* (Valley Forge, PA: Trinity Press International, 1994), 142.

10. Moltmann, *The Crucified God*, 82.

11. See the work of the Jewish historian Josephus (c. 37–100 CE) for a history of the Jewish revolt against Rome (63 BCE–74 CE) and the various political factions and parties that governed first-century Jewish Palestine. *The Works of Josephus, Complete and Unabridged*, trans. William Whiston (Peabody, MA: Hendrickson Publishers, 1987).

12. See the collection of essays in *Judaisms and Their Messiahs at the Turn of the Christian Era*, ed. Jacob Neusner, William S. Green, and Ernest Frerichs (Cambridge: Cambridge University Press, 1987); E. P. Sanders, *Judaism: Practice and Belief, 63 BCE–66 CE* (Philadelphia: Trinity Press International, 1992); and Helmut Koester, *Introduction to the New Testament*, vol. 1, *History, Culture and Religion of the Hellenistic Age* (New York: Walter de Gruyter, 1982).

13. See William Horbury, *Jewish Messianism and the Cult of Christ* (London: SCM Press, 1998).

14. See *The Old Testament Pseudepigrapha*, vol. 1, *Apocalyptic Literature and Testaments*, ed. James H. Charlesworth (New York: Doubleday, 1983), 70 (1 Enoch 90:18, 20).

15. See *The Old Testament Pseudepigrapha*, vol. 2, *Expansions of the "Old Testament" and Legends, Wisdom and Philosophical Literature, Prayers, Psalms and Odes, Fragments of Lost Judeo-Hellenistic Works*, ed. James H. Charlesworth (New York: Doubleday, 1985), 667 (Psalms of Solomon 17:21, 25).

16. In Josephus's political-military history, *The Wars of the Jews* (c. 75 CE), he identifies the Essenes as "the ministers of peace." See *The Works of Josephus*, 606 (*War* 2.8.6).

17. See *The Dead Sea Scrolls: A New Translation*, trans. Michael Wise, Martin Abegg Jr., and Edward Cook (San Francisco: HarperSanFrancisco, 1996), 167 (War Scroll 19:1, 3–5). It is generally agreed that the Qumran community that produced the Dead Sea Scrolls is the Essene sect named by Josephus as one of the three

leading "Judaisms"—along with the Pharisees and the Sadducees—flourishing from the second century BCE into the first century CE.

18. Jürgen Moltmann, *The Way of Jesus Christ: Christology in Messianic Dimensions,* trans. Margaret Kohl (San Francisco: HarperSanFrancisco, 1990), 74. Moltmann retrieves the politically engaged dimension of Jesus' understanding of Messiah by appealing to the *ruach*/Holy Spirit of God with its roots in the Spirit and Wisdom traditions of ancient Israel. The consequence of this line of argument is to give as much weight to the life and ministry of Jesus as is given to the death and resurrection when discussing Soteriology: "He is raised and present in the Spirit, not only as the one crucified, but also as the one baptized, as the healer, the preacher on the mount, the friend of sinners and tax-collectors, and the one whom the women accompanied to the moment of his death" (76).

19. John H. Yoder, *The Politics of Jesus: Vicit Agnus Noster* (Grand Rapids, MI: Eerdmans, 1972), 240.

20. Zaida Maldonado Pérez, "Visions of Hope: The Legacy of the Early Church," in *New Horizons in Hispanic/Latino(a) Theology,* ed. Benjamín Valentín (Cleveland, OH: Pilgrim Press, 2003), 44; see also her dissertation, "The Subversive Dimensions of the Visions of the Martyrs of the Roman Empire of the Second through Early Fourth Centuries" (Saint Louis University, 1999).

21. See Mark Lewis Taylor, *The Executed God: The Way of the Cross in Lockdown America* (Minneapolis, MN: Fortress Press, 2001), 70–98. Taylor argues that a contemporary political theology seeking genuine and effective change for social justice needs to free itself "from the fetters of Christendom" and reclaim "Christian faith as adversarial practice" by interpreting the "Galilean way of Jesus" as a way "that suffers and resists empire" (97). Thankfully, while Constantinian Christendom has dominated the Western theological landscape, "followers of Jesus who contest imperial ways have never been completely absent from history" (ibid).

22. See Jaroslav Pelikan, *The Christian Tradition: A History of the Development of Doctrine: The Emergence of the Catholic Tradition (100–600)* (Chicago: University of Chicago Press, 1971), 251–56; and J. N. D. Kelly, *Early Christian Doctrines* (San Francisco: HarperSanFrancisco, 1978), 301–9.

23. See Pelikan, *The Christian Tradition,* 233–34, 247–51; and Kelly, *Early Christian Doctrines,* 153–58, 318–23.

24. Sobrino, *Christology at the Crossroads,* 337.

25. See Pelikan, *The Christian Tradition,* 175–76; and Kelly, *Early Christian Doctrines,* 115–19.

26. Kelly, *Early Christian Doctrines,* 173.

27. Ibid., 283.

28. Ibid., 278.

29. Ibid., 279.

30. Ibid., 280.

31. See Sobrino, *Christology at the Crossroads*, 201–9.

32. Ibid., 202.

33. Ibid., 208–9.

34. See Leonardo Boff, *Trinity and Society* (Maryknoll, NY: Orbis Books, 1988); *Holy Trinity, Perfect Community*, trans. Phillip Berryman (Maryknoll, NY: Orbis Books, 2000); and Jürgen Moltmann, *The Trinity and the Kingdom*, trans. Margaret Kohl (Minneapolis, MN: Fortress Press, 1993).

35. See Taylor, *The Executed God*, 99–126.

36. Ibid., 108.

37. Luis G. Pedraja, *Teología: An Introduction to Hispanic Theology* (Nashville, TN: Abingdon Press, 2003), 127.

38. Pedraja, *Jesus Is My Uncle*, 123.

39. Ibid., 12.

40. Ibid., 69.

41. Ibid., 67.

42. Ibid.

43. Ibid.

44. Ibid., 72.

45. See Richard A. Horsley, *Galilee: History, Politics, People* (Valley Forge, PA: Trinity Press International, 1995); Horsley, *Archaeology, History, and Society in Galilee: The Social Context of Jesus and the Rabbis* (Valley Forge: PA: Trinity Press International, 1996); John Dominick Crossan, *The Historical Jesus: The Life of a Mediterranean Jewish Peasant* (reprint; San Francisco: HarperSanFrancisco, 1993); Geza Vermes, *Jesus in His Jewish Context* (Minneapolis, MN: Fortress Press, 2003); Marcus J. Borg, *Meeting Jesus Again for the First Time: The Historical Jesus and the Heart of Contemporary Faith* (reprint; San Francisco: HarperSanFrancisco, 1995); John P. Meier, *A Marginal Jew: Rethinking the Historical Jesus*, 3 vols. (New York: Doubleday, 1991–2001).

46. See Virgilio Elizondo, *Galilean Journey: The Mexican-American Promise*, 2nd ed., revised and enlarged edition (Maryknoll, NY: Orbis Books, 1983, 2000).

47. Taylor, *The Executed God*, 76.

48. Elizondo, *Galilean Journey*, 49.

49. Taylor, *The Executed God*, 107. Taylor draws upon the work of René Girard, *The Scapegoat*, trans. Yvonne Freccero (Baltimore: John Hopkins University Press, 1986), in defining this "scapegoat mechanism."

50. See Jon Sobrino, "The Crucified Peoples: Yahweh's Suffering Servant Today," in *Witnesses to the Kingdom: The Martyrs of El Salvador and the Crucified Peoples* (Maryknoll, NY: Orbis Books, 2003), 155–63.

51. Pedraja, *Jesus Is My Uncle*, 70–71.

52. Ibid., 88.

53. Ibid.

54. Gustavo Gutiérrez, *A Theology of Liberation: History, Politics, and Salvation,* rev. ed., trans. and ed. Sister Caridad India and John Eagleson (Maryknoll, NY: Orbis Books, 1988), xxxiv.

55. Pedraja, *Jesus Is My Uncle,* 88.

56. Pedraja, *Teología,* 128.

57. See H. Richard Niebuhr, *Christ and Culture* (New York: Harper Torchbooks, 1956); also James H. Cone, *God of the Oppressed,* rev. ed. (Maryknoll, NY: Orbis Books, 1997), 78–83. Cone offers a concise introduction and critique of Niebuhr's five paradigms, finding Niebuhr's definition of culture inadequate for liberation concerns yet praising Niebuhr for emphasizing "faith's involvement in, and transformation of, culture while remaining deeply aware of its own limitations" (81).

58. Niebuhr, *Christ and Culture,* 41.

59. Pedraja, *Teología,* 128.

60. Ibid., 128–29.

61. Ibid., 129.

62. Ibid.

63. Ibid.

64. Ibid., 102.

65. Ibid., 103.

66. Ibid., 105.

67. Eberhard Jüngel, *God's Being Is in Becoming: The Trinitarian Being of God in the Theology of Karl Barth,* trans. John Webster (Grand Rapids, MI: Eerdmans, 2001).

68. Pedraja, *Jesus Is My Uncle,* 106.

69. Ibid.

70. Ibid., 69.

71. Ibid., 106.

72. Pedraja, *Teología,* 77.

73. Ibid., 13.

74. Ibid., 17.

75. Pedraja, *Jesus Is My Uncle,* 83.

76. Ibid.

77. Ibid.

78. Pedraja, *Teología,* 158.

79. Ibid.

80. Pedraja, *Jesus Is My Uncle,* 110.

81. Ibid., 112.

82. Ibid.

83. Ibid., 113.

NOTES TO CHAPTER 6

1. Eugene F. Rogers Jr., "The Stranger as Blessing," in *Knowing the Triune God: The Work of the Spirit in the Practices of the Church,* ed. James J. Buckley and David S. Yeago (Grand Rapids, MI: Eerdmans, 2001), 265–66.

2. Luis G. Pedraja, *Jesus Is My Uncle: Christology from a Hispanic Perspective* (Nashville, TN: Abingdon Press, 1999), 106.

3. Mark Lewis Taylor, "Tracking Spirit: Theology as Cultural Critique in America," in *Changing Conversations: Religious Reflection and Cultural Analysis,* ed. Sheila Greeve Davaney and Dwight N. Hopkins (New York: Routledge, 1996), 137.

4. Ada María Isasi-Díaz, *En la Lucha/In the Struggle: Elaborating a Mujerista Theology* (Minneapolis, MN: Fortress Press, 1993), 42.

5. Ada María Isasi-Díaz, "Solidarity: Love of Neighbor in the 21st Century," in *Lift Every Voice: Constructing Christian Theologies from the Underside,* revised and expanded edition, ed. Susan Brooks Thistlewaite and Mary Potter Engel (Maryknoll, NY: Orbis Books, 1998), 39.

6. Ibid., 31.

7. Robert W. Jenson, "You Wonder Where the Spirit Went," *Pro Ecclesia: A Journal of Catholic and Evangelical Theology* 2, no. 3 (Summer 1993): 296–304.

8. For a historical survey of the development of the doctrine of the Holy Spirit, see Alasdair I. C. Heron, *The Holy Spirit* (Philadelphia: Westminster Press, 1983). For an introduction to the major issues in contemporary Pneumatology, especially the Western tradition's "forgetfulness of the Spirit," see Jürgen Moltmann, *The Spirit of Life: A Universal Affirmation,* trans. Margaret Kohl (Minneapolis, MN: Fortress Press, 1992), 1–14.

9. John D. Zizioulas, *Being as Communion: Studies in Personhood and the Church* (Crestwood, NY: St. Vladimir's Seminary Press, 1985), 19.

10. Ibid., 20.

11. For a defense of the *filioque* clause, see Karl Barth, *Church Dogmatics* I/1, 2nd ed., trans. G. W. Bromiley, ed. G. W. Bromiley and T. F. Torrance (Edinburgh: T & T Clark, 1975), 448–89; for a more muted defense of the *filioque* that addresses the Eastern church's theological objections, see Robert W. Jenson, *Systematic Theology,* vol. 1, *The Triune God* (Oxford: Oxford University Press, 1997), 146–61.

12. John Calvin, *Institutes of the Christian Religion,* 2 vols., trans. Ford Lewis Battles, ed. John T. McNeill (Philadelphia: Westminster Press, 1960), 537–38 (3.1.1).

13. Ibid., 1016 (4.1.4, 8).

14. Ibid., 695 (3.7.5).

15. Moltmann, *The Spirit of Life,* 217.

16. Ibid., 220.

17. Isasi-Díaz is not the first to discuss the work of the Holy Spirit as consti-

tutive of community, as evidenced by Moltmann's understanding of *koinonia* as the gift of the Spirit (see note 15). See also Friedrich Schleiermacher, *The Christian Faith*, trans. and ed. H. R. Mackintosh and J. S. Stewart (Philadelphia: Fortress Press, 1976), 560–81; and Paul Tillich, *Systematic Theology*, vol. 3, *Life and the Spirit/History and the Kingdom of God* (Chicago: University of Chicago Press, 1963), 149–61

18. Perhaps at this point a word of explanation is needed as to why Ada María Isasi-Díaz's *mujerista* theology is our starting point for discussing a Latino/a perspective on the doctrine of the Holy Spirit rather than the contributions of Latino/a Pentecostal theology, a movement whose underlying premise is that the Holy Spirit continues to guide and empower the church as the body of Christ. The rapid growth of Pentecostalism in Latin America and among U.S. Hispanics has contributed greatly to the formation of U.S. Latino/a theology. For example, see Eldin Villafañe, *The Liberating Spirit: Towards an Hispanic American Pentecostal Social Ethic* (New York: University Press of America, 1992); also Samuel Solivan, *The Spirit, Pathos and Liberation: Toward an Hispanic Pentecostal Theology* (Sheffield, England: Sheffield Academic Press, 1998). However, one of the major points I make in this chapter is that Western theology has long underemphasized Pneumatology. By engaging the theology of someone like Isasi-Díaz, who has not articulated an explicit and thorough Pneumatology, to expound the Holy Spirit's role in the work of liberation I hope to bring greater attention to the (often unacknowledged) importance of the Holy Spirit for the Christian life.

19. Karl Barth, *Church Dogmatics IV/1: The Doctrine of Reconciliation*, trans. G. W. Bromiley, ed. G. W. Bromiley and T. F. Torrance (Edinburgh: T & T Clark, 1969), 643.

20. Ibid., 650.

21. Ibid., 653.

22. Ibid., 661.

23. Ibid.

24. Isasi-Díaz, *En la Lucha/In the Struggle*, 186.

25. For an insightful article describing the complexities of Latino/a racial/ ethnic identity that debunks the myth that Latino/as (as the victims of racial discrimination) are nonracists, see Miguel A. De La Torre, "Masking Hispanic Racism: A Cuban Case Study," *Journal of Hispanic/Latino Theology* 6, no. 4 (May 1999): 57–73. Of particular relevance is his experience of being considered "white" in Cuba while being labeled racially "other" in the United States.

26. Isasi-Díaz, *En la Lucha/In the Struggle*, 187.

27. Ibid., 188. Citing Iris Marion Young's critique of the universalizing tendency in Anglo feminist theology in *Justice and the Politics of Difference* (Princeton, NJ: Princeton University Press, 1990), 165.

28. Ibid., 193.

29. Ibid., 194n21.

30. Ibid.

31. Ibid.

32. James H. Cone, "The Vocation of a Theologian," *Union News*, Winter 1991, 4.

33. Isasi-Díaz, *En la Lucha/In the Struggle*, 35.

34. Isasi-Díaz, "Solidarity," 32.

35. John Burnaby, ed., *Augustine: Later Works* (Philadelphia: Westminster Press, 1955), 157.

36. Ibid., 161.

37. Isasi-Díaz, "Solidarity," 32.

38. Ibid.

39. Ibid.

40. Ibid., 30.

41. Ibid.

42. Ibid., 32.

43. Isasi-Díaz, *En la Lucha/In the Struggle*, 146.

44. Orlando O. Espín, *The Faith of the People: Theological Reflections on Popular Catholicism* (Maryknoll, NY: Orbis Books, 1997), 66.

45. Isasi-Díaz, *En la Lucha/In the Struggle*, 146n17.

46. Ibid.

47. Espín, *The Faith of the People*, 67.

48. Ibid., 77.

49. Ada María Isasi-Díaz, "The Bible and *Mujerista* Theology," in *Lift Every Voice*, 274.

50. I am borrowing and adapting the threefold description of the Christian life in terms of the doctrines of justification, sanctification, and vocation developed by Karl Barth in his thorough discussion of the Doctrine of Reconciliation (see *Church Dogmatics IV/1–3*). Barth's analysis is itself indebted to John Calvin's discussion of the person and work of Christ in terms of the *munus triplex Christi*: prophet, priest, and king.

51. Calvin, *Institutes of the Christian Religion*, 551 (3.2.7).

52. See Calvin on the Christian life, *Institutes* (3.6–10).

53. Karl Barth, *Church Dogmatics IV/3.2*, trans. G. W. Bromiley, ed. G. W. Bromiley and T. F. Torrance (Edinburgh: T & T Clark, 1962), 681–82.

54. John Calvin, *Calvin's Commentaries*, vol. 14, reprint of the Edinburgh Edition, various editors and translators (Grand Rapids, MI: Baker Book House, 2003), 343 (Micah 6:6–8).

55. Ibid.

56. Gustavo Gutiérrez, *A Theology of Liberation: History, Politics, and Salvation*, rev. ed., trans. and ed. Sister Caridad India and John Eagleson (Maryknoll, NY: Orbis Books, 1988), 83–105.

57. Isasi-Díaz, "Solidarity," 33.

58. Ibid., 32.

59. Clodovis Boff, "Epistemology and Method of the Theology of Liberation," in *Mysterium Liberationis: Fundamental Concepts of Liberation Theology,* ed. Ignacio Ellacuría and Jon Sobrino (Maryknoll, NY: Orbis Books, 1993), 66.

60. Gustavo Gutiérrez, *We Drink from Our Own Wells: The Spiritual Journey of a People,* trans. Matthew J. O'Connell (Maryknoll, NY: Orbis Books, 1984), 115.

61. Ibid., 127.

62. Gutiérrez, *A Theology of Liberation,* 118.

63. Ibid., 117.

64. Ibid., 113.

65. Ada María Isasi-Díaz, "A New *Mestizaje/Mulatez*: Reconceptualizing Difference," in *A Dream Unfinished: Theological Reflections on America from the Margins.* ed. Eleazar S. Fernandez and Fernando F. Segovia (Maryknoll, NY: Orbis Books, 2001), 205.

66. Calvin, *Institutes of the Christian Religion,* 1023 (4.1.9).

NOTES TO THE CONCLUSION

1. Justo L. González, "In Quest of a Protestant Hispanic Ecclesiology," in *Teología en Conjunto: A Collaborative Hispanic Protestant Theology.* ed. José David Rodríguez and Loida I. Martell-Otero (Louisville, KY: Westminster/John Knox Press, 1997), 80.

2. Ibid., 83.

3. Gary Riebe-Estrella, "*Pueblo* and Church," in *From the Heart of Our People: Latino/a Explorations in Catholic Systematic Theology.* ed. Orlando O. Espín and Miguel H. Díaz (Maryknoll, NY: Orbis Books, 1999), 172.

4. See Orlando Espín, *Faith of the People: Theological Reflections on Popular Catholicism* (Maryknoll, NY: Orbis Books, 1997).

5. Riebe-Estrella, "*Pueblo* and Church," 181–83.

6. See Susan K. Wood, "Communion Ecclesiology: Source of Hope, Source of Controversy," *Pro Ecclesia: A Journal of Catholic and Evangelical Theology.* II, no. 4 (Fall 1993): 424–32. Also see Dennis M. Doyle, *Communion Ecclesiology: Visions and Versions* (Maryknoll, NY: Orbis Books, 2000).

7. Ibid., 425.

8. Ibid.

9. Ibid., 426.

10. See *Baptism, Eucharist and Ministry* (Geneva: World Council of Churches, 1982). Also see Max Thurian, ed., *Churches Respond to BEM* (Geneva: World Council of Churches, 1986); and *Baptism, Eucharist and Ministry 1982–1990* (Geneva: World Council of Churches, 1990).

11. *Baptism, Eucharist and Ministry,* 10.

12. Ibid., 428.

13. Susan K. Wood, "Robert Jenson's Ecclesiology from a Roman Catholic Perspective," in *Trinity, Time, and Church* (Grand Rapids, MI: Eerdmans, 2000), 178.

14. Ibid., 180.

15. Ibid., 182.

16. Ibid., 183.

17. Robert W. Jenson, *Systematic Theology,* vol. 1, *The Triune God* (Oxford: Oxford University Press, 1997), 205.

18. Wood, "Robert Jenson's Ecclesiology from a Roman Catholic Perspective," 182.

19. Ibid., 184.

20. Karl Barth, *Church Dogmatics IV/1: The Doctrine of Reconciliation,* trans. G. W. Bromiley, ed. G. W. Bromiley and T. F. Torrance (Edinburgh: T & T Clark, 1969), 661.

21. Dietrich Bonhoeffer, *Discipleship,* ed. Geffrey B. Kelly and John D. Godsey, trans. Barbara Green and Reinhard Krauss (Minneapolis, MN: Fortress Press, 2001), 225.

22. Robert W. Jenson, *Systematic Theology,* vol. 2, *The Works of God* (Oxford: Oxford University Press, 1999), 213.

23. Jenson, *Systematic Theology,* 1:206.

24. Jenson, *Systematic Theology,* 2:181.

25. Ibid., 177.

26. Ibid., 233.

27. Ibid., 242.

28. Wood, "Robert Jenson's Ecclesiology from a Roman Catholic Perspective," 187.

29. See Philip W. Butin, "Reformed Ecclesiology: Trinitarian Grace According to Calvin," *Studies in Reformed Theology and History* 2, no. 1 (1994).

30. Jenson, *Systematic Theology,* 2:213.

31. Ibid., 1:41.

32. Ibid., 181.

33. See Gustavo Gutiérrez, *A Theology of Liberation: History, Politics, and Salvation,* rev. ed., trans. and ed. Sister Caridad India and John Eagleson (Maryknoll, NY: Orbis Books, 1988); and Leonardo Boff, *Ecclesiologies: The Base Communities Reinvent the Church* (Maryknoll, NY: Orbis Books, 1986).

34. Gutiérrez, *A Theology of Liberation,* 146.

35. Ibid., 145.

36. See Roberto S. Goizueta, *Caminemos con Jesús: Toward a Hispanic/Latino Theology of Accompaniment* (Maryknoll, NY: Orbis Books, 1995), 173–211.

37. Gutiérrez, *A Theology of Liberation,* 150.

Index

Abelard, 197–198
Aesthetics, 162–163
Anderson, Victor, 112
Anselm, 7, 196, 198
Apartheid, 4, 11, 26, 119
Arius, 167
Athanasius, 167, 195
Atonement, 195–198, 201, 216
Augustine, 36, 224; on the origin of slavery, 36–37

Bañuelas, Arturo J., 91
"The Barmen Declaration," 252n13
Baptism, Eucharist and Ministry (BEM), 240, 246
Barth, Karl, 194, 214, 220, 231, 242; on the provisional nature of theological statements, 252n10
Bartolomé de Las Casas, 2
Battles, Ford Lewis, 163
Bevans, Stephen B., 252n11, 117
Beza, Theodore, 131
Biblical theology, 128
Biological *mestizaje*, 16, 17, 76, 92, 93, 105
Blackness, 2, 3, 30, 32, 35; equated with slavery, 33, 35–39
Boff, Clodovis, 232
Boff, Leonardo, 159, 245
Bonhoeffer, Dietrich, 242
Brown, Delwin, 118
Byron, Gay 32, 34

Calvin, John, 20, 119, 154, 216–217, 231, 235; affair of the placards, 121; on civil government, 119, 120–127; on the diaconate, 137–138; as model for public theology, 119–140; on pastoral praxis, 135–140; on poverty, 128–129, 136–138; on the power

of the sword, 124; principle of accommodation, 162; on the prophetic role of the pastor, 127–135; on Scripture as revelation, 252n9, 127–128
Calvinism, 119
Canon, 6, 10, 97; definition of, 6
Cappadocian Fathers, 148–149
Celsus, 144, 147
Chalcedonian Christology, 176, 198
Chalcedonian definition, 178–179, 193, 194, 199
Charisms, 249
Chávez, César, 153
Christ, 87, 88, 108, 131, 135, 140, 145, 154, 167, 174–175, 179, 184–186, 194–200, 220, 238–239, 250
Christian identity, 5
Christian life, 140, 146, 148, 229–231; as conversion to God's preferential option, 231–234
Christology, 20, 102, 167, 179, 180, 193, 199; definition of, 177–178; from above, 193; from below, 193; high and low types, 193; as *mestizaje* of the human and divine, 102; *mestizo* reconstruction of, 200–202; mujerista understanding of, 267–268n103
Church, 217–219, 236–250; as association, 242; biblical images of, 218; as communion, 242; as the work of the Holy Spirit, 220; identified with the risen body of Christ, 242, 243. See also *Ecclesia*
Civil religion, 112
Class, 90, 225
Collective memory, 62–63
Color difference, 2, 27
Color prejudice, 28, 29, 31, 33, 34
Color symbolism, 28, 29, 31–32
Colorism, 27

About the Author

Rubén Rosario Rodríguez is Assistant Professor of Theological Studies at Saint Louis University.